THE

EVERYTHING®

GET PUBLISHED BOOK

Everything and everyone you need to know to
become a successfully published author!

Peter Rubie

Adams Media Corporation
Avon, Massachusetts

An Everything® Series Book.
Everything® and everything.com® are registered trademarks of F+W Publications, Inc.

Published by
Adams Media, an F+W Publications Company
57 Littlefield Street, Avon, MA 02322. U.S.A.
www.adamsmedia.com

ISBN: 1-58062-315-8

Printed in the United States of America.

J I H G F E D

Library of Congress Cataloging-in-Publication Data
Rubie, Peter.
The everything get published book / by Peter Rubie.
p. cm. -- (An everything series book)
ISBN 1-58062-315-8
1. Authorship. 2. Authorship–Marketing. I. Title. II. Everything series
PN145 .R725   2000
808'.02–dc21   00-023952

This publication is designed to provide accurate and authoritative information with
regard to the subject matter covered. It is sold with the understanding that the publisher is not engaged in rendering legal, accounting, or other professional advice. If
legal advice or other expert assistance is required, the services of a competent professional person should be sought.
—From a *Declaration of Principles* jointly adopted by a Committee of the American
Bar Association and a Committee of Publishers and Associations

Illustrations by Barry Littmann.

*This book is available at quantity discounts for bulk purchases.
For information, call 1-800-872-5627.*

Visit the entire Everything® Series at everything.com

Table of Contents

Introduction:

Why Would Anyone WANT to Get Published These Days? vii
The Bare Mechanics: How Your Idea Becomes a Manuscript
    and Eventually Ends Up on a Bookstore Shelf viii

Part 1: Getting It on Paper 1

Chapter 1: The Basics 3
Writing Tools 4
Writing Seminars, Workshops, and Networking 5
Basic Things You Need to Know about the Publishing Industry . . 8
Publishing Terms 9
AWP Member Writing Programs 17
Associated Writing Programs Listing 18

Chapter 2: Types of Books 35
Fiction and Nonfiction 36
Categories and Genres 37
Are you an Expert about Something? 47
Good Ideas and Bad Ideas 48
Fiction Reading List 53

Chapter 3: Market Research, or How
to Study Your Market 59
Define Your Audience 60
Size Up the Competition 62
Know Your Audience 64
Talk to Booksellers 65
And the Title Is 66
What's Hot and Why It Really Isn't 66
How Many Copies Can YOU Help Sell? 68

Chapter 4: How to Translate Your Idea
into a Book Proposal 69
A Good Proposal Is a Good Sales Tool 71
Preparing a Nonfiction Proposal 73

Format 74
Benefits and Features 75
Preparing a Fiction Proposal 80
The Query Letter 81
Hooks 83
Non-Fiction Query Letter 83
Sample Proposals 87

Part 2: Getting It in Print 107

Chapter 5: Getting an Agent 109
What Does an Agent Do? 111
Finding and Working with an Agent 114
How to Contact an Agent 116
What to Expect from Your Agent 118
Where to Look for an Agent 120
Sample Author/Agent Agreement 121
List of Agents 126

Chapter 6: How a Publishing House Is Set Up 143
The Secrets of Editorial Meetings 147
Editorial Department 148
Sales and Marketing 149
Production Department 150
Submitting Without an Agent 152
Small Presses 153
"Sorry, This Just Doesn't Fit Our Current Needs . . ." . 154

Chapter 7: The Acceptance Process 157
The Contract 160
Sample Contract 162

Chapter 8: How Your Manuscript Becomes a Book . . . 191
Handing It In 192
What Next? 194
Beyond Copyediting 196

Chapter 9: Marketing and Publicity Swing into Action . . 199
How Your Book Gets into the Stores 200

The Numbers Game 201
What Your Publisher Will Do 203
What You Can Do to Help Yourself 204
Do You Have Famous Friends or Acquaintances
   Who'll Help Out? 205
Publicity and Sales Hints and Tips 206
Should I Hire a Publicist? 209
No Fidgeting: What to Do and Not to Do on
   Local and National TV 210

Chapter 10: Subrights and Royalties **213**
Types of Rights 215
Royalty Checks and Statements 220
Remainders 222

**Chapter 11: Alternative Ways of Getting
"Your Stuff" Out There** **223**
Nontraditional Publishing 224
The Difference Between Vanity Press and Self-Publishing 226
Book Packagers and Work for Hire 228
Electronic Publishing 230
What Is E-Publishing? 230
Three Types of E-Publishing 231
E-Books Pros and Cons 232
Choosing an E-Publisher 233
AEP Resources 236
AEP Membership Rules 237

Part 3: The Listing of Book Publishers **241**

**Chapter 12: Where to Find Book Publishers
in North America** **242**
Conglomerates 244
Mid-Level Publishers 248
Small Presses and University Presses 279
Additional Resources for Writers 317

Index 318

Introduction:

Why Would Anyone WANT to Get Published These Days?

I have always wanted to be a writer. My earliest memories are of bedtime stories being read to me by my mother, stories like *Alice in Wonderland, Winnie the Pooh,* and *The Wind in the Willows.* As a child I could be kept occupied with a couple of blank sheets of paper and an old typewriter. I'd happily clack out the first pages of stories until the grown-ups decided it was time to do something else.

Essay writing, drama, and English literature remained my favorite subjects, along with history, another form of storytelling. So it's hardly surprising that I decided not to major in economics but instead to major in journalism.

All the while I read voraciously, anything and everything I could get my hands on, "good" stuff and "bad." As a boy and into my teens, I haunted bookstores and libraries. I was never happier than when I was surrounded on all sides by stacks of books. My favorites included boys' adventure stories, comics, Conan Doyle, Ryder Haggard, Ray Bradbury, Richard Matheson, Ian Fleming, Charles Dickens, James Joyce, Philip K. Dick, Jack Schaeffer, Herman Hesse, Carlos Castaneda, and on and on. Had anyone told me, when I was 19 and about to take a job as a reporter on my first newspaper, that I could make a living reading novels, I would have dismissed them in disbelief. It was another 15 years before I discovered the truth of that statement. What's more, I also discovered in my 30s that I could make a living writing fiction. It was a simple step from being a journalist to becoming a publishing house editor to becoming a literary agent. No matter what else I do, I have always considered myself first and foremost a writer.

So what's the point of this story? Simply that most people who work in publishing either as industry professionals or as authors, have similar personal tales to tell. If you feel the same compelling urges about books, reading, and writing, chances are you're one of us.

Amazingly, most people share the same few reasons for wanting to be published. They think it's a road to fame and fortune, or

Book People

If you look carefully, you can always tell the publishing people in a bookstore: They're the ones who glance both ways over their shoulders to make sure no one's paying attention to them and then turn a book face out in a prominent spot on the shelf. Guaranteed, the book is either written by them, written by a friend, or written by a client.

they have an idea, pet theory, or story that they just *have* to get other people to read and appreciate. A professional writer is not the person who has his or her first book published; it's the individual with a second or third book on the shelves.

Authors sometimes tend toward being insecure and compulsive yet, on the page, their words exude a calm and confidence. But the truth is authors come in all shapes and sizes, colors, and persuasions, and everyone, potentially, has something to say that other people may want to read about. The *trick* is to figure out how to say it so that it appeals to the largest possible audience.

These days publishing is about making money, not making art or broadcasting propaganda. So before you commit yourself to the hard path of getting a book with your name on the spine onto the shelves of Barnes & Noble and your local independent store, make sure you know who your audience is, how big that audience will be, and why they are likely to spend money reading your book when there are thousands of others to choose from, some of which may be just like yours but by more experienced writers.

Daunted? Good.

Now you're ready to learn what needs to be done to get your book published. Writing at a publishable level is a craft, just like carpentry, and, just like carpentry, it can be learned. Bear that in mind as you read this book and any others on writing and publishing that you may come across. Just put in the right effort, listen to those who know what they're talking about, stay the course, and eventually you'll achieve your goal. Remember, until you're published, you're not the best judge of your own work.

The Bare Mechanics: How Your Idea Becomes a Manuscript and Eventually Ends Up on a Bookstore Shelf

Anyone can *want* to get published, just as anyone can want to be wealthy, but wanting isn't enough. Everyone thinks they can write (our literary agency gets some one thousand unsolicited queries per month, and we're just one agency among a couple of hundred!), and every writer without exception has had a variation on the same epiphany: They put down a book they had been reading with the thought, "I could write something like this!" And so the process starts.

Principally, writing is about *thinking* and the ability to put down on paper those thoughts in a clear, simple, and well-organized way.

If you want to get published, you need to practice putting down your thoughts on paper and then organizing and reorganizing them until they flow effortlessly into each other. To start earning money from writing, you need to work for a newspaper, or write briefs, newsletters, ad copy or do anything in which you have to write and think about ideas and words and how to make them as appealing as possible to the widest targeted audience. Words are your tools, and you need to learn how to use your tools effectively. To do that, you need to practice and then get as much feedback as possible.

I could write something like this!

There's a story about the jazz guitarist Wes Montgomery, who was once asked how much technique you need to play jazz. He answered, "You need as much chops (technical ability) as you have ideas to play." In other words, you must create effectively and to the utmost with the tools currently at your disposal. A limited vocabulary used effectively is much better than a large vocabulary used poorly. What do I mean by effectively? Know what you want to say, and then say it once clearly and unambiguously and move on. If you do that, your chances of getting published will improve radically.

Once your manuscript has been completed and polished, you can start sending it out. Most publishers don't accept unagented submissions these days, so you need to do some research on which literary agents represent the kind of book you've written and then send your manuscript to them.

Your book, of course, is brilliant, so it's mind-blowing to think that before you finally get a positive response, several agents will take months to respond to you and then reject your book.

"Aha!" you think. "Finally, someone who recognizes my genius." But the agent says your book has *potential*, and she wants you to make all sorts of changes.

Vacillating between euphoria and despondency, you set to work, because as much as you hate to admit it, the agent has made some good points about how to improve your book, even though you once thought it ready to hit the bookstores. Your next-door neighbor and your spouse thought it was fantastic, too, and they read all the time.

Anyway, determined to really nail it this time, you make the changes the agent suggested plus a couple more you've come up with, and send it off again. About 12 weeks later, the agent calls to say that the book is much stronger and she's going to start submitting it to publishers, so please photocopy three more copies and mail them out to her.

Fighting the urge to wear a beret and stick your pinky out as you speak, you tell your friends, the mailman, and the woman at the checkout of your local supermarket that you now have a "literary agent" and that "we're waiting for a publisher to make an offer on my book." Weeks go by and you still haven't had that million dollar offer. Fortunately, you're well balanced enough to realize that calling the agent every day is a no-no, and you manage to sit on your hands for a month before calling "just to say hi." The agent is understanding enough to say that the book's been rejected by a couple of houses already but that there's lots of interest in it whenever she calls editors and pitches the project to them.

Three months after the agent started submitting the book, the phone rings at 3:30 P.M. on a Wednesday afternoon. You are, of course, busy with something. "What?!" you growl into the phone.

You hear your agent say, "I've got an offer from an editor. Is this a good time to talk?" Your stomach turns, and you're convinced you've just insulted her irreversibly, so you sweetly apologize and say, "Not really, can I call you back in an hour or so?" You do your errands in a daze, run at least one red light by mistake, and think about quitting your day job. You even compose in your head your resignation letter to your boss.

The offer is only $10,000 for world rights, and it's certainly not the million plus you expected, but somehow none of that matters. What matters is that someone, a professional, thinks something you've written is *publishable* and, what's more, is prepared to pay you money for it! All that work, all that effort, all those people who mocked you and said you'd never amount to a hill of beans can go jump in a lake. Now you have your vindication! And you didn't tell your boss what to do with his job, so you still have one, thankfully. You realize in calmer moments that it may be awhile before you'll be able to write full time and earn a living from it.

The money, called an advance against royalties, is to be paid half on signing the publishing contract and half on delivery of a complete and acceptable manuscript, and your agent, meanwhile, has managed to get the editor to give up translation, foreign, and some other sub-rights so that you can sell your book abroad and get some more money from it. Things are looking up.

You chat with your editor, and she loves your book. She has some ideas for improving it, and once again, even though you thought it was perfect, she helps you see all sorts of things that can be done to make it better.

You do the work and send in the manuscript. About 8 weeks later, you get back the copyedited manuscript. Your beautiful typewritten, double-spaced manuscript has been defaced with a sheaf of yellow Post-Its with questions on them you need to answer, and the pages are now covered with so many black and red marks that it looks like a spider with ink on its feet crawled all over them. At one and the same time, you feel incensed at the copy editor's stupidity and humbled by the vastness of your ignorance and carelessness.

You make a final set of changes and return the manuscript to your editor. Some time later, you get your galley proofs. For the first time, you see your book set in type. You read the page proofs for spelling mistakes and return them. Then, 9 months after you signed your contract, the UPS guy knocks on your door with a box at his feet. You scribble a signature, and before he's pulled away from the curb, you rip open the box. Nestled among far too many Styrofoam peanuts are a dozen copies of *your book*.

You stand it up on the kitchen table, make yourself a cup of coffee, sit, prop your feet up, and stare lovingly at it for at least a half hour.

A few days later, you coyly browse the shelves of your local bookstore, and *there*, there it is, on the bookstore shelf with your name on the front cover. You introduce yourself to the bookstore owner and shyly suggest that if he wants, you'll autograph some copies for him.

Of course, there's more to it than this. But if getting your book published is your dream, this book will show you everything you need to know to get there.

Reading Pays Off

All those years of reading "trash" books and comics, as well as "good stuff" when you were a kid, will pay off in spades once you get involved in the publishing industry. Having read and enjoyed what has been done before will prove invaluable if you plan to write professionally or get a job in publishing.

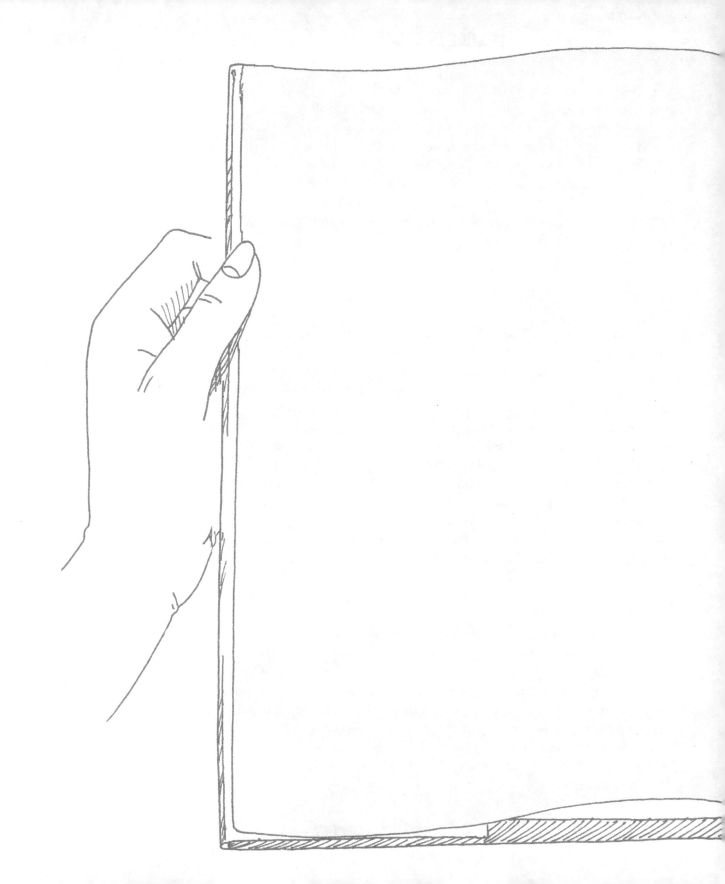

Part 1

~

GETTING IT
ON PAPER

CHAPTER 1

The Basics

Writing Tools

The most important tool is some sort of word processor. With all the revisions you'll have to do, the ease of use and neatness of a computer and a word processing program with a spell checker, plus a deskjet or laser jet printer, is really a must. It doesn't have to be the latest, cutting-edge equipment. It can be used and creaky and simple, because when all is said and done, all you need is a way to get words down on paper and then to correct them later.

Handwriting *anything* that is to be sent to an editor or agent is an absolute no-no. Most won't even bother to try and read what you've written.

After acquiring your computer, you should have the following books for reference: *Webster's Tenth New Collegiate Dictionary, Roget's Thesaurus, Bartlett's Familiar Quotations,* an atlas, and a library card.

If you want to be taken seriously as a writer, run, don't walk, to your nearest bookstore and buy a copy of Strunk and White's *The Elements of Style.* Take it home and read it from cover to cover.

This short little book is fantastic and should be compulsory reading for *every* writer of *anything,* regardless of how often he or she has been published. After you've read it, wait a few months, and then read it again. Read it often.

Also, subscribe to some magazines, including a writing magazine like *Writer's Digest* or the *Writer,* and get a couple of good books on writing. (Modesty forbids me from mentioning mine, so you didn't hear about them here. They're in the list at the end of this chapter, however, if you're interested.)

If you've never done any real writing, read some books on writing aimed at the level of a high school student. This is an excellent audience to imagine as you develop and write your book. Find a book with writing exercises and do them all.

An interesting exercise is to type out a few pages of something by your favorite writer. Things look different in typescript than they do when they're typeset, and you'll develop a better "eye" and a sense of how things should look in manuscript form. You'll also start to develop a feel for the use of language. It will begin to seem as though you are inventing the excerpt, not copying it.

Writing Seminars, Workshops, and Networking

Take some writing classes. First of all, they will remind you of all the things you thought you knew from high school but have forgotten. Secondly, you'll mix with people who are like-minded. Writing is a solitary pursuit, so if you get an opportunity to mix with others who think and talk writing just like you do, take advantage of it.

Go to writing conferences and listen, meet, and talk to others like yourself. These places are also great opportunities to listen to, mingle with, and occasionally meet with published authors, editors, and agents. Listen to what they have to say. Just remember that every published author was in exactly your position at some time in his or her life.

Attending writer's seminars, writing classes, and the like is important for an unpublished writer. Like any other performer, a writer is an entertainer, and as a young (i.e., inexperienced) writer you need to test your material in front of an audience and experience feedback. This can be tricky, because there's often a huge time lag between writing your piece and getting a response to it. Take any opportunity to shorten that time lag.

One of the best ways to start is to find a local writers group or workshop and join it. Failing that, try to form a small one of your own with a few other like-minded souls. Put an ad in the local paper or on the bulletin board of your local bookstore and see if the responses you get can turn up some likely candidates.

Toni Morrison, Karen Jay Fowler, and Amy Tan, for example, all started their writing careers as members of different writers groups. My business partner, Lori Perkins, started a group back in the early 1980s. It was fun to meet every week and take turns reading and listening, watching other people's books (as well as your own) grow like acorns into slender oak trees. Out of the regular six or so members who attended every week, three of us ended up

The Right Computer

Besides your brain, your most important tool is some sort of word processor. With all the revisions you'll have to do, the ease of use and neatness of a computer and a word processing program with a spell checker, plus a deskjet or laser jet printer is really a must.

Get a 56K modem or the best one you can afford for your computer so that you can use the Internet to do some *initial* research that you can later finish at the local library.

working full time in the publishing industry, and all but one ended up with published books under our belts.

Writers groups are also about reaffirming one's creativity, getting reassurance and feedback on your work, and developing confidence and individuality when it comes to putting down words on paper. Guaranteed, there will be someone in the group whose literary talent or skills make you green with envy. But the joke is, pull that person aside, and he or she will probably confess there's a quality to your writing he or she would just kill to be able to emulate.

Hang the following statement in a prominent place in your home where you can see it every day: *Writers write*. Regardless of what they write, there is a need to put down words on paper. Do it regularly, and do it often. Keep a journal, for example, or offer to write for free. As you get more experienced and better at what you do, the money will start to trickle in.

Come up with a writing routine, something that gets you "in the mood." Ernest Hemingway reportedly sharpened lots of pencils, while Thomas Wolfe took a walk. Emily Dickinson reputedly worked at night, when the rest of her household was asleep.

Unless you're going to do a stream-of-consciousness exercise, in which you write down everything that pops into your head as it happens, try to develop an idea of what you want to write about before you sit down to do it so that you don't end up staring at a blank computer screen for hours.

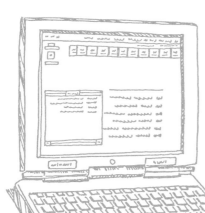

If you have a computer that's hooked up to the Internet, start searching for some sites by and about writing. If ever a medium appealed to and seems divinely designed for one group of people, it's the marriage between the Internet and people with aspirations to write.

There are loads of on-line writing groups of varying quality and friendliness. Two of the best places to start would be in forums on America Online and Compuserve. These two services in particular have a wide variety of writing groups that include unpublished and opinionated amateurs, as well as informed, generous, and well-published professionals.

Lastly, once you've gained some confidence and experience and think you're ready to be published,

It was a dark and stormy night

Web Sites for Writers

Here are some interesting and useful Internet writing sites that are worth visiting. All except the last one are free.

General:
http://ourworld.compuserve.com/homepages/prubie/Wrsites.htm
Peter Rubie's Web Page Guide to Publishing Sites and Sites Dedicated to Writers and Writing. (You can find links to many of the sites mentioned here on this page.)

www.bookwire.com/AAR/Links.html
AAR (The Association of Authors' Representatives), the Literary Agent's Association Web Site.

Writing Associations, Seminars, Schools:
www.gmu.edu/departments/awp
Associated Writing Programs—Serving Writers Since 1967

www.writersdigest.com/conferences/index.htm
Writer's Digest—Your On-Line Guide to Getting Published

www.shawguides.com/writing/
ShawGuides, Inc.—A Guide to Writers Conferences Nationwide

On-Line Writing Tools:
www.inkspot.com/craft
Craft of Writing

www.refdesk.com
Excellent reference material such as dictionaries, etc.

www.infoplease.com
Information Please—On-Line Dictionary, Internet Encyclopedia, and Almanac Reference

www.m-w.com/
Merriam-Webster's On-Line Dictionary and Thesaurus

http://thesaurus.com
Roget's Thesaurus On-Line

www.edunet.com/english/grammar/index.cfm
An On-Line English Grammar source

www.theslot.com
The Slot: A Spot for Copy Editors

Research and Other Writing-Related Sites:
www.pantheon.org/mythica/
Greek, Roman, and other Mythology On-Line at Encyclopedia Mythica

http://goon.stg.brown.edu/bible_browser/pbform.shtml
An On-Line Bible Browser

www.noveladvice.com/links.htm
NovelAdvice Web Page—Writing-Related Links

www.comlab.ox.ac.uk/archive/other/museums.html
The World Wide Web Virtual Library and Museums Source

This last resource charges $19.95 a year for access to its many facets:
www.novalearn.com/wirg/
The Writer's Internet Resource Guide

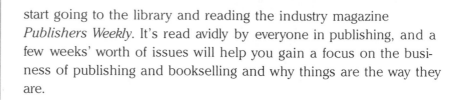

start going to the library and reading the industry magazine *Publishers Weekly*. It's read avidly by everyone in publishing, and a few weeks' worth of issues will help you gain a focus on the business of publishing and bookselling and why things are the way they are.

Basic Things You Need to Know about the Publishing Industry

Okay, let's be honest. Most of us—you, too, admit it—daydream about publishing a book, getting paid a ton of money for it, getting fantastic reviews ("The best thing since sliced bread!" *The New York Times*) and appearing on Jay Leno's show to talk wittily about it with Warren Beatty and Susan Sarandon. Hollywood falls at your feet, makes you an obscenely large offer of cash for the movie rights, and Leonardo DiCaprio and Kate Winslet end up starring in the film version. Hey, Margaret Mitchell did okay with *Gone With the Wind*, and so did Harper Lee with *To Kill a Mockingbird*, and both of these authors only ever wrote one book each. It *could* happen.

The great lure of publishing a book is that you can wander into any bookstore in the world, look around, and see that someone else has managed to achieve what you dream about, and not just one "someone," but thousands of them.

In fact, on average, fifty thousand books a year are published in the United States. So why not you?

The trick to getting published is to get the right idea in front of the right editor. That's essentially what agents do. They aren't really salespersons, they're much closer to matchmakers who manage authors' careers. Agents spend their time wooing, courting, cajoling, and fighting with editors on behalf of their clients, and they know better than most what an editor likes and needs, in terms of manuscripts.

So, in order to increase your chances of getting published, it's important that you spend some time getting to know the industry and how it works. Don't handicap yourself with fanciful notions about how publishing *should work*; learn how it *does* work, and you'll more than double your chances of getting published. Once you develop a professional attitude and an understanding of what everyone does in the industry, you'll be able to target your submissions with far greater precision and success.

Publishing is first and foremost a *business* and decisions are made not on how well written a book is but on how much money it will earn the publishing company. Quick, name the last prize winning literary novel to make the best-seller lists. Did you buy a copy? Did you pay full price at a small local bookstore or get it at a discount at a big national chain? Did you at least borrow a copy from the library and read it? How long was *The Celestine Prophecy* or *The Bridges of Madison County* on the lists? A lot longer than anything by Annie Proulx, Cheever, Irving, Beckett, or even Tom Wolfe, rest assured.

The best way for aspiring authors to begin to come to grips with publishing is to realize that publishing companies are businesses, and that writing, however artful, is also a business. You need to be specific and creative in targeting your audience. Then help the publishing company understand what a moneymaking opportunity publishing your book will be. When I say help them understand, I mean provide facts and figures that will make sales and marketing types start to drool with delight. Just offering your unvarnished opinion that this "is destined for the best-seller lists" will not do the trick. Trust me, we've heard it all before.

As a would-be author, your job is to learn your craft, gain real understanding of how publishing works, come up with a salable, focused idea, and present it in the most effective way.

Publishing Terms

Royalty Advance

A royalty advance is the money that an author is paid by a publisher for the license to print and sell the author's book. It is more accurately called an advance against royalties and is often paid in two or more payments, one after the signing of the publishing contract and the other after the acceptance by an editor of the finished manuscript. Some publishing companies try to delay the second payment until after the book is published.

However, the number of competing publishing companies is shrinking, creating a bias in favor of the buyer, and advances for

Reference Books

You should have the following books for reference:

- The latest version of *Webster's Ninth New Collegiate Dictionary*
- *Roget's Thesaurus*
- *Bartlett's Familiar Quotations*
- An atlas
- A library card

certain authors can be very high, so some companies are now splitting advances of over $100,000 into three or more payments; the final payment is made on publication.

The money is not a gift to the author, however. It is a calculated "best guess" by the publishing company as to what the author's book is worth in terms of royalties earned through X number of copies sold.

Royalty Rate

The author's "fee" or royalty advance for writing is "guesstimated" by the editor and included in the total costs of producing the book. For each copy sold, the author earns at a predetermined royalty rate that can escalate after a certain number of the book have been sold. (It can be, for example, 10 percent of the net price of the book for the first five thousand copies sold.) That earned income, collected like drops of water accumulating in a barrel, pays down the deficit of money already advanced to the author. The advance is not really a debt, though, because if the book does not earn back its royalty advance, the author does not owe the publishing company any money or have to pay back anything. The company takes a gamble, rolls the dice, and, if it loses, takes its financial beating like a man—almost.

The author of books that regularly fall into the red will quickly get smaller and smaller advances and, within a short space of time, have trouble getting anything he or she wrote published, regardless of its quality.

Sell Through

Sell throughs are the number of copies actually sold of a particular title. Publishers take "orders" from bookstores, who get books sent to them on consignment. The bookstore guesses how many copies of a particular title they will sell and then orders that number of books. They keep the title on the shelf for perhaps a month, and then if demand dries up, they ship back the remainder to the publisher.

All the sales figures are dutifully recorded on the bookstore's computers. Then, the next time a book by that author comes up, say, when the sales rep comes back to the store trying to sell the

It was a dark and stormy night

Writing Organizations

American Society of Journalists and Authors
1501 Broadway, Suite 302
New York, NY 10036
Voice: 212-997-0947
Fax: 212-768-7414
Internet: 75227.1650@compuserve.com
(JFORUM on CompuServe is ASJA's official on-line service)
Alexandra Cantor Owens, Executive Director
New address of the ASJA Web page: *http://www.asja.org/*

Author's Guild
330 West 42nd Street
29th Floor
New York NY 10036
212-563-5904
Fax: 212-564-5363
http://authorsguild.org

Novelists, Inc.
NINC is devoted to promoting the interests of published, professional novelists writing in all popular genres. Formed in 1989, NINC has grown from a small nucleus of dedicated authors working primarily in the romance genre to encompass over 650 published writers from every part of the industry. Minimum membership requirement is two published novels of popular fiction—at least one of which must have been published within the last five years—the average member has published a lot more.
www.ninc.com

author's latest book, the bookstore buyers will check their records and only order the number of books the last title by that author sold, regardless of the new book's potential for success.

Returns

Returns are copies of a book that are returned to the publisher by the bookstore once the store clears its shelves to make way for copies of new books to be sold. Publishers hate them.

The intricacies of selling books involve sell through rates, returns, discount rates to bookstore chains and less favorable discounts to small independent bookstores, and so on and so forth. If authors have heavy returns on their books, it can affect their ability to publish future books with their current or any other publishing company.

Hardcover, or Cloth

Publishers sell their books in a variety of formats, principally "cloth," or hardcover, and paperback.

Hardcover books usually sell for $22.95 on up and have cardboard covers. They are paid the most attention, reviewed more than any other type of book, and offer an author the most prestige.

There are also large-size books known as coffee table books; they are usually collectible and often heavily illustrated rather than text based. Except in special circumstances, say, when the author hits some sort of best-seller list, hardcovers also sell less actual units than any other type of book sold. Depending on who markets it, and how enthusiastically, an average hardcover novel sells between three thousand and ten thousand copies. Authors can earn as little as $1,000 or as much as several million.

Paperback

Paperback books break down into two main types: trade or hardcover-size formats (usually 6 by 9 inches) and mass market.

Trade format books fill the gap between mass market and hardcover and are often used for high-quality fiction or a certain type of practical nonfiction such as child rearing advice, Zen Buddhism, commercial but intellectually stimulating titles, and the like. On

It was a dark and stormy night

National Writer's Union
www.nwu.com

National Offices:

National Office East
113 University Place, 6th Floor
New York, NY 10003
Voice: 212-254-0279
Fax: 212-254-0673
Email: nwu@nwu.org

National Office West
337 17th Street, #101
Oakland, CA 94612
Voice: 510-839-0110
Fax: 510-839-6097
E-mail: nwu@nwu.org

NWU Locals:

Most union members participate in union activities
through their NWU local.
(Sub-locals are locals in the
process of organization.)
At-Large Local
800-417-8114
(This is the local for all
members who do not live
near one of the geography-
based locals.)

Boston Local-4
650 Beacon Street, 4th Floor
Boston, MA 02215
Voice: 617-266-7729
Fax: (617) 266-6414
E-mail: nwu4@channel1.com

Chicago Local-12
P.O. Box 2537
Chicago, IL 60690
773-348-1300

Los Angeles Local
12335 Santa Monica Blvd.
Los Angeles, CA 90025
310-281-6901

Miami Organizing Committee
305-895-0010

New Jersey Local
C/O Eric Lerner
20 Pine Knoll Drive
Lawrenceville, NJ 06848
609-883-8878

New York Local-1
275 Seventh Avenue,
20th Floor
New York, NY 10001
Voice: 212-929-2241
Fax: 212-807-6245
E-mail:
nwuny@echonyc.com

Oregon Local
P.O. Box 10821
Eugene, OR 97440
541 485-9692
Web: Oregon Local Home Page

Philadelphia Local
P.O. Box 1916 Southeastern
Philadelphia, PA 19399
610-282-9744
E-mail:
nwuphil@libertynet.org
Web: Philadelphia Writers
Home Page

San Francisco Bay Area
Local-3
337 17th Street, #101
Oakland, CA 94612
Voice: 510 839-1248
Fax: 510-839-6097
E-mail: nwusf@igc.org
Web: Local-3 Home Page

Santa Cruz/Monterey Local-7
P.O. Box 2409
Aptos, CA 95001
831-457-7488
Web: Local-7 Home Page

Seattle Local
P.O. Box 19743
Seattle, WA 98109
206-282-9744

Southeast Michigan
P.O. Box 10407
Detroit, MI 48210
313-438-1829

Twin Cities Local-13
P.O. Box 50507
Minneapolis, MN 55403
612-879-4114

Tucson Sub-Local
P.O. Box 40341
Tucson, AZ 85717
520-325-6966

Vermont Local
150 Cherry Street
Burlington, VT 05401
802-658-9667
E-mail: GColbyVT@aol.com

Washington, D.C. Local-2
1757 N Street, NW
Washington, D.C. 20036
202-466-8866

Westchester/Fairfield NY
Local
P.O. Box 559
Ardsley, NY 10502

Western New England Local-5
P.O. Box 132
Greenfield, MA 01302
Voice: 413-586-8844
Fax: 413-243-3066
Web: Local-5 Home Page
E-mail:
jackhandler@juno.com

average they sell anywhere from ten thousand to twenty-five thousand copies and cost approximately $13 to $15 each.

Mass market books are aimed at the lowest common denominator and the highest possible sales. In nonfiction, mass market books are often *National Enquirer* or *People* magazine-type material or reprints of successful (or sometimes not so successful but nevertheless well publicized) hardcovers. In fiction, they are usually genre books (science fiction, mystery, romance, horror, Westerns, etc.). Both types are widely available in bookstores, supermarkets, and so forth.

They are usually priced in the $6 range. Mass market paperbacks were developed in the 1950s and boomed into the 1960s and 1970s. They are in large part responsible for the evolution of the publishing industry from the sometimes snobbishly elite "gentleman's" club of the pre–World War II era to the female-dominated arena of today.

Mass market books sell from twenty-five thousand copies to one hundred thousand, though more copies are often returned to the publisher than are actually sold. A 40 percent sell through is considered average for a mass market paperback print run.

Publishing List

Publishers generally announce the publication of their authors' latest books in the fall and spring. They do so with as much fanfare as they can muster.

Titles on the spring book list come out roughly from April to September; those on the fall list come out roughly from October through the following March, although the months covered vary from publisher to publisher.

Some publishers have rethought this system, introducing a third season to cover the summer months. Their hope is to attract the attention of booksellers at a time when no major books are due to be launched.

Vertical Publishing

A large number of publishing companies have converged and become part of groups and conglomerates. In the last 20 years, publishing has moved from individual hardcover houses and individual paperback houses—a structure known as horizontal publishing—to companies that buy books that they can publish first as hardcovers and then as a paperback—a structure known as vertical publishing. Doubleday and Dell are such an oak tree and ivy team, for example, as are New American Library and Dutton or Simon and Schuster and Pocket Books, to mention but a few. However, many companies also publish both hardcover and mass market under the same name, such as Warner Books or Bantam.

Conglomerates

Publishing has headed more and more in the direction of conglomerates, as bigger companies gobble up smaller. It has always been a business that has a large financial risk attached to it for the publishing companies. In many instances, a handful of commercially successful books carry the financial burden of the rest of the publishing house list, allowing the company to publish smaller selling but more prestigious quality literature, be it fiction or nonfiction, and maintain its credibility as a house that supports serious books on cultural, artistic, and scientific topics of importance to us as a society. These financial "also rans" sometimes break even and sometimes never make back the money spent on them.

One of the consequences of the changing economics of book publishing is the coalescing of smaller companies into bigger ones. Giant diversified groups, so the theory goes, do not suffer so acutely from a shortage of cash and can even up the balance of power when dealing with large bookstore chains, such as Barnes & Noble or Crown, in terms of the discounts the chains demand for stocking and selling the publishing company's books.

Some conglomerates believe in the power of cross-fertilization, that is, that the various businesses within the group will benefit from a particular book's acquisition. Another type of conglomerate has arisen as a result of a sort of corporate cooperative, in which several companies have banded together but remained editorially independent, as though they are different rooms in a house owned by an overarching financial authority.

As they greedily gobble up one of their rivals, conglomerate heads always declare that the various editorial departments will function inde-

INFORMATION

Did You Know...

A book that is "remaindered" is sold at a deep discount in a store prior to the book going out of print.

pendently and become stronger and increase the diversification of book titles available to the reading public. This resolve lasts about 6 to 9 months. What then usually happens is that various imprints within the new combined entity are collapsed into one another and the streets of Manhattan run red with the blood of sacked editors yet again. On one occasion, the firing of the editorial staff took place in alphabetical order, and no one unconnected with the company was allowed into the building while the carnage took place.

Quite commonly, the first people to go are the sales staff as sales forces are combined into a selling behemoth. What this means is that the various independent editorial departments find themselves presenting their new acquisition projects at editorial boards that include the same sales force representatives as the rival imprints within the same publishing group two floors up, and the sales force rep says, "We already have a book like this from imprint X. Why should we compete with ourselves?" If, of course, book A is successful, the conglomerate sales people usually can't get enough of them, and that's all they want the editors to buy.

Book Clubs

Book clubs sell, by direct mail, hardcover and paperback books to members at special club discount prices. They achieve these prices by buying large numbers of the book from the publisher at a high discount, reducing the author's standard royalty but also requiring their club members to buy X number of books per year.

Some book clubs reprint their own editions of books. This practice ensures that the author gets a higher than usual book club royalty rate but only happens if the book club thinks it can sell vast numbers of a title to its membership, say, the new Stephen King or Danielle Steel. Such books are often called main selections and alternate main selections. Book clubs often cater to specific areas, such as history, gardening, cooking, religion, computers, and so on.

Subsidiary Rights

Subsidiary rights break down into a variety of potential money-making extras, from translations to dramatic and film or audio and magazine reprints. These can be especially lucrative if the author managed to retain these rights for himself or herself when the book was originally sold to the publisher.

If the publishing company has a share of these rights, an agreed-upon percentage of the money earned from the sale of these rights (say, 50/50 or 75/25 in favor of the author) will be split between the author and the company. If the royalty advance has not yet been fully paid back, the author's share of these sales will go toward paying off that royalty advance. Once the advance has been paid back, if the book continues to sell, the author will receive twice yearly royalty statements accompanied by checks.

AWP Member Writing Programs

The Associated Writing Programs (AWP) is a national, nonprofit literary organization for the benefit of writers, writing programs, teachers of writing, and lovers of literature. It was founded in 1967 and presently supports over eighteen thousand writers at over three hundred member colleges and universities and eighty writers conferences and festivals.

The core services include publication of *The Writer's Chronicle*, the AWP Job List, and the AWP Official Guide to Creative Writing Programs. It also offers a career placement service, available for members only, and sponsors an annual conference and a number of annual writing competitions.

Anyone can become a member for a subscription of $57 for 1 year or $99 for 2 years. This entitles you to *The Writer's Chronicle* magazine as well as the AWP Job List. For more detailed and up-to-date information, check out the AWP Web site.

While the AWP list of creative writing programs is the most comprehensive compilation of undergraduate and graduate writing programs, it does not rank creative writing programs in terms of quality.

Contact AWP at: Tallwood House, MSN 1E3
George Mason University
Fairfax, VA 22030
703-993-4301
Fax 703-993-4302
http://www.awp@gmu.edu

Books About Writing

The Elements of Storytelling by Peter Rubie
How to Tell a Story by Peter Rubie & Gary Provost
The Tyranny of Words by Stuart Chase
The Writer's Handbook (any year you can get your hands on)
The Elements of Style by Strunk and White
The Hero with a Thousand Faces by Joseph Campbell
Character Analysis by Wilhelm Reich
Memories, Dreams, Reflections by C. G. Jung
The Art of Fiction by John Gardner
On Becoming a Novelist by John Gardner
On Moral Fiction by John Gardner
The Screenwriter's Workbook by Syd Field
Make Your Words Work by Gary Provost
What If? by Anne Bernays and Pamela Painter
Starting From Scratch by Rita Mae Brown
I'd Rather Be Writing by Marcia Golub
Writing for Story by Jon Franklin
How to Get and Keep the Right Agent for You by Lori Perkins

Following is a listing of AWP members by state. For the most up-to-date information on the schools and their writing programs, check out the AWP Web site at *www.gmu.edu/departments/awp/*

Associated Writing Programs

ALASKA
Ronald Spatz, Director
Creative Writing Program
University of Alaska-Anchorage
3211 Providence Drive
Anchorage, AK 99508
907-786-4356
Fax: 907-786-4383
http://www.uaa.alaska.edu/cwla

Frank Soos, Writing Program Codirector
University of Alaska-Fairbanks
P.O. Box 755720
Fairbanks, AK 99775-5720
907-474-7193
Fax: 907-474-5247
http://zorba.uafadm.alaska.edu/english/

ALABAMA
Dennis Covington, Director
University of Alabama-Birmingham
217 Humanities Building
900 South 13th Street
Birmingham, AL 35294-1260
205-934-5293
Fax: 205-975-8125
http://www.uab.edu/

Michael Martone
University of Alabama-Tuscaloosa
Creative Writing Program
P.O. Box 870244
Tuscaloosa, AL 35487-0244
205-348-5526
Fax: 205-348-1388
http://www.as.ua.edu/english

Dennis Rygiel
Department of English
Auburn University
9030 Haley Center
Auburn, AL 36849-5203
334-844-4620
Fax: 334-844-9027
http://www.auburn.edu/academic/liberal_arts/english/au_english.html

Lynne Burris Butler, Director
University of North Alabama
Department of English
UNA P.O. Box 5175
Florence, AL 35632-0001
256-765-4494
Fax: 256-765-4239
http://www.una.edu/

ARKANSAS
Carl Brucker, Director
Department of English and Foreign Languages
Arkansas Tech University
142 Witherspoon Hall
Russellville, AR 72801-2222
501-968-0484
Fax: 501-964-0812
http://www.atu.edu/

James Whitehead
University of Arkansas, Fayetteville
Department of English
Writing Program
Kimpel Hall 333
Fayetteville, AR 72701
501-575-4301
http://www.uark.edu/depts/english

Doris Norman Holmes
University of Arkansas at Pine Bluff
Department of English, Speech, and Drama
Pine Bluff, AR 71611
870-543-8000

ARIZONA
Jewell Parker Rhodes, Director
Creative Writing Program
Arizona State University
Department of English
P.O. Box 870302
Tempe, AZ 85287
602-563-3751
Fax: 602-965-2012
http://www.asu.edu/clas/english/

Robert Houston
University of Arizona
Creative Writing Program
Department of English
P.O. Box 210067
Tucson, AZ 85721-0067
520-621-3880

Fax: 520-621-7397
David Coy, Director
The Writing School
Arizona Western College
P.O. Box 929
Yuma, AZ 85364
520-726-1000
http://www.awc.cc.az.us/

Dr. Allen Woodman, Director
Northern Arizona University
Creative Writing Program
Department of English
P.O. Box 6032
Flagstaff, AZ 86011
602-523-5661
http://www.nau.edu/

Lisa K. Miller
Phoenix College
Department of English
1202 West Thomas Road
Phoenix, AZ 85013
602-285-7345
Fax: 602-285-7368

CALIFORNIA
Eloise Klein Healy
Antioch University Los Angeles
MFA in Writing Program
13274 Fiji Way
Marina Del Rey, CA 90292
800-7-ANTIOCH or 310-578-1080, ext. 226
Fax: 310-822-4824
http://www.antiochla.edu

Jack Hicks
University of California-Davis
Department of English
Creative Writing Program
303 Sproul Hall
Davis, CA 95616
530-752-1658
Fax: 530-752-5013
http://www.english.ucdavis.edu

Arielle Anne Read, Graduate Program Coordinator
University of California-Irvine
MFA Programs in Writing
Department of English and Comparative Literature
Irvine, CA 92697-2650
949-824-6718
Fax: 949-824-2916

Christopher Buckley
University of California-Riverside
2209 Watkins Hall
Creative Writing Department
900 University Avenue
Riverside, CA 92521-0318
909-787-2414/4291
Fax: 909-787-3933
http://www/chass.ucr.edu/crwt.htm

Carole Oles
California State University-Chico
Department of Writing and English
West 1st and Salem Streets
Chico, CA 95929-0830
916-898-5124
http://www.csuchico.edu

Charles Hanzlicek, Director
Creative Writing Program
California State University-Fresno
5425 North Backer Avenue
P.O. Box 98
School of Arts and Humanities
Fresno, CA 93740-8001
209-278-2553
Fax: 209-278-7143
http://www.csufresno.edu

Suzanne Greenberg, Director
Creative Writing Department
California State University-Long Beach
English Department
Long Beach, CA 90840
562-985-4243
Fax: 562-985-2369
http://www.csulb.edu

Dr. Mary Bush
California State University-Los Angeles
Department of English
5151 State University Drive
Los Angeles, CA 90032-8629
323-343-4140
Fax: 323-343-6740

Jack Lopez, Director
Department of English
Creative Writing Program
California State University-Northridge
18111 Nordhoff Street
Northridge, CA 91330
818-677-3431
Fax: 818-677-3872
http://www.csun.edu/

Mark Axelrod
Chapman University
333 North Glassell Street
Orange, CA 92866
714-997-6750
http://www.chapman.edu/comm/english

Adrienne Sharp
El Camino College
16007 Crenshaw Boulevard
Torrance, CA 90506
310-660-3192

Jim Dodge
Humboldt State University
Creative Writing Program
Department of English
Founders Hall 209
Arcata, CA 95521
707-826-5906
http://www.humboldt.edu/

Donald A. Put, Director
Idyllwild Arts Academy
P.O. Box 38
52500 Temecula Road
Idyllwild, CA 92459
909-659-2171, ext. 380
Fax: 909-659-5463

Sandra Alcosser
San Diego State University
Creative Writing Program
5500 Campanile Drive
San Diego, CA 92182-8140
619-594-5443
Fax: 619-594-4998
http://www.rohan.sdsu.edu/dept/writing/

Maxine Chernoff
San Francisco State University
Creative Writing Program
School of Humanities
1600 Holloway Drive
San Francisco, CA 94132-4162
415-338-1891
Fax: 415-338-7030
http://www.sfsu.edu/~cwriting

William Babula, Dean
Sonoma State University
School of Arts and Letters
Arts and Humanities, Nichols Hall #380
Rohnert Park, CA 94928
707-664-2146
http://www.sonoma.edu/

James Ragan, Director
University of Southern California
Professional Writing Program
Waite Phillips Hall 404
Los Angeles, CA 90089-4034
213-740-3252
Fax: 213-740-5775
http://www.usc.edu/

Paul Douglass, Chair
San Jose State University
College of Arts and Humanities
Department of English
1 Washington Square
San Jose, CA 95192-0090
408-924-4424
Fax: 408-924-4580
http://www.sjsu.edu/

Edward Kleinschmidt
Santa Clara University
Department of English
St. Joseph's Hall
500 El Camino Real
Santa Clara, CA 95053
408-554-4939
Fax: 408-554-4837

Frank Gaspar, Director
Long Beach City College
Creative Writing Program
Department of English
4901 East Carson Street
Long Beach, CA 90808
562-938-4111

Chana Bloch, Director
Mills College
Creative Writing Program
5000 MacArthur Boulevard
Oakland, CA 94613-1301
510-430-2219
Fax: 510-430-3398
http://www.mills/edu
Acad_INFO/ENG
ENG_GR/enggr.homepage.html

Ross Talarico
National University
Department of Writing and Communications
11255 North Torrey Pines Road
La Jolla, CA 92037-1011
619-642-8471
Fax: 619-642-8715

Adam Cornford, Chair/Poetics
New College of California
Poetics Program
School of Humanties
776 Valencia Street
San Francisco, CA 94110
415-437-3458
Fax: 415-626-554

Dr. Renee M. Kilmer
Southwestern Community College
Dean of Language Arts
900 Otay Lakes Road
Chula Vista, CA 91910
619-421-6700, ext. 5307
http://www.swc.edu/

Joy Manesiotis
University of Redlands
Writing Program
1200 E. Colton Avenue
P.O. Box 3080
Redlands, CA 92373-0999
909-793-2121
Fax: 909-793-2029
http://www.redlands.edu/

Eavan Boland
Stanford University
Creative Writing Program
Department of English
Stanford, CA 94305-2087
650-723-2637
Fax: 650-723-3679
http://www.stanford.edu/

Sheila Cole Robinson, Director
Saddleback College
Creative Writing Program
Department of English
28000 Marguerite Parkway
Mission Viejo, CA 92692
949-582-4837
Fax: 949-347-1663

Diem Jones, Director
Saint Mary's College of California
P.O. Box 4686
Moraga, CA 94575
925-631-4088
Fax: 925-631-0938
http://www.stmarys-ca.edu/

CONNECTICUT
Dr. J. Tom Hazuka
Central Connecticut State University
Creative Writing Program
Department of English
Willard Hall
1615 Stanley Street
New Britain, CT 06050
860-832-2762
Fax: 860-832-2784
http://www.ccsu.edu/

Charles Hartman and Blanche Boyd
Creative Writing Program
Connecticut College
270 Mohegan Avenue
New London, CT 06320-4196
860-439-2350
Fax: 860-439-5340
http://www.conncoll.edu/

Wally Lamb, Director
University of Connecticut
337 Mansfield Road
English Department/Arjona, U-25
Storrs, CT 06269-1025
860-486-2141
Fax: 860-486-5130
http://www.uconn.edu/

Kim Bridgford, Director
Fairfield University
Department of English
DMH-130
North Beson Road
Fairfield, CT 06430
203-254-4000, ext. 2795
Fax: 203-254-4131
http://www.fairfield.edu/

Tim Parrish, Director
Southern Connecticut State University
Writing Program
Department of English
501 Crescent Street
New Haven, CT 06515-1355
203-397-4550
Fax: 203-392-6731

J. Frederick Pfeil, Director
Trinity College
Department of English
300 Summit Street
Hartford, CT 06106-3141
860-297-2455
Fax: 860-297-5258
*http://www.trincoll.edu/
homepage.html*

COLORADO
David Mason
Colorado College
Department of English
Colorado Springs, CO 80903
719-389-6502
Fax 719-389-6833

Leslee Becker, Director
Colorado State University
Creative Writing Program
359 Eddy Building
Fort Collins, CO 80523-6010
970-491-7374
Fax: 970-491-5601

Marilyn Krysl, Director
University of Colorado-Boulder
Creative Writing Program
Department of English
P.O. Box 226
Boulder, CO 80309-0226
303-492-5213
Fax: 303-492-3904
http://www.colorado.edu/

Cole Swensen
University of Denver
Writing Program
Department of English
Pioneer Hall
Denver, CO 80208
303-871-2898
Fax: 303-871-2853
http://www.du.edu/english/creativewriting.html

FLORIDA
Jocelyn Bartkevicius
Department of English
FA-301
University of Central Florida
P.O. Box 16-1346
Orlando, FL 32816-1346
407-823-2212
Fax: 407-823-6582
http://www.ucf.edu/

Les Standiford, Chair
Florida International University
Creative Writing
Department of English
North Miami Campus
3000 NE 151 Street
North Miami, FL 33181
305-919-5857
Fax: 305-919-5734
http://www.asl1s.fiu.edu/cwp

Mark Winegardner, Director
Florida State University
Creative Writing Program
Department of English
Tallahassee, FL 32306-1580
904-644-0240
http://english.fsu.edu/crw

William Logan, Director
University of Florida
Department of English
P.O. Box 117310
Gainesville, FL 32611-7310
352-392-0777
Fax: 352-392-0860
http://web.english.ufl.edu/crw

Fred D'Aguiar
University of Miami
Creative Writing
Department of English
P.O. Box 248145
Coral Gables, FL 33124
305-284-2182
Fax: 305-284-5635
http://www.as.miami.edu/english

Kurt Wilt, Director
Saint Leo College
Creative Writing Directors
P.O. Box 6665
Saint Leo, FL 33574-6665
352-588-8294
Fax: 352-588-8440
http://www.saintleo.edu/

Don Morrill
University of Tampa
Department of Creative Writing
Department of English
401 West Kennedy Boulevard
Tampa, FL 33606-1490
813-253-3333, ext. 3557
Fax: 813-258-7292
http://www.utampa.edu/

GEORGIA
James Smith, Director
Creative Writing Program
Armstrong Atlantic State University
11935 Abercon Street
Savannah, GA 31419-1997
912-921-5633
Fax: 912-927-5399
http://www.it.armstrong.edu/

Sandra Meek
Berry College
Department of English
P.O. Box 5010
Mount Berry, GA 30149-5010
706-802-6723
Fax: 706-802-6722
http://www.berry.edu/academic/
hass/english/

Frank Manley, Director
Creative Writing Program
Emory University
N209 Humanities Building
Atlanta, GA 30322
404-727-4683
Fax: 404-727-2605
http://www.emory.edu/

Tom Sauret
Gainesville College
P.O. Box 1358
Division of Humanities
Gainesville, GA 30503
770-718-3674
Fax: 770-718-3832

Julie Checkoway Thomsen
University of Georgia
Department of English
Park Hall 102
Athens, GA 30602-6205
706-542-2659
Fax: 706-542-2181
http://www.uga.edu/~jcheckow/
creative.html

Martin Lammon
Georgia College and State University
Creative Writing Program
P.O. Box 44
Milledgeville, GA 31061
912-445-3176
Fax: 912-445-5961
http://al.gcsu.edu

Lee Hetrick
Georgia Perimeter College
The Chattachoochee Review
2101 Womack Road
Dunwoody, GA 30338
770-551-3166
Fax: 770-551-7471

Eric Nelson
Georgia Southern University
P.O. Box 8026
Statesboro, GA 30460
912-681-0739
Fax: 912-681-0783

John Holman, Director
Creative Writing Program
Georgia State University
Department of English
University Plaza
Atlanta, GA 30303-3083
404-651-2900
Fax: 404-651-1710
http://www.gsu.edu/

Tony Grooms, Director
Kennesaw State University
Creative Writing Program
Department of English
1000 Chastain Road
Marietta, GA 30144-5591
770-423-6440/6297
Fax: 770-423-6524
http://www.kennesaw.edu

Chester Fontenot
Mercer University
Department of English
1400 Coleman Avenue
Macon, GA 21207
912-752.2562
Fax: 912-752.2457

Janice Eden
Macon State College
Humanities
100 College Station Drive
Macon, GA 31206-5144
912-471-2700
Fax: 912-757-3624

Anne B. Warner
Spelman College
Department of English
P.O. Box 745
350 Spelman Lane
Atlanta, GA 30314-4399
404-876-3245, ext. 2148

Dr. Joshua McKinney
Valdosta State University
Department of English
1500 Patterson Street
Valdosta, GA 31698
912-333-7352
Fax: 912-333-7389

HAWAII
Susan Schultz
University of Hawaii at Manoa
Writing Program
Department of English
1733 Donaghho Road
Honolulu, HI 96822
808-956-7619
Fax: 808-956-3083
http://www.hawaii.edu/

IOWA
Frank Conroy, Director
University of Iowa Writers' Workshop
102 Dey House
507 North Clinton Street
Iowa City, IA 52242-1000
319-335-0416
Fax: 319-335-0420
http://www.uiowa.edu/~iww

Paul Diehl
University of Iowa
Nonfiction Writing Program
308 English-Philosophy Building
Iowa City, IA 52242-1492
319-335-0473
Fax: 319-335-2535
http://www.uiowa.edu/~nwp

Barbara Haas
Iowa State University
Department of English
203 Ross Hall
Ames, IA 50011
515-294-6814
Fax: 515-294-1966

IDAHO
Tom Trusky
Boise State University
Department of English
1910 University Drive
Boise, ID 83725
208-426-1246 or 800-824-7017, ext. 1199
http://www.idbsu.edu/english

Mary Clearman Blew
University of Idaho
Creative Writing Program
Department of English
Brink Hall, Room 200
Moscow, ID 83844-1102
208-885-7337
Fax: 208-885-5944

Okey Goode
Lewis and Clark State College
Writing Program
Department of Language and Literature
500 8th Avenue
Lewiston, ID 83501
208-799-2307
Fax: 208-799-2324
http://www.lcsc.edu/

ILLINOIS
Janet DeSaulniers
The School of the Art Institute of Chicago
MFA in Writing Program
37 South Wabash Avenue
Chicago, IL 60603-6110
312-899-5094
Fax: 312-899-5095
*http://www.artic.edu/saic/
saichome.html*

Kevin Stein, Director
Department of English
Bradley University
Peoria, IL 61625
309-677-2480
Fax: 309-677-2330
http://www.bradley.edu/

Garnett Kilberg Cohen
Columbia College
600 South Michigan Avenue
Chicago, IL 60605
312-344-8100
Fax: 312-344-8001

Deborah Roberts
Columbia College-Chicago
Fiction Writing Department
600 South Michigan Avenue
Chicago, IL 60605-1996
312-344-7615

Eugene Wildman
University of Illinois, Chicago
Department of English (MC 162)
601 South Morgan Street
Chicago, IL 60607-7120
312-413-2229
http://www.uic.edu/

Paul Friedman, Director
University of Illinois at Urbana, Champaign
Creative Writing Program
Department of English
608 South Wright Street
Urbana, IL 61801
217-333-2391

Ron Fortune
Illinois State University
Creative Writing Program
Department of English
Campus P.O. Box 4240
Normal, IL 61790-4240
309-438-3667
Fax: 309-438-5414

James Plath
Illinois Wesleyan University
Department of English
P.O. Box 2900
Bloomington, IL 61702-2900
309-556-3352
Fax: 309-556-3411
http://www.iwu.edu/

Robin Metz
Knox College
Creative Writing Program
Department of English
P.O. Box K-50
Galesburg, IL 61401
309-341-7419
Fax: 309-343-7090
http://www.knox.edu/

Mary Kinzie, Director
Northwestern University
Writing Majors
Department of English
215 University Hall
Evanston, IL 60208-2240
847-491-7294
Fax: 847-467-1545
http://www.english.nwu.edu

Kent Haruf
Southern Illinois University
Writing Program
Department of English
Carbondale, IL 62901-4503
618-453-6861
Fax: 618-453-3253
http://www.siu.edu/

INDIANA
Michael Carson, Director
University of Evansville
Creative Writing Program
Department of English
1800 Lincoln Avenue
Evansville, IN 47722-0001
812-479-2968
Fax: 812-479-2320
http://www.evansville.edu/

David Wojahn
Department of English
Indiana University
442 Ballantine Hall
Bloomington, IN 47405
812-855-8224
Fax: 812-855-9535
http://www.indiana.edu/~engweb/index.html

Karen Kovacik
Indiana University/Purdue U. of Indianapolis
Department of English
CA 502L
425 University Boulevard
Indianapolis, IN 46202
317-274-9831
Fax: 317-274-2347

William O'Rourke, Director
University of Notre Dame
Creative Writing Program
356 O'Shaughnessy Hall
Notre Dame, IN 46556-0368
219-631-7526
Fax: 219-631-4268

Marianne Boruch, Director
Purdue University
Creative Writing Program
Department of English
Heavilon Hall
West Lafayette, IN 47907
317-494-3740
http://www.purdue.edu/

Richard Hill, Director
Taylor University
Creative Writing
Department of English
500 West Reade Avenue
Upland, IN 46989-1001
765-998-4971
Fax: 765-998-4930
http://www.taylor.edu/

Marc Hudson and Joy Castro
Wabash College
301 West Wabash Avenue
P.O. Box 352
Crawfordsville, IN 47933-0352
765-361-6232

KANSAS
Amy Sage Webb and Philip Heldrich
Creative Writing Program
Emporia State University
Department of English
P.O. Box 4019
Emporia, KS 66801-5087
316-341-5216
Fax: 316-341-5547
http://www.emporia.edu/cw/index.htm

Carolyn Doty
University of Kansas
Creative Writing Program
3114 Wescoe Hall
Department of English
Lawrence, KS 66045
785-864-4520

Jonathan Holden
Kansas State University
Creative Writing Program
Department of English
106 Denison Hall
Manhattan, KS 66506-0701
785-532-6716
Fax: 785-532-7004
http://www.ksu.edu/

Richard S. Spilman, Director
Wichita State University
Creative Writing Program
Department of English Box 14
1845 North Fairmount
Wichita, KS 67260-0014
316-978-3130
Fax: 316-978-3548

KENTUCKY
Jeffrey T. Skinner, Director
University of Louisville
Creative Writing Program
Department of English
Brigham Humanities 315
Louisville, KY 40292
502-852-6801
Fax: 502-852-4182
http://www.louisville.edu/

Lynne Taetzsch
Morehead State University
Department of English
U.P.O. Box 645
Morehead, KY 40351
606-783-2136
Fax: 606-783-2678
*http://www.morehead-st.edu/colleges/
humanities/eflp*

Squire Babcock
Murray State University
Department of English
P.O. Box 9
Murray, KY 42071-0009
502-762-4730
Fax: 502-762-4545

LOUISIANNA
Mona Lisa Saloy, Director
Dillard University
Department of English
2601 Gentilly Boulevard
New Orleans, LA 70122-3097
504-286-4689
http://www.dillard.edu/

Joanna Leake, Director
University of New Orleans
Creative Writing Workshop
College of Liberal Arts
New Orleans, LA 70118
504-280-7454
Fax: 504-280-6468
http://www.uno.edu/

Jerry L. McGuire, Director
University of Southwestern Louisiana
Creative Writing Program
Department of English
Drawer 44691
Lafayette, LA 70504-4691
318-482-5478
Fax: 318-482-6096
http://www.usl.edu/

Peter Cooley, Director
Tulane University
Department of English
122 Norman Mayer Hall
New Orleans, LA 70118
504-862-8174
Fax: 504-862-8958
http://www.tulane.edu/

Patrice Melnick
Xavier University of Louisiana
Department of English
Palmetto Street
New Orleans, LA 70125
504-485-5161
Fax: 504-485-7944

MASSACHUSETTS
Suzanne Matson
Boston College
Department of English
Carney Hall
Chestnut Hill, MA 02167
617-552-3716
Fax: 617-552-4220
http://www.bc.edu/

Dr. Iain Crawford, Chair
Department of English
Bridgewater State College
Tillinghast Hall
Bridgewater, MA 02325

John Skoyles
Emerson College
Writing, Literature and Publishing Division
Department of English
100 Beacon Street
Boston, MA 02116-1523
617-824-8750
Fax: 617-824-7856
http://www.emerson.edu/

Brad Watson
Harvard University
Creative Writing Program
Barker Center
12 Quincy Street
Cambridge, MA 02138
617-495-8958
Fax: 617-496-8737
http://www.harvard.edu/

Agha Shahid Ali
University of Massachusetts at Amherst
Department of English
Barlett Hall
Amherst, MA 01003-0515
413-545-0643
Fax: 413-545-3880

Edwin J. Thompson, Chair
Department of English
University of Massachusetts at Dartmouth
285 Old Westport Road
North Dartmouth, MA 02747-2300
508-999-8273
Fax: 508-999-9235
http://134.88.18.11/welcome.html

James Paradis
Massachusetts Institute of Technology
Program in Writing and Humanistic Studies
14-E303
77 Massachusetts Avenue
Cambridge, MA 02139-4307
617-253-7894
Fax: 617-253-6910
http://web.mit.edu/humanistic/
www/homepage.htm

Corinne Demas
Mount Holyoke College
Department of English
South Hadley, MA 01075
413-538-2146
Fax: 413-538-2138

Stuart Peterfreund
Northeastern University
Creative Writing Programs
406 Holmes Hall
360 Huntington Avenue
Boston, MA 02115-5005
617-373-2512
http://www.neu.edu/

MARYLAND
Madison Smartt Bell
Goucher College
Creative Writing Program
Dulaney Valley Road
Towson, MD 21204
410-337-6282
http://www.goucher.edu/cwpromo

Larry Bielawski
Goucher College
MFA Program Director
CNF Low-Residency Program
1021 Dulaney Valley Road
Baltimore, MD 21204
410-337-6344
Fax: 410-337-6461

Nancy Ryan, Director
Johns Hopkins University
The Writing Seminars
135 Gilman Hall
Baltimore, MD 21218-2690
410-516-7562
http://www.jhu.edu/

Dr. Neil Alperstein, Chair
Loyola College
Department of Writing/Media
4501 North Charles Street
Baltimore, MD 21210-2528
410-617-2528
Fax: 410-617-2198
http://www.loyola.edu/

Donald Berger
University of Maryland
4140 Susqhehanna Hall
Department of English
College Park, MD 20742
301-588-6875
Fax: 301-314-7539
http://www.umd.edu/

Michael Waters
Salisbury State University
1101 Camden Avenue
Salisbury, MD 21801
410-543-6540
Fax: 410-543-6068
http://www.ssu.edu/

Clarinda Harriss
Towson State University
Department of English
Towson, MD 21252-0001
410-830-2869
http://www.towson.edu/

Robert Mooney
Washington College
300 Washington Avenue
Chestertown, MD 21620
410-778-7897

MAINE
Wesley McNair, Director
University of Maine at Farmington
Department of Language and Literature
Roberts Learning Center
112 Main Street
Farmington, ME 04938-1720
207-778-7454
Fax: 207-778-7452
http://www.umf.maine.edu/

MICHIGAN
William P. Osborn
Grand Valley State University
1 Campus Drive
Allendale, MI 49401
616-895-3070
Fax: 616-895-3430

Eric Torgersen
Central Michigan University
Department of English
Mt. Pleasant, MI 48859
517-774-3171
Fax 517-774-1271

Gerry LaFemina
Kirtland Community College
10775 North St. Helen Road
Roscommon, MI 48653-9699
517-275-5121, ext. 376
Fax: 517-275-8745

Heather Sellers
Hope College
Department of English
126 East 10th Street
P.O. Box 9000
Holland, MI 49422-9000
616-395-7620
Fax: 616-395-7134

Linda Gregerson, Director
University of Michigan
Creative Writing Program
Department of English
3187 Angell Hall
Ann Arbor, MI 48109-1003
734-764-6330
Fax: 734-763-3128
http://www.umich.edu/

Diane Wakoski, Director
Michigan State University
Creative Writing Program
Department of English
201 Morrill Hall
East Lansing, MI 48824-1036
517-355-7570
http://www.msu.edu/

Teresa Kynell
Northern Michigan University
Department of English
Writing Program
1401 Presque Avenue

Marquette, MI 49855-5363
906-227-2711
Fax: 906-227-1096
http://www.nmu.edu/English

Dr. Arnie Johnston, Chair
Department of English
Western Michigan University
619 Sprau Tower
Kalamazoo, MI 49008-5092
616-387-2571
Fax: 616-387-2562
http://www.wmich.edu/english

MINNESOTA
Cynthia Malone
College of St. Benedict
37 South College Avenue
St. Joseph, MN 56374
320-363-5384
Fax 320-363-6095

W. Scott Olsen, Director
Creative Writing Program
Concordia College
Department of English
901 South 8th Street
Moorhead, MN 56562
218-299-3812
http://www.concordia.edu/

Daniel Nodes
Hamline University
Grad Liberal Studies
845 Snelling
1536 Hewitt Avenue
St. Paul, MN 55104-1284
612-523-2901
Fax: 612-523-2490
*http://web.hamline.edu/graduate/
b/s/index.html*

Diane Glancy
Macalester College
Creative Writing Program
Department of English
1600 Grand Avenue
St. Paul, MN 55105-1899
651-696.6516
Fax: 651-696-6430
http://www.macalester.edu

Richard Robbins, Director
Creative Writing Program
Minnesota State University at Mankato
Department of English
230 Armstrong Hall
Mankato, MN 56002-8400

507-389-1354
Fax: 507-389-5362
http://www.mankato.msus.edu

Leslie Cooney, Program Coordinator
University of Minnesota
Creative Writing Program
209 Lind Hall
207 Church Street SE
Minneapolis, MN 55455
612-625-6366
Fax: 612-624-8228
*http://English.cla.umn.edu/CreativeWriting/
Program*

Lin Enger
Moorhead State University
1104 7th Avenue South
Moorhead, MN 56563
218-236-4689
Fax: 218-236-2236

Dr. Leslie A. Miller
University of Saint Thomas
2155 Summit Avenue #30F
St. Paul, MN 55105-1096
612-962-5600
Fax: 612-962-5623

Beth Weatherby
Southwest State University
Writing Center
Department of English
Marshall, MN 56258
507-537-7251
Fax: 507-537-7154

Mark Allister
St. Olaf College
1520 St. Olaf Avenue
Northfield, MN 55057-1001
507-646-3438

MISSOURI
Rose Marie Kinder
Central Missouri State University
Department of English and Philosophy
Martin 336
Warrensburg, MO 64093
660-543-4425
Fax: 660-543-8554
http://www.cmsu.edu/

Ginger Jones
Lincoln University
820 Chestnut
P.O. Box 29
Jefferson City, MO 65102-0029

573-681-5234
Fax: 573-681-5040
http://www.lincoln.edu/trappa/index.html

Sherod Santos, Director
University of Missouri at Columbia
Creative Writing Program
Department of English
107 Tate Hall
Columbia, MO 65211
573-882-6421
Fax: 573-882-5785

James McKinley, Director
University of Missouri at Kansas City
Department of English
5100 Rockhill Road
Kansas City, MO 64110-2499
816-235-1000

Mary Troy, Director
University of Missouri at St. Louis
MFA Program
8001 Natural Bridge
St. Louis, MO 63121
314-516-6845
http://www.usml.edu/divisions/artscience/
english/creative.htm

Michael Burns, Director
Southwest Missouri State University
Department of English
901 South National
Springfield, MO 65804
417-836-5107
http://www.smsu.edu/

Judith P. Clark, Director
Stephens College
Languages and Literature
Campus Box 2034
1300 East Broadway
Columbia, MO 65215
573-442-2211, ext. 4668
Fax: 573-876-7248
http://www.stephens.edu/

Guinn Batten
Washington University in St. Louis
Creative Writing Program
Department of English
One Brookings Drive, Campus Box 1122
St. Louis, MO 63130-4899
314-935-7130 (Derek Webster-contact)
Fax: 314-935-7461
http://www.wustl.edu/english

Wayne Zade
Westminster College
Writing Program
Department of English
501 Westminster Avenue
Fulton, MO 65251-1299
573-592-5287
Fax: 573-592-1217
http://www.westminster.edu/

MISSISSIPPI
Rich Lyons
Mississippi State University
Creative Writing Program
Department of English
Drawer E
Mississippi State, MS 39762
601-325-2362
Fax: 601-325-3645

Frederick Barthelme, Director
University of Southern Mississippi
Center for Writers
P.O. Box 5144 USM
Hattiesburg, MS 39406-5144
601-266-4321
Fax: 601-266-5757
http://sushi.st.usm.edu/MRW

MONTANA
Kate Gadbow
University of Montana
Creative Writing Program
Department of English
Missoula, MT 59812-1013
406-243-5231
Fax: 406-243-4076
http://www.umt.edu

NORTH CAROLINA
Luke Whisnant
Writing Program
East Carolina University
Department of English
2201 General Classroom Building
Greenville, NC 27858-4353
252-328-6516
Fax: 252-328-4889
http://www.ecu.edu

Kevin Boyle
Elon College
CB 2252
Elon College, NC 27244
336-538-2749
Fax 336-538-6811
http://www.elon.edu

Richard Chess, Director
University of North Carolina at Asheville
Department of Language and Literature
Karpen Hall CPO 2130
1 University Heights
Asheville, NC 28804-3299
828-251-6411
Fax: 828-251-6603
http://www.unca.edu/lit

Marianne Gingher
University of North Carolina at Chapel Hill
Creative Writing Program
Department of English
Greenlaw CB 3520
Chapel Hill, NC 27599-3520
919-962-0468

James Clark, Director
University of North Carolina at Greensboro
MFA Writing Program
Department of English
134 McIver Building
P.O. Box 26170
Greensboro, NC 27402-6170
336-334-5459
Fax: 336-334-3281
http://www.uncg.edu/eng/mfa

Mark Cox, Director
University of North Carolina at Wilmington
Creative Writing Program
Department of English
601 South College Road
Wilmington, NC 28403-3297
910-962-3331
Fax: 910-962-7186
http://www.uncwil.edu/writers/

Dr. Tom Lisk, Department Head
Creative Writing Program
Department of English
P.O. Box 8105
North Carolina State University
Raleigh, NC 27695-8105
919-515-3866
Fax: 919-515-1836
http://www.ncsu.edu

Peter Turchi
Warren Wilson College
MFA Program for Writers
P.O. Box 9000
Asheville, NC 28815-9000
704-298-3325
http://www.warren-wilson.edu/

NORTH DAKOTA
Jay Meek
University of North Dakota
Creative Writing Program
Department of English
Grand Forks, ND 58202
701-777-2703
http://www.und.edu/

NEBRASKA
Charles Fort
University of Nebraska at Kearney
Thomas Hall
Room 202
Kearney, NE 68849-1320
308-865-8299
Fax: 308-865-8806

Grace Bauer
University of Nebraska at Lincoln
Department of English
202 Andrews Hall
Lincoln, NE 68588-0333
402-472-0993
Fax: 402-472-9771
http://www.unl.edu/english/index.htm

Richard Duggin
University of Nebraska at Omaha
Writers' Workshop WFAB 315
Omaha, NE 68182-0324
402-554-4801
Fax: 402-554-3436
*http://www.unomaha.edu/
~fineart/wworkshop/wrkshop.html*

Mary Helen Stefaniak
Creative Writing Program
Creighton University
Department of English
2500 California Plaza
Omaha, NE 68178
402-280-2306
Fax: 402-280-2143
http://www.mockingbird.creighton.edu/new

NEW HAMPSHIRE
Margaret Love-Denman, Director
University of New Hampshire
Hamilton Smith Hall
95 Main Street
Durham, NH 03824-3574
603-862-0261
Fax: 603-862-3563
http://www.unh.edu/

Linda Butler
New Hampshire Institute of Art

148 Concord Street
Manchester, NH 03104-4826
603-623-0313
Fax: 603-641-1832

NEW MEXICO
Sharon Oard Warner
University of New Mexico
Department of English
Humanities 223
Albuquerque, NM 87131
505-277-6348
Fax: 505-277-5573
http://www.unm.edu/~english

Christopher Burnham
New Mexico State University
Department of English
P.O. Box 3001
Dept. 3E
Las Cruces, NM 88003-0001
505-646-1814
Fax: 505-646-7725
http://www.nmsu.edu/

NEW JERSEY
David Lloyd
Rowan University
201 Mullica Hill
Professional Writing Department
College of Communication
Glassboro, NJ 08028-1701
Fax: 609-256-4439

Karl Garson
Writers' Project, Inc.
P.O. Box 3098
Princeton, NJ 08543-3098
609-275-2947
Fax: 609-275-1243

NEVADA
Richard Wiley
University of Nevada, Las Vegas
4505 Maryland Parkway
P.O. Box 455011
Las Vegas, NV 89154-5011
702-895-3533
Fax: 702-895-4801
http://www.unlv.edu/
Susan Palwick
University of Nevada, Reno
Department of English/098
Reno, NV 89557-0031
702-784-6689

NEW YORK
Gayle Whittier
Binghamton University

Creative Writing Program
Department of English
Binghamton, NY 13902-6000
607-777-2168
Fax: 607-777-2408
http://www.binghamton.edu/

Nancy Black
Brooklyn College
2900 Bedford Avenue
Creative Writing
Department of English
Brooklyn, NY 11210-2814
718-951-5195
http://www.brooklyn.cuny.edu/

Frederick Tuten
City College of New York
Department of English
Writing Program
138th Street at Convent Avenue
New York, NY 10031
212-650-7000
Fax: 212-650-7649

Joseph Duemer, Director
Clarkson University
P.O. Box 5750
Potsdam, NY 13699
315-268-3967
http://www.clarkson.edu/

Alan Ziegler
Columbia University
School of General Studies
615 Lewiston Hall
New York, NY 10027
212-854-3774
http://www.columbia.edu/

Richard Locke, Director
Columbia University School of the Arts
415 Dodge Hall
2960 Broadway
New York, NY 10027
212-854-4392
http://www.columbia.edu/cu/arts/writing

Kenneth McClane
Cornell University
Department of English
Goldwin Smith 250
Ithaca, NY 14853-3201
607-255-6800
Fax: 607-255-6661
http://www.cornell.edu/

Naomi Guttman, Director
Hamilton College

Creative Writing Program
Department of English
Clinton, NY 13323
315-859-4780
Fax: 315-859-4390
http://www.hamilton.edu/

Marian MacCurdy
Ithaca College
Writing Program
Park Hall
Danby Road
Ithaca, NY 14850
607-274-3569
Fax: 607-274-3935
http://www.ithaca.edu/hs/writing/writing1/

Susan Gubernat, Director
Nassau Community College
Department of English
Bradley Hall
One Education Drive
Garden City, NY 11530-6793
516-572-7185
Fax: 516-572-8134

Melissa Hammerle
New York University
Creative Writing Program
Department of English
19 University Place
Room 310/2nd Floor
New York, NY 10003-4502
212-998-8806
Fax: 212-995-4864
*http://www.nyu.edu/gsas/english/
creativewriting*

Ruth Danon
New York University
SCE, Liberal Arts
50 West 4th Street
225 Shimkin Hall
Washington Square
New York, NY 10012-1165
212-998-7093
Gerald McCarthy
St. Thomas Aquinas
Route 340
Sparkill, NY 10976
914-398-4134

Susan Guma, Director
Sarah Lawrence College
Graduate Studies
1 Mead Way
Bronxville, NY 10708-5999

914-337-0700
FAX: 212-979-5951
http://www.slc.edu/

William Hathaway
Southampton College
Division of Humanities-MFA
239 Montauk Highway
Southampton, NY 11968
516-287-8424
Fax: 516-287-4049

Natalia Rachel Singer
St. Lawrence University
Hallmark Program in Creative Writing
Department of English
Richardson Hall
Canton, NY 13617
315-229-5898
Fax: 315-229-5328

Amy Lee, Director
State University of New York at Albany
Graduate Studies
Department of English
HU 335, 1400 Washington Avenue
Albany, NY 12222
518-442-4055, ext. 4069
Fax: 518-442-4599
http://www.suny.edu/

David Kelly
State University of New York at Geneseo
Creative Writing Program
Department of English
One College Circle, Blake E
Geneseo, NY 14454-1451
716-245-5272
Fax: 716-245-5181
http://www.suny.edu/

Brooks Haxton, Director
Syracuse University
Creative Writing
Department of English
401 Hall of Languages
Syracuse, NY 13244-1170
315-443-9482
Fax: 315-443-3660
*http://wwwhl/depts/english/
default.html*

OHIO
Elton Glaser
University of Akron
Department of English
Olin Hall 301

Akron, OH 44325-1906
330-972-7470
Fax: 330-972-8817
http://www.uakron.edu/

Wendell Mayo, Director
Creative Writing Program
Bowling Green State University
Department of English
Bowling Green, OH 43403
419-372-8370
Fax: 419-372-6805
*http://www.bgsu.edu/
departments/english*

Mary Grimm
Case Western Reserve University
Department of English
11112 Bellflower Road
Cleveland, OH 44106-7117
216-368-2355
Fax: 216-368-2216
http://www.cwru.edu/

John Drury
Department of English
Creative Writing Program
University of Cincinnati
P.O. Box 21-0069
Cincinnati, OH 45221-0069
513-556-3946
Fax: 513-556-5960
http://www.uc.edu/

Neal Chandler, Director
Creative Writing Program
Cleveland State University
Euclid Avenue at East 24th Street
Cleveland, OH 44115
216-687-4522
Fax: 216-687-6943

David Baker, Director
Creative Writing Program
Denison University
Department of English
Granville, OH 43023
740-587-6419
Fax: 740-587-6417
http://www.denison.edu/

Joyce Dyer
Hiram College
P.O. Box 67
Hiram, OH 44234
330-569-5152
Fax: 330-569-5130

Maggie Anderson, Director
Kent State University
Department of English
P.O. Box 5190
113 Satterfield
Kent, OH 44242-0001
330-672-2067
Fax: 330-672-3152
http://www.kent.edu/

Michelle Herman, Director
Ohio State University
Creative Writing Program
Department of English
421 Denney Hall
164 West 17th Avenue
Columbus, OH 43210-1370
614-292-2242
Fax: 614-292-7816
*http://www.english.ohio-state.edu/areas/
creative_writing*

Mark Halliday, Director
Ohio University
Department of English
209 Ellis Hall
Athens, OH 45701
740-593-2758
Fax: 740-593-2818

Dr. Norman Chainey
Otterbein College
Creative Writing Program
303 Towers Hall
Westerville, OH 43081
614-823-1560
http://www.otterbein.edu/

Eric Goodman, External Director
Miami University
Creative Writing Program
Department of English
356 Bachelor Hall
Oxford, OH 45056
513-529-6500
Fax: 513-529-1392
http://www.muohio.edu/

Joel Lipman
University of Toledo
Department of English
2801 West Bancroft
Toledo, OH 43606-3390
419-530-4050/2318
Fax: 419-530-4440
http://www.utoledo.edu/

OKLAHOMA
Dr. Lynette Wert
University of Central Oklahoma

Department of Creative Studies
100 University Drive
Edmond, OK 73034-0184
405-341-2980, ext. 5667
http://www.ucok.edu/

J.M. Davis
University of Oklahoma
Department of English
760 Van Vleet Oval #113
Norman, OK 73019-0240
405-325-6254
Fax: 405-325-0831

Mark Cox, Director
Creative Writing Program
Oklahoma State University
Department of English
205 Morrill Hall
Stillwater, OK 74078-4069
405-744-6235
Fax: 405-744-6326
*http://www.writing.okstate.edu/
english*

OREGON
Emily Orlando
Clackamas Community College
19600 South Molalla Avenue
Oregon City, OR 97045
503-657-6958, ext. 2285
*http://www.clackamas.cc.or.us/
INSTRUCT/ENGLISH*

Anne Dawid
Lewis and Clark College
Creative Writing Program
Department of English
0615 SW Palatine Hill Road, #58
Portland, OR 97219
503-768-7404
Fax: 503-768-7418

Dorianne Laux
University of Oregon
Program in Creative Writing
144 Columbia Hall
Eugene, OR 97403-1286
541-346-0536
Fax: 541-346-0537

Tracy Daugherty
Oregon State University
Creative Writing Program
Department of English
238 Moreland Hall
Corvallis, OR 97331-5302
541-737-1657

Fax: 541-737-3589
http://osu.orst.edu/dept/english/

PENNSYLVANIA
Cynthia Hogue
Stadler Center for Poetry
Bucknell University
Lewisburg, PA 17837
570-577-1853
Fax: 570-577-3760
*http://www.bucknell.edu/
departments/pr/admissions/
stadler.html*

Patricia Dobler
Carlow College
Department of English
3333 5th Avenue
Pittsburgh, PA 15213-3109
412-578-6346
Fax: 412-578-6019
http://www.carlow.edu/

Jim Daniels, Director
Creative Writing Program
Carnegie Mellon University
Department of English
Pittsburgh, PA 15213-3890
412-268-2850
Fax: 412-268-7989
http://www.cmu.edu/

Dr. Elaine Reed
Kutztown University
Creative Writing Program
Department of English
Kutztown, PA 19530-0730
610-683-4353
Fax: 610-683-4354

Joseph Nicholson, Director
Lock Haven University
Creative Writing Program
Raub Hall
Lock Haven, PA 17745
717-893-2640

G.W. Hawkes, Director
Lycoming College
Creative Writing Program
Department of English
Williamsport, PA 17701-5192
717-321-4114
Fax: 717-321-4389

Gregory Djanikian
University of Pennsylvania
Creative Writing Program

Department of English
Philadelphia, PA 19104-6273
215-898-7347
http://www.english.upenn.edu/

William J. Cobb, Director
Pennsylvania State University
Creative Writing Program
Department of English
117 Burrowes Building
University Park, PA 16802-6200
814-865-9681

Lynn Emanuel, Director
University of Pittsburgh
Creative Writing Program
Department of English
52G CL
Pittsburgh, PA 15260
412-624-4036
Fax: 412-624-5539
http://www.pitt.edu/

Paula Closson Buck, Director
University of Pittsburgh at Bradford
Creative Writing Program
300 Campus Drive
Bradford, PA 16701-2812
814-362-7514
Fax: 814-362-7684
http://www.pitt.edu/

Judith Vollmer, Director
University of Pittsburgh at Greensburg
Department of English
1150 Mt. Pleasant Road
Greensburg, PA 15601-5860
412-624-6118
Fax: 412-836-7133
http://www.pitt.edu/

Dr. Carroll Grimes
University of Pittsburgh at Johnstown
450 Schoolhouse Road
Johnstown, PA 15904-2912
814-269-7137
Fax: 814-269-7196

John Meredith Hill, Director
University of Scranton
Creative Writing Program
Department of English
Scranton, PA 18510-4644
717-941-7619

Lee Tobin McCain
Seton Hill College
Seton Hill Drive
Greensburg, PA 15601

724-830-1040
Fax: 724-830-1294
http://www.setonhill.edu/~academic/grad/fsh5/html

Dr. Alan Singer, Director
Temple University
Creative Writing Program
1020 Anderson Hall
1117 West Berks Street
Philadelphia, PA 19122-6090
215-204-1796
Fax: 215-204-9620
http://www.temple.edu/

Gary Fincke
Susquehanna University
Selinsgrove, PA
570-372-4164
Fax: 570-372-2774
http://www.susqu.edu

RHODE ISLAND
C.D. Wright
Program in Creative Writing
Brown University
P.O. Box 1852
Providence, RI 02912-1535
401-863-3260
Fax: 401-863-1535
http://www.brown.edu/

Jane Lunin Peril
Providence College
Department of English
Providence, RI 02918-0001
401-865-2490
fax: 401-865-2823
http://www.providence.edu/

Thomas Cobb
Rhode Island College
600 Mt. Pleasant Avenue
Providence, RI 02825
401-456-8115
http://www.ric.edu/

SOUTH CAROLINA
Rick Mulkey
Converse College
580 East Main Street
Spartanburg, SC 29302-1931
864-596-9186
Fax: 864-596-9221
http://www.converse.edu

John MacNicholas
University of South Carolina at Columbia

Creative Writing Program/Graduate English
Humanities Building
Columbia, SC 29208
803-777-5063
Fax: 803-777-9064
http://www.scarolina.edu/

SOUTH DAKOTA
Brian Bedard, Director
University of South Dakota
Creative Writing
Department of English
212 Dakota Hall
414 East Clark
Vermillion, SD 57069-2390
605-677-5486
Fax: 605-677-6409
http://www.usd.edu/

TENNESSEE
Thomas Russell
The University of Memphis
Creative Writing Program
Department of English
Patterson Hall Room 463
Memphis, TN 38152
901-678-4589
Fax: 901-678-2226

Tina Barr
Rhodes College
Creative Writing Program
Palmer Hall, 3rd Floor
2000 North Parkway
Memphis, TN 38112
901-843-3979
http://www.rhodes.edu/

Wyatt Prunty, Director
University of the South, Sewanee
Creative Writing Program
S.po/735 University Avenue
310 St. Luke's Hall
Sewanee, TN 37383-1000
615-931-1141
Fax: 615-598-1145
http://www.sewanee.edu/

Marilyn Kallet, Director
University of Tennessee at Knoxville
Writing Program
Department of English
301 McClung Tower
Knoxville, TN 37996-0430
423-974-6933
Fax: 615-974-6926
http://www.utenn.edu/

TEXAS
Albert Haley, Director
Creative Writing Program
Abilene Christian University
Department of English
Abilene, TX 79699
915-674-2262
Fax: 915-674-2408
http://www.acu.edu/

Dr. William V. Davis
Department of English
Baylor University
P.O. Box 97404
Waco, TX 76798
254-710-1768
Fax: 254-710-3894
http://www.baylor.edu/

Robert A. Fink
Hardin-Simmons University
Creative Writing Program
P.O. Box 15114
Abilene, TX 79698
915-670-1214

Kathleen Cambor
University of Houston
Writing Program
Department of English
Houston, TX 77204-3012
713-743-2952
Fax: 713-743-3215
http://www.uh.edu/

Bob McCranie
Red River Review
1729 Alpine Drive
Carrollton, TX 75007
http://www.RedRiverReview.Com

James B. Sanderson
Lamar University-Beaumont
Creative Writing Program
Department of English
P.O. Box 10023
Beaumont, TX 77710
409-880-8598
Fax: 409-880-8591
http://www.lamar.edu/

Dr. Leslie M. Williams
Midland College
Main Campus
3600 North Garfield
Midland, TX 79705-6397
915-685-4624
Fax: 915-685-4769

Dr. Gary D. Swaim
North Lake College
5001 North MacArthur Boulevard
Irving, TX 75038-3899
972-273-3551
Fax: 972-273-3583

Bruce Bond
University of North Texas
Department of English
P.O. Box 311307
Denton, TX 76203-1307
940-565-2050
Fax: 940-565-5355
http://unt.edu/engl/

Paul Ruffin
Sam Houston State University
Texas Review Press
Suite 458
1901 Sam Houston Avenue
Huntsville, TX 77341
409-294-1403
Fax: 409-294-1408
http://shsu.edu

C.W. Smith, Director
Southern Methodist University
Creative Writing Program
Department of English
Dallas, TX 75275
214-768-2000
Fax: 214-768-1234
http://www.smu.edu/

Tom Grimes, Director
Southwest Texas State University
Creative Writing Program
601 University Drive
San Marcos, TX 78666-4616
512-245-7681
Fax: 512-245-8546
http://www.swt.edu/MFA.html

Laurie Drummond and Alan Altimont
St. Edwards University
Writing Program
3001 South Congress Avenue
Austin, TX 78704-6489
512-416-5833/448-8564
Fax: 512-448-8492
http://www.stedwards.edu/hum/writprog.html

Leslie Ullman, Director
University of Texas, El Paso
Writing Program
Department of English
Hudspeth Hall, Room 113

El Paso, TX 79968
915-747-5529
Fax: 915-747-6214

Janet McCann
Texas A & M University
Creative Writing Program
Department of English
College Station, TX 77843-4227
409-845-8316
Fax: 409-862-2292
http://www-english.tamu.edu/cw

James Magnuson, Director
Michener Center for Writers
University of Texas, Austin
702 East Dean Keeton
Austin, TX 78713-7330
512-471-1601
Fax: 512-471-9997
http://www.utexas.edu/

Walter McDonald, Director
Texas Tech University
Writing Program
Department of English
P.O. Box 43091
Lubbock, TX 79409-3091
806-742-2500 or 2501
Fax: 806-742-0989
http://www.english.ttu.edu

Peter Balbert, Chair
Trinity University
Department of English
715 Stadium Drive
San Antonio, TX 78212-7200
210-736-7517
Fax: 210-736-7578
http://www.trinity.edu/

UTAH
Sally T. Taylor, Director
Department of English
Brigham Young University
3146 Jesse Knight Humanities Building
Provo, UT 84602
801-378-3181
Fax: 801-378-4720
http://english.byu.edu/

Jacqueline Osherow
University of Utah
Writing Program
Department of English
255 South Central Campus Drive, Room 3500
Salt Lake City, UT 84112-0494

801-581-6168
Fax: 801-585-5167
http://www.utah.edu/

Natasha Sajo
Westminster College of Salt Lake City
2840 South 1300 East
Salt Lake City, UT 84105
801-488-1654
Fax: 801-466-6916

VIRGINIA
William Miller, Director
Creative Writing Program
George Mason University
Department of English
MSN 3E4
Fairfax, VA 22030-4444
703-993-1160
http://www.gmu.edu/

R.H.W. Dillard
Hollins College
Creative Writing Program
Department of English
P.O. Box 9677
Roanoke, VA 24020-1677
540-362-6316
Fax: 540-632-6097
http://www.hollins.edu/

Susan V. Facknitz
James Madison University
Creative Writing Program
Department of English
Keezell Hall
MSC 1801
Harrisonburg, VA 22807
540-568-6202
Fax: 540-568-2983
http://www.jmu.edu/

Dr. Michael Pearson
Old Dominion University
Creative Writing Program
Department of English
Hampton Boulevard
Norfolk, VA 23529
757-683-4770
http://courses.lib.odu.edu/engl/mfa

Jim Peterson
Randolph-Macon Woman's College
Creative Writing Program
Department of English
2500 Rivermont Avenue
Lynchburg, VA 24503-1526
804-947-8513

Fax: 804-947-8138
http://www.rmwc.edu/

Paul Hanstedt
Roanoke College
Department of English
221 College Lane
Salem, VA 24153-3794
540-375-2380
http://www.roanoke.edu/

John Gregory Brown, Director
Sweet Briar College
Creative Writing Program
Department of English
Sweet Briar, VA 24595
804-381-6434
Fax: 804-381-6173
http://www.sbc.edu/

Douglas Day and Charles Wright,
Codirectors
University of Virginia
Creative Writing Program
Department of English
219 Bryan Hall
Charlottesville, VA 22903-4444
804-924-6675
Fax: 804-924-1478
http://www.engl.virginia.edu

Marita Golden
Virginia Commonwealth University
Department of English
P.O. Box 842005
Richmond, VA 23284-2005
804-828-1329
Fax 804-828-2171
http://www.has.vcu.edu/eng/grad/

Edward Falco and Catherine Soniat
Virginia Polytechnic Institute and State
University
Creative Writing Program
Department of English
Blacksburg, VA 24061-0112
540-231-6501
Fax: 540-231-5692
http://www.vt.edu/

VERMONT
Liam Rector
Creative Writing Program
Bennington College
Bennington, VT 05201
802-440-4454
Fax: 802-440-4453
http://www.bennington.edu/

Paul Selig
Goddard College
123 Pitkin Road
Writing Program
Plainfield, VT 05667 -9700
802-454-8311
Fax: 802-454-8017
http://www.goddard.edu/

Mark Cox, Faculty Director
Louise Crowley, Administrative Director
Vermont College of Norwich University
The MFA in Writing
Montpelier, VT 05602
802-828-8840
Fax: 802-929-8649
*http://www.norwich.edu/grad/
writing/*

WASHINGTON D.C.
Myra Sklarew, Codirector
Creative Writing Program
American University
4400 Massachusetts Avenue NW
Department of English
Washington, D.C. 20016-8047
202-885-2990
Fax: 202-885-2938
*http://www.american.edu/
academic.depts/cas/lit/mfa-lit.htm*

Norma Tilden
Georgetown University
Department of English
P.O. Box 571131
Washington, D.C. 20057

David McAleavey
George Washington University
Creative Writing Program
Department of English
Washington, D.C. 20052
202-994-6180
Fax: 202-994-7915
http://www.gwu.edu/

David Everett
Johns Hopkins University
Part-time Graduate Writing Program
1776 Massachusetts Avenue NW
Washington, D.C. 20036-2280
202-452-0758
Fax: 202-530-9857
http://www.jhu.edu/pgp-as

Kenneth Carroll
Writers Corps, Washington D.C.
1331 H Street NW, Suite 920
Washington, D.C. 20005-4703

202-347-1734
Fax: 202-347-3350

WASHINGTON
John Keeble
Eastern Washington University
Creative Writing Program, MS 1
Spokane Center
705 West 1st Avenue
Spokane, WA 99201
509-623-4245
http://www.ewu.edu/

Peter Chilson
Washington State University
Department of English
P.O. Box 645020
Pullman, WA 99164-5020
509-335-2163
Fax: 509-335-2582
http://www.wsu.edu/~english

Linda Bierds
University of Washington
Writing Program
Department of English/Box 354330
Seattle, WA 98195-4330
206-543-9865
Fax: 206-685-2673
http://www.washington.edu/

Robin Hemley
Western Washington University
MS 9055
Department of English
Bellingham, WA 98225-9055
360-650-3236
Fax: 360-650-4837
http://www.wwu.edu/

Chuck Luckmann
Skagit Valley College
Mount Vernon Campus
2405 East College Way
Oak Harbor, WA 98277
360-416-7696

WISCONSIN
Clint McCown, Director
Creative Writing Program
Department of English
Beloit College
700 College Street
Beloit, WI 53511-5596
608-365-3391
*http://www.beloit.edu/
~academic/majors/eng/eng.html*

Peter Blewett
Cardinal Strich College
6801 North Yates Road
Milwaukee, WI 53217-3985
414-410-4193
Fax 414-410-4239

Karl Elder, Director
Lakeland College
Creative Writing Program
Department of English
P.O. Box 359
Sheboygan, WI 53082-0359
920-565-1276
Fax: 920-565-1206
http://www.lakeland.edu/

C.J. Hribal
Marquette University
P.O. Box 1881
Department of English
Milwaukee, WI 53233
414-288-7179
Fax: 414-288-5433
http://www.mu.edu/

Ronald Wallace
University of Wisconsin, Madison
Creative Writing Program
Helen C. White Hall
600 North Park Street
Madison, WI 53706
608-263-3800
Fax: 608-263-3709
http://www.wisc.edu/

Sheila Roberts, Coordinator
University of Wisconsin, Milwaukee
Creative Writing Program
P.O. Box 413
Department of English
Milwaukee, WI 53211
414-229-4511
Fax: 414-229-2643
http://www.uwm.edu/Dept/English

Donna Lewis, Secretary
University of Wisconsin at Whitewater
Department of Modern Languages and
Literatures
800 West Main Street
Whitewater, WI 53190-2121
414-472-5050
Fax: 414-472-1419

WEST VIRGINIA
James Harms, Director
West Virginia University
Writing Program
Department of English
230 Stansbury Hall, Box 6296
Morgantown, WV 26506-6296
304-293-1307, ext. 451
http://www.wvu.edu/

Irene McKinney
West Virginia Wesleyan College
Creative Writing Program
Department of English
Buckhannon, WV 26201-2995
304-473-8329
Fax: 304-473-8187
http://www.wvwc.edu/

WYOMING
Vicki Lindner, Director
University of Wyoming
Writing Program
Department of English Box 3353
Laramie, WY 82071-3353
307-766-2384
Fax: 307-766-3189

CANADA
Derk Wynand
University of Victoria
Department of Writing
P.O. Box 1700 STN CSC
Victoria, BC V8W 2Y2
250-721-7306

Dr. Wyman Herendeen
University of Windsor
Writing Program
401 Sunset Avenue
Windsor, Ontario
Canada N9B 3P4
519-253-4232
Fax: 519-973-3676
http://www.uwindsor.ca/

GREAT BRITAIN
Mahendra Solanki
Department of English and Media Studies
Nottingham Trent University
Clifton Lane
Nottingham NG11 8NS
United Kingdom
+44 (0) 115-941-8418, ext. 3397
Fax: +44 (0) 115-848-6632
*http://human.ntu.ac.uk/foh/pg/
mawrit.html*

Types of Books

Best-selling novelist John D. MacDonald once said that he shunned writers' conferences because he always heard one of two comments from the writers who came up to talk with him. The first comment was "Let me give you a great idea for a novel." The second was "I'm thinking about writing a book."

It's something everyone who is published has experienced in similar circumstances. As for the first comment, every published writer worth his or her salt has more ideas than they know what to do with; the trick is sorting out those that are good and commercial from those that are bad and unsellable. What's more, individuals in their right mind would not lay themselves open to charges that somehow they "stole" someone else's idea. You can't anyway. Ideas are ten-a-penny. Anyone can take an idea and run with it. What makes one book publishable and another unpublishable, using the same idea, is what the author has done with that idea.

As for the second comment, in his book *The Insider's Guide to Getting Published,* literary agent John Boswell reports that MacDonald told him, "Can you imagine someone coming up to the painter Andrew Wyeth and saying, 'I do a little painting myself every now and then. Whom should I approach, the Guggenheim or the Met?' Writing for me is a profession, but for some reason everyone thinks they should be able to do it. I guess it's because everyone writes letters or postcards or laundry lists. So, they figure, why not a book?"

Well, okay let's start there. Why not a book?

Fiction and Nonfiction

I'll begin by defining the two types of book that publishers publish: fiction and nonfiction.

Fiction is an invention, usually in the form of a story, that may or may not be based on real things that happened to you or someone else. There are broadly three types of fiction formats: short stories—usually no longer than 30 double-spaced manuscript pages and often much shorter; novellas—which range from 30 to 150 manuscript pages; and novels—from about 250 manuscript pages and on up. In reality, a good length to aim for in a novel is between 250 and 450 manuscript pages. Usually novels are the only thing that publishers are interested in looking at in the fiction category.

Nonfiction is anything that is *not* fiction. That is, it's all true and based on research and/or expert opinion. Pay attention to that last part—*expert* opinion; that means not just an opinion on something you think you have insight into, but *expert* opinion.

This book is a classic example of nonfiction: You're reading it because I'm considered an expert in the field (who am I to argue when a publisher wants to give me money for writing a book; it is one of the things I do for a living, after all); my opinions are worth paying some attention to and are considered thoughtful by my peers, who know as much if not more than I do about publishing; and I've backed up my opinions with research and hard fact.

Categories and Genres

An average of fifty thousand books a year are published in the United States. Some are hardcover (or cloth), many more are paperback, both mass market (the small-sized books that fit in your pocket) and trade (the larger sized ones that almost look like hardcovers). All are very different, but they have one thing in common: Each book can be slotted into a category, or genre.

Probably 98 percent of books written fall into some category. Why? Because readers gravitate toward a certain kind of reading experience. I'm sure if you stop and think about it, every time you go to the library or the bookstore you have some idea of what you want to read before you start browsing the book stacks.

Genres developed as a way of marketing and selling mass market paperbacks. As a result, even mainstream novels, when reprinted as mass market paperbacks, need to be slotted into a genre of some sort.

Browsing bookshelves with an eye to studying genre can be very revealing, especially if you're thinking about writing your first book. One of the first questions an editor asks of a manuscript is, What genre is it? Without knowing that, how is the editor or bookstore owner going to know on which shelf in the bookstore to put the book? And how will the editor be able to convince colleagues that a book he wants to buy is a commercially viable project?

INFORMATION

Did You Know...

A *genre* is a marketing term that divides and categorizes books so that they are easily placed together in a store. Westerns, romances, and mysteries are examples of genres.

It's important that you know who your audience is and that you study that group. Haunt bookstores and libraries to familiarize yourself with the various genres; read a lot of books in as many genres as you can. If you're not reading a particular genre, it's almost certain you shouldn't be writing in it.

Your first successfully published book will, almost inevitably, be centered around some category that you really love. You don't "write what you know," as the old saw has it; you *draw upon* what you know, but you *write what you read.*

When a book comes out, it's not really competing with all the other books in the store. It's only competing with all the other books in the same genre. So, without diverging too much from what's expected, you ought to be thinking about how you're going to make your book different from others like it. And that difference comes from knowing your genre well enough that you can spot a "hole," or good idea.

Books are generally written with a specific audience in mind. Self-help books, for example, have a strong female readership, while nonfiction adventure books, such as man against nature (e.g., *Into Thin Air* or *The Perfect Storm*) are largely bought and read by men. Only books that become big sellers transcend these limitations.

A common mistake inexperienced writers make is to assume that because, say, a romance develops in their cop novel, the book must also be a romance. That's why when you ask an unpublished writer what her book is about, she sometimes says things like, "It's this. But it's also that. And then it's this third thing as well."

If you decide to write a romance, for example, think about what it is that's always true about romance novels. Genre refers to the main focus of the type of story that's being told. If the story is set on the American frontier in the 1880s, for example, and it involves, say, ranchers and squatters, and gunfighters, and greedy railroad barons, you are writing a Western. It doesn't matter if the hero falls in love and has a torrid affair with one of the robber baron's daughters; *it's not a romance unless the main focus of the story is squarely centered on the romance between the two characters.*

You could have a story about two cowboys who come across evidence of a werewolf attacking and killing, first, their cattle and, later, settlers. This might be considered a *cross-genre* novel, but really it is just a horror novel set in the American West. Similarly, a story about a cowboy who has to solve the murder of a friend would be a mystery or crime novel with a Western setting.

Romance

Romance fiction has a strict form, usually variations on this theme: Girl meets boy, girl loses boy, girl finds boy again. You can write to the publishers of such fiction, and they'll send you guidelines that will tell you how they like their books to be structured.

In general, the reader of romance fiction expects that both the hero and heroine will be alive and well and thoroughly in love with each other at the end of the story. The protagonists shouldn't be separated for long periods, and the story should end at a point in their story in which there is the most hope for their relationship.

Romance touches something universal that we're all looking for in our own ways. The quality of the book is determined by the perceptiveness of the writer and his or her ability to put words on paper. You also need to be able to create strong female characters who speak to the genre's predominantly female readership.

Horror

Who is the biggest selling novelist of the last decade? Stephen King, of course, followed closely by Anne Rice, Clive Barker, and Dean Koontz. Horror fiction, once a part of science fiction and fantasy, has grown to become a major genre in its own right.

Horror fiction has been best described by author Peter Straub as "the thin ice of life." While it was a strong selling genre for authors to break into a couple of years ago, recently the only horror novels being published are from well-established writers. Horror's appeal is to take everyday things and magnify them, exposing our fears so that we can examine them safely. Ultimately, horror is about confronting and dealing with our fear of death.

Think About This . . .

Your book may be well written, but does it follow the rules of its genre? If not, why not?

Science Fiction and Fantasy

By the early 1990s, science fiction and fantasy books were multibillion-dollar generators of profit for publishing houses. Sci-fi (or SF, for short) and fantasy, while around for a long time, took off as a genre after the striking success of the movie *Star Wars* in 1977. In many ways, it has also paved the way for how publishing in general has developed in the 1990s.

SF and fantasy are "author driven," which means, simply, that readers pay attention to who wrote the book they last read and enjoyed and make efforts to find something else by that author. Author driven material overcomes one of corporate publishing's biggest problems, that is, how to mass market a commodity (i.e., a book) in an industry that for most of its existence has been defined by its idiosyncratic nature. The generalized approach to selling books through the cult of personality, which is now dominating publishing, first developed in the SF and fantasy genre, and then spread to the other genres as SF's marketing success grew.

Many people involved in publishing SF and fantasy cling to the notion that aping the success of others is more important, because of potential financial rewards, than encouraging the development of what John Silbersack, former HarperPrism executive editor and vice president, once described as the "literature of revolution."

Westerns

Westerns are clearly definable by their covers, which often show cowboys with side arms, American Indians in full warpath regalia, wagon trains, and rearing horses against backgrounds reminiscent of the American Southwest. Westerns are a peculiar brand of story, partly gritty, partly historical, partly mythological.

The Western is about the opening of the frontier, roughly between 1840 and 1900, and the perils and tribulations of those who gambled, often with their lives and their fortunes, in order to establish themselves and their dreams. There is a natural conflict at the heart of every Western, be it man against man, man against nature, or man against himself. These conflicts are concerned with morality and the challenges of survival. Westerns are not an easy genre to break into, though, because there are only a handful of editors working in the field, and their lists are already pretty full.

Historicals

It is not a far trip from the Western to the historical novel. The serious historical novelist needs to be able to weave a fictional plot into real historical events without distorting the historical characters who appear.

To succeed, historical fiction and nonfiction have to be written by a recognized scholar, or someone with credentials of some sort, say, a Ph.D.

A historical novel's appeal involves the chance for readers to meet real people as they were and understand something of what happened back then. The historical writer strives to maintain the customs, culture, and knowledge of the period.

In a time of political correctness, it's sometimes difficult to maintain honesty while portraying past cruelties and ignorance. Perhaps for that reason, historical novels are much tougher to write and sell now than they were previously. Most historical novels are best slanted toward other genres, such as historical romance or historical mystery, to make them more commercially viable.

Crime Novels

Mystery or crime novels fall into a very popular genre with millions of devoted fans. There are "tough guy" mysteries, sometimes referred to as hardboiled—such as those written by Raymond Chandler, Dashiell Hammett, or Mickey Spillane—that feature a cynical private investigator, or PI; and there are soft mysteries, sometimes called cozies, which usually feature an amateur sleuth, typically along the lines of an Agatha Christie, John Dickenson Carr, or *Murder She Wrote* kind of puzzle story.

Then there are police procedurals, in which the usually gritty detail of what cops do to bring criminals to justice is more prominent than the puzzle. One of the first examples of police procedurals is Ed McBain's 87th Precinct series. These days, most editors agree that successful new crime novels are more concerned with interesting characters and settings than with just an intriguing mystery.

The Literary Novel

Literary or mainstream fiction is a genre like any other. It's a hard area to sell in because the competition and standards are extremely tough and the available publishing "slots" relatively few. The reason is that the publisher can't find an identifiable audience. There's no group of individuals that walk up to a bookstore clerk and say, "Hey, do you have any mainstream novels?"

Fancy yourself as a literary novelist? You're in competition with books like *The Shipping News* by E. Annie Proulx, *Portrait of the Artist as a Young Man* by James Joyce, *For Whom the Bell Tolls* by Ernest Hemingway, *The Name of The Rose* by Umberto Eco, *Jazz* by Toni Morrison, *The Joy Luck Club* by Amy Tan, *The World According to Garp* by John Irving, and so on. Some people confuse *literate* with literary, but they're not the same thing. All books, whether fiction or nonfiction, should be literate, that is, gracefully well written.

The literary novel survives on the reputation and consummate skill of the writer, on book reviews and blurbs from other more famous writers, and on word of mouth. If you're a beginner, you're not likely to have any of that going for you. There have been and continue to be plenty of examples to prove me wrong, but the authors are probably not reading this book, and they're almost certainly not making a living writing fiction exclusively.

Thrillers

Thrillers require a protagonist who is in a lot of danger, what Stephen King calls in *Misery* (his horror novel that is also about how to write good fiction) "get out of that" storytelling. In other words, the car is about to go over the cliff with our hero lying unconscious in the backseat—get out of that. Every time the protagonist does something in a thriller, it is like going from the frying pan into the fire; there's danger on every single page.

Readers of this kind of book expect thrills and spills, and if you don't provide them, you're going to create a very disappointing book. Classic thrillers you should be familiar with include John Buchan's *The Thirty-Nine Steps*, Richard Condon's *The Manchurian Candidate*, and Frederick Forsythe's *The Day of the Jackal*.

Books for Children and Young Adults

Children's books broadly fall into three categories: picture books for the very young, chapter (chap) books for roughly ages 7 to 14 (middle grade), and young adult (YA) for teenagers.

A lot of beginning writers think children's books are easy to write, but they're wrong. It's actually one of the most demanding of genres. Inexperienced writers often assume that tales for children should be "good for them" and write simplistic morality tales. But kids are a tough audience, and they're not easily fooled. They want stories that speak *to* them, not *at* them, and they loathe blatant moralizing.

In general, kids love books that afford an escape into fantasy. The Harry Potter books are the biggest selling children's books on both sides of the Atlantic.

YA books also deal seriously and candidly with issues that teens face today. These issues are very important, from incest and teen violence to alienation and loss of innocence, and need to be handled with great sensitivity and insight.

Nonfiction

Narrative nonfiction (i.e., character driven nonfiction) has a similar structure to that of a piece of fiction. A good commercial nonfiction piece should have a narrative spin that also encompasses a debate on a topic of national interest that grows from the story. A good example of this would be *The Burning Bed* and the issue of domestic abuse.

Nonfiction should also offer a positive spin on even the most negative topic. Readers don't want to plunk down $25 for a book only to be told that life is hopeless. While that approach can work effectively in a magazine or newspaper because it is balanced by other more upbeat pieces in the same issue, a book rises or falls on its own merits.

A book of nonfiction must have lots of information and can't just be a soapbox for you. People have to trust you as a guide to the topic you're writing about before they'll bother to read what you have to say. That's why most successful nonfiction is written by experts of one sort or another.

True Crime

Ever read *In Cold Blood* by Truman Capote? Is it nonfiction or fiction? It's a true story, after all, though it's considered the first narrative nonfiction book to use fictional techniques to tell a true story. The experts who write true crime successfully are or have been lawyers, cops, investigators, journalists, forensic specialists, and so forth. The stories are often psychosexual in nature or symbolic of some facet of our culture that the crime has exposed.

Biography

There are broadly three types of biography: interpretive, objective, and dramatic. All try to reveal the essence of the subject. Interpretive biographies interpret the events and actions of a subject's life through a psychological prism. Objective biographies gather facts and documents about how the subject lived. Dramatic biographies use fictional techniques to recreate the subject and his or her times.

In general, a biography has to have a theme, and its subject has to fit into the context of the times the subject lived in. More than that, the subject of a biography should also be a symbol of some sort for the spirit of his or her age. The book should bring out some thematic element of that culture it represents. Broadly, a good biography is one that illuminates and shows the times in addition to the person.

The biographer must have the skills of a storyteller to construct a compelling narrative, a diplomat to deal with the many witnesses who can shed light on the subject's life, and a detective to ferret out research on the subject. The biographer must be devoted to his or her subject and yet objective enough to explore the dark nooks and crannies of the life in question and employ literary and psychological brilliance to create a book that the subject could honestly admit was an accurate portrayal of his or her life.

Memoirs

A woman I know stopped me in the elevator one day and said, "I've written a memoir about growing up in this neighborhood. Would you like to read it?"

Now we get several manuscripts a week along these lines, nearly all of which we reject. So I asked her, "Was there any trauma in your family? Did you suffer rape or incest or serious disease?"

The woman was horrified and turned in a huff, believing that I had slighted and ridiculed her. In fact, memoirs are about traumatic events in a writer's life that a writer of exquisite skill can transform into an experience we can all share. It is the nearest thing to poetry a writer of prose can do. Read Isabelle Allende's *Paula*, about the sickness and coma her daughter suffered. Could you honestly write something that powerful about your life?

Memoirs are about a child's sickness, a father's death, a loss of honor or career. We read another's pain because the writer's sensibility allows him or her to extract from the dreadful experience powerful universal emotions that illuminate our lives.

Editors who buy memoirs do so because the writer has successfully transferred the experience to the page in a strong emotional way. And in so doing the writer, like the alchemists of old, has transmuted the experience from base lead into gold.

How-to Books

How-to books are one of the best genres to write to break into publishing. This nonfiction genre is probably the largest and also one of the most successful. How-to books embrace a wide field, from knitting and hobbies to health, finance, sports, and parenting. So while your book may well fall under the broad category of How-to, try to be as specific as you can about who your audience is, and what is different about your book on the subject.

Reference Books

I'm not talking just about dictionaries and encyclopedias here. This category also includes lighter books such as *The One Hundred Stupidest Questions Ever Asked*, or books like Dave Feldman's *Why Do Dogs Have Wet Noses?* These kinds of books are sold to libraries and schools, as well as bookstores.

Cookbooks

Most cookbooks are written by people who own restaurants, have become famous as chefs, have their own TV show, or are in the public eye already in some fashion, perhaps as food writers or some such. The publishing company can then cash in on the name recognition of the author. Any chance at all in this field will start with some success at the regional or local level, and the book will echo this success in some way.

Travel Books

Travel books include narratives of adventures, travel guides, and destination guides. They provide information on hotels, restaurants, places to go, interesting sights to see, and so forth.

Travelogues often provide lyrical descriptions of faraway places. They're aimed at an audience known as the "armchair travelers."

Travel guides are nondestination books that tell you how to travel in a particular way, such as traveling by donkey across Tibet or by train across China, as in Paul Theroux's *Riding The Iron Rooster*.

Destination guides are like the *Everything Guide to Washington D.C.* They include what to see, where to stay and eat, and so forth.

Pop Culture

Pop culture books have become very popular as we head into the new millennium, trying to understand who we are, what cultural forces are shaping our identity, and what messages the mass media of our time is sending us. To write in this genre successfully, you need to have some expertise, often reflected by a passion for a subject that has made you something of an expert. The trick becomes parlaying that passion (let us not call it an obsession, please) into a book that others will read and enjoy, and learn from.

Humor

Cartoon books like *Dilbert* or Gary Larson's *Far Side*, and books with humorous observations on life like *Dave Barry on Computers* or Paul Reiser's *Babyhood* are lumped together as humor. You're on your own here. Do others think you're funny? Can you make an overworked editor smile enough to see the commercial potential in your scribblings? It's probably easier to do stand-up comedy in a comedy club, though not by much. Humor is possibly the most subjective category in the industry, so good hunting for your humor soul mate in publishing.

Are You an Expert about Something?

You need to have some sort of credentials to write nonfiction. A parish priest could write a major work on religion and get it published; a teacher could write a book about education; a journalist could do a book about, say, the medical establishment; a parent of a sick child could research all there is to know abut the disease and then write about it. You need to have some edge, however small, beyond your interest in the topic, though. In general, those who are passionate about something also tend to have studied it a lot and are often experts by default.

Fashion in genres comes and goes in phases. True crime, for example, is a category that while once very popular is now harder to sell. A genre can be "hot," and then it is overbought and becomes hard to sell for a while. The genre becomes "dormant" until a book comes along that reinvigorates the category beyond the work of the established few authors who have luckily continued to write and sell in that area, keeping it "ticking over."

For example, true crime books can sometimes be reshaped as current event stories if the story (like *The Burning Bed*) is broad enough and symbolic enough to become more than just the sum of what happened. It's the writer's job to learn the art of the newspaper reporter, not only capturing the spirit of what was said and done, but also capturing it accurately without boring readers with unnecessary detail or speech in the process.

Good Ideas and Bad Ideas

So I'm at lunch with my friend Maggie a few years ago—she's buying because her newspaper gave her a bigger expense account than mine—and after a lull in the conversation, I finally come out with, "I'm thinking of writing a book."

Typical of Maggie, her first reaction was not "Oh, really, about what?" but "Don't tell me about it, do it." "Okay," I said, rising to the challenge, "I will."

I went home, grabbed my typewriter and some blank paper, and began what I had been doing for years, the opening paragraph of a novel. Several years, some false starts, and a lot of angst later, I finished it. Maggie read it, thought it was great, and then I moved to America. It was, of course, unsellable. But it was my first book, and I learned a huge amount doing it, principally, what not to do.

The problem now was what to write next? Ideas eluded me for a while, and I began to feel desperate. I read magazines, newspapers, other books, but nothing seemed to help.

Then I had this idea about a terrorist who had ESP, and my friend Jim Cohen thought it would be cool to have a cop who also had ESP tracking him down. "Let's make the terrorist a man and the cop a woman," I said. So we developed the idea into a synopsis. Then I wrote the first draft, Jim rewrote it into a second draft, I edited that, he edited mine, and eventually we were both content (or perhaps it was exhausted, I forget) with the prose and the story. Two years and twenty-two submissions later, our agent sold it. Lo and behold, my first novel, *Mindbender*, was published in 1988.

You may not believe it now, but once you work at developing book ideas, they'll start tumbling out of you. When that happens, you must be willing to throw all but the best ones away.

The problem is not coming up with an idea. The problem is determining which idea will sell and then whether this idea will work best as nonfiction or fiction, a book, a short story, a screenplay, a magazine article, or what have you.

Once you begin to develop your "idea muscle," ideas will start to flow. This can be quite frustrating because you'll realize you can't possibly develop every idea you have. So how do you decide which ones to work on?

In the absence of a compelling idea that won't let go, you grope around looking for something to start work on. You watch TV, read newspapers, listen to the radio, eavesdrop on other people's conversations, start thinking *what if* that happened this way instead?

What if a policeman tracking down a serial killer during the London Blitz comes to think the killer is a werewolf? This was the starting idea for my novel *Werewolf*.

H. G. Wells asked himself, "What if a man could travel in time?" Then he sat down and wrote *The Time Machine*.

Once you've gotten into the habit of coming up with book ideas, one of the best ways to decide which ones to play with and which to ignore is to focus on those ideas that seem to insistently nag at you. In other words, each time you try to ignore the idea, it comes back a little more formed and shaped and insistent than before, until eventually you have no choice but to sit down and write your story.

With nonfiction book ideas, you must first consider who your audience is: Is it men? Is it women? Is it men and women? Remember that men and women have different ideas about what they want to get out of or learn from books.

Is the idea one that will sell twenty thousand to thirty thousand copies? Will it appeal to a broad, though distinctive audience? A good rule of thumb is to ask yourself, Am I affected by this topic? If not, is someone I know—a friend or relative perhaps—affected by it? Will the audience be passionate about the subject? If you can answer yes to these questions, then your nonfiction idea has passed its first hurdle. An audience that is only mildly interested probably won't buy the book in large enough numbers to make it worth publishing.

INFORMATION

Did You Know...

A *series* is made up of two or more books linked by the same character, the same "world" within the books, or a brand name.

Identifying Bad Ideas

So how do you decide what makes a bad idea? Most bad ideas come into existence because the writer was drawn to them for the wrong reasons. Here's the first test: Have you come across your idea in someone else's books or seen it on the TV or in the movies? If so, someone's beaten you to it, and chances are it's not worth writing about.

There are three things that can tip you off that your idea is probably a bad one: familiarity, importance, and truth. What these three things have in common is that they are based on the writer's needs and not the reader's needs. Bad ideas appeal to inexperienced writers because they make life easier for the writer.

Familiarity

Just because something's familiar and you have particular access to it doesn't automatically make it a good idea. Narrative nonfiction—unlike journalism, in which the event itself is the important piece of information to focus on—is about the meaning of the event. The significance lies in what you make of the event and how it affects you as a person.

Importance

An idea may be important to you because it comes from your life. Take, for example, a woman who for ten years watches her husband slowly waste away from cancer and, then, when he's gone, decides to write about a woman watching her husband die of cancer. This scenario is a literary agent or editor's nightmare. You hate to tell somebody that a wrenching experience such as that, not to mention ten years of one's life, is not interesting enough to sustain even an article, let alone a good book idea.

But we've all been doing something with our lives, be it baking white bread, drilling holes in bamboo flutes, picking strawberries in the broiling sun, whatever. Am I saying that you can't write a good book about someone dying of cancer? Of course not. Any idea you write about should be important to you, but it doesn't automatically follow that any idea that is important to you is a good idea.

Truth

If editors and agents had a nickel for every time a young writer responded to criticism with a plaintive, "But it's *true*," we'd all be *very* wealthy people. An idea is not a good idea just because it's true: "Yo, Pete. My cousin Chuckie? He had a 6-inch nail driven into his skull by some guy in a bar. And you know what? It cured his headaches!"

Sometimes an idea that's true isn't even necessarily believable. Again, you could make up a story about a guy who cures people's headaches by driving 6-inch nails into their skulls, but it really wouldn't get you very far. Just because it's true doesn't make it a good idea.

Identifying Good Ideas

Study your genre or your topic and know it well enough to be familiar with what's been done and *what hasn't*. What's fresh and new and yet familiar enough to still fit into the main body of books published in this area?

In other words, start looking for holes. What's a hole? A hole is something that hasn't been done quite that way before. Find a hole, and you will usually find a good idea in there somewhere.

So, what exactly are the reader's needs? What are some qualities of a good idea that will encourage a reader to plunk down his or her good money and buy your book?

First, people read fiction and narrative nonfiction (such as biographies) to escape their own lives. Strong stories, whether fiction or nonfiction, take you to new worlds and introduce you to new and interesting people and ideas. A guy who works at an insurance company all day long doesn't want to come home and read about an insurance company. (Look at the work of Franz Kafka if you don't believe me.) Instead, he might want to read about how characters resolve high-powered ethical and moral dilemmas that he hopes he will never be faced with but that call up powerful emotional responses. For example, do I save the three hundred people on the approaching train that will crash if I don't lower the bridge and crush my 6-year-old daughter who has crawled out onto the track? Or do I save her and kill all the people on the train instead?

Second, readers want to read about active characters. Movies are made and stories told, both fiction and nonfiction, about the person who takes action. There are no stories about the person who just sits back and observes the action without getting involved or reacting to the events of the story. Make sure your characters *do* something to affect what's going on in the story. It's not what happens to the character that makes her interesting. *It's what she does about it.* Without an active character there is no emotional power to a narrative. In a word, it becomes *boring.*

Third, readers want characters with clear and definable goals. What does this character want? It should be something very specific, something that the reader can imagine.

Finally, there has to be something important at stake. What will victory cost the characters in your story? If you're asking people to sit down and read a three-hundred- or four-hundred-page book, there better be something really important at stake. If there isn't, your readers will be angry and disappointed.

In many ways, stories, whether true or invented, can be thought of as biographies of watershed events in the central character's life. The story begins with the trauma, or watershed event, and ends when the trauma is resolved, or the watershed event ends. And because it's about a character, it also involves our feelings for and about this person.

The High Concept Idea

A high concept idea is an idea that is usually outrageous yet compelling and can be stated in one sentence.

Here are two examples:

- A Memphis law firm is laundering money for the Mafia, and a young lawyer who tries to leave the firm is threatened with death. (*The Firm*, John Grisham)
- A group of explorers, investigating disturbances at sea, are captured by a megalomaniacal captain in a high-tech deep-sea submarine.

The last example would not be high concept now, but in its day—1870—when Jules Verne wrote *Twenty Thousand Leagues under the Sea*, it certainly was.

There's nothing new about high concept:

- A bookish young prince, driven crazy by the death of his father, the king, discovers that his mother and his uncle conspired to murder his father and steal his throne. (*Hamlet*, William Shakespeare)

Not every story has to be high concept, but the idea of marketing your work this way is becoming more and more important, and it certainly boasts the fierceness of a book's focus.

Fiction Reading List

It always amazes me that unpublished writers confess that while they want to be published, they don't have the time to read. If you're not sure what you should be reading, below is a list of fiction titles to get you going.

I'm sure loads of people will disagree wildly with what I've included and what I've left out, but this list is meant to stir up some form of debate about good books and bad, and what should be included and what left out. If you have favorites that you think should be included, be vociferous in your opinion—send me an e-mail. Feel free to post this list, rip it to shreds, or praise it to the heavens. But at least read some of the books I've included here; they're worth it.

The Canterbury Tales by Geoffrey Chaucer
The Collected Plays of William Shakespeare
Robinson Crusoe by Daniel Defoe
Gulliver's Travels by Jonathan Swift
Pride and Prejudice by Jane Austin
Ivanhoe: A Romance by Sir Walter Scott
Frankenstein, or The Modern Prometheus by Mary Wollstonecraft Shelley

Exercises to Develop Ideas

Here are a few ways to come up with ideas for stories, whether fiction or nonfiction:

- Scour newspapers, magazines, and other sources of current events.
- Invent lives for strangers you observe as you go about your daily business.
- Think about something that happened to you or someone you know. What would have happened if things had gone differently?
- Spontaneously write an opening "hook" or sentence.
- Rewrite fairy tales and legends as modern stories.
- Go to trade shows and find out what's hot in the industry (any industry that has a trade fair that catches your fancy) that hasn't quite made it into the consciousness of the general public.
- Browse the bookshelves of your local bookstores and familiarize yourself with a particular topic. What's missing from the shelves that you think you could provide?

Twice-Told Tales and/or *The Scarlet Letter* by Nathaniel Hawthorne

The Stories of Edgar Allen Poe

Alice's Adventures in Wonderland and *Through the Looking Glass* by Lewis Carroll

Little Women by Louisa May Alcott

Tess of the D'Urbervilles by Thomas Hardy

The Adventures of Tom Sawyer and *The Adventures of Huckleberry Finn* by Mark Twain

Collected Stories and Essays of Ambrose Bierce

Treasure Island and *Doctor Jekyll and Mr. Hyde* by Robert Louis Stevenson

She or *King Solomon's Mines* by H. Rider Haggard

The Picture of Dorian Gray by Oscar Wilde

The Adventures of Sherlock Holmes by Sir Arthur Conan Doyle

The Red Badge of Courage by Stephen Crane

The Time Machine: An Invention and *Goodbye Mr. Chips* by H. G. Wells

War and Peace by Leo Tolstoy

The Collected Short Stories and Plays of Anton Chekhov

Crime and Punishment by Fyodor Dostoevsky

The Water Babies by Charles Kingsley

Just So Stories and *The Jungle Book* by Rudyard Kipling

Dracula by Bram Stoker

Lord Jim and/or *The Secret Agent* by Joseph Conrad

Cabbages and Kings by O'Henry

The Wind in the Willows by Kenneth Grahame

The Secret Garden by Frances Hodgson Burnett

Ethan Frome by Edith Wharton

Riders of the Purple Sage by Zane Grey

Sons and Lovers by D. H. Lawrence

The Collected Poems of Wilfred Owens

Portrait of the Artist as a Young Man and *The Dubliners* by James Joyce

This Side of Paradise and *The Great Gatsby* by F. Scott Fitzgerald

The Sun Also Rises, *The Old Man and the Sea*, and *For Whom The Bell Tolls* by Ernest Hemingway

Peter Pan by J. M. Barrie

The Stranger by Albert Camus

The Immoralist by Andre Gide

Narciss and Goldamund and *Siddhartha* by Herman Hesse

Orlando by Virginia Woolf

The Dain Curse and *The Maltese Falcon* by Dashiell Hammett

Collected Stories of W. Somerset Maugham

I Claudius and *Claudius the God* by Robert Graves

The Little Foxes by Lillian Hellman

U.S.A. by John Dos Passos

Cry, the Beloved Country by Alan Paton

The Grapes of Wrath and *Of Mice and Men* by John Steinbeck

The Day of the Locust by Nathaniel West

Down and Out in Paris and London, *1984*, *Animal Farm*, and
     The Road to Wiggan Pier (and other essays and stories) by
     George Orwell

The Lady in the Lake by Raymond Chandler

The Catcher in the Rye by J. D. Sallinger

The Invisible Man by Ralph Ellison

The Group by Mary McCarthy

Go Tell It on the Mountain by James Baldwin

Lord of the Flies by William Golding

The Collected Stories, Plays and Poems of Dylan Thomas

To Kill a Mockingbird by Harper Lee

Briefing for a Descent into Hell and *The Fifth Child* by Doris
     Lessing

In Cold Blood by Truman Capote (not a novel, but chilling non-
     fiction written with fictional techniques)

The Fixer and *The Natural* by Bernard Malamud

Catch 22 by Joseph Heller

Sophie's Choice and/or *The Confessions of Nat Turner* by
     William Styron

The Illustrated Man, Dandylion Wine, and *The Martian
     Chronicles* by Ray Bradbury

I Am Legend by Richard Matheson

Burr by Gore Vidal

A Clockwork Orange by Anthony Burgess

The Spy Who Came in from the Cold and *The Perfect Spy* by
    John le Carré
Grendel by John Gardner
The Hobbit and *Lord of the Rings* by J. R. R. Tolkein
Watership Down by Richard Adams
The Joy Luck Club by Amy Tan
Childhood's End by Arthur C. Clarke
Ragtime by E. L. Doctorow
Time After Time by Jack Finney
The Prince of Tides and/or *The Great Santini* by Pat Conroy
The Color Purple by Alice Walker
Jazz by Toni Morrison
Past Caring and *In Pale Battalions* by Robert Goddard

Nonfiction Reading List

Biography
The Lives of John Lennon, Albert Goldman
No Ordinary Time: Franklin and Eleanor Roosevelt, Doris
    Kearns Goodwin

Business
Just Do It: The Nike Spirit in the Corporate World, Donald Katz
Knock 'Em Dead, 2000, Martin Yate

Cooking
The Way to Cook, Julia Child
The Beat This! Cookbook, Ann Hodgman

General Reference
*Letitia Baldridge's Complete Guide to New Manners for the
    '90s,* Letitia Baldridge
Imponderables: The Solution to the Mysteries of Everyday Life,
    David Feldman

History
Undaunted Courage, Stephen Ambrose
The Civil War: A Narrative, Shelby Foote

Humor

Big Trouble, Dave Barry
Couplehood, Paul Reiser

Parenting

Touchpoints: Your Child's Emotional and Behavioral Development, T. Berry Brazelton
Dr. Spock's Baby and Child Care, Benjamin Spock

Popular Culture

Raised on Rock: Growing Up at Graceland, David Stanley, Mark Bego
The Encyclopedia of Bad Taste, Jane & Michael Stern

Psychology

The Verbally Abusive Relationship, Patricia Evans
Reviving Ophelia: Saving the Selves of Adolescent Girls, Mary Pipher

Religion, Spirituality, and New Age

The Hero With a Thousand Faces, Joseph Campbell
The Good Book: Reading the Bible with Mind and Heart, Peter Gomes
Small Miracles: Extraordinary Coincidences from Everyday Life, Yitta Halberstam and Judith Leventhal

Science

A Natural History of the Senses, Diane Ackerman
Surely You're Joking, Mr. Feynman!: Adventures of a Curious Character, Richard Feynman
The Diversity of Life, E.O. Wilson

Self-Help

Confidence: Finding It and Living It, Barbara DeAngelis
When Bad Things Happen to Good People, Harold S. Kushner

Book Club

Check out these reading sources on the Web as a start to discussing books:

www.bookbrowser.com/Resources/ReadingGroups.html
BookBrowser, Reader's Resources, Reading Groups

www.net-language.com/read-club.htm
An On-Line Reading Club

Sports

A Good Walk Spoiled: Days and Nights on the PGA Tour, John Feinstein

Summer of '49, David Halberstam

Travel

Under the Tuscan Sun, Frances Mayes

To the Ends of the Earth: The Selected Travels of Paul Theroux, Paul Theroux

Selected Nonfiction Classics

Twenty Years at Hull-House, Jane Addams

Let Us Now Praise Famous Men, James Agee and Walker Evans

The Second Sex, Simone de Beauvoir

The Holy Bible, standard revised edition

Ball Four: My Life and Hard Times Throwing the Knuckleball in the Big Leagues, Jim Bouton

Bury My Heart at Wounded Knee: An Indian History of the American West, Dee Alexander Brown

In Cold Blood: A True Account of a Multiple Murder and Its Consequences, Truman Capote

How to Win Friends and Influence People, Dale Carnegie

Silent Spring, Rachel Carson

The Second World War, Winston Churchill

The Souls of Black Folk, W.E.B. Du Bois

The Meaning of Relativity, Albert Einstein

The Diary of a Young Girl, Anne Frank

The Interpretation of Dreams, Sigmund Freud

The Feminine Mystique, Betty Friedan

The Affluent Society, John Kenneth Galbraith

Satyagraha (Non-Violent Resistance), Mohandas K. Ghandi

The Story of My Life, Helen Keller

There Are No Children Here, Alex Kotlowitz

On Death and Dying, Elizabeth Kubler-Ross

The Autobiography of Malcolm X, Malcolm X

The Joy of Cooking, Irma S. Rombauer

And the Band Played On: Politics, People, and the AIDS Epidemic, Randy Shilts

Night, Elie Weisel

CHAPTER 3

Market Research, or How to Study Your Market

Okay, you think you've got a good idea. The first big question you need to answer for yourself is, Is this idea really a book, or will it work better as a magazine article or short story? If you're sure you can write several hundred pages (at least 250, double-spaced) without struggling and padding, then you may well have an idea that will sustain a book.

Having decided that, what you've got to do now is start the process of growing that little seedling (your idea) into a sapling (your proposal), which promises in turn to become a beautiful tree (your book). This will take time, care, some serious objectivity, and a lot of thought on your part. When all else is said and done, writing is not just about putting down words on paper gracefully and clearly. It's also about *thinking*.

The reason that most of us continue to work in the publishing industry at a time when it's in such turmoil is that we love what we do with a passion. The vast majority of our colleagues, be they editor, agent, or published writer, are brilliant, witty, interesting people who are fun to hang out with.

But our love affair is not really with books ("What!" I hear you gasp). Books are just the outer form of what really matters. At its heart, publishing is about ideas.

It's a heady thought to realize that the publishing industry is really a marketplace for ideas, especially those with strong emotional impact. I derive great pleasure from the notion that I'm working in an industry in which the written product of our best thinkers commands financial as well as intellectual attention. It's an industry in which a good idea can sell when it's not that well written, and an idea that's overly familiar or mundane, with little emotional impact, will not.

Define Your Audience

You must come at your idea from the perspective of a potential reader. Catching the reader's attention is a function of not just how well you write your proposal or your book but also of how well you structure and think through your idea.

It was a dark and stormy night

Web Sites for Marketing Research

Below are some Web sites that may be helpful in tracking down marketing information. They also offer up-to-the-minute news about the publishing industry.

www.amazon.com
Amazon.com Books—the oldest and biggest on-line bookstore

www.barnesandnoble.com
Barnes & Noble—your neighborhood bookseller now in competition with Amazon.com

www.bookbrowse.com
BookBrowse.com—excerpts of bestsellers and much more.

www.ingrambook.com
Ingrams is one of two major book distributors in the United States and Canada (the other is Baker & Taylor). Once you're at their site, go to the "Book Kahoona," which will give you free top fifty lists on a wide variety of subjects.

www.nyt.com
The New York Times on the Web (You can access their book review section and also look at their top thirty bestseller lists.)

www.bookwire.com
R. R. Bowker's BookWire site (The site deals mostly with subscription, but you can get some basic information for free, and it has gateways to the AAR agents site, *Publishers Weekly,* and many others.)

www.bookwire.com/AAR./links
Association of Authors' Representatives' links to other publishing sites

www.bookwire.com/pw/pw.html
Publishers Weekly home page

www.uop.edu/misc/bookpub.html
Book Publishers on the Web

When you start to develop your idea, the most important questions are who will buy this book and what category does it fall into? In other words, from the outset, define your audience.

So how does an unpublished writer improve his or her chances of getting published? The answer is: Make sure your idea is told in such an emotionally gripping way that it will appeal to as wide an audience as possible. Enough people must be so interested in what you have to say that they'll spend enough of their hard-earned cash to make it worth a publisher's while to produce and sell your book.

Size Up the Competition

The first thing you should do is see whether there are other books on your topic and, if there are, how successful they've been. Go on-line to Amazon.Com or Barnes&Noble.Com and do a check on the category or subject you intend to write about. After you've done that, visit your local bookstores and browse the shelves. Has anyone written something like your book and published it recently? What are the names of the publishers who publish books like the one you propose? Who are the big selling authors in this genre, and what are the titles of their latest and/or most successful books?

Go to the library and check out *Books in Print*. In particular, look up books that have been published on your topic in the last 5 or so years. The results can be daunting and need to be interpreted, but the most important thing about *Books in Print* is that it's an exhaustive catalog. Concentrate not on the academic and "barely in print" titles, but on those by mainstream and small press publishers that you can find relatively easily in any neighborhood bookstore of some quality. Remember, the point is to size up your audience and see whether your idea has been done already.

With your *Books in Print* list in hand, start browsing the shelves of your local bookstores. Sit in one of those comfy chairs in a corner with a stack of books and a calming, flavorful tea. Check through the stack to see whether the names of any editors or agents are mentioned on the acknowledgment pages. Make a note of them.

Pay particular attention to competing and complementing books. You'll need all this information when you construct your proposal.

You need to compare your idea objectively against what has been already published in this area. What does your book add to the field? If it's only your thoughts and philosophies, unless you're an expert whose opinion is sought after by colleagues in the field, the likelihood is that your book might be a tough sell. If, however, you know your subject well enough that you realize there's a "hole"—for example, no one's ever written an A-Z or a beginner's guide in . . . whatever—you're probably onto a good thing.

Now for some subtle "detective-like" stuff. Look at the books that have been published already on the subject. Do they fit a pattern? Can you fit into or manipulate that pattern to your own advantage? For example, are all the books expensive hardcovers? Could there be room for a cheap paperback that would appeal to a large mass of people? Publishers always determine the price and style of the book, but in your proposal, you can always suggest the broad aim of the book and temper its language and appeal to fit more easily into a type of book.

Are any of the books new? When was the publication date of the last book on your topic? Look inside and find the copyright page. Somewhere there you'll find a date. Sometimes it'll say, "©1999, By ——" and sometimes the book may have a name like *Angel Woofs* (I make this up, of course!), but inside may say something like, "First published as *All Dogs Go To Heaven*, ©1999, 1974, By ——." What this means is that the book was originally published under another name in 1974 and has been reprinted under a new name in 1999.

Consider that it can take as long as 2 years from the time a book proposal is contracted by a publishing company to the time it reaches a bookstore. So that book copyrighted 1999 may well contain, at best, 1998 information. In other words, it *could* be out of date.

Has anything really changed in the field in the intervening period that might make publishing a more up-to-date book worthwhile? One of the big problems with publishing books in the computer and Internet field, ironically, is that things change *so fast* it's

INFORMATION

Did You Know...

A *backlist* book is any book that's continuing to sell after 6 months on bookstore shelves, or into the next catalog season.

A *frontlist* book is any new book, particularly something with high expectations from the publisher, that is featured as an up-and-coming book in a publisher's latest catalog.

almost impossible for a book to keep up; as a result, publishers tend to try and find topics that will have a long and more stable backlist life.

Ideally, you want to write a book that will have good frontlist potential (people will be excited to see it when it's first published). But you also want to write a book that has staying power, or is a good backlist candidate (despite the attention other newer books being published may attract, your book will maintain a strong selling life after the initial enthusiasm has died away and it's left pretty much to its own devices, whistling "Dixie" on the shelves.)

Know Your Audience

Books that sell well invariably touch some sort of communal nerve. Successful books on a subject not only tackle the problem in a simple and inventive way but also speak to the reader in a reassuring and positive way that makes the reader feel empowered.

Once you approach your book from your reader's viewpoint, you force yourself to become more objective. And that should help you to re-examine, reshape, and, if necessary, restructure your idea.

In general, it's worth remembering that certain constants apply, particularly in the nonfiction field. People who like cookbooks, for example, don't just buy one and use it. They tend to collect them. Similarly, people who buy weight loss or parenting books usually do so for a reason—that is, they have a problem they're trying to solve. So regardless of the fact that they may have bought six other books on the topic before buying yours, the other six didn't work for them, and they're hoping that yours will provide the key to the problem they're grappling with, be it a difficult child or an inability to keep weight down.

So how many readers do you think you'll get for your book idea? Do you really think, for example, that at a minimum, fifteen thousand people would buy it in a trade paperback format?

Keep an eye on magazines and newspapers. If you see that there's been a noticeable rise in the sales of hair beauty products or a lot of articles about new trends and so forth, perhaps there might be a corresponding interest in a new book on the topic. You must let your passion for a topic drive you, but you must also be objective about its sales potential. Just how many people are really into bird watching? Surprisingly (if you're not an ornithologist yourself), there are several million, and they spend lots of money on books and equipment about birds and birding.

Talk to Booksellers

Bookstore owners and managers generally love to talk to authors if they have the time. Talk to your local bookstore people and find out what sells well in your region. See if you can discover what backlists well locally and what book prospects excite bookstore customers. Pitch your idea to the bookstore owner and see what sort of reaction you get.

If there are a lot of new books on a topic, maybe it's not such a good idea for you to write this book, *unless* you really do have something different to say. On the other hand, all those new books on a topic also indicate that publishers think the topic is a hot seller, so they might be interested in something different on the topic. Bear in mind that subjects get overbought and that hot now is often cold later.

Get on the phone and call publishing houses for their latest catalogs. You can find the numbers of many publishers in the back of this book. Or check out the *Literary Market Place (LMP)* at your local library.

Publishers are usually happy to send prospective authors free catalogs. It's a lot easier to help educate a writer than cope with inappropriate and unprofessional submissions that take up valuable time to examine and reject, and clutter up office space.

Once you get the catalogs study them carefully. They'll tell you what the publishers intend to publish in the upcoming season. Is there a book on your subject? Study the entry carefully. Are they making a big deal of it? Does it get a full page? Are there marketing and advertising plans? Pay attention to the author's qualifications. How do yours compare?

Hot Books to Look For

Here are a few examples of strong selling titles:

- *The Seven Habits of Highly Effective People*
- *Chicken Soup for the Soul*
- *Life's Little Instruction Book*
- *What to Expect When You're Expecting*
- *Prozac Nation*
- *When Bad Things Happen to Good People*
- *Eat More, Weigh Less*
- *Toxic Parents*

And the Title Is . . .

Another thing to pay attention to is the title of your book. As a start, if you're working on nonfiction, see whether you can come up with something that has *How, What,* or *When* in it.

A good title should be both informative and provocative. You should know at once what the book is about; at the same time, ideally, you should strike just the right chord with the reader.

I have had editors reject proposals purely on the basis of not liking the title, though they quite liked the book idea. (I've said editors are smart people, and they are. I didn't say *every* editor was smart.) A couple of editors I had to deal with over the years had clearly never been introduced to the concept of (gasp!) *editing*! "If you don't like the title, change it," I said to them, barely containing my exasperation. But the task, it seemed, was beyond them.

What's Hot and Why It Really Isn't

The big question I'm sure you keep asking, despite everything you've read in this chapter so far, is, Just what is it that publishers want *right now*? But as I said before, by the time you get to read this, anything that's hot is going to be, at best, lukewarm, and more probably arctic cold.

Here's a rough timetable to give you some idea of how things work:

From idea to research to book proposal: 1 to 2 months
From book proposal to literary agent: 3 months
From agent to editor and book contract: 6 months (if you're lucky)
From contract to delivery to editor: 6 months (This is pushing it; it's often more like 9 months to a year.)
From transmission by editor to finished book on the shelves: 9 months
Total Time: 2 years, give or take a few months

You might think from this that you could go straight to the editor and gain some time. But the truth is, agents know exactly who in a publishing house is looking for material and what his or her tastes are, so the agent will probably shorten the time it takes to get an editor to accept the book. They can also send to more than one editor at a time. It's tougher for an author to do that. Your proposal could languish in an editorial "slush" pile (the *slush* pile is what the sack loads of unsolicited manuscripts at a publishing house are called) for at least 6 months before it gets rejected and you have to start the process all over again.

So how do you stay ahead of the curve? First of all, nonfiction is sold on a proposal and sample chapter; a first novel has to be completed. What's more, sales and marketing types much prefer nonfiction to fiction because nonfiction generally has a much longer backlist life and, therefore, will make the company more money over the long run, unless the novel becomes a big seller.

For the last couple of years, fiction has been something of a gamble. You toss in the ball and watch it spin around the roulette wheel. If you hit, you get a contract, but more than likely you won't. However I know this won't put you off because 95 percent of submissions to editors and agents are from unpublished novelists.

Be warned, however, that everyone wants to write fiction, and every publisher that publishes fiction wants to find another John Grisham, Stephen King, Tom Clancy, or Danielle Steel. But there are only so many of these types to go around and only a handful of publishers who can afford them. The best chance you have of getting published is with good nonfiction. That won't put you off, though, and that's probably a good thing in the end. Remember, editors are looking for outstanding books, particularly those with a strong voice and strong characters that an audience can get involved with.

Try to home in on niche publishing. This involves identifying a specific area that will appeal to that audience (e.g., new age, new age health, and computer and technology for dummies). A return to the turn of the century, Jack London-esque, man-against-the-elements and/or nature kind of nonfiction is also doing well. In general, as the baby boomer generation ages, it has more time to read, and since it "came of age" in the 1960s, it has always been a generation that is fascinated with itself and its problems.

At present, genre fiction is much more likely to sell than any other, and the genres that are a little easier to break into tend to be these:

Mystery and Crime
Romance
Sci-fi and Fantasy
Middle Grade and YA Fiction

Try to test the waters for new areas that may prove lucrative for the book field. For example, even though thrillers and horror fiction are in a slump, both genres are really waiting for the right person to come along with a new take on things and reinvigorate the genre. How do you do that? I'll know it when I see it. Otherwise, if I knew the answer to that question, I wouldn't be telling you. I'd be writing it myself!

How Many Copies Can YOU Help Sell?

Aim to add as much value as you can to your book idea. Don't be shy about letting potential editors know if you have a regular newspaper of magazine column or a constituency of some kind that could be tapped into as a potential market for your book.

This is especially true if you teach a course or regularly hold a seminar on the topic you're writing about. Publishers are looking for book sales, and anything that promises to pay for itself is looked upon with much kinder eyes than something that will be a greater financial risk for the publishing house.

If you're not an expert in an area, go out and find one. Use your intelligence, read magazines, and keep up with current events and trends. If you are the expert, try to get a well-known (and, ideally, well-respected) colleague or expert to endorse your idea or at least promise to look at your book with an eye to endorsing it when it's finally published. Even if you're Jane Bloggs and highly respected in your field, if Stephen Hawking says he'll write you a blurb or better yet an introduction to your book, your chances of getting published increase markedly.

Finally, add a brand name if you can. Are there any national organizations, museums, clubs, whatever, that you have access to whose name might increase a book's visibility and marketability? Such a connection could be helpful in attracting a publisher's attention.

CHAPTER 4

How to Translate Your Idea into a Book Proposal

This is where the work you've done on-line and in the library and bookstore will start to pay off. The first thing to understand is that *a book proposal is primarily a sales tool.* It describes the structure of your proposed book and includes a sample chapter to demonstrate the voice, or tone, of the piece.

It's usually done for nonfiction books, though there are circumstances in which an unpublished novelist can try to get a book contract on the strength of a proposal for a fiction series and, say, a hundred pages of the novel. However, it's unlikely that an unpublished, first-time writer will sell a piece of fiction on the strength of a proposal. Because there are so many accomplished writers with finished fiction manuscripts, the question becomes, Why would an editor bother with something that's not ready?

A nonfiction book is essentially about the appeal and marketability of an idea. It's less concerned with a writer's ability to put down words on paper.

However, what will catch people's attention first and foremost is a strong voice in the work. If an editor or agent gets caught up in the world of the writer—whether it's in fiction or nonfiction—from the first sentence, the writer is way ahead of the game.

Besides a good plot and strong characters, fiction needs some flair and style to its narrative tone. It is much more idiosyncratic in its appeal.

When editors buy books in proposal form, they are taking a gamble that the finished book will resemble what they think they've paid for and that the writer will manage to complete the book on deadline or, even worse, at all. Buying an unfinished (or, in some cases, barely started) book by an unpublished and unagented writer is a huge act of faith on an editor's part. And that's before dealing with the complications and trauma of having an editor leave a publishing house halfway through a project. The book can suddenly become an unwanted stepchild of a new editor who has a completely different view of how it should be written and published.

In 1998, a great deal of publicity was focused on the HarperCollins decision to cancel a number of author contracts.

Everyone in the publishing world was up in arms, complaining about the terrible thing that HarperCollins had done. But the truth was that nearly all the canceled contracts were for books that were *years* late, for which signing payments had been paid with no sign that the finished books would ever be delivered. In most cases, while authors are supposed to pay back the portion of the royalty advance they've so far received (what's called in the contract a "first proceeds" clause, designed to deal with just such a situation), the reality is they end up keeping the money until they sell the book elsewhere, if they ever do. They then repay the publisher from the first proceeds of the new sale.

A Good Proposal Is a Good Sales Tool

The first thing to think about when writing a book proposal is that at any given time editors have hundreds to look at. Our literary agency receives close to a thousand queries and proposals a month. Editors at publishing houses receive almost as many.

So your proposal had better stand out, and it had better be well prepared and professionally presented. If it isn't, I guarantee the next guy's will be. There it is, next in line to be read in that wobbly, towering stack of manila envelopes beside the pizza box. It's eight o'clock at night, and the editor and her assistant are closing out a 12-hour day with after-hours work, tackling the mail stacks before the envelopes somehow reproduce like rabbits and get completely out of hand. The editor—and the agent (who's doing much the same thing at the same time in his office)—are looking for decent ideas, professionally presented, by a writer who looks like he or she can deliver what he or she promises.

With all that mail, you'd think such promising material would be easy to find, but it isn't. That's why if you do a terrific job on your proposal, you start way ahead of the pack.

The basic philosophy behind writing a book proposal is to describe the book you want to write and provide the editor with sufficient ammunition in the form of facts and figures for her or him to convince colleagues in both editorial and sales and marketing at an editorial board meeting not only that the proposed

INFORMATION

Did You Know...

When you send in your manuscript or book proposal to an editor or agent, you have *submitted* it; the process is called a *submission*.

If the author does not have an agent, publishing houses call such submissions *unagented*.

book is a quality piece of work, but also that it will *make money for the publishing company*.

A golden rule of writing a book proposal is, Don't assume anything. The editor may not remember, until you point it out, that there's a strong link between your book and a current bestseller. Your book, however, is unique because _____ (fill in the blank).

If your mother and your boss have promised to buy five thousand copies each and you know others who can get multitudes to buy your book, mention it; if you are best friends with Stephen King or Danielle Steel, and they'll give you a blurb, say so; if you've won the Nobel prize, or the Pulitzer, or just first or second place in a writing competition, let us know (Dr. Johnson once said he liked being considered the "second best writer in England" after William Shakespeare. "It means someone had to think about it," he said.); if your book has a huge and clearly identifiable audience, point it out; if it helps to quote from the *New York Times*, or *The Birder's Weekly*, do it. And make sure you do all of this fairly close to the beginning of your proposal.

A good book proposal is, in essence, a justification for why your book should be published. Marshal all your facts and figures about competing books, marketing material, the book's uniqueness, and so on. And then present it all in the most effective and positive light.

Demonstrate that you know your subject, but beware of getting so caught up in the demonstration that you cannot see the forest for the trees. Once you start getting too technical or too involved in minutiae, it can seem that you're trying too hard. A good proposal should be about twenty-five to thirty pages long, including a sample chapter. You can push it to forty pages, but any longer than that and you're in danger of overwriting.

If you can, mention how long the book will be and how long it will take you to write it. For example, "I estimate my seventy-five-thousand-word book on *Lecherous Lemurs* will take approximately 9 months to complete."

There is an accepted structure for a book proposal that broadly follows this structure:

- A brief cover letter
- A title page

- A hook and then an overview of the project
- A marketing analysis
- A brief description of competing books
- A half-page narrative biography of the writer(s)
- A table of contents (TOC)
- A narrative description of each chapter listed in the TOC
- An estimated book length and delivery date
- A writing sample demonstrating the voice of the proposed book

Preparing a Nonfiction Proposal

Your proposal should offer just enough information in an accessible and, it is hoped, entertaining manner to convince the reader you know your subject and can write well about it. It should also be well organized in a logical progression of ideas and facts and, ideally, reflect the tone and style of the final book.

All nonfiction books have one thing in common: They pose a question and then answer it. In other words, they propose a simply stated thesis that the text of the book will focus on proving.

When you write fiction, the stronger and more impressive you make your villain, the more impressive your protagonist becomes as he or she overcomes obstacles the villain places in his or her path on the road to achieving his or her ultimate goal. Something of the same principle applies in writing nonfiction, too: Present the strongest arguments against your thesis and then defeat them. One-sided arguments rarely hold a reader's interest or imagination as effectively as a well-turned debate.

A nonfiction proposal should be about an idea that has universal appeal and could sell at least ten thousand or more copies. Anything narrower in appeal and you're in the realm of small press and niche publishing books.

It's worth remembering that on average it can take perhaps 2 years from the signing of a nonfiction book contract to the book appearing on the shelves, so your book idea must be appealing enough that in 2 or 3 years, people will still be excited about it.

Another book recently published on your subject may not necessarily be a fatal blow to your book idea. In fact, you may find

Submitting to Small Presses

Your proposal should follow the same structure when submitting to small presses, but you need to be certain that you have targeted your proposal to the right house and its interests, rather as you would if proposing a magazine article to a magazine. You wouldn't send an article suitable for *Playboy* to *Reader's Digest*, for example. Find out what the small press house publishes *before* you submit to it. Ideally, target a specific editor who will be interested in your project. How do you do that? Call a publisher and talk to an editorial assistant.

once you've read the published book that the author treats the subject differently from the way you intend to treat it.

It's important that you let editors and agents know that this other book is in the marketplace and why it won't be a problem for your book idea. If an editor, in ignorance of this other book because you failed to mention it in your proposal, puts forward your idea in an editorial meeting and someone around the table says, "But so-and-so just published a book exactly like this," that editor will have been made to look foolish and ill prepared. Guess whose book they're *not* going to buy, and which author they're not going to want to work with in the future?

Work on the table of contents early. As you develop the proposal, you'll continually need to revise it, but it'll provide an excellent overall map to the project while you're working, as well as a guide to its final form when completed.

Format

The proposal should be in a 12-point clean pica or elite typeface, double-spaced, with 1-inch margins all the way around. Better to have more pages and fewer words on the page, which is easier on the eyes, than to cram a load of small-sized words on one page in an effort to make the proposal look shorter than it is.

There should be a header on every page, with a catchword and your name in the top left-hand corner, and consecutive and continuous page numbering in the top right-hand corner. Ideally, each section of the proposal should start on a new page. Make sure that you have included your name, address, and telephone numbers on the title page.

Don't bind or staple your proposal. If you want to keep it together, use a clip and/or slip it into a folder, or use a piece of cardboard as a backing and slip a large rubber band around everything.

Remember, if you manage to get an agent, or if an editor picks up on your proposal, he or she is going to need to make copies for colleagues, editorial meetings, submissions, and so on, and won't want to mess around unstapling a manuscript.

Enclose any material relevant to either you as a writer or your proposal subject. These materials include press clippings, testimonial letters, proofs of book sales (if the book is self-published), brochures, or PR material.

Benefits and Features

A book proposal can be broken down into two broad categories: benefits and features. Here's an example of a descriptive set of features: "This is a high quality green, four wheel drive, independent suspension sport pickup truck." Here are the benefits of the truck: "This truck not only makes you look good when you take your family to church on Sundays, but it'll haul anything and everything you need to or from the back pastures the rest of the week."

The Benefits Sections of Your Proposal

Title Page

Center your title and the subtitle of the book proposal. Under that, add your name, an address, and telephone number, and voice and fax if you have it (perhaps even an e-mail address). Make yourself easy to reach. Does your answering machine work? Is there a professional message on the machine when an editor or agent does get through? All these things count.

Byline

Make sure that every page of the proposal is bylined in some fashion and easily recognizable with continuous numbering (except for the first page). If an editorial assistant drops the pages by accident, he or she should be able to reconstruct the proposal easily. Try to avoid pictures and graphics unless they are extremely well done and relate directly to the proposal's subject.

The Hook Overview

The first overview is the hook—a one-sentence or one-paragraph in-a-nutshell description of the book that helps the editor sell the book to colleagues in 30 seconds or less.

INFORMATION

Did You Know...

A *synopsis* is a narrative summation of your fiction, "telling" the story rather than "showing" it.

The Larger Overview

The second overview is a development of the first. If colleagues say, "This sounds interesting, tell us more," you then provide the editor with broad facts and figures (if applicable) and a general overview of the project. This overview is a much stronger sales tool than your manuscript because it allows you to state not only what the book is about (features) but also why it's important (benefits). How will your book appeal to and help readers? Why does the world need another book on this topic? If you answer these questions, you establish your book's identity and commercial worth. Make sure your passion for and interest in your topic shines through.

Think about an overview in these terms:

- Why is there a need for this book? What's the problem? What's the hole that needs to be filled? What suffering can you help alleviate in your readers' lives? What information do they lack? What predicament exists in society, or what vacuum needs to be filled? In what new ways can your readers be entertained? State your case as dramatically as you can without being overly sensational. Startle us from the outset and make us consider your topic with fresh eyes.
- How will your book meet this need or fill this hole? Don't answer these questions with hype or rhetoric. Nobody's interested in your opinion of how great this book idea is. What you have to do is convince us with solid content summed up in a paragraph of two.
- How is your book different from others in the field?
- Why are you the best person to write this book?
- How long will the manuscript be, and how long will it take you to write it?

Close your overview with something that sums up the benefits or merits of the book, reminding the reader of the book's importance. Try to do all this in no more than four double-spaced pages, ideally, two.

Marketing Analysis

In this section, you need to explain who the audience is for your book. That is, who's going to go into a store and plunk down $6 for a paperback (or $13 for a trade paperback, or $22 for a hardcover) version of your book. What evidence can you offer that your assessment is accurate? Use facts and figures you have researched. How many people belong to organizations or subscribe to magazines that deal with this topic? What other books out there have proven there is a successful and eager audience for your proposed book? Why will these people still be interested in reading about your topic in 2 years or even 5 years (publishers call a book's backlist life)? Give the statistics about groups who may be interested in buying copies of the book. Go on-line; haunt the library. You have to be factual and realistic. It won't help to be sloppy or overly general in your assessment. If you have experience or knowledge in selling, marketing, or promoting, mention that. Do you have a seminar that you take around, or do you lecture to groups of people regularly? What can you do to translate your experiences into book sales? A strong marketing plan accompanying a book proposal will go a long way in helping to sell the proposal. Are you a member of organizations who will help publicize your book and, ideally, buy lots of copies? Could you help sell bulk quantities of your book to organizations that might want to give them away as gifts to members? Do you have a connection to well-known people who might endorse your book and help increase book sales that way?

Competing Books

What you need is a list of a half dozen or so of the most successful and most recent books published in the field you propose to write about. Nothing breeds success like success, particularly if you have a new take on a successful idea. In your comments about the books, mention title, author, year of publication, publisher, a one- or two-sentence description and a line pointing out the difference between your book and the published book. Every competing book gives you an opportunity to make a new point about your book idea, so take advantage of the situation. Again, use the library and the Internet for your research. Browse the bookstores in your area; befriend bookstore owners; chat with book people in general. If there is nothing in the field to compare with your book, make certain you convince editors and agents that there really is a market for the book and that you're the first person to have spotted a "hole" and decided to fill it.

The Features Section

Table of Contents

The table of contents shows how the book will be organized and what it will say. A simple table of contents will list the number of chapters you intend to have in your book and what the subtitle of each chapter will be (e.g., Chapter 1: Joe is Born; Chapter 2: Joe Goes to School; Chapter 3: Joe Discovers Baseball for the First Time). The TOC provides an at-a-glance guide to the book's content and organization and perhaps a glimpse of the wit or seriousness you intend to bring to the project through your subtitling. At least 75 percent of a book proposal's success lies in its organization. You may have a great idea, but if you present it poorly, it shows not only a poor writing ability but also poor thought processes. And in nonfiction, a logical exploration of an idea and an easily graspable progression of thought is more or less what you are offering, beyond the originality of the idea in question. Agents and editors look for books that are logical, well written, and have a well-organized plan that is obvious and accessible to its readers. For example, a client of mine decided to do a book about parent activism in educational reform by profiling a dozen or so schools around the country that have been turned around by parent activism. In the end, however, we decided to identify a dozen or so problems that schools faced—from the need for more schools and teachers to the need to improve a school's looks—and then show what parents have done to solve these problems. The reader was more immediately interested in a book of problems and solutions, than in profiles of success stories.

Chapter-by-Chapter Descriptions

Now that you've nailed down the overall structure of your book, write a half- to one-page description of what you plan to cover in each chapter. The key here, as throughout the proposal, is your ability to write succinctly yet dynamically about your subject. In general, state your premise and then explain how you will develop it. Make sure that your passion and interest for your subject comes through. An effective second-person voice can work (e.g., "Have you ever thought about what life would be like without access to water? Your life and the lives of those around you would be vastly different").

Sample Chapters

This is pretty self-explanatory. A nonfiction book needs a mixture of narrative, emotion, and logic to work well. So it doesn't matter what chapters you include. Aim at about fifteen to twenty pages. No more than two chapters need to be included. If you use partial chapters, make sure everyone knows they are not the complete version of the chapter.

Author Biography

Nowadays you have to be an expert or a professional writer who is working in collaboration with one or more experts to get a nonfiction book successfully published. You have to be an expert because you will be competing with others who are experts who have published books in this field, even if their books aren't very good. So establish you credibility both as a writer and as an expert in the topic you are proposing. That may mean writing articles on the topic you propose in your book and getting them published in magazines before you start querying editors and agents with your book idea. Try to write your bio in the third person rather than first person, unless you have a life experience that makes your view particularly valid.

The Cover Letter

The cover letter should be brief, warm, and probably contain the hook. It should include your address, phone numbers, and other relevant information (e.g., that you're a prize-winning writer, a member of this or that group, and an expert in the topic you propose and that you were referred by a writer or agent). Mention the book's title and what kind of book it is, the estimated length of the finished book, and how long it will take you to write it. Include a stamped self-addressed envelope (SASE) if you want your work returned. Never, ever send original material. Always make sure you keep the originals at home and you submit clean, crisp copies. Accidents happen, so be forewarned and prepared.

Preparing a Fiction Proposal

The fiction proposal is a simpler document, but it should follow much the same format as nonfiction. In nonfiction, what we're selling is an idea, well-organized and well-presented. In fiction, we need to reassure an editor that an idea for a novel can be expanded successfully to a book length, usually three hundred to four hundred manuscript pages, double-spaced, and that a quality manuscript can be delivered on time. Because meeting deadlines is so important in fiction particularly, editors generally prefer to see a completed novel rather than trust to luck on an unfinished or proposed manuscript. Alas for you, there are many accomplished writers with finished manuscripts to choose from, who are eager to get published. An exception to this might be if you're writing fiction based on your widely recognized field of expertise (e.g., you're a NASA astronaut writing a sci-fi thriller).

A fiction proposal from a novice writer is best created after at least the first draft of a manuscript has been completed. If an editor or agent expresses an interest in seeing the rest of the manuscript, you can strike while the iron is hot and send them the book immediately.

Most fiction proposals that succeed in getting an author published come from experienced writers who an editor knows can provide a well-written manuscript. In such circumstances, an editor is not worried about whether the author can write a good novel but whether this novel has a chance of being a commercial success.

In many cases, fiction proposals that are successful are for genre works such as mysteries. They propose a single title but also outline a series idea and main character(s). They provide details of the principal book being proposed as well as details of at least one or two more books in the series showing how the series will be developed.

At the very least, a fiction proposal should provide a short hook and a brief overview and synopsis as well as sample pages. The narrative synopsis of the story should paint in broad strokes the beginning, middle, and end of your story. A chapter-by-chapter breakdown is not necessary and can be cumbersome to read. The proposal should also include a bio of the author that emphasizes writing experience and publications, and so on, and the *first* eighty to one hundred pages of the book. If the first few chapters aren't the best in the book, the reader will never get to it, regardless of the brilliance of the rest of the novel. If a writer of fiction chooses to send chapters other than the first chapters to an editor or agent, the obvious conclusion is that the first chapters need work and, consequently, that the book isn't ready for submission.

The Query Letter

Check out this scenario: A good one-sentence hook in a query letter describing a project catches an agent's eye; the agent calls you and says he intends to represent you and your book; you celebrate by taking your spouse out to that chic Italian restaurant you've been meaning to try.

When he pitches your book, your agent (doesn't the sound of that give you a thrill?) uses your hook because it had such an effect on his decision to represent you and your book. The editor reads the proposal with enthusiastic anticipation because, as the agent knows, she's a sucker for books just like the one he's sent her. Sure enough, she loves it, and decides to try to make an offer on the book. To do that, she has to go to an editorial board and convince others in her company to go along with her enthusiasm. What's the bait she uses to convince her colleagues to buy your book? Why, that one-line hook you wrote. She throws it out during the meeting and manages to convince everyone that this is a book they should buy not only because it's good but also because *it will make the company money*.

When your book is finally published, the publisher's sales representative visits his bookstore accounts and tries to interest the store owner in the new, eagerly awaited best-seller by . . . and what about *this* newcomer? The sales rep now has about 30 seconds to

describe your book and get the bookstore owner to take a bunch of copies. How's the rep going to get that owner enthused about stocking your book? And what's the bookstore owner going to say to the customer to excite her about your book? You got it. More than likely, they'll use the hook you came up with in your query letter that got you an agent in the first place.

Query letters (or cover letters as they're sometimes called) can be very effective pieces of succinct writing. In truth, if you can't write a decent query letter, it's highly doubtful you'll be able to write a good book. It's an advertisement for your ability to write, structure, *and* think.

At the least, a query should mention the hook (i.e., what the book is about), who you are, and why you're the best person to write this book. It should thank the agent or editor for his or her time. The tone should be warm and friendly, and the whole letter should fit comfortably on one page. At the end of the letter, include a brief paragraph mentioning writing credits, if you're lucky enough to have some.

If the query letter is about fiction, then it should have some flavor of the book in its tone and show off (in a restrained way) your ability to catch a reader from the outset and hold his or her interest.

Following are some examples of what I mean. Consider this query letter for a novel:

> Dear Sir,
>
> I recently wrote a novel about a group of 12-year-old kids who years before murdered a man who had been abusing one of the group.
>
> Now Jimmy, the leader of the group, has died in mysterious circumstance, and it looks like their deep dark secret's finally been revealed. Someone, it seems, is out for revenge. Who is it and who will be next?

This is quite a good idea, and I'd probably ask to see a sample of the manuscript with a synopsis of the story. But the writing is not overly compelling. Now, compare the above with the following. The first thing to notice is that this writer has bothered to find out my name and spell it correctly.

> Dear Mr. Rubie,
>
> We never meant to kill old Starrett. It really was just an accident. But when you're 12 years old and becoming a helpless victim, something's bound to happen when your friends try to help you.
>
> The day I found Marisa sitting on the parapet of the railroad bridge, her body wracked with huge sobs, waiting to jump in front of the approaching train, I knew we had to do something.
>
> But who do you turn to when the grown-ups ignore you, and the town cop's the guy causing all the problems?

Which version excites and interests you the most?

Hooks

A hook provides you with a clear beginning and strong focus for your work. Here are some examples:

- What would you do if you could live your life over again, knowing what the future will be? (That's Ken Grimwood's hook for his novel *Replay*.)
- Terrorists threaten to blow up the Super Bowl from a blimp. (*Black Sunday*, Thomas Harris)
- Suppose an English seaman is shipwrecked off the coast of Japan and becomes a pawn in a power play to take over the island. (*Shogun*, James Clavell)
- On Christmas Eve, a miserly old man is visited by three ghosts who show him his past, present, and miserable future unless he mends his ways. (*A Christmas Carol*, Charles Dickens)

Non-Fiction Query Letter

Here are a couple of examples of non-fiction queries.

LETTER #1

Dear Mr. Rubie:

So many cat books, who can tell one from another? Such incomplete information, such misleading "facts." What's a pet owner to do? *The A to Z of Cats* is the answer.

During my 25 years as a veterinary surgeon I've searched for a book that I could recommend to the cat owners and prospective owners I come in contact with every day. It's true some combination of books comes close, but—until now—no one book has contained all the critical information that cat owners should have at their fingertips.

If you are among the vast millions of Americans (over 30 percent of the population) who owns a cat, you owe it to yourself and your pet to read *The A to Z of CATS*.

Besides my busy practice as a feline oncologist, I've contributed articles to *Zoo Life* and other magazines for several years. I enclose a full biography and samples of the latest articles I've had published, plus a table of contents for the proposed book, some detailed market analysis, and a list of competing books that shows why my book will fill a gap unfilled up to now. Cat facts don't change, so this book will have a long shelf life for any publishing company that decides to publish it.

I look forward to hearing from you soon.

Yours sincerely,

Jerry Leopard
ENC

LETTER #2

Dear Mr. Rubie:

Thank you so much for taking my call the other afternoon. I appreciate how busy you are and the time you took to discuss my narrative non-fiction idea with me. Your enthusiasm was encouraging. It was your background as a journalist and your reputation as an agent who specializes in high quality non-fiction *(Witchunt, How The Tiger Lost Its Stripes, From Steel to Cyberspace)* that encouraged me to contact you in the first place.

As you suggested, please find enclosed *The Last Watchman,* the heretofore untold story of the CIA's involvement in the ill-fated Somali U.N. mission led by U.S. troops in 1993.

As I mentioned when we spoke, *Blackhawk Down* has become a huge success, telling the story of a fateful battle in Mogadishu, Somalia between U.S. forces and the Somali war lords.

The Last Watchman details the CIA's role in the futile attempt of the U.N. to establish President Bush's New World Order, from the perspective of experienced field officers who were on the scene.

I began my journalistic career as a correspondent for *Stars and Stripes.* Since then, over the last 15 years I have worked for major newspapers, such as the *Jerusalem Post,* the *London Independent,* and the *Herald Tribune.* I have had stories published in *Time,* and *The London Sunday Times* color magazine, as well as reported for the BBC World Service.

I covered the Somalia "campaign" in its entirety, and have extensively interviewed all of the people mentioned in the book. All my notes are carefully documented and sourced.

Enclosed with this letter, please find a narrative biography of myself, a table of contents, and two sample chapters as you requested.

I look forward to hearing from you soon, and thank you in advance for your time and consideration.

Regards,

Sam Estates, 4th
ENC

It was a dark and stormy night

Fifteen Do's and Don'ts of Proposal Writing

1. DO find out a person's correct name and title before you send him or her your proposal and query letter.

2. DON'T misspell names and technical words in particular. Do some research.

3. DO make sure you put the correct postage and address labels on both the letter you send out AND the SASE you include.

4. DON'T use antiquated equipment if the printed copies it produces are hard to read.

5. DON'T handwrite anything, except your signature.

6. DO make sure the proposal is easy to look at and read, with double spacing and 1-inch margins all around.

7. DO come to the point quickly in your query letter, and keep it short.

8. DON'T bother to make statements like, "I've registered the proposal with X, so no one can steal it," or "I'll only take a minimum of $250,000 for this book." If it's good enough to steal, it's good enough to represent. If not, who cares? And as far as price is concerned, you'll get what you're offered. Accept it or not, as you please.

9. DON'T inundate an editor or agent with a shopping list of ideas at one time, on the basis of "If you don't like this, then try that."

10. DO behave professionally, and try to help the agent or editor to help you.

11. DO try and remember you're not the only writer the agent or editor has to deal with. The volume of mail and telephone calls they have to go through is *enormous.*

12. DON'T "get your knickers in a twist," as they say in England, about the need to rush your book proposal into print. It ain't gonna happen! By the time the book's ready, if the subject is that timely, it'll be too late. No one will remember or care what your book was about. You're better off writing a magazine or newspaper article.

13. DON'T submit e-mail proposals unless you're asked to.

14. DON'T send full manuscripts unless invited.

15. DON'T call every day asking if they've either received the manuscript, or read it yet.

Sample Proposals

Following are a couple of sample proposals.

Non-Fiction Proposal

The first is the proposal for a nonfiction book I wrote, which was published in 1998 by *Writer's Digest*. If you compare the proposal with the book, you'll discover that the finished book differed from the proposal, though not in substantial ways. Books, after all, are organic creatures that develop as you write them. This proposal, however, was what prompted editor Jack Heffron to buy the book.

INFORMATION

Did You Know...

SASE means self-addressed stamped envelope. Make sure you always include one with the correct postage if you want your submission returned.

How to Tell a Story
The Secrets of Writing Captivating Tales

A Book Proposal
By Peter Rubie and Gary Provost

In a Nutshell

What makes one aspiring novelist or writer of narrative nonfiction more likely to succeed than another? How does a writer develop a great idea for a story? *In an increasingly tough publishing market, how can a writer get that edge that will get him published and keep him being published? How to Tell a Story*, by Peter Rubie and Gary Provost, is the first book on dramatic structure in fiction and nonfiction to answer those questions and more.

Overview

Almost every time my friend Gary Provost and I got together and talked about teaching writing, the conversation would eventually get around to whether or not it was possible to teach students story sense.

Why is it that one person can tell you about his flight from an erupting volcano and bore you to death, while someone else can tell you why she had to do the same laundry three times last Thursday and have you hanging on every word? How is it that two people can tell the same joke, and one person can have you rolling in the aisles while the other makes you squirm in your seat?

Clearly, some people are born with a gift for storytelling or story sense. Indeed, many people believe that story sense is the one thing that *can't* be taught, that it is a God-given talent. And yet, a great many writers, whether they're journalists or novelists, somehow manage to acquire the ability to tell a good story well. Put a group of experienced reporters or writers of fiction in a room and feed them a bunch of ideas for stories, and almost invariably the good ones will pick the *same idea* and want to do something with it. What's more, in an industry that is defined by the idiosyncratic taste of editors and agents, *everyone* "gets" a good idea the first time they hear it or see it.

So what is this mystical storytelling talent and how do you learn it? What makes one aspiring novelist or writer of narrative nonfiction more likely to succeed than another? How does a writer develop a great idea for a story and how does he pick it out from the hundreds of other story ideas he gets? *In an increasingly tough publishing market, how can a writer get that edge that will get him published and keep him being published?*

This book will answer these and other questions with a strong emphasis on *published* and, in the case of movies, widely released and well-known examples.

How to Tell a Story is not about style, dialogue, description, or viewpoint, subjects that Gary and I have both written about in other books. *How to Tell a Story* is about the dramatic forces that make a story work. It is about what creates excitement for the reader, why the reader will get involved with the story and feel *compelled* to turn the page. Story sense, at its simplest, is about the most interesting way to tell a good story, whether that story is invented (fiction) or adapted from real life (narrative nonfiction).

And what, you ask, is a good story? It's something that takes us somewhere we haven't been before, in the company of people we learn to care about, who are forced to deal with adversity.

It doesn't matter how much the reader of this book knows, or doesn't know, about style, description, viewpoint, and so on because story sense is about understanding dramatic structure. The book will have a great many examples to illustrate the points we're making and will be written in a chatty and humorous tone.

How to Tell a Story is about developing and recognizing a great idea and how to turn it into a compelling narrative that will make even jaded publishing professionals sit up and get excited.

Marketing Angle

Despite the many books on writing that are available in the stores, the concept and approach of *How to Tell a Story* is unique. Nothing currently on the market uses this approach to teaching writing. The material has been honed and tested through years of being successfully published ourselves, plus the hands-on teaching and editing experience Gary and I have had with "wannabe" writers, as well as more experienced professional writers. The purpose of *How to Tell a Story* is to teach writers how to write compelling, high-quality stories that have the potential for both commercial success and literary acclaim in today's tough publishing market.

Because the book will deal with dramatic structure, it will appeal to writers of fiction (novels, short stories, screenplays, and plays) and narrative nonfiction (such as true crime, biography, history, and documentaries) alike. The audience will include the many thousands of people who wish to be published or who have managed to sell a first book but have had trouble following up that success with a sellable next book.

Who We Are

Gary Provost was arguably the leading teacher of writing in the United States. Gary had published thousands of articles and dozens of books, including most recently, Stephen Bogart's biography of his father, actor Humphrey Bogart (Dutton), a new mystery series with Berkeley (the first one, *Baffled in Boston*, came out in late 1995), and had been contracted to write Kelsey Grammer's biography *So Far . . .* (Dutton) just before he succumbed to a heart attack.

Gary was also a contributing editor and regular columnist for *Writer's Digest* magazine, and the director of the Writer's Retreat Workshop and Write It/Sell It seminars. He won the National Jewish Book Award for Children's fiction and was nominated for a Newbery Medal.

I met Gary several years ago when he asked me to be a guest lecturer at his seminars, first when I was the fiction editor at Walker and Company (where novels I edited won the Shamus Award for Best First Novel, were voted among the top ten novels in the Southwest, and were nominated for an Edgar Award and a Pen Hemingway Award, among others) and later in my current occupation as a literary agent.

I began writing as a journalist in England in 1969, when I was 19 years old, eventually working in Fleet Street and for BBC Radio News, before moving to the United States, where I was editor in chief of a Manhattan newspaper. I later became a book doctor and freelance editor working for such companies as Doubleday, Dutton-Signet, TOR, Houghton Mifflin, and Pocket. I have published two novels, written several screenplays, and published a number of nonfiction books and articles, the latest of which is *The Elements of Storytelling* (John Wiley). I also lecture on the craft of fiction at a number of universities, writers conferences, and workshops, to some acclaim.

Over the last few years, Gary developed a body of work on writing fiction and narrative nonfiction at his Writer's Retreat Workshops. Except for the material on goals and subplotting, which was written for *Writer's Digest* magazine, none of this material has been published. It is also the basis of Gary's Video Novel Workshop and his story sense seminars. It is this material, along with my own teaching and publishing experiences (author, editor, and literary agent), that with Gary's wife Gail's help I propose to put into book form.

How to Tell a Story
By Gary Provost & Peter Rubie

Table of Contents

Chapter 1 Coming Up with Ideas
Chapter 2 Understanding Genres I: Fiction
Chapter 3 Understanding Genres II: Nonfiction, screenplays, and other narrative forms
Chapter 4 The Hook
Chapter 5 Plotting
Chapter 6 Goals
Chapter 7 Writing in Scenes
Chapter 8 Conflict
Chapter 9 Subplotting and Themes
Chapter 10 Characterization
Chapter 11 Pace
Chapter 12 Structure
Chapter 13 Systems
Chapter 14 Fourteen Steps to Writing Your Story

Chapter Outline of How to Tell a Story

Chapter 1: Coming Up with Ideas

Here's an idea: Let's talk about ideas.

We will write about the process of coming up with an idea and how to test its value. How can you tell whether it should be written as fiction, nonfiction, or a screenplay? We will start by warning off writers from having a FIT, that is, the 3 "great ideas."

Familiarity—Importance—Truth

F. Ideas that you have special access to or are familiar with. (My cousin's brother's auntie's lodger robbed ten laundromats—what a great idea for a true crime story.)

I. Ideas that are important to you. (I spent 20 years delivering pizza—what a great idea for a novel.)

T. Ideas that happen to be true. (My uncle Fred really was married 15 times—what a great idea for a movie.)

On the positive side, we will introduce readers to WAGS. WAGS, you ask?

W is for the World you take your reader to.

A is for Active, not passive, characters.

G is for clear and definable Goals.

S is for the Stakes that are high.

Chapter 2: Understanding Genres I: Fiction

We will explain the difficulty in trying to sell a mid-list or mainstream novel these days. We will talk about the different genres or categories and show the reader why they exist.

Readers of most novels are trying to recreate an experience similar to the one they had with the last book that really grabbed them. We will explain that each category has its own conventions and that the most successful genre writer will be someone who has an intimate knowledge and understanding of the genre he or she is writing in.

We will talk about why a writer has a better chance of selling her novel if it's in a category, and we will suggest ways a writer can slant his or her mainstream novel into a category. After we have explained this in the context of the novel, we will show the reader that all narrative forms, whether it's fiction or nonfiction, have genres.

Chapter 3: Understanding Genres II:
Nonfiction, screenplays, and other narrative forms

In a continuation of the last chapter, we will explain that like fiction, narrative nonfiction and other narrative forms also have their genres.

We will discuss how to tell whether your idea will best be suited as a magazine article or a book. A good commercial nonfiction book should contain three things:

1. A narrative spine
2. A debate over a topic of broad national interest that grows from the story (e.g., *The Burning Bed* and domestic abuse)
3. A positive spin on even the most negative topic in order to attract an audience who will plunk down $25 or more in a bookstore to read your book.

Again, we will emphasize that each category (biography, history, true crime, screenplay, theatrical play, etc.) has its conventions, and we will discuss ways to tackle each genre, showing how the same idea can differ in dramatic structure from medium to medium. And we will offer plenty of examples, from *Inherit the Wind* (the Scopes Monkey trial), *Rope* (based on Leopold and Loeb murder case), and *In Cold Blood* to *The Physics of Star Trek*.

Chapter 4: The Hook

We will explain why a writer should be able to reduce his or her book to one or two dynamic sentences. We will explain the importance of focus in a narrative and that the writer must look for the element that makes his story different from the one next to it on the shelf.

We will give examples of good and bad hooks and show the reader how he can use elements of his plot list to come up with a great hook.

Chapter 5: Plotting

We will tell readers the ten crucial plot points of 90 percent of all successful fiction and how this can be used to shape a narrative nonfiction piece, a screenplay, or a play.

The Inciting Incident
The Prize
The Strategy
The Conflict
The Stakes
The Bleakest Moment
The Lesson
The Decision
The Unconscious Goal
The Back Story

We will give examples of each and then take the reader through examples, showing how all these plot points create structure. Here, as throughout the book, we will draw our examples from novels, stories, films, plays, and narrative nonfiction.

Chapter 6: Goals

Imagine a soccer game without any goals at each end of the field. How long are you going to watch guys pass the ball to each other, intercept and tackle, and show off their skill at ball control? Not very long, because you won't know how each event relates to their goals or what their goals are.

What if . . . a man walks into a store and says hello to a woman. He buys gum and a newspaper, walks out, then returns several minutes later and starts a conversation with her about local garbage collection policy. She asks him about himself, he buys a soda, and so on. At the end of the scene, the writer writes, "Donald walked out, pleased that his wife had not recognized him in his disguise."

Donald's goal was to trick his wife. Trouble is, we didn't know that until the scene was over, so most likely we skipped over the scene. However, if we'd known at the beginning what Donald's goal was, the scene would have had tension and interest.

Characters in stories have major goals (e.g., bring the murderer to justice); intermediate goals (e.g., climb the mountain where the murderer's hiding); and minor goals (e.g., learn how to climb mountains). Without knowing what a character's goal is, that is, what the character *wants*, a reader has no way of making sense of the story she's reading, nor will she feel compelled to read further.

To remind yourself about your characters, put this sign over your desk:
What does he/she want?

Chapter 7: Writing in Scenes

Whether you are writing fiction or nonfiction, the powerful influence of screenplays and plays can be seen in the idea of constructing your story as a series of related scenes. Here we will talk about the importance of writing narrative in scenes. We'll show the reader what a scene is and what a scene is not.

Each scene has a reason for being where it is in a narrative and contains conflict and plot movement. A scene occurs in a time and place and is a microcosm of the whole novel or story. We will discuss scenes of low temperature and high temperature, with lots of examples, of course.

Chapter 8: Conflict

We will tell the reader that conflict is the basis of all narrative prose, whether it is fiction or nonfiction—no conflict, no story. We will tell readers that while they might go out of their way to avoid conflict in real life, they must infuse it into their narratives.

In a less expanded form, some of this chapter was published by *Writer's Digest* in Gary's article "Just Say No" (enclosed).

We will tell readers that opposition must be substantial, that conflict involves fights for dominance and against submission, close spaces, ticking clocks, and people at odds while forced to share a common goal—such as Sidney Poitier and Tony Curtis in *The Defiant Ones* (black and white prisoners who hate each other but are chained together while escaping from the prison guards hunting them) or a slob and a "neatnik" in the same apartment in *The Odd Couple*, plus several nonfiction examples.

Chapter 9: Subplotting and Themes

We will explain that subplots are not just "additional stories" chosen at random to give characters something to do while they're waiting for the main story to unfold. Subplots and themes are very much related to main plots.

Stories are *about* things, and once the writer has an idea what his or her story is about, these themes can be echoed in subplots, either as complementary ideas or as contradictory ideas. Subplots are related to main plots and "dance" with them. Again, there will be lots of examples to illustrate. We will explain that if a subplot never links up to a main plot, it's not a subplot but an additional plot.

Chapter 10: Characterization

Everything in a story is a function of character, and everything in the narrative, from viewpoint to description, will tell the readers something important about the character.

True character, however, is what the character reveals about herself under the pressure of the story. The character is changed by the events of the story, ending in a different place to where she began. You can change a great many things about a character, woman to man (e.g., as in Virginia Woolf's *Orlando*), kid to adult, black to white, but you cannot change true character without changing the story. The way the character emerges is what the story is about.

Chapter 11: Pace

This is about the movement of the story. We will encourage readers to be aware of what they are writing. It's fine to detail small actions ("He walked across the room. He sat down. He lit a cigarette."). But make sure that each new sentence has information that serves the reader and the plot. ("He pulled out his pen" is okay, but "It was long, blue, shiny, chipped at one end, and cool to his touch" is not okay unless the pen is significant to the story in some way.)

We will talk about how to self-edit your work, cutting words to pick up the pace, and offer tips to those who tend to tell a story too fast.

Chapter 12: Structure

We will talk about the building blocks of dramatic structure and how they apply to fiction and nonfiction alike:

The Sequence
The Scene
Exposition
The Half-Scene
The Swing
The Action

Each element will be illustrated, and we will show how each builds to become the next largest element and, eventually, the whole.

Chapter 13: Systems

Here we will discuss the idea that a writer's narrative is a systematic whole. It is organic and not just a bunch of events that have little or nothing in common, such as they all happened to a guy named Harvey or they all happened on Monday.

We will explain what editors mean when they say a narrative is "too episodic" and will give writers an objective, measurable way to tell whether this is true of their stories.

We will show that a system means that each element in the story puts pressure on all the other elements of the story. We will talk about using systematic thinking to create a back story that will work for the reader's story. We will talk about the problem of the inciting incident for a scene occurring within the scene, thus making the writing self-contained and episodic.

Chapter 14: Fourteen Steps to Writing Your Story

We will make the point that this is not the only way to write, but it does work and is worth trying. We have worked out a pretty good approach for writing a novel that works for us and has gotten us published. The same plan can also be applied to short stories, screenplays, or plays.

Among the fourteen steps, which we won't bother to outline here, are rewriting, creating scenes on index cards, writing a first draft without judging it, and working on a scene in your head, away from the keyboard, before you begin.

Gary Provost
Peter Rubie

Fiction Proposal

The second proposal is for a work of fiction, a mystery series called *Ghostwriter*, by Noreen Wald. Noreen had published *Contestant* (Avon), a nonfiction book, but she had not published any fiction. She received a three-book contract from Berkeley Prime Crime on the strength of this proposal, although the writing sample was longer than that included here. The editor at Berkeley was her old editor from Avon who had moved to a new job. Did this have a positive effect on selling the series? Maybe. But others still had to be convinced before an offer was made.

Bought as a paperback original, since its publication, the first book has been picked up by the Detective Book of the Month Club and reprinted in a hardcover edition, received nominations for several awards, and basked in the glory of some great reviews and quotes.

And what makes it all the more remarkable is that Noreen's professional writing career didn't start until she was well into her late 50s. (I can tell you that because she has a new nonfiction book coming from St. Martin's Press called *How To Be Sexy at 60!*)

GHOSTWRITER
by Noreen Wald

If Susan Isaacs morphed with Mary Higgins Clark, the result would be the Ghostwriter.

Synopsis and Series Overview

For Jake O'Hara, murder will never be cozy again. She accepts a highly invisible assignment, as a ghost for the world's bestselling mystery writer, Kate Lloyd Connors. The same afternoon, Barbara B, Jake's friend and fellow member of Ghostwriter's Anonymous, is found dead . . . her skull crushed by a wicked blow to the head with a signed copy of *The Godfather.* Then a second Ghostwriter Anonymous member, Emmie R, who disappeared after sending a mysterious e-mail to Jake, turns up bludgeoned to death with *Crime and Punishment*.

Who wants the ghosts dead? And why? Barbara had been threatened by the mob, after ghosting a jailed Mafia don's daughter's book, but based on Emmie's cryptic message, Jake's convinced that the answers to her questions are in Kate Lloyd Connors's Sutton Place mansion. Could Emmie have been Kate's last ghost?

Kate's household of loony literary look-alikes is alive with suspects: Caroline Evans, Kate's sexy 18-year-old adopted daughter, who swears, in her Cockney accent, that there's cyanide in the sour cream; Vera Madison, the sinister housekeeper, zealously devoted to Connors; the veddy British male secretary, Jonathan Arthur—beware of men with two first names; and Patrick Hemmings, a handsome hypnotist, who's doing regression and parts therapy—his sessions may well be hands-on—with both Caroline and Kate.

Jake, determined to solve the ghosts' murders, enlists the help of her mother, Maura Foley O'Hara, a former Miss Reinhold runner-up, and the family's favorite fortune-teller, Gypsy Rose Liebowitz. The O'Haras and Gypsy Rose are longtime residents of Carnegie Hill, and the murder investigation, crisscrossing the neighborhood's museum and mansion-filled streets, is a valentine to the area. Gypsy Rose owns a new age bookstore, combining tea leaf and literary readings. Maura works there part-time, but her real job is finding a husband for Jake: "Christ was dead at 33, you're not even engaged."

On that same fateful Saturday, unbeknownst to her mother, Jake's turned on—big time—by three hot prospects. Dennis Kim, an entertainment attorney and Jake's childhood crush, divorced, reappears; however, he represents one dead ghost and one live suspect. How deeply is he involved? Patrick Hemmings, the hypnotherapist with the best butt in Manhattan, keeps Jake spellbound, but suspicious. And homicide detective Ben Rubin tweaks Jake's sneaks, though it's possible he believes she's guilty.

The Ghostwriters Anonymous members work on accepting their anonymity, but they twelve step to the sound of a different drummer. The fellowship includes Ginger S—Jake's good friend and a cookbook ghost—who describes people as food and makes Martha Stewart look incapable; Modesty M—a Gothic romance ghost—a closet misogynist who revels in misery, her own and others; and Jane D—a self-help ghost—so serene she's often asleep at meetings. The program's tradition of confidentiality prevents one ghost from knowing what her best friend is doing and complicates Jake's search for the killer.

Emmie's cryptic e-mail message—"Skim milk masquerades as cream"—completes Caroline's earlier Gilbert and Sullivan quote—"Things are seldom as they seem"—and the couplet becomes Jake's mantra.

The clues don't add up. Ivan, a Hungarian waiter and Emmie's lover, delivers an envelope to Jake. It contains a 1958 newspaper clipping of a death by drowning in northern Michigan. Emmie told Ivan it was important, but what does it reveal? Jake's super-sleuth mom learns Connors formed a new corporation, Aubergine, with a silent partner. Who is it? Vera, the grim housekeeper, would do anything to protect Kate—does that include double murder? Jonathan has a publisher for the ugly expose of his glamorous aging, Edgar Award winning . . . but ghost written . . . employer. Did Emmie find out about his book? Were she and Barbara killed to shut them up? Patrick's been sleeping in both mama and daughter's bed. Had Emmie succumbed to his spell, too? Is crazy Caroline really the never married Kate's biological granddaughter? Could someone be blackmailing Kate?

As Jake works on Kate's current book, she gets closer to the truth. And there's more than a ghost of a chance that she's on the killer's short list. She receives threatening e-mail, then is shoved in front of a Fifth Avenue bus.

At a seance in Gypsy Rose's tearoom/bookstore, Maura, Jake, and the other ghosts communicate telepathically with Emmie, who reveals the killer's initial, "W."

Only problem is, there's not a suspect in sight with that initial.

Jake's sure Kate Lloyd Connors has a deadly secret. She arranges a meeting in Kate's Sutton Place library, but when Jake arrives, Kate is dead. A powerful blow to her head with the complete anthology of her famous society-sleuth Suey O's mysteries. Heavy enough to split the thickest skull.

Against Detective Rubin's strong warnings, Jake digs deeper into Kate's past and unearths a pile of dirt. Ripe for blackmail. Even while suspecting Patrick, Jake allows him to do regression therapy with her, hoping to uncover a nagging clue buried in her subconscious. When she rummages through Dennis's office files and discovers the name of Kate's silent partner—Virginia Wolfe—Jake knows who done it.

In a tense and dangerous confrontation, Jake meets with the murderer in the killer's natural habitat, her Carnegie Hill kitchen, and narrowly escapes being carved to death. Ben Rubin arrives in time for the first nick.

The motive? Money. Ginger S, Jake's old friend and former co-ghost, has been blackmailing Kate Lloyd Connors for almost a decade. As a young girl in upper Michigan, Kate had allowed her sexually abusive father to drown while ice fishing. Stood there, on that long ago, cold February morning, and laughed as he floundered in the freezing water of Lake Ontario. Ginger, employed as Kate's first ghost, long before any of the current crop of crazies had come to work for her, found the old clippings, researched the story, and used the information to extort hundreds of thousands of dollars from the beloved, international Queen of Murder-Most-Cozy. The corporation was set up to fund Ginger's dream. A television show. Network. Prime Time. "Cooking in the Kitchens of the Rich and Famous." Poor Emmie had stumbled on Ginger's scheme and confided in Barbara, her Ghostwriters Anonymous sponsor. Both ghosts were dead ducks.

"How did you know?" Maura asks Jake. What Jake couldn't remember until Patrick's posthypnotic suggestion was that Ginger Simon had changed her name. Ginger once told Jake that her real last name was the same as another writer's, but never said which one. As soon as Jake learned Kate's silent partner's name was Virginia Wolfe, she knew it had to be Ginger. Ironic that Ginger used a nom de plume, considering ghosts go unnamed.

"Things are seldom as they seem," Jake explains to Maura and Gypsy Rose. "Skim milk masquerades as cream. Ginger fooled everyone. A blackmailer. Maybe. She did love money. But a murderer. I still can't believe it."

Jake's mother says, "Ginger snapped."

I'll Take Manhattan

Jake O'Hara doesn't vanish after the *Ghostwriter's* final proofs. She writes a true crime bestseller based on the murder of Kate Lloyd Connors and finally sees her name on a book cover. She spends a bundle on a beach house on Shelter Island, then takes an interim job as a feature editor at *Manhattan* magazine to help maintain her two residences, while she finishes her second book. Jake knows going back to ghosting would be considered a slip in Ghostwriters Anonymous, so the 6-month editorship, filling in for a friend on maternity leave, is perfect.

Her first day on the job, Richard Peter, the magazine's acerbic book critic, and one of New York's ten most hated men, is murdered at his computer. Stabbed in the back. Jake discovers the body. Homicide Detective Ben Rubin isn't a bit surprised. Jake seems to court murder. Meanwhile, Ben's father has started to court Jake's mother, but Ben's not thinking of Jake as a sister.

The magazine's music critic Anthony Prato's swan song comes the next evening. He's killed in his box at the Met, during Aida's death scene, while his date's in the john. Jake, her mother, and Gypsy Rose Liebowitz are in the mezzanine, when a blood-curdling scream, coming not from the onstage tomb but from a box above them, stops the show.

To tell the truth, Jake's finding editing a bloody bore and is delighted to once again be in the middle of a Manhattan murder mystery.

Lullaby of Broadway

Dennis Kim has an offer so intriguing, even Jake O'Hara can't refuse. Writing the book for the musical *Suey O*, to be based on Kate Lloyd Connors's society sleuth, who, as everyone knows, is based on Jackie O. Since Jake ghosted the last book, in the long-running series *A Killing in Katmandu*, she's typecast as the playwright. That's what Dennis says. Jake's not so sure.

But, it's an exciting project. Every over-the-hill movie actress wants to star as Suey O. The casting question catches the public's fancy, rivaling the search for Scarlett. Jake's mother and Gypsy Rose Liebowitz beg Jake to just say yes. Jake knows Dennis represents some unsavory angels, but just as starstruck as Maura and Gypsy Rose, she accepts.

The search for Suey O narrows down to six of the world's most famous and beautiful, albeit aging, movie stars. When Colleen Grahame, one of the candidates, dies of a "heart attack", no one is suspicious. She had to be 65 and has existed for decades on diet pills and Remy Martin. However, Morgan Wagner's "suicide" belongs in Homicide. This case is out of Ben Rubin's precinct, but, knowing Jake, he plans to spend his off-duty hours on Broadway.

Ghostwriter
Noreen Wald
Chapter One

"You could kill Wagner in the kitchen," my mother said, "that way you could throw the bloody clothes in the washer and clean up everything in the sink. You know, use lots of Clorox. And don't forget the dishwasher's good for any weapons stained with clinging body tissues." Mom: the meticulous murderer.

"We'll talk about it after the company leaves," I said. She looked disappointed. I gave her a hug. "Let's not mix business with pleasure. Right now, why don't you mix me a martini?"

"Okay, but let's work on it later tonight for an hour or so." Mom headed to the dining room bar. Over her shoulder she added, "Oh, Jake, some guy called while you were at Gristede's; he wanted to discuss hiring you for a job. I told him to drop by the party." That's my mother, hustling business in front of twenty guests.

"The thing of it is, you see, it's a delicate matter, my employer would need the arrangement to be handled in the best of taste."

The fop irked me. Who was he and what did he want from me? And why couldn't he get to the point, if there was one.

"I represent," he hesitated, brushing an invisible fleck from his well-cut Ralph Lauren jacket. I just knew he'd paid retail. No upstate discount malls for this fine specimen, 72 and Madison—Polo's flagship—would be his store of choice.

"Yes," I prompted.

"Well, as I was saying, it's a tad difficult to be discreet and . . ."

"Forget discreet. Try forthcoming." My voice had acquired a less-than-gracious edge. Not good. After all, he did represent a possible client and a cash advance. God knows I could use the business.

I flashed the full set of my just bleached teeth, good thing today's dentists took Visa, and motioned to the white leather couch. Rooms-to-Go . . . no payment till January 2000. By then, I could be dead or rich or anywhere in between.

Credit, the American way. My instant attitude adjustment seemed to relax him. Smiling back, he pulled a slim gold cardholder from the inside pocket of his navy jacket and handed me a cream-colored engraved card.

Clicking cocktail glasses and high-pitched chitchat surrounded us. Jonathan Arthur, I read, thinking—beware of men with two first names. His address was on Sutton Place.

"Hello, Jonathan." I held out my right hand as my left tucked his card in my blue blazer pocket. It occurred to me that Jonathan and I were dressed like twins, gray gabardine pants, white linen collarless shirts, and black loafers. He'd added a tomato red scarf to his blazer's breast pocket. Two dapper dandies. "I'm Jake O'Hara."

"Indeed, you are." He sat, then primly arranged his trouser folds.

Mom passed by with a tray full of drinks. I grabbed my long overdue martini, mumbled thanks, took a gulp, plopped into the Casablanca chair next to the couch, and gave Jonathan my full attention. "What can I do for you?" I suspected it was going to be a long night.

The cocktail hour was mother's longtime ritual. The third Friday of every month, she invited the lesser-literary-lights of our acquaintance—we knew few bright lights—to our big prewar co-op on 92nd Street. Mom still believed that 1957 had been the last great year for songs. "The Stars Fell on Alabama" filled the room as the lesser-literary-lights discussed their yet to be published manuscripts. Everyone had a work-in-progress, some for as long as 30 or 40 years.

Mr. Kim, the local greengrocer cum poet, and I had been comparing the patriotic verse of Walt Whitman and Rupert Brooke when Jonathan Arthur had waltzed in, and Mom had two-stepped him over to me.

Graceful carriage in motion, military posture in repose. No slouch. Jonathan sat straight and tall, knees together, hands folded in his lap. Sister Mary Alice would have awarded him an A in deportment.

What can I do for you?—had sounded like a reasonable query, worthy of an answer, but Jonathan appeared stumped. I tapped the rattan arm of my chair and drained the rest of my martini. Still smiling.

"This will be confidential—I need to know straight away, you don't discuss your clients or your contracts?"

"Jonathan, I don't do guest shots on Rosie. If I blabbed, I wouldn't be in business." Of course, at the moment, I had neither a client nor a contract, that's why Jonathan, however annoying, was being offered a cordial shoulder and another drink. He warmed to both.

"Let me be candid, Jake."

Thank God!—"Please do." My smile would have to be chopped off.

"I'm familiar with some of your work. Oh, not from you, of course! But in our circle, the word gets out. My employer is most impressed with your 'reported' body of work. She thinks you kill cute."

"I never thought of it that way. Jonathan, just who is your employer?"

He checked over both shoulders to make sure he wouldn't be overheard, then in an awestruck tone, he whispered, "Kate Lloyd Conners . . ."

I, equally awed, said, "No shit." America's Queen of Mystery apparently wanted to hire me as a ghostwriter. Wait till my mother heard this!

Mom and all lovers of the murder-most-cozy genre adored Kate Lloyd Conners, panted for her next release, and had turned her into a multimillionaire, best-selling author. Her heroine, society sleuth Suey O, was the widow of a wealthy, Irish-American senator. Any resemblance to Jackie O—definitely intended. Suey's murder suspects skied at Biarritz, sailed the Aegean, gambled at Monte Carlo, and shopped at Bergdorfs. Her victims included a reigning monarch's secret mistress and the secretary of state's former husband. Wherever the international jet set met death, Suey-on-the-spot solved the case. The cookie-cutter formula, illogical plots, and stereotypical characters were a lot of fun. I'd never confessed to Mom that I loved them, too. Reading Kate Lloyd Connors, like devouring Milky Ways, was a secret vice.

"Well, Jonathan, I'd be delighted to have a chat with Ms. Connors."

"She's most anxious to see you. Is luncheon at one, tomorrow, too soon? The address on my card is Kate's townhouse. I live there."

"Fine, I'll see you then."

Jonathan Arthur rose, almost clicked his heels in a half bow, and forged his way to the door.

Lord love a duck, I thought, does the great Kate Lloyd Connors need a ghost? Has she used ghosts before? And why me? Our styles were as disparate as our incomes. I looked forward to our meeting.

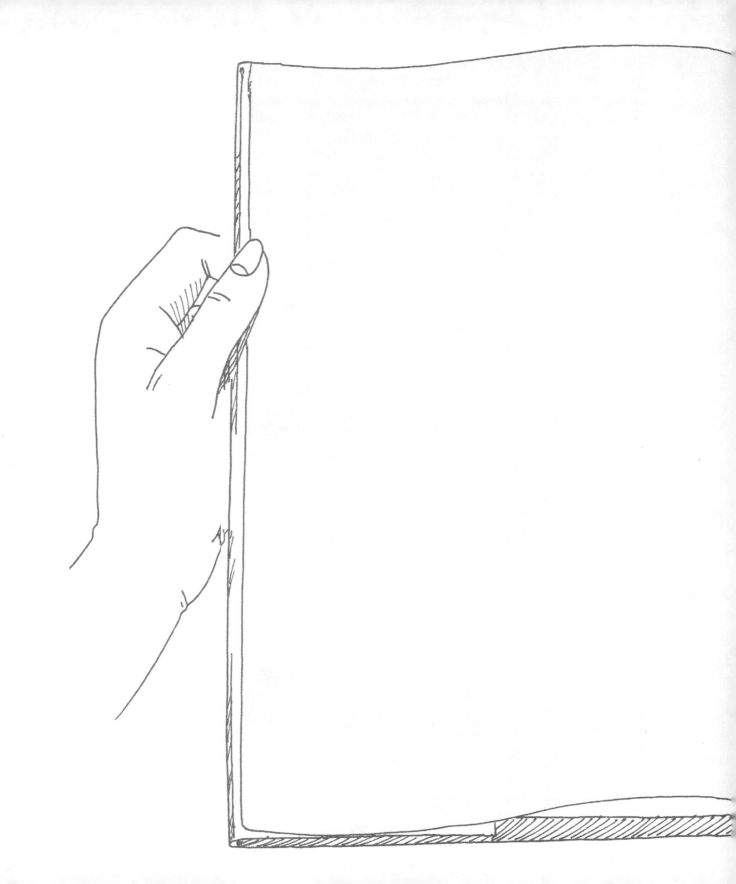

Part 2

~

GETTING IT
IN PRINT

CHAPTER 5

Getting an Agent

Okay, you've done all this work, got your proposal and your query letter just right, and now you're ready to submit. But people are advising you to get an agent. Are they mad? Why would you want to give away 15 percent of your money after all the hard work you've done? What exactly do these interlopers *do* for their money, anyway? Write a few letters, make a few phone calls—money for old rope, as they say in England. Apart from which, you say to yourself, *I* hear *anyone* can claim to be an agent. How do you tell a good one from a shyster?

These are all good questions. The plain truth is that writers write, editors edit, and agents agent, and it's very difficult to mix these elements successfully at the same time. It's not a good idea to write a book and then try to agent it yourself.

I've been a journalist, a publishing house editor, a book doctor, a published writer of fiction and nonfiction, and, currently, a literary agent. You'd think with all that experience under my belt that if I didn't know better, I should at least know *something* about the publishing business when it comes to representing myself. However, you'd be wrong. Let me tell you a story.

Once upon a time . . . my agent and business partner (I represent her; she represents me; it sounds a bit incestuous, I know, but it does work, believe it or not) was going through something of a personal crisis and was not as focused on work as usual.

Meanwhile, I was offered a book deal by an editor, Ms. A, with whom I thought I had a good relationship. We developed a proposal, and the book was accepted. I submitted the manuscript, and over the course of the next couple of months learned, to my horror, that I was being edited not only by Ms. A, the elderly but experienced editor, but also by Ms. B, a woman in her 40s, and Ms. C, an opinionated young woman just out of college. They would request a change, I'd make it, and I'd get the manuscript back with someone else's handwritten comments scrawled in the margin asking why I'd made the change!

Being edited by committee, especially when everyone on that committee has her own agenda, is excruciating. I was so close to the work by then that I was pulling out my hair in exasperation.

"I don't care if I'm edited by Genghis Khan," I cried, "just pick *one* person for me to work with and let me get on with it!" No such luck. My relationship with the publishing company rapidly started going down the tubes. I began embracing Buddhism, chanting the mantra "Better published than not published," in an effort to see the silver lining in the darkening cloud hovering over me.

To make matters worse, I realized one day that they weren't going to let me see the copyedited manuscript, which meant in effect that they would make whatever changes they wanted to my book—and some of Ms. C's had been pretty bizarre—and put out a book that was supposed to be my philosophy of how to write fiction, based on my expertise, as they thought the audience should have it, not as I had written it. I felt as though I'd been transported in my sleep to a Hollywood B movie screenwriter's hell. That's where the producer has his girlfriend star in the film, and he exclaims: "Hey, in *my Romeo and Juliet* they both survive and set up house in Simi Valley! The Will-meister would love it, trust me, baby. Just sign here, would you?"

Fortunately, at this point Lori came back into the picture. One of the things an agent spends a lot of time doing is solving problems with and for clients or, as they say in the business, putting out fires. By this point I had a nice two-alarm fire raging.

Lori spoke with editor A and, when she realized what a nightmare the company was putting me through and what they intended to do to the book, helped me move the book to another company. She even got them to let me keep the money they had already paid me.

The new publisher changed barely a word of what I'd written and made some suggestions that I thought made good sense. I got on like gangbusters with my new editor. *The Elements of Storytelling* was published to good reviews and nice comments. You can still buy it in the stores, and twice a year I get a royalty check with my royalty statement. All's well that ends well—because of my agent.

Without my agent, none of this would have been possible. Let this be a lesson to you. It certainly was for me.

What Does an Agent Do?

The big question for unpublished writers is, What exactly do agents do and how do I find a good one?

INFORMATION

Did You Know...

A *royalty* is the percentage of money that is earned off the sale of a book and that a publisher pays to an author.

The best agents help to manage their clients' careers. Agents should more properly be thought of as authors' representatives. In fact, the agents guild is called the Association of Authors' Representatives (AAR). It has a cannon of ethics, demanding qualifications a new agent has to meet before his or her name is put to a vote for acceptance into the association, and if you do something unethical, such as lie during a book auction, they'll throw you out on your ear.

Doesn't sound like much of a punishment, but publishing is a small industry that thrives on gossip and rumor (the technical term for it is *buzz*, but don't let that fool you), and stories that show people in a bad light, particularly involving unethical behavior, can be very damaging. For an agent, it can severely curtail his or her ability to conduct business effectively (read: editors won't buy books from them).

There's a common misconception that agents spend all their time developing new material and new clients for publishers. Unpublished writers think that if you just take your place in line, they'll get to you eventually. Alas, it's not really true, unless the agent is setting up a new business or is new to an agency and building a client list.

Agents spend *some* of their time in the evenings and on weekends doing that, but only after they've finished reading the latest material sent to them by their clients. Most agents have a full complement of clients, often as many as forty or fifty writers, and while they're always on the lookout for good new material, they have plenty to do just keeping on top of their existing workload. That means your new material has to be really special. However, if it is, you *will* attract the attention of agents and editors.

Unagented writers don't seem to realize that when an agent takes on a new client, the agent is taking on a *negative asset*. The client will actually *cost* the agent money—in time, energy, mailing fees, telephone calls, photocopying proposals, and so forth—before the agent ever sees a dime of the commission he or she earns from a sale.

What agents do during the day is spend a lot of time developing new contacts with editors and publishers and renewing old ones. They pitch projects by clients, write query letters on behalf of the client and the project, check royalty statements, pursue outstanding royalty advances, go through the fine print of contracts, put out "fires," negotiate deals . . . the list is exhaustive.

Agents also attend lunch meetings, attend book parties, speak at writers conferences, and make it their business to meet and get to know as many publishing house acquiring editors (and contracts people as well) as they can. The essence of the job is match-making—putting the right project with the right editor at the best house—so you better know who the editors are, as well as their likes and dislikes.

Each publishing house has its own personality and specialties and is continually reinventing itself in order to gain as large a share of the market as possible. These days editors move around a lot. Then there are all the mergers and acquisitions that have taken place in the last couple of years and the reshaping of giant companies such as Bantam, Doubleday, Dell and its imprints with Random House (and all its imprints).

You can guarantee that in the next couple of years publishing won't much resemble what it looked like a few years ago. In the face of all this industrial volatility, agents provide a font of cutting-edge knowledge and a haven of stability for authors.

Agents make it their job to keep up with where editors are currently working, what they like, and what they are *looking for* (not necessarily always the same thing) and, in certain circumstances, actually help to create books for their authors that editors seem keen to acquire.

Publishing lunches are important because, rather like platonic dating, they offer an opportunity for agent and editor to get to know each other's tastes and styles without the phone ringing or someone barging into the office with something to sign, a crisis to solve, or a reminder that you're late for yet another meeting.

Publishers value agents so highly that editors usually pay for lunch. Why? Because just as writers can't effectively concentrate on writing and selling at the same time, editors can't edit a book, look after a variety of projects at various stages of completion in the

INFORMATION

Did You Know...

A *literary agent* is also called an *author's representative*. They earn their money solely from a commission, which is a percentage of an author's earned royalties.

publishing process, and also screen unknown new properties, all at the same time.

Editors have to rely on agents to bring them hot new properties and help fix problems that may be on the horizon. They rely on agents to do some of the screening for them. Ensuring that agents keep the editors in the loop and send the editors their most exciting new projects and authors is worth at least the price of a lunch.

Agents also commonly submit a project to more than one editor at the same time, and the editors know this and accept it, though they don't much like authors trying to do the same thing. It's hard for an editor to discuss, editorially, with an unagented writer, how much he loves a book and then have to switch gears and tell that same writer in harsh terms all the book's weaknesses in order to try and negotiate as small a royalty advance as possible for the book.

Cool heads and objectivity are needed to do that job. It's not personal; it's about business, and that's the most important thing an agent does for an author—take care of business.

Once an editor makes an offer on a book, the agent informs everyone else who has it that she and the author have an offer. If they're lucky, they can get an auction going, with editors bidding against each other to buy the book. If every editor but one drops out, the agent sometimes has a number of persuasive arguments she can make to get the editor to increase the proposed royalty advance.

Having negotiated the deal in broad measure, the agent, once the publishing contract arrives, turns into a paralegal and examines the contract closely. She'll discuss technical details either with the editor or the publishing company's contract staff in an effort to get the client the best deal possible, taking care of contingency disasters that almost certainly will never happen but nevertheless need to be prepared for.

Finding and Working with an Agent

What should you look for in a good agent? One of the best questions to ask is: Does the agent make a living from commissions on sales to publishers?

Ten Reasons Why You Need a Good Agent

1. It's an agent's job to know which editor at which house is interested in projects like yours or is looking for projects like yours.

2. An agent can nearly always get a better deal for your book than you can, even if the initial contact is yours.

3. An editor knows that if you have an agent, it's because the agent sees something commercially viable in your work. Your agent's enthusiasm and professional reputation will count for something in selling your book.

4. An agent is well versed in the tools of getting a book out into the marketplace. She knows the best timing for a submission and what to say over the phone and write in a cover letter, and she has the ability to develop a little buzz about your book.

5. Even if you're a lawyer, unless you know publishing law, publishing contracts can be difficult to understand and negotiate. An unagented writer or lawyer not versed in publishing contracts might not be able to achieve those same favorable terms.

6. Agents will get you the best deal, and that often means retaining subsidiary rights—which agents can then sell and earn extra money for you through their subagents in foreign and translation markets and the movie and TV arena, and so on, without sharing the proceeds of those sales with the publisher.

7. An agent commonly submits a project to several editors at the same time (called multiple submissions).

8. An agent can run interference for you with a troublesome editor and/or publishing house employee. If you don't think this means much now, wait until you learn they've decided to take your literary novel, *Sister Marie and the Convent in the Ghetto*, and retitled it *Biker Nun in Hell*, with matching cover art.

9. Your agent keeps track of who owes you money, how much, and when it's due to be paid.

10. A good agent will be a career manager and adviser and will encourage and guide you in your literary endeavors. Remember, an agent only makes money if you do.

If an agent charges a "reading fee," my advice is to steer well clear. Reputable agents, with one or two notable exceptions, don't charge reading fees, nor do they provide "reader's reports." The whole concept of charging for reading is questionable to begin with. How can you give someone an unbiased opinion on his or her work if you're interested in representing it but also charge for editorial advice? It's a conflict of interest that leads to authors buying their agents' time and attention with very likely little to show for their money at the end of the project, except hard lessons learned.

Agents look for writers who have put together a terrific project, have "their act together" as writers, and are ready to be published. They then help them polish their projects and sell them, thus beginning, it is hoped, a wonderful and enduring partnership.

The hard truth is that if you can't get an agent interested in your work without paying for some sort of "service," you're almost certainly not ready to be published yet, and you'll have a hard time getting a publisher interested. Agents are not in the business of teaching writers how to write or helping unpublished writers find a publisher, or even earn a living. Their job is to get you the best deal possible for a book.

Best advice: Don't spend your money on these services; spend it instead on taking writing classes or working with a reputable book doctor who will teach you how to fix your project. A good place to start, if you're looking for a book doctor, is the Editorial Freelance Association (212-929-5400; *www.the-efa.org*).

How to Contact an Agent

After you've done your research and compiled a list of agents who represent the kind of book you've written and who you're interested in having represent you and your book, you should find a way to catch their eye. Simply writing a letter and mailing it in makes the odds of your being picked out of the pile much lower. It may also take months before you get a response.

Every agent is different in their wants and needs, and many established agents find their new clients through referrals from colleagues and existing clients because this is the best way to meet those demands of quality.

If you can't get someone to refer you (which is highly probable), the next best thing is to cold call the agent late in the afternoon, say after 4pm their time but before 5:30pm. (This is a good time because the day is winding down, most important calls to editors have been made, and the agent may be preparing to spend the rest of the work day talking to clients and potential clients.)

If the agent takes your call, gird your loins, and in your most professional, pleasant, and succinct manner, pitch them your book in a sentence or two. Don't ramble, and don't shoot the breeze—time is money. It's probable that rather than get the agent, you'll talk to an assistant instead. Before you get weird on the phone or insistent that you must speak to Ms. So-and-So, remember: the assistant may well be an agent in training herself and looking for clients of her own to develop. If she takes you on you'll end up with an agent who wants you, and the big agent you were originally after who will be supervising the assistant's submissions; and secondly, she probably knows her boss's taste well, because she is responsible for helping to go through the unsolicited mail and will be able to tell you whether or not you're wasting your time, or the agent's time. If she says your idea seems right for her boss, you now have a recommendation from someone the agent is going to pay attention to. Make sure this referral is prominently at the front of any query letter you send in.

If all goes well, the agent will tell you to send in your material to his or her attention, and will be intrigued enough to look at it ahead of much of the other unsolicited mail. (In fact, it has now been "solicited," something that jumps you well ahead of other writers.)

Make sure you ask the agent what they would like to see and then give them what they asked for. There's nothing more aggravating than saying to a prospective client, "I'd like a narrative synopsis showing the beginning, middle, and end, a bio, and the first 30 or so pages," and then having a 900 page manuscript land on your desk with a note saying, "I feel you need to read the whole thing to get the full impact of my brilliant and original work, so I've taken the liberty of sending you the whole thing."

If I had wanted to read the whole manuscript I would have asked to see it! Guess what happens next to that writer's project . . . .

INFORMATION

Did You Know...

Multiple submissions means sending out the same submission to more than one person at the same time.

Exclusive submission means sending the submission out to only one person at a time.

What to Expect from Your Agent

First of all, has the agent actually *read* your book or book proposal and can she talk intelligently about it? Is she enthusiastic, and does she *get* it? Yes, undoubtedly she will have suggestions to make something either clearer or more focused, or more commercially viable, but are you comfortable that she really understands what you're trying to do and sympathizes with your efforts?

Sometimes an agent is just starting out, and in many cases, new agents are the best bet for new writers. But because they are new agents does not mean they are new to the publishing business. Many are former editors or publishing house employees who know the business, how it's conducted, and a lot of the people in it.

There are basically three types of literary agents: former editors and editorial types who develop and shape projects with writers; agents who prefer selling to editorial work and are into the "gavotte," the hard bargaining that can take place during a book deal negotiation dance; and entertainment lawyers, who basically just do the deal for the writer. Very successful authors sometimes use lawyers because it's cheaper for them to pay an hourly rate than a 15 percent commission. That does not work well for less-well-paid authors for obvious reasons.

Publishing relationships between agent/writer and editor/writer suffer many of the same problems that romantic relationships collapse under. Don't ignore each other, communicate whenever possible, be considerate and respectful, say thank you occasionally, but be aware that everyone has other demands put on him or her. Respect each other's need for privacy but also expect that your agent will respond quickly if there is a problem that needs to be fixed. Learn to trust each other.

Ask around and get an agent with a strong reputation, one who will give you some attention when you need it. That doesn't mean necessarily he'll call you back immediately, but your agent should certainly respond within a few days. If you make repeated calls to an agent and don't get a reply, that's a clue something's going sour in the relationship.

Your agent will often be someone you like, but he or she is not your friend, nor is friendship a good basis for a business rela-

It was a dark and stormy night

Questions to Ask
a Potential Agent

You may wish to pose to a new agent (when the two of you are contemplating establishing a business relationship) the following twelve questions. Bear in mind that most agents are *not* going to bother to take the time to answer these questions unless they've decided to represent you.

The following list is reprinted with permission of the Association of Authors' Representatives, Inc.

1. Are you a member of the Association of Authors' Representatives?

2. How long have you been in business as an agent?

3. Do you have specialists at your agency who handle movie and television rights? Foreign rights?

4. Do you have subagents or corresponding agents in Hollywood and overseas?

5. Who in your agency will actually be handling my work? Will the other staff members be familiar with my work and the status of my business at your agency? Will you oversee or at least keep me apprised of the work that your agency is doing on my behalf?

6. Do you issue an agent-author agreement? May I review the language of the agency clause that appears in contracts you negotiate for your clients?

7. How do you keep your clients informed of your activities on their behalf?

8. Do you consult with your clients on any and all offers?

9. What are your commission rates? What are your procedures and time frames for processing and disbursing client funds? Do you keep different bank accounts separating author funds from agency revenue? What are your policies about charging clients for expenses incurred by your agency?

10. When you issue 1099 tax forms at the end of each year, do you also furnish clients upon request with a detailed account of their financial activity, such as gross income, commissions and other deductions, and net income, for the past year?

11. In the event of your death or disability, what provisions exist for my continued representation?

12. If we should part company, what is your policy about handling any unsold subsidiary rights in my work?

tionship. Agents are not shrinks, sources of emotional or psychological support, or even personal editors. A good agent may exhibit some or all of these abilities because it is a job that involves nurturing, but don't expect it and don't ask for it. If you have problems, figure them out before you get together with your agent. Her job, remember, is to sell your work. If you have nothing to sell, there isn't much she can do for you.

New York City is the heart of American publishing, and most of the publishing industry is based there. However, there are many good agents based outside of the city. Those not based in New York usually make regular trips into the city to meet with editors. However, most of the work is done by phone and fax. Better a good agent outside the city than a mediocre one based in New York.

Where to Look for an Agent

Here's something to think about: Get agents to chase you. "What's that?" you say.

A lot of writers are chasing agents who are too busy to respond most of the time. These agents have their hands full just with their regular clientele. They *are*, however, on the lookout for successful writers who are unrepresented.

These writers are published in magazines and anthologies, have written book reviews for local or national newspapers, have gotten their names in print somewhere (and often more than once), and in their bylines, it says something like "Kathleen Blodget is currently working on a nonfiction book about pain relief management" or "a novel about dinosaurs, who now walk among us disguised as humans."

Go to writer conferences and network. Enter competitions and win prizes. Get your writing noticed by people whose opinion counts for something and can talk to friends or colleagues in the business about you and your work.

One of the best ways to get a good agent is to try to find out who is starting up on his own or has just joined an established agency. These days, with editors losing jobs in the volatile seismic earthquakes that are wracking the publishing industry at the moment, many of these former editors are setting themselves up as agents and are on the lookout for new clients.

One of the best ways to find a good agent is by word of mouth. Try querying members of an organization such as AAR, though not all good agents are members.

AAR is a not-for-profit trade organization of literary and dramatic agents. It was formed in 1991 through the merger of the Society of Authors' Representatives, founded in 1928, and the Independent Literary Agents Association, founded in 1977. The association's objectives include keeping agents informed about conditions in publishing, the theater, the motion picture and television industries, and related fields; encouraging cooperation among literary organizations; and assisting agents in representing and defending their authors' interests.

Another good source is the *Literary Market Place* (LMP); it, too, has rules about who can be listed as an agent in its pages.

Sample Author/Agent Agreement

There is a debate among agents as to whether or not to have letters of agreements with authors. Every agent has an agency clause that is inserted into a successful publishing contract. The clause basically says that the agent is the agent of record for that book and that all the money will be funneled through the agent, who will take an agreed-upon commission from the gross amount before remitting the rest to the client. In rare cases, the agreement will state that the publisher will send the commission to the agent and separately send the client the rest of the money due after the agent's commission is deducted.

The basis of any successful agent/author relationship, just like a marriage, is trust. Although authors often insist upon it, in fact, a letter of agreement is more in the agent's interest than the client's. It protects the agent from many things, including doing all the work and having the client waltz away at the last moment and reap the rewards from the agent's work without the agent earning any money. And it can

tie up an author to work exclusively with an agent when the agent is not the best person to represent a certain project. Like a marriage, once the marriage is over, regardless of the piece of paper legalizing the union, the author/agent relationship has nowhere to go but to hell if it continues when neither party trusts or can work with each other anymore.

Below is a sample agency clause that would be inserted in a publishing contract. This is the one we use at Perkins, Rubie and Associates, but they're all much the same.

Sample Agency Clause

The Author hereby confirms that s/he has irrevocably appointed and designated **Perkins, Rubie and Associates** (hereafter referred to as the "Agent") of 240 West 35th Street, Suite 500, New York, NY 10001 as the Author's sole Agent throughout the world with respect to the Work and all rights herein. The Author hereby authorizes and directs the Publisher to pay and forward all statements and monies accruing from the Publisher to the Agent, and the Publisher agrees to do so. The Author hereby empowers the Agent to act on the Author's behalf in all matters arising from or pertaining to this Agreement and/or the Work. The Author hereby irrevocably agrees to pay the Agent, and the Author hereby irrevocably authorizes the Agent to receive and retain, and the Author hereby irrevocably assigns and transfers to the Agent an amount equal to fifteen percent (15%) of all monies accruing, payable, or paid to the Author under this Agreement and otherwise accruing from the Publisher or Author with respect to the Work, and the Publisher hereby accepts and agrees to honor said assignment and transfer. Any sum payable by the Publisher under this Agreement and paid to the Agent pursuant to this paragraph shall constitute a valid discharge of the Publisher with respect thereto. The Author warrants that he has secured the rights that he has given the Agent clearance to represent on the Author's behalf. The Author indemnifies the Agent and holds him harmless from any legal action that may result from the contents or presentation of the books.

Sample Letter of Agreement

Here's a sample letter of agreement. You'll notice it echoes a lot of what is in the agency clause.

Dear _____,

Please regard this letter as a declaration of a business relationship between _____ ("you") and _____**Agency ("us")**.

We agree to take you on as a client of _____**Agency** and will make our best efforts to guide you and enthusiastically represent your work in the publishing and related industries both in North America and abroad through our foreign agents; should you so desire we will also put forth our best efforts to get you representation with our motion picture and television associates.

You authorize us to direct a Publisher to pay and forward all statements and monies accruing from the Publisher to us. You empower us to act on your behalf in all matters arising from or pertaining to any Agreement with a Publisher. You warrant that you have secured the rights that you've given us permission to represent on your behalf. You further indemnify us and hold us harmless from any legal action that may result from the contents or presentation of your books.

For our efforts, _____**Agency** will take 15% (fifteen percent) of any monies earned, which shall be written into any publishing contract we are successful in making on your behalf. A commission for any movie or TV deals we are successful in making for you with a Hollywood co-agent will be split 50/50 between the co-agent and ourselves. Foreign sales will be charged at 20% (10% for the foreign agent and 10% for _____**Agency**).

_____**Agency** will remit payments to the Author, after deducting Agency commission, no later than 14 days after monies have been received and deposited in the bank. The Agency will send the Author copies of all royalty statements, checks, and contracts received from the Publisher concerning a work.

All photocopying, and other mutually agreed-upon expenses (not to exceed $200), will be paid by you when billed by us or deducted by us from funds received by us for your account.

Any controversy, claim, or dispute between the Agency and the Author that cannot be resolved will be taken to Arbitration and the differences resolved under the laws of the State of New York.

We agree not to sign any contract or make any commitment on your behalf without your written or oral agreement.

Either party is free to notify the other that they wish to terminate this agreement, as long as it is done in writing and with one month's notice.

Sincerely,

_____**Agency**

ACCEPTED AND AGREED TO:

_____ _____
Name   SS# or Federal ID

Reprinted with permission of the Association of Authors' Representatives.

1. The members of the Association of Authors' Representatives, Inc. are committed to the highest standard of conduct in the performance of their professional activities. While affirming the necessity and desirability of maintaining their full individuality and freedom of action, the members pledge themselves to loyal service to their clients' business and artistic needs, and will allow no conflicts of interest that would interfere with such service. They pledge their support to the Association itself and to the principles of honorable coexistence, directness, and honesty in their relationships with their co-members. They undertake never to mislead, deceive, dupe, defraud, or victimize their clients, other members of the Association, the general public, or any person with whom they do business as a member of the Association.

2. Members shall take responsible measures to protect the security and integrity of clients' funds. Members must maintain separate bank accounts for money due their clients so that there is no commingling of clients' and members' funds. Members shall deposit funds received on behalf of clients promptly upon receipt, and shall make payments of domestic earnings due clients promptly, but in no event later than ten business days after clearance. Revenues from foreign rights over $50 shall be paid to clients within ten business days after clearance. Sums under $50 shall be paid within a reasonable time of clearance. However, on stock and similar rights, statements of royalties and payments shall be made not later than the month following the member's receipt, each statement and payment to cover all royalties received to the 25th day of the previous calendar month. Payments for amateur rights shall be made not less frequently than every six months. A member's books of account must be open to the client at all times with respect to transactions concerning the client.

3. In addition to the compensation for agency services that is agreed upon between a member and a client, a member may, subject to the approval of the client, pass along charges incurred by the member on the client's behalf, such as copyright fees, manuscript retyping, photocopies, copies of books for use in the sale of other rights, long distance calls, special messenger fees, etc. Such charges shall be made only if the client has agreed to reimburse such expenses.

4. A member shall keep each client apprised of matters entrusted to the member and shall promptly furnish such information as the client may reasonably request.

5. Members shall not represent both buyer and seller in the same transaction. Except as provided in the next sentence, a member who represents a client in the grant of rights in any property owned or controlled by the client may not accept any compensation or other payment from the acquirer of such rights, including but not limited to so-called "packaging fees," it being understood that the member's compensation, if any, shall be derived solely from the client. Notwithstanding the foregoing, a member may accept (or participate in) a so-called "packaging fee" paid by an acquirer of television rights to a property owned or controlled by a client if the member: a) fully discloses to the client at the earliest practical time the possibility that the member may be offered such a "packaging fee" which the member may choose to accept; b) delivers to the clients at such time a copy of the Association's statement regarding packaging and packaging fees; and c) offers the client at such time the opportunity to arrange for other representation in the transaction. In no event shall the member accept (or participate in) both a packaging fee and compensation from the client with respect to the transaction. For transactions subject to the Writers Guild of America (WGA) jurisdiction, the regulation of the WGA shall take precedence over the requirements of this paragraph.

6. Members may not receive a secret profit in connection with any transaction involving a client. If such profit is

received, the member must promptly pay over the entire amount to the client. Members may not solicit or accept any payment or other thing of value in connection with their referral of any author to any third party for any purpose, provided that the foregoing does not apply to arrangements made with a third party in connection with the disposition of rights in the work of a client of the member.

7. Members shall treat their clients' financial affairs as private and confidential, except for information customarily disclosed to interested parties as part of the process of placing rights, as required by law, or, if agreed with the client, for other purposes.

8. The AAR believes that the practice of literary agents charging clients or potential clients for reading and evaluating literary works (including outlines, proposals, and partial or complete manuscripts) is subject to serious abuse that reflects adversely on our profession. For that reason, members may not charge clients or potential clients for reading and evaluating literary works and may not benefit, directly or indirectly, from the charging for such services by any other person or entity. The term "charge" in the previous sentence includes any request for payment other than to cover the actual cost of returning materials.

List of Agents

It is unfortunately true that anyone can hang out a shingle and call themselves an agent, take on clients, charge them money for this and that, make outrageously optimistic claims ("I'll make you a best-selling star, my dear!"), and never get anyone published.

The following is a list of agents who are members of AAR. Because of its Canon of Ethics and its strict professionalism, you can be assured that all are reputable agents worthy of recommendation.

Membership in the AAR is restricted to agents whose primary professional activity for the 2 years preceding application for membership in the AAR has been as an authors' representative or a playwrights' representative.

To qualify for membership, an applicant must have sold ten different literary properties during the 18-month period preceding application. Member agents must adhere to the AAR's Canon of Ethics, and associate members are full-time employees of a sponsoring agent member.

This list was accurate as of fall 1999.

Carole Abel
Carole Abel Literary Agent
160 West 87th Street
New York, NY 10024
(Literary, Adult)

Dominick Abel
Dominick Abel Literary Agency
146 West 82nd Street, 1B
New York, NY 10024
(Literary, Adult)

Linda Allen
Linda Allen Literary Agency
1949 Green Street, #5
San Francisco, CA 94123
(Literary, Adult)

Miriam Altshuler
Miriam Altshuler Literary Agency
RR#1 Box 5
5 Old Post Road
Red Hook, NY 12571
(Literary, Adult)

Betsy Amster
Betsy Amster Literary Enterprises
2151 Kenilworth Avenue
Los Angeles, CA 90039
(Literary, Adult)

Giles Anderson (Associate
    Member)
Scott Waxman Agency, Inc.
1650 Broadway
Suite 1011
New York, NY 10019
(Literary, Adult)

Cheryl E. Andrews (Associate
    Member)
Flora Roberts, Inc.
157 West 57th Street
Penthouse A
New York, NY 10019
(Literary, Adult, Dramatic)

Steve Axelrod
The Axelrod Agency, Inc.
66 Church Street
Lenox, MA 01240
(Literary, Adult)

Julian Bach
IMG—Julian Bach Literary Agency
22 East 71st Street
New York, NY 10021
(Literary, Adult, Children's)

Richard Balkin
The Balkin Agency
P.O. Box 222
Amherst, MA 01004
(Literary, Adult)

Lisa Bankoff
International Creative Management
40 West 57th Street
New York, NY 10019
(Literary, Adult)

Virginia Barber
Virginia Barber Agency, Inc.
101 Fifth Avenue
New York, NY 10003
(Literary, Adult)

Dave Barbor
Curtis Brown, Ltd.
Ten Astor Place
New York, NY 10003
(Foreign)

Loretta Barrett
Loretta Barrett Books Inc.
101 Fifth Avenue
New York, NY 10003
(Literary, Adult)

Faye Bender (Associate Member)
Doris S. Michaels Literary Agency,
    Inc.
1841 Broadway
Suite 903
New York, NY 10023
(Literary, Adult)

Mel Berger
William Morris Agency, Inc.
1325 Avenue of the Americas
New York, NY 10019
(Literary, Adult)

Amy Berkower
Writers House
21 West 26th Street
New York, NY 10010
(Literary, Adult)

Meredith Bernstein
2112 Broadway
Suite 503A
New York, NY 10023
(Literary, Adult)

Pam Bernstein
Pam Bernstein & Associates, Inc.
790 Madison Avenue
Suite 310
New York, NY 10021
(Literary, Adult)

Matthew Bialer
William Morris Agency, Inc.
1325 Avenue of the Americas
New York, NY 10019
(Literary, Adult)

Vicky Bijur
333 West End Avenue
New York, NY 10023
(Literary, Adult)

Agnes Birnbaum
Bleecker Street Associates, Inc.
532 LaGuardia Place, #617
New York, NY 10012
(Literary, Adult)

David Black
David Black Literary Agency
156 Fifth Avenue
Suite 608
New York, NY 10010-7002
(Literary, Adult)

BethAnn Blickers
Helen Merrill, Ltd.
425 West 23rd Street, #1F
New York, NY 10011
(Dramatic)

Judy Boals
Berman, Boals & Flynn, Inc,
A Talent & Literary Agency
208 West 30th Street
Room 401
New York, NY 10001
(Dramatic)

Anne Borchardt
Georges Borchardt, Inc.
136 East 57th Street
New York, NY 10022
(Literary, Not accepting manuscripts)

Georges Borchardt
Georges Borchardt, Inc.
136 East 57th Street
New York, NY 10022
(Literary, Adult)

Carl Brandt
Brandt & Brandt Literary Agents
1501 Broadway
New York, NY 10036
(Literary, Adult)

Helen Brann
The Helen Brann Agency, Inc.
94 Curtis Road
Bridgewater, CT 06752
(Literary, Adult)
Patti Breitman
Nonfiction Publishing Projects
12 Rally Court
Fairfax, CA 94930
(Literary, Not accepting manuscripts)

Helen Breitwieser (Associate
    Member)
William Morris Agency, Inc.
1325 Avenue of the Americas
New York, NY 10019
(Literary, Adult)

Andrea Brown
P.O. Box 429
El Granada, CA 94018-0429
(Literary, Children's)

Elliot Brown, Esq.
Franklin Weinrib Rudell Vassallo
488 Madison Avenue
New York, NY 10022

Jane Jordan Browne
Multimedia Product Development, Inc.
410 South Michigan Avenue
Suite 724
Chicago, IL 60605
(Literary, Adult, Children's)

Knox Burger
Knox Burger Associates, Ltd.
39-1/2 Washington Square South
New York, NY 10012
(Literary, Adult)

Sheree Bykofsky Associates, Inc.
Sheree Bykofsky
11 East 47th Street
New York, NY 10017
(Literary, Adult)

Christopher Byrne (Associate
    Member)
Harold Ober Associates, Inc.
425 Madison Avenue
New York, NY 10017
(Literary, Adult)

Ben Camardi
Harold Matson Company, Inc.
276 Fifth Avenue
New York, NY 10001
(Literary, Adult, Dramatic)

Moses Cardona (Associate Member)
John Hawkins & Associates, Inc.
71 West 23rd Street
Suite 1600
New York, NY 10010
(Literary, Adult)

Michael Carlisle
William Morris Agency, Inc.
1325 Avenue of the Americas
New York, NY 10019
(Literary, Adult)

Jennifer Carlson (Associate Member)
Henry Dunow Literary Agency
22 West 23rd Street, 5th Floor
New York, NY 10010
(Literary, Adult)

Michael Carlisle
William Morris Agency, Inc.
1325 Avenue of the Americas
New York, NY 10019
(Literary, Adult)

Jennifer Carlson (Associate Member)
Henry Dunow Literary Agency
22 West 23rd Street, 5th Floor
New York, NY 10010
(Literary, Adult)

Maria Carvainis
Maria Carvainis Agency, Inc.
235 West End Avenue
New York, NY 10023
(Literary, Adult, Children's)

Martha Casselman
P.O. Box 342
Calistoga, CA 94515-0342
(Literary, Adult)

Julie Castiglia
Julie Castiglia Literary Agency
1155 Camino del Mar
Suite 510
Del Mar, CA 92014
(Literary, Adult)

Jane Chelius
Jane Chelius Literary Agency
548 Second Street
Brooklyn, NY 11215
(Literary, Adult)

Faith Hampton Childs
Faith Childs Literary Agency, Inc.
915 Broadway
Suite 1009
New York, NY 10010
(Literary, Adult)

Michael Choate (Associate member)
Lescher & Lescher, Ltd.
47 East 19th Street
New York, NY 10003
(Literary, Adult)

Nancy Coffey
Pinder Lane & Garon-Brooke
Associates, Ltd.
159 West 53rd Street
New York, NY 10019
(Literary, Adult, Dramatic)

Ms. Rob Cohen
The Cohen Agency
348 West 56th Street, #2B
New York, NY 10019
(Literary, Adult)

Ruth Cohen
Ruth Cohen, Inc. Literary Agency
P.O. Box 7626
Menlo Park, CA 94025
(Literary, Adult, Children's)

Susan Cohen
Writers House
21 West 26th Street
New York, NY 10010
(Literary, Adult, Children's)

Sam Cohn
International Creative Management
40 West 57th Street
New York, NY 10019
(Dramatic)

Joanna Lewis Cole
Literary Agent
404 Riverside Drive
New York, NY 10025
(Literary, Children's)

Don Congdon
Don Congdon Associates, Inc.
156 Fifth Avenue
Suite 625
New York, NY 10010
(Literary, Adult)

Michael Congdon
Don Congdon Associates, Inc.
156 Fifth Avenue
Suite 625
New York, NY 10010
(Literary, Adult)

Eileen Cope (Associate Member)
Lowenstein-Morel Associates, Inc.
121 West 27th Street
Suite 601
New York, NY 10001
(Literary, Adult)

Robert Cornfield
Robert Cornfield Literary Agency
145 West 79th Street
New York, NY 10024
(Literary, Adult)

Claudia Cross (Associate Member)
William Morris Agency, Inc.
1325 Avenue of the Americas
New York, NY 10019
(Literary, Adult)

Richard Curtis
Richard Curtis Associates, Inc.
171 East 74th Street
New York, NY 10021
(Literary, Adult)

Jane Cushman
JCA Literary Agency, Inc.
27 West 20th Street
Suite 1103
New York, NY 10011
(Literary, Adult)

Liz Darhansoff
Darhansoff & Verrill
179 Franklin Street, 4th Floor
New York, NY 10013
(Literary, Adult)

Rose Elizabeth DePasquale (Associate
    Member)
Maria Carvainis Agency, Inc.
235 West End Avenue
New York, NY 10023
(Literary, Adult)

Richard Derus (Associate Member)
Claudia Menza Literary Agency
1170 Broadway
New York, NY 10001
(Literary, Not accepting manuscripts)

Donna Dever (Associate Member)
Pam Bernstein & Associates, Inc.
790 Madison Avenue
New York, NY 10021
(Literary)

Sandra Dijkstra
Sandra Dijkstra Literary Agency
1155 Camino Del Mar
Suite 515
Del Mar, CA 92014
(Literary, Adult)

Jonathan Dolger
The Jonathan Dolger Agency
49 East 96th Street, 9B
New York, NY 10128
(Literary, Adult)

Candida Donadio
Donadio & Ashworth, Inc., Literary
    Representatives
121 West 27th Street
Suite 704
New York, NY 10001
(Literary, Adult, Children's)

Janis Donnaud
Janis A. Donnaud and
    Associates, Inc.
525 Broadway, 2nd Floor
New York, NY 10012
(Literary, Adult)

Sarah Douglas
Flora Roberts Inc.
157 West 57th Street
Penthouse A
New York, NY 10019
(Literary, Adult, Dramatic)

Darlene M. Dozier (Associate Member)
Martha Casselman Literary Agent
P.O. Box 342
Calistoga, CA 94515-0342
(Literary, Adult)

Dick Duane
Pinder Lane & Garon-Brooke
    Associates, Ltd.
159 West 53rd Street
New York, NY 10019
(Literary, Adult, Dramatic)

Jennie Dunham
Russell & Volkening, Inc.
50 West 29th Street
New York, NY 10001
(Literary, Adult, Children's)

Henry Dunow
Henry Dunow Literary Agency
22 West 23rd Street, 5th Floor
New York, NY 10010
(Literary, Adult)

Jane Dystel
Jane Dystel Literary Management
One Union Square West
Suite 904
New York, NY 10003
(Literary, Adult)

Anne Edelstein
Anne Edelstein Literary Agency
404 Riverside Drive
New York, NY 10025
(Literary, Adult)

Anne Engel (Associate Member)
Jean V. Naggar Literary Agency, Inc.
216 East 75th Street
New York, NY 10021
(Literary, Adult)

Ms. Gareth Esersky
Carol Mann Agency
55 Fifth Avenue
New York, NY 10003
(Literary, Adult)

Felicia Eth
555 Bryant Street
Suite 350
Palo Alto, CA 94301
(Literary, Adult)

Joni Evans
William Morris Agency, Inc.
1325 Avenue of the Americas
New York, NY 10019
(Literary, Adult)

Mary Evans
Mary Evans, Inc.
242 East Fifth Street
New York, NY 10003
(Literary, Adult

Eileen Fallon
Fallon Literary Agency
240 West 35th Street
Suite 500
New York, NY 10001
(Literary, Not accepting manuscripts)

Melena Fancher (Associate Member)
Barbara Lowenstein Associates, Inc.
121 West 27th Street
Suite 601
New York, NY 10001
(Literary, Adult)

Sarah Feider (Associate Member)
Barbara Hogenson Agency
165 West End Avenue
Suite 19-C
New York, NY 10023

Leigh Feldman (Associate Member)
Darhansoff & Verrill
179 Franklin Street, 4th Floor
New York, NY 10013
(Literary, Adult)

Diana Finch
Ellen Levine Literary Agency, Inc.
15 East 26th Street
Suite 1801
New York, NY 10010-1505
(Literary, Adult, Children's)

Joyce Flaherty
816 Lynda Court
Street Louis, MO 63122
(Literary, Adult)

Evan M. Fogelman
The Fogelman Literary Agency
7515 Greenville Avenue
Suite 712
Dallas, TX 75231
(Literary, Adult)

Jason Fogelson
William Morris Agency, Inc.
1325 Avenue of the Americas
New York, NY 10019
(Dramatic)

Emily Forland (Associate Member)
The Wendy Weil Agency, Inc.
232 Madison Avenue
Suite 1300
New York, NY 10016
(Literary, Adult)

Peter Franklin
William Morris Agency, Inc.
1325 Avenue of the Americas
New York, NY 10019
(Dramatic)

J. Warren Frazier (Associate Member)
John Hawkins & Associates, Inc.
71 West 23rd Street
Suite 1600
New York, NY 10010
(Literary, Adult)

Jeanne Fredericks
Jeanne Fredericks Literary Agency
221 Benedict Hill Road
New Canaan, CT 06840
(Literary, Adult)

Jean Free (Associate Member)
Pinder Lane & Garon-Brooke
    Associates
159 West 53rd Street
New York, NY 10019
(Literary, Adult, Dramatic)

Robert Freedman
Robert A. Freedman Dramatic Agency,
    Inc.
1501 Broadway
Suite 2310
New York, NY 10036
(Dramatic)

Sharon Friedman
Ralph Vicinanza, Ltd.
111 Eighth Avenue
Suite 1501
New York, NY 10011
(Literary, Adult, Children's)

Ms. Molly Friedrich
The Aaron M. Priest Literary Agency
708 Third Avenue, 23rd Floor
New York, NY 10017-4103
(Literary, Not accepting manuscripts)

Candice Fuhrman
Candice Fuhrman Literary Agency
2440C Bush Street
San Francisco, CA 94115
(Literary, Adult)

Russell Galen
Scovil Chichak Galen Literary Agency, Inc.
381 Park Avenue South
Suite 1020
New York, NY 10016
(Literary, Adult)

Ellen Geiger
Curtis Brown, Ltd.
Ten Astor Place
New York, NY 10003
(Literary, Adult)

Jane Gelfman
Gelfman Schneider
250 West 57th Street
Suite 2515
New York, NY 10107
(Literary, Adult)

Peter Ginsberg
Curtis Brown, Ltd.
1750 Montgomery Street
San Francisco, CA 94111
(Literary, Adult)

Debra Goldstein
William Morris Agency, Inc.
1325 Avenue of the Americas
New York, NY 10019
(Literary, Adult)

Arnold Goodman
Goodman Associates
500 West End Avenue
New York, NY 10024
(Literary, Adult)

Elise Simon Goodman
Goodman Associates
500 West End Avenue
New York, NY 10024
(Literary, Adult)

Irene Goodman
Irene Goodman Literary Agency
521 Fifth Avenue, 17th Floor
New York, NY 10017
(Literary, Not accepting manuscripts)

Robert Gottlieb
William Morris Agency, Inc.
1325 Avenue of the Americas
New York, NY 10019
(Literary, Adult)

Christopher Gould
Broadway Play Publishing
56 East 81st Street
New York, NY 10028-0202
(Dramatic)

Ashley Grayson
Ashley Grayson Literary Agency
1342 18th Street
San Pedro, CA 90732
(Literary, Adult, Children's)

Carolyn Grayson
Ashley Grayson Literary Agency
1342 18th Street
San Pedro, CA 90732
(Literary, Adult, Children's)

Francis Greenburger
Sanford J. Greenburger Associates
55 Fifth Avenue, 15th Floor
New York, NY 10003
(Literary, Adult)

Tal Gregory (Associate Member)
Darhansoff & Verrill
179 Franklin Street, 4th Floor
New York, NY 10013
(Literary, Adult)

Maxine Groffsky
Maxine Groffsky Literary Agency
853 Broadway
Suite 708
New York, NY 10003
(Not accepting manuscripts)

Ronald Gwiazda (Associate Member)
Rosenstone/Wender
3 East 48th Street
New York, NY 10017
(Literary, Adult)

Faith Hamlin
Sanford J. Greenburger Associates
55 Fifth Avenue, 15th Floor
New York, NY 10003
(Literary, Adult)

Jeanne Hanson
Jeanne K. Hanson Literary Agency
5441 Woodcrest Dr.
Edina, MN 55424-1649
(Literary, Not accepting manuscripts)

Mary Harden
Harden Curtis Associates
850 Seventh Avenue
Suite 405
New York, NY 10019
(Dramatic)

Elizabeth Harding (Associate
   Member)
Curtis Brown, Ltd.
Ten Astor Place
New York, NY 10003
(Literary, Children's)

Laurie Harper
Sebastian Literary Agency
1450 Sutter Street, #534
San Francisco, CA 94109
(Literary, Adult)

Joy Harris
The Joy Harris Literary Agency, Inc.
156 Fifth Avenue
Suite 617
New York, NY 10010
(Literary, Adult, Dramatic)

A. L. Hart
Fox Chase Agency, Inc.
Five Radnor Corporate Center
100 Matsonsford Road
Suite 441
Radnor, PA 19087
(Literary, Adult)

Jo C. Hart
The Fox Chase Agency, Inc.
Five Radnor Corporate Center
100 Matsonsford Road
Suite 441
Radnor, PA 19087
(Literary, Adult)

Anne Hawkins (Associate Member)
John Hawkins & Associates, Inc.
71 West 23rd Street
Suite 1600
New York, NY 10010
(Literary, Adult)

John Hawkins
John Hawkins & Associates, Inc.
71 West 23rd Street
Suite 1600
New York, NY 10010
(Literary, Adult)

Linda Hayes
Columbia Literary Associates
7902 Nottingham Way
Ellicott City, MD 21043
(Literary, Adult)

Rosalie Grace Heacock
Heacock Literary Agency, Inc.
1523 Sixth Street
Suite 14
Santa Monica, CA 90401
(Literary, Adult, Children's)

Merilee Heifetz
Writers House
21 West 26th Street
New York, NY 10010
(Literary, Adult)

DeAnna Heindel (Associate Member)
Georges Borchardt, Inc.
136 East 57th Street
New York, NY 10022
(Literary, Adult)

David Hendin
David Hendin Literary Enterprises
P.O. Box 990
Nyack, NY 10960
(Literary, Adult)

Richard Henshaw
Richard Henshaw Group,
Authors' Representatives
264 West 73rd Street
New York, NY 10023
(Literary, Adult)

Jeff Herman
The Jeff Herman Agency, Inc.
332 Bleeker Street
Suite G-31
New York, NY 10014
(Literary, Adult)

Patrick Herold (Associate Member)
Helen Merrill, Ltd.
425 West 23rd Street, 1F
New York, NY 10011
(Literary, Adult, Dramatic)

Gail Hochman
Brandt & Brandt Literary Agents
1501 Broadway
New York, NY 10036
(Literary, Adult)

Berenice Hoffman
Berenice Hoffman Literary Agency
215 West 75th Street
New York, NY 10023
(Literary, Adult)

Barbara Hogenson
Barbara Hogenson Agency
165 West End Avenue
Suite 19-C
New York, NY 10023
(Literary, Adult, Dramatic)

Bert Holtje
James Peter Associates, Inc.
P.O. Box 772
Tenafly, NJ 07670
(Literary, Adult)

Pamela A. Hopkins
Hopkins Literary Associates
2117 Buffalo Road
Suite 327
Rochester, NY 14624
(Literary, Adult)

Cornelius Howland (Associate Member)
Virginia Barber Agency, Inc.
101 Fifth Avenue
New York, NY 10003
(Literary, Adult)

Alleen Hussung (Associate Member)
Samuel French, Inc.
45 West 25th Street
New York, NY 10010
(Dramatic)

Jennifer Jackson (Associate Member)
Donald Maass Literary Agency
157 West 57th Street, Suite 703
New York, NY 10019
(Literary, Adult)

Emilie Jacobson
Curtis Brown, Ltd.
Ten Astor Place
New York, NY 10003
(Literary, Adult, Children's)

Sharon Jarvis
Sharon Jarvis Literary Agency
Toad Hall, Inc.
RR 2 Box 16B
Laceyville, PA 18623
(Literary)

Booker Jones (Associate Member)
Roslyn Targ
105 West 13th Street, 15E
New York, NY 10011
(Literary, Adult)

Elizabeth Kaplan
Ellen Levine Literary Agency
15 East 26th Street, Suite 1801
New York, NY 10010-1505
(Literary, Adult)

Katharine Kidde
Kidde, Hoyt & Picard
335 East 51st Street
New York, NY 10022
(Literary, Adult)

Mary Alice Kier
Cine/Lit Representation
7415 181st Place SW
Edmonds, WA 98026
(Literary, Adult)

Linda Kirland (Associate Member)
Samuel French
45 West 25th Street
New York, NY 10010
(Literary, Adult)

Harvey Klinger
Harvey Klinger, Inc.
301 West 53rd Street
New York, NY 10019
(Literary, Adult)

Edward Knappman
New England Publishing Associates
P.O. Box 5
Chester, CT 06412
(Literary, Adult)

Elizabeth Frost Knappman
New England Publishing Associates, Inc.
P.O. Box 5
Chester, CT 06412
(Literary, Adult)

Ginger Knowlton
Curtis Brown, Ltd.
Ten Astor Place
New York, NY 10003
(Literary, Adult Children's)

Perry Knowlton
Curtis Brown, Ltd.
Ten Astor Place
New York, NY 10003
(Literary, Adult)

Timothy Knowlton
Curtis Brown, Ltd.
Ten Astor Place
New York, NY 10003
(Literary, Dramatic)

Linda Konner
Linda Konner Literary Agency
10 West 15th Street Suite 1918
New York, NY 10011
(Literary, Adult)

Barbara S. Kouts
Literary Agent
P.O. Box 558
Bellport, NY 11713
(Literary, Adult, Children's)

Stuart Krichevsky
Stuart Krichevsky Literary Agency, Inc.
381 Park Avenue South, Suite 819
New York, NY 10016
(Literary, Adult)

Linda M. Kruger
The Fogelman Literary Agency
7515 Greenville Avenue
Suite 712
Dallas, TX 75231
(Literary, Adult)

Carolyn Krupp
IMG—Julian Bach Literary Agency
22 East 71st Street
New York, NY 10021
(Literary, Adult)

Frances Kuffel (Associate Member)
Jean V. Naggar Literary Agency, Inc.
216 East 75th Street
New York, NY 10021
(Literary, Adult)

Linda Kirland Kurland (Associate Member)
Samuel French, Inc.
45 West 25th Street
New York, NY 10010
(Dramatic)

Bernard Kurman
Rights Unlimited, Inc.
101 West 55 Street
Suite 2D
New York, NY 10019
(Literary, Adult)

Norman Kurz (Associate member)
Barbara Lowenstein Associates, Inc.
121 West 27th Street
Suite 601
New York, NY 10001
(Literary, Adult)

Heide Lange
Sanford J. Greenburger Associates
55 Fifth Avenue, 15th Floor
New York, NY 10003
(Literary, Adult)

Laura Langlie (Associate Member)
Kidde, Hoyt & Picard
335 East 51st Street
New York, NY 10022
(Literary, Adult)

Vicki Lansky
The Book Peddlers
15245 Minnetonka Boulevard
Minnetonka, MN 55345-1510
(Literary, Not accepting manuscripts)

Robert Lantz
The Lantz Office
888 Seventh Avenue
New York, NY 10106
(Dramatic)

Michael Larsen
Michael Larsen/Elizabeth Pomada,
   Literary Agents
1029 Jones Street
San Francisco, CA 94109
(Literary, Adult)

Owen Laster
William Morris Agency, Inc.
1325 Avenue of the Americas
New York, NY 10019
(Literary, Adult)

Sarah Lazin
Sarah Lazin Books
126 Fifth Avenue
Suite 300
New York, NY 10011
(Literary, Adult)

Ned Leavitt
The Ned Leavitt Agency
70 Wooster Street
New York, NY 10012
(Literary, Adult)

Fran Lebowitz (Associate Member)
Writers House
21 West 26th Street
New York, NY 10010
(Literary, Adult, Children's)

Jane Lebowitz (Associate Member)
Mildred Marmur Associates, Ltd.
2005 Palmer Avenue
Suite 127
Larchmont, NY 10538
(Literary, Adult)

Lettie Lee
Ann Elmo Agency, Inc.
60 East 42nd Street
New York, NY 10165
(Literary, Adult, Dramatic)

Lillian Lent (Associate Member)
Frances Goldin Literary Agency
57 East 11th Street
Suite 5B
New York, NY 10003
(Literary, Adult)

Robert Lescher
Lescher & Lescher, Ltd.
47 East 19th Street
New York, NY 10003
(Literary, Adult)

Susan Lescher
Lescher & Lescher, Ltd.
47 East 19th Street
New York, NY 10003
(Literary, Adult)

Ellen Levine
Ellen Levine Literary Agency, Inc.
15 East 26th Street
Suite 1801
New York, NY 10010-1505
(Literary, Adult)

James A. Levine
James Levine Communications, Inc.
307 Seventh Avenue
Suite 1906
New York, NY 10001
(Literary, Adult, Children's)
Samuel Liff

William Morris Agency, Inc.
1325 Avenue of the Americas
New York, NY 10019
(Dramatic)

Wendy Lipkind
Wendy Lipkind Agency
165 East 66th Street
New York, NY 10021
(Literary, Adult)

Chris Lotts (Associate Member)
Ralph M. Vicinanza, Ltd.
111 Eighth Avenue
New York, NY 10011
(Literary, Adult)

Nancy Love
Nancy Love Literary Agency
250 East 65th Street
New York, NY 10021
(Literary, Adult)

Barbara Lowenstein
Barbara Lowenstein Associates, Inc.
121 West 27th Street
Suite 601
New York, NY 10001
(Literary, Adult)

Kirsten M. Lundell (Associate Member)
Loretta Barrett Books, Inc.
101 Fifth Avenue
New York, NY 10003

Selma Luttinger
Robert A. Freedman Dramatic Agency, Inc.
1501 Broadway
Suite 2310
New York, NY 10036
(Dramatic)

Donald Maass
Donald Maass Literary Agency
157 West 57th Street
Suite 703
New York, NY 10019
(Literary, Adult)

Jay Mandel (Associate Member)
Virginia Barber Agency, Inc.
101 Fifth Avenue, 11th Floor
New York, NY 10003
(Literary, Adult)

Carol Mann
Carol Mann Agency
55 Fifth Avenue
New York, NY 10003
(Literary, Adult)

Janet Wilkens Manus
Manus & Associates Literary Agency, Inc.
417 East 57th Street
Suite 5D
New York, NY 10022
(Literary, Adult)

Jillian W. Manus
Manus & Associates Literary Agency, Inc.
430 Cowper Street
Palo Alto, CA 94301
(Literary, Adult)

Denise Marcil
Denise Marcil Literary Agency, Inc.
685 West End Avenue
New York, NY 10025
(Literary, Adult)

Dorothy Markinko
McIntosh & Otis, Inc.
310 Madison Avenue
New York, NY 10017
(Literary, Children's)

Elaine Markson
Elaine Markson Literary Agency, Inc.
44 Greenwich Avenue
New York, NY 10011
(Literary, Adult)

Marilyn Marlow
Curtis Brown, Ltd.
Ten Astor Place
New York, NY 10003
(Literary, Adult, Children's)

Mildred Marmur
Mildred Marmur Associates Ltd.
2005 Palmer Avenue
Suite 127
Larchmont, NY 10538
(Literary, Adult)

Evan Marshall
The Evan Marshall Agency
6 Tristam Place
Pine Brook, NJ 07058-9445
(Literary, Adult)

Tonda Marton
Elisabeth Marton Agency
One Union Square
Room 612
New York, NY 10003-3303
(Dramatic)

Jonathan Matson
Harold Matson Company, Inc.
276 Fifth Avenue
New York, NY 10001
(Literary, Adult)

Jed Mattes
Jed Mattes, Inc.
2095 Broadway, #302
New York, NY 10023-2895
(Literary, Adult)

Margret McBride
Margret McBride Literary Agency
7744 Fay Avenue
Suite 201
San Diego, CA 92037
(Literary, Adult)

Gerard McCauley
Gerard McCauley Agency, Inc.
P.O. Box 844
Katonah, NY 10536
(Literary, Adult, Children's)

Anita McClellan
Anita D. McClellan Associates
50 Stearns Street
Cambridge, MA 02138
(Literary, Adult)

Jennie McDonald
Curtis Brown, Ltd.
1750 Montgomery Street
San Francisco, CA 94111
(Literary, Adult)

Patricia McLaughlin (Associate Member)
The Shukat Company, Ltd.
340 West 55th Street
Suite 1A
New York, NY 10019
(Literary, Adult, Dramatic)

Claudia Menza
Claudia Menza Literary Agency
1170 Broadway
New York, NY 10001
(Literary, Not accepting manuscripts)

Amy Victoria Meo
Richard Curtis Associates, Inc.
171 East 74th Street
New York, NY 10021
(Literary, Adult)

Marianne Merola
Brandt & Brandt Literary Agents
1501 Broadway
New York, NY 10036
(Literary, Adult)

Doris S Michaels
Doris S. Michaels Literary Agency, Inc.
1841 Broadway
Suite 903
New York, NY 10023
(Literary, Adult)

Martha Millard
Martha Millard Literary Agency
293 Greenwood Avenue
Florham Park, NJ 07932
(Literary, Adult)

Howard Morhaim
Howard Morhaim Literary Agency
841 Broadway
Suite 604
New York, NY 10003
(Literary, Adult)

Ellen Morrissey (Associate Member)
Betsy Nolan Literary Agency
224 West 29th Street, 15th Floor
New York, NY 10001
(Literary, Adult)

Jean Naggar
Jean V. Naggar Literary Agency, Inc.
216 East 75th Street
New York, NY 10021
(Literary, Adult)

Muriel Nellis
Literary and Creative Artists Agency, Inc.
3543 Albemarle Street NW
Washington, D.C. 20008
(Literary, Adult)

Betsy Nolan
Betsy Nolan Literary Agency
3426 Broderick Street
San Francisco, CA 94123
(Not accepting manuscripts)

Ken Norwick, Esq.
Norwick & Schad
One Madison Avenue, 30th Floor
New York, NY 10010

Neil Olson
Donadio & Ashworth, Inc.
121 West 27th Street
Suite 704
New York, NY 10001
(Literary, Adult)

Fifi Oscard
Fifi Oscard Agency, Inc.
24 West 40th Street
New York, NY 10018
(Literary, Adult, Dramatic)

Tony Outhwaite
JCA Literary Agency, Inc.
27 West 20th Street
Suite 1103
New York, NY 10011
(Literary, Adult)

Gilbert Parker
William Morris Agency, Inc.
1325 Avenue of the Americas
New York, NY 10019
(Dramatic)

Richard Parks
The Richard Parks Agency
138 East 16th Street, 5B
New York, NY 10003
(Literary, Adult)

Lori Perkins
Perkins, Rubie Associates
240 West 35th Street
Suite 500
New York, NY 10001
(Literary, Adult)

Laura Blake Peterson
Curtis Brown, Ltd.
Ten Astor Place
New York, NY 10003
(Literary, Adult, Children's)

Samuel L.Pinkus (Associate Member)
McIntosh and Otis, Inc.
310 Madison Avenue
New York, NY 10017
(Literary, Adult)

Elizabeth Pomada
Michael Larsen/Elizabeth Pomada,
    Literary Agents
1029 Jones Street
San Francisco, CA 94109
(Literary, Adult)

Andrew Pope (Associate Member)
Curtis Brown, Ltd.
Ten Astor Place
New York, NY 10003
(Literary, Adult)

Lori A. Pope (Associate Member)
Faith Childs Literary Agency
915 Broadway
Suite 1009
New York, NY 10010
(Literary, Adult)

Marcy Posner
William Morris Agency, Inc.
1325 Avenue of the Americas
New York, NY 10019
(Literary, Adult)

Patricia Powell
Harold Ober Associates, Inc.
425 Madison Avenue
New York, NY 10017
(Literary, Adult)

Marta Praeger (Associate Member)
Robert A. Freedman Dramatic
1501 Broadway
Suite 2310
New York, NY 10036
(Dramatic)

Helen F. Pratt
Helen F. Pratt, Inc.
1165 Fifth Avenue
New York, NY 10029
(Literary, Children's, Adult)

Jean Price
Kirkland Literary Agency, Inc.
P.O. Box 50608
Amarillo, TX 79159-0608
(Literary, Adult, Children's)

Mr. Aaron Priest
The Aaron M. Priest Literary Agency
708 Third Avenue, 23rd Floor
New York, NY 10017-4103
(Literary, Adult)

Susan Ann Protter
110 West 40th Street
Suite 1408
New York, NY 10018
(Literary, Adult)

Evva Pryor
McIntosh & Otis, Inc.
310 Madison Avenue
New York, NY 10017
(Literary, Adult)

Victoria Gould Pryor
Arcadia
20A Old Neversink Road
Danbury, CT 06811
(Literary, Adult)

Louise Quayle (Associate Member)
Ellen Levine Literary Agency, Inc.
15 East 26th Street
Suite 1801
New York, NY 10010-1505
(Literary, Adult, Children's)

Susan Raihofer (Associate Member)
David Black Literary Agency
156 Fifth Avenue
Suite 608
New York, NY 10010-7002
(Literary, Adult)

Mrs. Joan Raines
Raines & Raines
71 Park Avenue
Suite 44A
New York, NY 10016
(Literary, Not accepting manuscripts)

Theron Raines
Raines & Raines
71 Park Avenue
Suite 44A
New York, NY 10016
(Literary, Adult)

Susan Ramer
Don Congdon Associates, Inc.
156 Fifth Avenue
Suite 625
New York, NY 10010
(Literary, Adult)

Helen Rees
Helen Rees Literary Agency
123 North Washington Street, 5th Floor
Boston, MA 02114
(Literary, Adult)

Joseph Regal
Russell & Volkening, Inc.
50 West 29th Street
New York, NY 10001
(Literary, Adult)

Jody Rein
Literary Agency
7741 South Ash Court
Littleton, CO 80122
(Literary, Adult)

William Reiss
John Hawkins & Associates, Inc.
71 West 23rd Street
Suite 1600
New York, NY 10010
(Literary, Adult, Children's)

Ann Rittenberg
Ann Rittenberg Literary Agency, Inc.
14 Montgomery Place
Brooklyn, NY 11215
(Literary, Adult)

Flora Roberts
Flora Roberts Inc.
157 West 57th Street
Penthouse A
New York, NY 10019
(Literary, Adult, Dramatic)

James E Rogers Jr (Associate Member)
Ellen Levine Literary Agency, Inc.
15 East 26th Street
Suite 1801
New York, NY 10010-1505
(Literary, Adult)

Rita Rosenkranz
Literary Agency
285 Riverside Drive
Apartment 5E
New York, NY 10025
(Literary, Adult)

Howard Rosenstone
Rosenstone/Wender
3 East 48th Street
New York, NY 10017
(Literary, Adult, Dramatic)

Gail Ross
Lichtman, Trister, Singer & Ross
1666 Connecticut Avenue, NW
Suite 501
Washington, D.C. 20009
(Literary, Adult)

Carol Susan Roth
Literary Representation
1824 Oak Creek Drive
Palo Alto, CA 94304
(Literary, Adult)

Jane Rotrosen
Jane Rotrosen Agency
318 East 51st Street
New York, NY 10022
(Literary, Adult)

Damaris Rowland
The Damaris Rowland Agency
510 East 23rd Street, #8-G
New York, NY 10010
(Literary, Adult)

Peter Rubie
Perkins, Rubie Associates
240 West 35th Street
Suite 500
New York NY 10001
(Literary, Adult)

Pesha Rubinstein
Pesha Rubinstein Literary Agency, Inc.
1392 Rugby Road
Teaneck, NJ 07666
(Literary, Adult, Children's)

Robin Rue
Writers House
21 West 26th Street
New York, NY 10010
(Literary, Adult)

Raphael Sagalyn
Raphael Sagalyn, Inc.
4825 Bethesda Avenue
Suite 302
Bethesda, MD 20814
(Literary, Adult)

Victoria Sanders
Victoria Sanders Literary Agency
241 Avenue of the Americas
Suite 11H
New York, NY 10014
(Literary, Adult)

Charles Schlessinger
Brandt & Brandt Literary Agents
1501 Broadway
New York, NY 10036
(Literary, Adult)

Wendy Schmalz
Harold Ober Associates, Inc.
425 Madison Avenue
New York, NY 10017
(Literary, Adult, Children's)

Harold Schmidt
343 West 12th Street
Suite 1B
New York, NY 10014
(Literary, Adult)

Deborah Schneider
Gelfman Schneider
250 West 57th Street
Suite 2515
New York, NY 10017
(Literary, Adult)

Susan Schulman
Susan Schulman Literary Agency
2 Bryan Plaza
Washington Depot, CT 06794
(Literary, Adult, Dramatic)

Timothy Seldes
Russell & Volkening, Inc.
50 West 29th Street
New York, NY 10001
(Literary, Adult)

Edythea Ginis Selman
Literary Agent
14 Washington Place
New York, NY 10003
(Literary, Adult, Children's)

Richard Selman (Associate Member)
Edythia Ginis Selman Agency
14 Washington Place
New York, NY 10003
(Literary, Adult)

Denise Shannon
Georges Borchardt, Inc.
136 East 57th Street
New York, NY 10022
(Literary, Adult)

Scott Shukat
The Shukat Company, Ltd.
340 West 55th Street
Suite 1A
New York, NY 10019
(Literary, Adult, Dramatic)

Elinor Sidel (Associate Member)
John Hawkins & Associates, Inc.
71 West 23rd Street
Suite 1600
New York, NY 10010
(Literary, Adult)

Rosalie Siegel
International Literary Agent, Inc.
One Abey Dr.
Pennington, NJ 08543
(Literary, Adult)

Irene Skolnick
Irene Skolnick Agency
22 West 23rd Street, Fifth Floor
New York, NY 10010
(Literary, Adult)

Nikki Smith
Smith-Skolnik Literary Management
303 Walnut Street
Westfield, NJ 07090
(Literary, Adult)

Karen Solem (Associate Member)
Writers House
21 West 26th Street
New York, NY 10010
(Literary, Adult)

Elyse Sommer
Elyse Sommer
110-34 73rd Road
P.O. Box 1133
Forest Hills, NY 11375
(Literary, Adult)

Philip Spitzer
Philip G. Spitzer Literary Agency
50 Talmage Farm Lane
East Hampton, NY 11937
(Literary, Adult)

Kitty Sprague
Knox Burger Associates, Ltd.
39-1/2 Washington Square South
New York, NY 10012
(Not accepting manuscripts)

Peter Steinberg (Associate Member)
Donadio & Ashworth, Inc.
121 West 27th Street
Suite 704
New York, NY 10001
(Literary, Adult)

Gloria Stern
Gloria Stern Agency
2929 Buffalo Speedway
Suite 2111
Houston, TX 77098
(Literary, Adult)

Douglas Stewart (Associate Member)
Curtis Brown, Ltd.
Ten Astor Place
New York, NY 10003
(Literary, Adult)

Robin Straus
Robin Straus Agency, Inc.
229 East 79th Street
New York, NY 10021
(Literary, Adult)

Dan Strone
William Morris Agency, Inc.
1325 Avenue of the Americas
New York, NY 10019
(Literary, Adult)

Emma Sweeney
Harold Ober Associates, Inc.
425 Madison Avenue
New York, NY 10017
(Literary, Adult)

William Talbot (Associate Member)
Samuel French, Inc.
45 West 25th Street
New York, NY 10010
(Dramatic)

Mr. Jack Tantleff
The Tantleff Office
375 Greenwich Street
Suite 700
New York, NY 10013
(Dramatic)

Roslyn Targ
Roslyn Targ Literary Agency, Inc.
105 West 13th Street, 15E
New York, NY 10011
(Literary, Adult, Children's)

Clyde Taylor
Curtis Brown, Ltd.
Ten Astor Place
New York, NY 10003
(Literary, Adult)

Patricia Teal
Patricia Teal Literary Agency
2036 Vista del Rosa
Fullerton, CA 92831
(Literary, Adult)

Craig Tenney
Harold Ober Associates, Inc.
425 Madison Avenue
New York, NY 10017
(Literary, Not accepting manuscripts)

Robert Thixton
Pinder Lane & Garon-Brooke
   Associates, Ltd.
159 West 53rd Street
New York, NY 10019
(Literary, Adult, Dramatic)

Geri Thoma
Elaine Markson Agency
44 Greenwich Avenue
New York, NY 10011
(Literary, Adult)

Claire Tisne (Associate Member)
Virginia Barber Agency, Inc.
101 Fifth Avenue
New York, NY 10003
(Literary, Adult)

Jennifer Treusch (Associate Member)
Flora Roberts Inc.
157 West 57th Street
Penthouse A
New York, NY 10019
(Literary, Adult, Dramatic)

Laura Tucker (Associate Member)
Richard Curtis Associates, Inc.
171 East 74th Street
New York, NY 10021
(Literary, Adult)

Charles R. Van Nostrand
Samuel French, Inc.
45 West 25th Street
New York, NY 10010
(Dramatic)

Michelle A. Vant (Associate Member)
Maria Carvainis Agency, Inc.
235 West End Avenue
New York, NY 10023
(Literary, Adult)

Ralph Vicinanza
Ralph Vicinanza, Ltd.
111 Eighth Avenue
Suite 1501
New York, NY 10011
(Literary, Adult)

David Vigliano
David Vigliano Literary Agency
584 Broadway
Suite 809
New York, NY 10012
(Literary, Not accepting manuscripts)

James C. Vines
The Vines Agency
684 Broadway
Suite 901
New York, NY 10012
(Literary, Adult, Children's)

Liza Pulitzer Voges
Kirchoff/Wohlberg, Inc.
866 United Nations Plaza
New York, NY 10017
(Literary, Not accepting manuscripts)

Mary Jack Wald
Mary Jack Wald Associates, Inc.
111 East 14th Street
New York, NY 10003
(Literary, Adult, Children's)

Elizabeth Wales
Levant & Wales Literary Agency, Inc.
108 Hayes Street
Seattle, WA 98109
(Literary, Adult)

Hannah Wallace (Associate Member)
Rosenstone/Wender
3 East 48th Street
New York, NY 10017
(Literary, Adult)

Thomas C. Wallace
The Wallace Agency
177 East 70th Street
New York, NY 10021
(Literary, Adult)

Jennifer Rudolph Walsh
Virginia Barber Agency, Inc.
101 Fifth Avenue
New York, NY 10003
(Literary, Adult)

Maureen Walters
Curtis Brown, Ltd.
Ten Astor Place
New York, NY 10003
(Literary, Adult)

Ms. Harriet Wasserman
Harriet Wasserman Literary
    Agency, Inc.
137 East 36th Street
New York, NY 10016
(Literary, Adult)

Mitchell S. Waters (Associate Member)
Curtis Brown, Ltd.
Ten Astor Place
New York, NY 10003
(Literary, Adult, Children's)

Scott Waxman
Scott Waxman Agency
1650 Broadway
Suite 1011
New York, NY 10019
(Literary, Adult)

Wendy Weil
The Wendy Weil Agency, Inc.
232 Madison Avenue
Suite 1300
New York, NY 10016
(Literary, Adult)

Phyllis Wender
Rosenstone/Wender
3 East 48th Street
New York, NY 10017
(Literary, Adult, Dramatic)

Phyllis Westberg
Harold Ober Associates, Inc.
425 Madison Avenue
New York, NY 10017
(Literary, Adult)

Rhoda A. Weyr
Rhoda Weyr Agency
151 Bergen Street
Brooklyn, NY 11217
(Literary, Adult)

Eugene Winick
McIntosh and Otis, Inc.
310 Madison Avenue
New York, NY 10017
(Literary, Children's)

Edwin John Wintle (Associate Member)
Curtis Brown, Ltd.
Ten Astor Place
New York, NY 10003
(Literary, Adult)

Audrey A Wolf
Audrey A. Wolf Literary Agency
1001 Connecticut Avenue NW
Washington, D.C. 20036
(Literary, Adult)

Mary Yost
Mary Yost Associates, Inc.
59 East 54th Street, #72
New York, NY 10022
(Literary, Adult)

Nancy K. Yost (Associate Member)
Barbara Lowenstein Associates, Inc.
121 West 27th Street
Suite 601
New York, NY 10001
(Literary, Adult)

Susan Zeckendorf
Susan Zeckendorf Associates, Inc.
171 West 57th Street
New York, NY 10019
(Literary, Adult)

Albert Zuckerman
Writers House
21 West 26th Street
New York, NY 10010
(Literary, Adult, Children's)

CHAPTER 6

How a Publishing House Is Set Up

So now your proposal, sent in by your agent, is sitting on an editor's desk waiting to be read. It's worth taking a few moments to understand how a typical publishing house is set up and why things move with the speed of molasses in winter most of the time.

Downstairs in the lobby of the new office building that the publishing house has just moved all its imprints and departments into, stand security guards dressed in navy blue jackets. Their job it is to check everyone's ID and sign in visitors. You cannot move or "pass go" to get to the elevator banks until an over polite security type gets on the phone to the person you're visiting and then gives you a "visitor" sticker for your lapel and permission to enter the building.

On the tenth floor, beyond a glass door with a combination lock that has a code that has to be keyed in to be opened, are the *editorial* offices. Once inside, the hallway walls prominently display the latest books published by the company and its sister and sibling imprints. The editors' offices look a lot like that of your agent. Inside each editor's office, floor to ceiling shelving that often takes up at least two out of four walls groans with published books and manuscripts to be read, manuscripts to be edited, and copies of edited books transmitted and in "the system." On the editor's desk and also that of his assistant sit piles of paper, in trays and out of them. Often on the only free chair in the editor's office sit more manuscripts and papers. In a corner, somewhere, are filing cabinets; outside the office are more filing cabinets.

Your manuscript arrives as part of a huge daily delivery of letters and parcels that are doled out by staff in the mail room. If you're lucky, the editors get their mail the same day it arrives, but sometimes the mail room decides to move at its own pace. (The guy in charge, having survived two office moves, several mergers, and downsizings in the last couple of years, and a hernia operation, is unfazed by the concept of urgency in mail delivery to editors who

Manuscripts

may not even be employed by the company anymore. When challenged, he says rather resentfully, "We're getting to it," and indicates the sacks full of mail piled unsorted by the door as the mail room worker hefts in yet another load of mail.) So it may be a couple of days before an editor gets to read all his mail.

Usually the mail is opened and logged in by his editorial assistant. Senior editors get their own assistants; other editors sometimes have to share.

The assistants often sit in open cubicles, with their computer screens and telephones the most obvious equipment on their desks, next to piles of paper (did I mention that already?), under neon strip lighting, in a long line facing the offices of the editors, who get to have windows.

If the submission the assistant logs in is a manuscript or proposal the editor is eagerly awaiting, the editor will take it home that night, or very soon anyway, and respond as quickly as he can. More usually, the submission will languish in a pile on a shelf, waiting to be read, having been sorted by an agreed-upon priority system. Solicited agented mail tends to get a higher priority than unsolicited, which will be read before "over the transom" unagented mail.

Very often, especially when it comes to fiction, the assistant will give the manuscript a first read. The assistant's experience grows by doing this type of work, and she will eventually get promoted to assistant editor and, after that, full editor. (She may have to move to other houses, though, to get those promotions. That's one reason editors change jobs a lot.)

The assistant will give each submission serious consideration, because she's looking for promising material. Finding a solid seller is like panning for gold, but that's how she will make her name in the company and in the industry in general, so she has an incentive to find good projects. Her editor is relying on her help.

Because she's worked for the editor for a while now, and has typed all his letters, and helped him with the day-to-day details of acquiring and rejecting material, as well as followed up on the transmittal details of books in the system, she has a pretty good

sense of what the editor likes and is looking for and, more importantly, what the editor does not like or want.

My assistant, for example, knows I'm a sucker for really good writing. She knows never to bother passing along to me a novel that starts with a rape scene or literary fiction by someone without any credentials whatever, or essay collections or general nonfiction by people with no credentials on topics they have no real expertise in. She also knows that I don't do romance or women's fiction, or anything to do with sports, or gossip-based nonfiction (*Bedroom Secrets of the Kennedy Clan Revealed!*).

Many writers have quaint notions about publishing that have about as much to do with the modern realities of being an editor as Civil War soldiering has to serving in Vietnam. Somehow, a romantic idea got abroad that editors (nearly all male) either sit around in post-collegiate camaraderie, wearing cardigans and smoking pipes, engaging in Dorothy Parker-like witty repartee, or spend their time like literary gold prospectors, combing the slush pile in search of the next best-selling "Great American Novel" and its author. The truth is that these days, publishing (and those who buy books, by all accounts) is overwhelmingly female, and most of an editor's time is taken up with producing and moving "merchandise," not "books."

Glamour? Well, there are occasional publication parties, industry conferences, business lunches, and glimpses of TV green rooms (once a decade); but the reality of an editor's life is a daily grind of meetings, building a positive consensus for books whose merits seem obvious to you, feeling guilty that you haven't read all that has been sent to you quickly enough, not paying enough attention to your private life, and not finding enough time to read published books that you really want to read (which is why you went into publishing in the first place).

Each day is taken up with endless meetings: editorial meetings to acquire the book; scheduling meetings to figure out if the publication of a book is on track and when to publish it; and book cover conferences to discuss the jacket design. Then there are catalog copy and book flap copy that must be written for your books; presentations for sales reps at a sales conference that must be prepared; problems and emergencies that have to be swiftly dealt with; phone calls to authors and agents that must be returned; and new proposals that have to be read, from agents who are nagging you not to be so slow. Editing is somehow done at home when you steal a day here and there, and reading is often done in bed at 10 P.M., while back in the office the word is out: "Find best-sellers. Get another Grisham or Steel or Patricia Cornwell if you want to keep your job."

I once had a senior editor friend tell me over lunch in all seriousness that what he was looking for were first novels that could sell a first printing of one hundred thousand copies or more. My response was to slap my forehead and say, "Well, why didn't you say so. I thought all you wanted were these little $5,000, five thousand print run books you've been buying from me instead!"

Thankfully, he saw the foolishness of his comment and laughed. My business partner, on the other hand, actually had an editor turn down an option on a book by writers the editor had previously published, because he stated he feared the book would be *too* commercially successful! Go figure.

Now you know something of what an editor's life is like. The moral of these stories is, The more professional your submission and thus the easier you make an editor's job, the more likely he or she will be able to help you turn your project into a published book.

The Secrets of Editorial Meetings

Once the editor finds something that "speaks" to him, he has to start a campaign to get others in the company to see the commercial merit in the project that he sees. The editor will photocopy the proposal, or perhaps have his assistant make a copy of the manuscript, which will then be circulated to other editors and the sales and marketing director, perhaps with a note from the editor explaining what he finds appealing and publishable about the project.

A publishing company has two conflicting needs that continually have to be resolved. The first is the editorial desire to publish a project of literary merit. For an editor who is considering buying a

INFORMATION

Did You Know...

Print run refers to the number of books a publisher decides to print at a given time. *First printing* means the first time the book is issued. Second printing (third printing, etc.,) refers to the number of times the publisher "goes back to press" in order to satisfy booksellers' and readers' demands for a book.

book, the question is, Should this book be published? The other conflicting demand is defined by the sales director, for whom the question is, How many copies can I get into the bookstores and is this book promotable?

If sales and marketing are not keen on a book, or just plain don't like it, they can veto the acquisitions process or, at the least, severely cripple it by making sure there's a very low print order.

One of the problems of conglomerate publishing is that while editorial departments remain "independent" of each other, the sales forces collapse into one unit and are reduced. Suddenly at editorial meetings it is not the enthusiasm of the editors at a house that counts but a sales director who says, "But imprint X is already doing a book something like this. Do we really want to publish two books on the same topic?" Thus, the project is nixed. Unless, of course, imprint X's book does so well that everyone in sales and marketing wants more books just like it.

A major paradox of contemporary publishing is that everyone wants to publish a trendsetting book, but no one wants to be so far ahead of a trend that the book-buying public is running to catch up.

Editorial Department

The *editorial department* is headed by the editorial director who answers to the publisher. A good publisher has the responsibility of balancing the financial books and watching the bottom line and often has a good editorial eye as well, at least in terms of recognizing potential moneymakers when his staff bring them up at editorial meetings.

The next in charge after the editorial director is the executive editor, and below her are a number of senior editors, editors, associate editors, and editorial assistants.

The acquisition of a new book usually requires the agreement of the editorial director as well the whole editorial board, which includes the sales

director, and sometimes also the publisher, who may act as the de facto head of the editorial board.

Senior editors, particularly if they have their own imprint, can at times buy books they love, up to a certain price, but they rarely exercise that option without first getting a couple of other editors on their side.

Editors are becoming concerned that as publishing corporate types emphasize the bottom line more and more, in the future an editor's job security will be tied to the sales records of the books they buy. Buy enough flops and you'll likely be out on your ear after your annual review. Such pressures color one's judgment.

As well as acquiring and editing books, the editorial department is often responsible for the overall coordination of other activities in the publishing house. This is usually the responsibility of the managing editor, who oversees the progress of a manuscript as it passes through the various stages needed to turn it into a published book.

Sales and Marketing

After editorial, the department that has the most impact on how and what books are bought and sold is *sales and marketing*.

Publishing, whether newspaper, magazine, or book, has always been an uneasy alliance between art and commerce, and since the advent of huge royalty advances to authors, the input of the marketing department has become more and more crucial to book acquisition.

When I was an editor I would go to my publisher (when I wanted to buy a book) and say, "It's great. It's a potential prize winner!" And my boss would look at me and rather laconically say, "And . . .?" And I would add, "But this author can really write! We have to publish this book." And Sam would say, "And . . .?"

After a while I realized that literary merit was one thing but that emphasizing the bottom line was what made everyone smile and got me what I wanted. I learned to do profit and loss statements (P&Ls) and manipulate the figures as much as possible in my favor without actually creating a total fiction in the process. After all,

Did You Know...

Sell through means the numbers of books a bookstore ordered that customers actually bought.

Returns are books ordered by a store that are returned to the publisher for a credit.

eventually I would be called to account if my books hemorrhaged money for the company.

These days publishing is all about numbers—getting stock out and making sure it doesn't get returned. That's the job of sales and marketing. The marketing department explores different and innovative ways to sell books, coordinating publicity and promotional campaigns, and figuring out ways of getting the reading public to pay attention to a new book and new author.

In some cases these days, book buyers for major bookstore chains suggest to publishing company sales reps the kinds of book they want to sell. The reps report back to the head of sales and marketing, and she in turn informs editorial of the kind of books they ought to be buying. And before you know it, the tail is trying to wag the dog.

This is not to suggest that those in that chain do not have valid roles and valid opinions. Editors *should* spend time listening and talking with book buyers and sellers. However, a finely honed balance of power seems to be tipping more in favor of sales and marketing (i.e., commerce and conservatism) and away from editorial (i.e., art, creativity, and innovation). Lacking the will and the courage to potentially fall on their faces in an effort to publish new and inventive things, companies lose the ability to find and exploit new talent and reap the considerable rewards that can accrue as a result.

Sales and marketing's most crucial decision is made when a manuscript is first acquired. Very often the proposal that sold that book will be used as the basis for the sales and marketing campaigns, which are put into gear way before the final manuscript is turned in. If the proposal is woolly or unfocused, then the subsequent marketing campaign may well reflect that lack of focus and the book will not do well.

Production Department

Next comes the *art department*. This department creates dust jackets and book covers, and the work is largely produced by freelance artists from guidelines given them by art directors and acquiring editors. It is unlikely that the artist has read the book. At cover design meetings, everyone must sign off on the art before it is put into the system.

Rarely will a publishing company pay attention to an author's ideas about what should be on the cover. Authors are usually wrong and lack any real understanding of the task of the book cover, and publishing companies are exceedingly jealous of their control over how a book will look in its finished version. The best they'll sometimes do is give "cover consultation." This usually means they'll listen to what you have to say and then ignore it, half the time. Submitting sample jacket sketches is a sure sign of amateurism on a writer's part.

The *production and design department* designs the look of the book: the typeface, the page margins, and the design of each chapter page, facing pages, and so forth. They coordinate with the printer and are responsible for turning the manuscript into something you recognize in a bookstore.

The *promotion department* creates advertisements that usually boast of a book's success or announce the latest book by a best-selling author with an eager and impatient audience waiting for its publication. They also create point-of-sale display materials for bookstores, book fairs, and the like.

The *publicity department* gets copies of the book to reviewers and others, arranges media coverage, schedules book tours, and tries to shout loudly about a book to anyone who will listen.

The sad truth is that these departments have limited resources and personnel, and they pick and choose which books they will expend effort on and which books will sit on the vine, like grapes, and wither from inattention. The odds are that your book will sit on the vine, so you must be in the vanguard of promoting and publicizing your book. Keep in regular touch with the sales and marketing and publicity departments; they will probably assign someone to work with your book. But don't expect them to do much for your book, they're just too overworked. However, where you lead, they will follow. Many a successful book became that way because of an author's, not a company's, efforts to initially get a book noticed.

INFORMATION

Did You Know...

Crashing a book means publishing it within weeks, rather than months, as is normal. Instant books, that is, books that are time sensitive (such as biographies of famous people who have died unexpectedly), are often crashed.

If you've given the publishing company any rights to your book—for example, paperback rights or book club rights, which are commonly held by publishing companies—it's the people in the *subsidiary rights department* who are responsible for selling them on your behalf. The proceeds are usually split 50/50 between you and the publishing company. Other rights are split in ways that the publishing house and an author agree upon during the contract negotiations.

If the company also has foreign or translation rights, once again, the subsidiary rights people are the ones who will sell them. Very often, with high royalty advances paid for books, the money from such "subrights" sales goes toward a company recouping some of their initial outlay to an author.

Lastly, there is the *distribution department*, which receives finished books from the printer and in coordination with leads from sales and marketing, distributes copies of the book to various places around the country, and sometimes outside of the country.

Submitting Without an Agent

What happens when you can't get an agent but you are convinced you have a strong seller on your hands? What are you to do? It is possible to get published without an agent, and many people have done it successfully. You need to know *how* to do it and what areas are open to you. Many authors in children's literature, for example, are unagented, at least at first.

University presses often have editors who make it their business to attend professional conferences of all sorts, be it historical, medical, engineering, scientific, whatever, and they know who are the top dogs in particular fields. These editors cultivate relationships with leading academics and, in some cases, actively help them create and write books on subjects in which the authors have expertise. In such cases, editors find you, rather than the other way around. If you want to catch an editor's attention, make sure that you have an outstanding resume in your field of expertise and that you have published articles already on the subject, as well as lectured on it.

Small Presses

A growing field for novice writers is the small press arena. If you have a seminar or strong regional presence, exploit it regionally.

Small press publishing companies are springing up all over with experienced editorial staff and very specific philosophies about the kinds of books they want to publish and can publish well. For example, one of the most successful books in the 1990s didn't come from a major conglomerate; it was an unagented manuscript that was picked up by a small publisher in Florida called Health Communications. The book? *Chicken Soup for the Soul*, and the many sequels it spawned.

Niche publishing, or publishing with a specific focus, has become more and more important in the modern publishing landscape. Running Press, for example, was started for—you guessed it—runners. Sierra Club Books publish environmental guides. And Harvard Common Press is interested in books focusing on New England and the Northeast.

Then there are companies such as Prima, Chronicle, and Renaissance in California; Taylor in Texas; and Walker in New York. All are bigger than many small presses but still medium sized enough that they are interested in seeing proposals and books from authors who are willing to accept modest advances for being published well. An added advantage to this route is that with some luck and careful work you can establish a track record of escalating sales (what we call giving a book "legs") that will attract the attention of major publishers and perhaps eventually get you a contract with them.

To catch an editor's attention, reread the chapter on submitting book proposals. In short, find out an editor's name, write a dynamite query letter and proposal, mail the material in, then sit back and wait for a response.

Think About This . . .

Most authors have a second job in addition to writing professionally. Few earn enough money to live comfortably just on the money earned from writing books.

If a small press makes you an offer, you could negotiate it on your own. It's a wise writer who, with an offer in hand, returns to her search for an agent, this time telling potential agents that she has an offer from publisher *X*. Almost certainly an agent will respond quickly and positively to you.

If you feel you have to negotiate things yourself, the chapter on contracts will give you some idea of what to ask for, but it takes a long time to learn to do contracts well, so don't fool yourself that it's easy—it isn't. You will make mistakes that can have repercussions for the rest of a book's life.

"Sorry, This Just Doesn't Fit Our Current Needs . . ."

There are many reasons a book or book proposal is rejected, but by far the most common is that the writer was ill prepared, either in technical ability or technical information in the proposal.

On average, something like 90 to 95 percent of material sent to editors and agents is rejected. That's a tough market to crack, you might think. But looked at another way, it means that if you have a polished and well-written book idea, you're in competition not with all the others who submit but with the 5 to 10 percent whose material cries out to be taken seriously by editors and agents. Now *that's* a much more workable situation.

Publishers will never write to you and say something like this:

Dear ———

Thank you for submitting your manuscript *The Life and Times of Fred the Roach.* We were impressed by the vast extent of your knowledge in the roach and pest field and can certainly appreciate that your 30 years as an exterminator have made you an expert in the field. It's also true, as you point out, that to the best of our knowledge there has never been a definitive book on roaches and extermination by a working professional.

We were most impressed with your suggestion that your book could mirror in the book world the success of the movies *Antz* and *A Bug's Life*, particularly when, as you so rightly point out, many millions of people in the United States suffer from sometimes severe pest infestations. You're quite right, too, that on the face of it, there would seem to be a large and ready-made audience for your book.

Unfortunately, only part of the manuscript was in a form of English we could understand; the rest of it was so poorly spelled and ungrammatical that we had trouble understanding the context of your sentences much of the time.

We had difficulty distinguishing whether this was nonfiction or fiction, and telling your narrative from the point of view of each bug became rather tedious and confusing after a while. There are, after all, so many of them in the hive that you so accurately recreate.

We must confess that we also found the lack of a continuous narrative a severe drawback, and after page 150, the book became somewhat tedious. There seemed to be no end of important technical detail and some gruesome though effective death scenes involving highly toxic chemicals and bone-snapping rat traps, but the lack of a real hero or villain is a particularly tough obstacle to overcome.

All in all, you might be well advised to consider taking some writing lessons and go back to the drawing board plotwise if you continue to have ambitions to get this book published.

However, even were you to successfully accomplish this, there is probably no real point in resubmitting to us. As we specialize in feminist cookbooks, even a well-written book on roaches might be difficult for us to publish at this time.

We wish you all good fortune in your writing career . . .

Sincerely,

The Editor

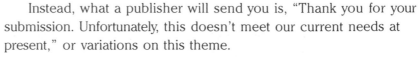

Instead, what a publisher will send you is, "Thank you for your submission. Unfortunately, this doesn't meet our current needs at present," or variations on this theme.

The reasons for this rejection could be some of the reasons outlined in the letter above, or it could be simply that other books on that topic have been recently published by the company or are in the system. Perhaps the publisher had a bad experience with a book such as you suggest.

If you write and ask an editor to give you a reason for rejecting your book, he'll likely ignore your letter. Most editors don't have the time to critique or analyze your work if it's not for them. Rejections are not personal; they're about the suitability of that project with that particular agent or publishing house. There is also no point in writing a rude letter in response to a rejection letter, however exasperated you feel. My advice: Success is the best revenge. Get your book published elsewhere. If it's as good as you think, someone will pick it up and publish it.

If you get a rejection with a handwritten note from an editor, or a comment of any kind, pay attention to it. Editors and agents don't do these things unless they see promise.

Take heart, pay attention to what's suggested, and then go back to the fight with renewed vigor. Obviously, if you've gone from getting standard rejections to personalized ones, you're heading in the right direction.

Publication will happen eventually. Believe it.

CHAPTER 7

The Acceptance Process

Remember back in the introduction we talked about the process of how a manuscript becomes a book? Now that you've read this far, let's revise that scenario a little more realistically.

I said then that 3 months after the agent started submitting the book, you get a phone call at 3:30 P.M. on a Wednesday afternoon. Realistically, this will probably happen after 6 to 9 months of submissions and rejections, unless the book, is snapped up quickly after initial submission.

You hear your agent say, "I've got an offer from an editor. Is this a good time to talk?" She tells you that the offer is $15,000 for world rights. You barely hear your agent say that the advance against royalties is to be paid half on signing the publishing contract and half on delivery of a complete and acceptable manuscript and that there are details she still has to negotiate with the editor. Your agent, however, asks, "Do you want to accept the offer?"

"What choices do we have?" you ask. Your agent explains that one other house may still be interested, but that the book has been rejected by some twelve houses to date, and the offer from Company A is a fair one. It's not great, but the editor knows her stuff and is great to work with, and you'll learn a lot by going through the process. They'll publish your book well. As far as a royalty advance is concerned, if the book turns out to be as successful as everyone expects, then you'll make money in royalties from copies sold.

Obviously, you want as much money up front as you can get. However, that money has to be paid back in some form or other, usually in copies sold and royalties earned, or through subrights sales. If you want to make a career as a writer, sometimes starting modestly is best because a book that makes money and has good sales figures puts an author into a much stronger position for her next book.

An author who gets a huge royalty advance for her first book but doesn't sell enough copies to earn back the royalty advance will have a much harder time getting the same kind of advance for her next book. Obviously, it's better to get more for your next book than less.

The agent says that in all fairness she doesn't think she can improve the offer significantly because the only other editor who's interested works for Company B, which is famous for not paying high advances. They would be willing to go up as high as, say, $12,500 for world rights.

You think about it, discuss the situation with your spouse, and decide, wisely, that a bird in the hand . . . So you call your agent back and tell her that if she can't do any better to go ahead and accept the offer.

The agent now has a bottom line to work from that is acceptable to the client. Neither editor knows the details of who she is in competition with, though she does know that at least one other house is interested in buying the property. The agent is hoping that using that knowledge will provide enough of an impetus for Company A, who made the offer, to improve their offer. Perhaps the agent can get the offer up another $5,000 through wrangling, wheedling, and a little bullying, but at this stage of the game, progress is going to be measured by how effectively the agent can turn the contract to her client's advantage.

So now you wait for the contract to arrive—and you wait, and you wait, and you wait some more. Finally, maybe 6 to 8 weeks after the phone call from your agent, your contract arrives.

What took so long? Well, a number of people, including your editor, the editorial director, the publisher, the contracts manager, and the chief financial officer, all have to sign off on it. It could be on someone's desk for ages while they're on vacation, out of town, ill, or just plain busy. Contracts departments in particular are usually small, do the contracts for all the editors in a house, and are usually logjammed. Checks are usually cut once a week toward the end of the week. If the okayed contract arrives on your editor's desk the day after checks have been cut for that week, you'll have to wait another week before you see your money.

Study your contract; call your agent up and ask her to explain the clauses you don't understand. You sign all three or four copies of the contract (adding your social security number), initial the paragraphs in which any changes have been made, and then return the contracts to your agent.

Pay attention to the length of the book the company wants, that is, the number of words stated as acceptable in the contract. Also note the delivery date.

About a month or so later, you'll get your countersigned contract from your agent—with the signing check, usually about 1/2 to 1/3 the total advance, minus your agent's commission. The pub-

Your Contract

A contract should contain at least the following information:

- The title of your work

- The specific rights being purchased (e.g., print, electronic, reprint rights, translation, etc.)

- The exact fee offered for your work, how it will be paid out, and when you can expect to receive it

- Your obligations and liabilities (Some companies specify issues of accuracy, originality, and libel. Make sure you can reasonably meet such demands.)

lisher has written your agent a check. She cashes it, takes out the commission, and writes you a check from her own company.

The Contract

What follows is a sample contract with comments in **bold face** on what the major clauses mean and what you should do or can do about certain things. This is not intended as an exhaustive study of contracts. Several books have been written on the subject by lawyers and more experienced agents versed in publishing law. This chapter is designed only to help you *understand* some of the more important things that are in a contract and why they should or should not be there.

Go into contract negotiations knowing what you want and why you want it. Contracts are about many things, but mainly they're concerned with making sure that each party gets what it needs out of the contract and that contingency plans are in place for awkward or difficult situations down the road. The contract should specify the principles of precise ownership and the responsibilities of each party in the contract.

The first thing to realize is that a publishing contract is heavily weighted in favor of the publishing house. They drew it up, after all. Their boilerplate contract is usually horrible and is intended to take a share of everything that the publisher can get its hands on, as far as a book's moneymaking potential is concerned. What's more, they don't think twice about trying to tie up a writer, as far as future work is concerned, to suit their needs with barely a thought about the author's needs as a working writer.

Every agent worth his salt has changes that he makes to each house's standard publishing contracts, each of which is different, establishing precedents with the many houses that he does business with.

There are, however, areas that each contract has in common, and it's these areas I'll discuss. In general, it's not acceptable for a publisher to just send you a check and then claim that certain rights have been automatically transferred to the publisher by your acceptance of that payment.

Contracts may be transmitted by fax or e-mail. These days if both parties are in agreement, a faxed signature can be considered legally binding. E-mail is trickier; it may lack the editor's signature, and you'll have to print it out to sign it.

BOOK TITLE: _____

AUTHOR: _____

PUBLISHER/EDITOR:

_____

ROYALTY ADVANCE: $ _____

❑ ½ on signing $ _____

❑ ½ on d&a of ms $ _____

❑ _____ on d&a of an outline

❑ _____ other

❑ Option: Sample chapter and outline

_____

TERRITORY:

❑ North America _____

❑ World English _____

❑ World _____

AUTHOR COPIES

❑ 20 copies to author and 10 to agent

❑ 10 copies to author and 5 to agent on other

   editions _____

ROYALTIES (ON RETAIL PRICE):

❑ Hardcover 10%, 12½ %, 15% (on 1st 5,000,

   2nd 5,000, thereafter)

_____

❑ Trade 7½ % or _____

❑ Mass market 8% or _____

❑ Electronic 10% or _____

❑ Escalators: " _____ %" up to " _____,000"

   then " _____ %" after.

❑ Best-seller bonus _____

❑ Pass through on subsidiary rights

OTHER:

❑ Split cost of indexing 50/50 author and

   publisher

❑ Reversion of Publisher rights after 18

   months if no printing happens or book

   falls out of print _____

❑ We keep Dramatic _____

❑ We keep Audio: ___ Abridged ___ Unabridged

❑ We Keep Electronic other than verbatim

_____

❑ We sell rights: _____

❑ Book Clubs 50/50 _____

❑ 1st Serial 90/10 or _____

❑ 2nd Serial 50/50 or _____

❑ We keep Merchandising _____

OTHER RIGHTS WE GET:

❑ Author Consultation on MS, cover copy, &

   cover design _____

❑ Publish within 18 months _____

❑ Author has right to retain own legal counsel

_____

❑ No Joint Accounting _____

Sample Contract

The issues in the sample contract that follows include some of the more pervasive contract problems throughout the industry. The agent's job is to make the best deal available to an author—not necessarily the best imaginable. Many things in this boilerplate are negotiable, but certainly not all. Negotiating with a big house in particular, say a Random House imprint or a Putnam Penguin imprint, is a little like getting into bed with a band of gorillas. You have to be very careful they don't crush you when they embrace you, and if they say no, reasonable or not, you don't have much leverage to convince them to change their minds other than saying that "the deal is off." For many authors that's not a very viable option, unless the deal really stinks.

This is a fictional contract for "*XXX* Publishing House," and while I've tried to make it as accurate as possible, different houses have different boilerplate contracts that include and exclude a number of things. This particular contract is heavily weighted in favor of the publishing house, and negotiating with this company may well be an arduous experience.

XXX Publishing House

AUTHOR'S AGREEMENT

Agreement made this _____ day of _____ , 20____
between *XXX* Publishing House, a corporation with its principal place of
business at *XXX* Street, *XXX, XX XXXXX* (the "Publisher"), and
_____ (the "Author")
concerning the publication of a Work presently entitled
_____ (the "Work").

**#1. Here the company is detailing when the manu-
script should be submitted, and any other relevant
deadlines. Indexing is difficult to do properly (and is
a pain in the behind as well). Try to negotiate a two-
thirds to one-third split in favor of the author, and be
happy when you're offered 50/50.**

1. DELIVERY OF THE MANUSCRIPT. The Author agrees to deliver to the Publisher
on or before _____ the completed manuscript of the Work con-
sisting of a minimum of _____ words together with all drawings,
photographs, illustrations, maps, charts, and indexes, in form and content sat-
isfactory to the Publisher. If Author elects not to construct an index for the
Work, the Publisher shall have the right to have an index prepared, the cost
of which shall be charged to the Author's royalty account.

**#2. There next follows the Grant of Rights. This is an
important clause because it details which territories
you have allowed the publisher to sell its version of
your book into. Broadly the terms are "US and
Canada," also called "North American rights," and**

American dependencies such as Guam, Puerto Rico, US Virgin Islands, and so forth; and "World English," which is any English-speaking country, such as North America, Great Britain, Australia, South Africa, and so forth. The percentage splits between author and publisher for these sales, which will be handled by the publisher and are detailed in Appendix A. And finally, there is World Rights, which similarly allows the publishing company a negotiated percentage of all the foreign and translation rights to your book. Any American publisher can also export a copies of its English language version of a book into a foreign country. Which means you may be able to find on, say, American Army bases in Germany, American version of book, and still sell German language translations of the same book.

Audio. This is a subright that you would want to retain if possible. There are two types of audio right: abridged, which is the more commercially viable, and unabridged, which is the complete text of the book. There is also dramatic readings and dramatized readings. All of these should be distinguished. At the least, the percentage split should be improved from 50/50 if possible. Note that the publishing house, if they own the recording, wants to make the author record the tape for free for them—"participate without cost"—though the extent of that participation is left undefined. It needs to be defined. It can take days to record a book well, and a professional actor would be paid to do the work. The author ought to get some compensation for his or her time as well.

Electronic. **This is another of those new areas of rights that's becoming more and more problematic. You should try to reserve these rights as well. Royalties received by the author on e-books are defined as 15 percent of the amount received. However it gets more interesting: often electronic book rights are listed among the various subrights and are split 50/50 between author and publisher. So, if the publishing House license e-rights out, then the author will get 50 percent of the sale; but if the e-book is treated as a publisher's "edition," they'll only give the author 15 percent. It's up to the agent to negotiate what they want; it is a business rather than a legal question. There's no industry standard.**

2. GRANT OF RIGHTS. In consideration of the mutual promises set forth herein including the compensation as provided in Appendix A, which is attached to and is made part of this Agreement, the Author grants and transfers to the Publisher, for the duration of the copyright in the Work, the following exclusive rights:

(1) to reproduce, publish, distribute, and sell the Work and all subsequent revisions and editions thereof in the English language and all other languages throughout the world, including in book form, adaptation, anthology, collected works, book club, digest, abridgement, condensation, serialization, syndication, periodical, audio, video, performance, dramatic, motion pictures, animation, radio and television, theater, filmstrip, microfilm, microcard, Braille and large type, foreign language editions, recorded readings, visual projections, information-storage and retrieval systems, all electronic versions (including without limitation software, electronic books or "e-books," interactive or multimedia versions, other

screen-display technologies, as well as verbatim text-only electronic editions), all other mechanical reproduction and transcription (including print-on-demand versions), all versions in any and all media and all technologies now existing or which may in the future come into existence, and all other derivative works whether by itself or in combination with any other material; as well as to use the title and characters of the Work as the basis for trademarks or trade names for other products or in connection with merchandise in all forms; and

(2) to grant licenses to third parties to exploit any of the rights granted herein.

3. AUTHOR'S WARRANTIES AND INDEMNITIES.

A. WARRANTIES. The Author represents and warrants (a) that the Work has not been published in whole or in part; (b) that the Author has full power to enter into this agreement; (c) that the Work is not, and prior to the normal expiration of copyright will not be, in the public domain in whole or in part; (d) that the Work is and will be original and the Author is its sole author and creator; (e) that no third party has or will have any claim to or interest in the Work as a co-author or otherwise; (f) that the Author has not previously assigned, pledged or otherwise encumbered the rights granted hereunder; (g) that the Work will not violate any right of privacy or publicity nor infringe upon any statutory or common-law copyright and will not otherwise be injurious or in contravention of law; (h) that the Author has used and will use all reasonable care in the creation, research, and preparation of the Work to ensure that all facts and statements in the Work are true and correct in all material respects; and (i) that no instruction, formula, direction, recipe, prescription, or other matter contained in the Work will cause injury or damage.

The Publisher shall be under no obligation to make an independent investigation to determine whether the foregoing warranties and representations are true and correct, and any independent investigation by or for the Publisher, or its failure to investigate, shall not constitute a defense to the Author in any action based upon a breach of any of the foregoing warranties.

The Author's warranties shall not apply to any material that the Publisher may supply for the Work.

The Author's warranties and the Author's other responsibilities under this Agreement shall be in effect throughout the term of this Agreement and shall survive its termination.

B. INDEMNITY. In the event of any claim, action or proceeding based upon an alleged violation of any of the Author's warranties the Publisher shall have the right to defend the same through counsel of its own choosing, and to settle any claim, action or proceeding with the Author's prior approval, such approval not to be unreasonably withheld. The Author shall hold harmless and indemnify the Publisher, any seller of the Work, and any licensee of the Publisher against any costs, damages or losses, including reasonable attorney's fees arising out of defending against any claims, actions or proceedings which, if sustained, would constitute a breach of the warranties set forth above.

It's important you know who bears the expense of insurance. You need to know the limits of the policy, as mentioned but not defined in (iii). According to (iv), the author may be required to pay most if not all of the cost. The policy seems to be limited. If *XXX* Publishing House were hit with a lawsuit, just before

your case came along, insurance may not be available to cover you as well.

The Author shall have the right to select separate counsel at his own expense provided that the conduct of the defense shall remain under the Publisher's control. In the event any such claim, action or proceeding is instituted, the Publisher and Author agree to give each other prompt written notice thereof; and the Publisher may withhold payment of any reasonable amounts due the Author under this Agreement to conduct the defense thereof.

4. PREPARATION OF THE WORK

A. COMPLETED COPY. The Author will deliver to the Publisher two (2) clean and legibly typed, double-spaced, sequentially page-numbered, complete copies of the manuscript, together with an exact duplicate of the Work on a computer disk in IBM compatible or Apple standard word processing format on or before the Delivery Date. Any photographs, illustrations, maps, charts, drawings and indexes specified by mutual agreement to be included in the Work shall be delivered to the Publisher in a form and of a quality suitable for reproduction. If the Author shall fail to supply any such materials promptly or in proper form, the Publisher shall have the right to supply same at the Author's expense. The Author will obtain at the Author's expense and deliver to the Publisher at the same time as the completed manuscript written permission for any and all material in the Work which is the copyrighted property of another, such permission to cover the territories and rights granted to the Publisher herein.

#4B This says that if the author doesn't deliver the manuscript by the deadline, he must repay any money he's collected from them. This would clearly be something to negotiate, if possible. Also, read a certain

way, this next clause says that an author doesn't automatically get the opportunity to fix a delivered manuscript the publishing house judges unacceptable (note the phrase "in its sole judgment" and all the "or" clauses). The publishing house can reject an unacceptable manuscript the first time it's submitted. Again, this is a contingency situation that should be addressed in the author's favor.

B. FAILURE TO DELIVER OR UNSATISFACTORY MANUSCRIPT. If the Author fails to deliver the completed manuscript by the Delivery Date or any extended delivery date agreed to in writing by both parties, or if, in the Publisher's sole judgment, the delivered manuscript is unsatisfactory, the Publisher may terminate this Agreement by giving written notice thereof to Author whereupon the Author shall repay all amounts which may have been advanced hereunder.

5. PUBLICATION OF THE WORK.

#5A. The 18-month publishing window is common. However, in this clause, there's no stated *obligation* to publish if the publishing house decides not to. The author's options if the publishing house does not publish would either be (1) to go with another publishing house and pay back The publishing house or (2) to give The publishing house 6 months or more to publish. If they still don't publish the book, the author can keep the money the publishing house already paid as a "cancellation fee" and forego the on-acceptance payment (if there was supposed to be one). So the publishing house can choose simply not to publish, as happened when HarperCollins canceled over a

hundred contracts in 1998. It would be a good idea to try to define more closely a definitive publication period more in line with the writer's needs than those of the publishing house.

A. PUBLICATION DATE. The Publisher agrees to publish the Work at its expense in such style and manner and at such price as it shall deem suitable within eighteen (18) months of its acceptance of the Work, unless publication is delayed by (i) Author's failure to return proofs of the Work within ten (10) days after having received them for review hereunder; or (ii) circumstances beyond the Publisher's reasonable control. In either case the delay in publication will not exceed the delay caused by such circumstances.

Should the Publisher fail to publish the Work before the expiration of said period, its failure shall be just cause for the Author to terminate this Agreement upon sixty (60) days' written notice to the Publisher and, unless Publisher shall publish the Work within such sixty (60) day period, all rights (except for any licenses already granted by the Publisher) shall revert to the Author, and Author as his sole remedy shall retain all sums paid to him pursuant to this Agreement.

Should the Publisher publish the Work within such sixty (60) day period the parties agree the Publisher shall have met its obligation to timely publish hereunder, and the Author's termination shall be of no force or effect.

#5B. You should insert a phrase that says something like "the author will see the copyedited manuscript and make changes." The revision clause should be amended to include some intent by the publisher to pay the author for extensive revisions to his work.

B. AUTHOR'S CORRECTIONS IN PROOF. The Publisher shall send the Author proofs of the Work, and the Author agrees to read, correct, and return them promptly but in no case later than ten (10) days after having received them from Publisher. The Author agrees to pay the cost of alterations made by the Author in excess of ten percent (10%) of the cost of composition. Any such charges shall be charged to the Author's royalty account or applied against any sums due or accruing to the Author under this Agreement except that if the Publisher so requests, payment will be made by the Author in cash or by check upon presentation by the Publisher of an itemized bill. The Author will not be charged for printer's or Publisher's errors.

C. COPYEDITING. The Author authorizes the Publisher to make the manuscript of the Work conform to its standard style in punctuation, spelling, capitalization, and usage.

> **#5D. The author should try to negotiate the inclusion of the phrase "author will be given the opportunity for timely consultation on cover design" here. It's not much, but it's something toward shaping what the publishing house decides to put on the front cover of your book.**

D. STYLE OF PUBLICATION. The Publisher shall determine the style and manner of publication including but not limited to design, form, printing, production, price, sale, promotion, and distribution of free copies.

E. PROMOTION OF THE WORKS. The Publisher may use and authorize others to use the Author's name, likeness, and biographical information in the sale and promotion of the Work.

F. AUTHOR TO EXECUTE DOCUMENTS. The Author shall, when requested by the Publisher, execute all documents which may be necessary or appropriate to enable the Publisher to exercise or deal with any of the rights granted here-under.

#5G. Your agent will probably want to insert "and ten free copies to the Agent". These will be used for sub-rights submissions by the agent. The copies mentioned here are personal copies for the author and should not impinge upon copies that the author wants the publicity and promotional department to send to reviewers and people who will or have provided blurbs for the book.

G. AUTHOR'S FREE COPIES. The Author shall receive twenty-five (25) free copies of the Work on first publication in book form, and may purchase further copies of the Work for personal use (not for resale within the book trade) at a fifty percent (50%) discount on the then current retail price. The author may order any other books on the Publisher's list for personal use at a twenty percent (20%) discount on the current retail price. Payment, including freight costs, must accompany all such orders.

H. AUTHOR'S ORIGINALS. The Publisher shall not be liable for any damage that may occur to the Author's manuscript (or to other illustrations or materials) and Author hereby acknowledges and agrees that to ensure the safety of the manuscript and related materials, Author should retain and safeguard Author's own private copies thereof, including at least one hard copy and at least one computer disk copy of the Work.

I. ARTWORK. All right, title and interest in and to all artworks to be included in the Work as supplied by Publisher (except line drawings, charts, diagrams, and similar illustrations prepared by the Author at his or her expense and submitted in essentially finished form) shall be and remain that of the Publisher and may be used by the Publisher in any other Work in Publisher's sole discretion.

6. COPYRIGHT AND PERMISSIONS

A. REGISTRATION AND NOTICE. The Publisher will insert in every copy of the Work in the name of the Author the copyright notice required for protection under the Universal Copyright Convention and will require the same of its licensees and will register copyright for the Work in the Author's name in the United States within ninety (90) days of its publication at Publisher's sole expense. The Author shall provide the Publisher, upon its request, any documents which shall be necessary in order to enable the Publisher to obtain or enforce copyright in the Work.

B. PRIOR PUBLICATION. If the Author grants or has granted any rights to others to publish or otherwise exploit part or all of the Work before the Publisher's publication, the Author will promptly notify the Publisher of the dates of such publications and will deliver to the Publisher legally recordable assignments of the copyright or of the rights granted as deemed necessary by the Publisher.

C. SELECTIONS FOR PROMOTION. If the Publisher believes it will benefit the Work, for promotional purposes, to publish or to permit critics, reviewers, or others to publish or otherwise use excerpts, it may do so without charge to them or payment to the Author. The Publisher may also permit charitable organizations to reproduce or record the Work without charge in appropriate forms for the physically handicapped. In the event of the disposition of performance rights (i.e. dramatic, musical, radio, television, motion picture and allied rights) the Publisher may grant to the purchaser the right to publish excerpts and summaries of the Work for advertising and exploiting such rights, provided that such grant shall require the purchaser to take all steps necessary to protect the copyright of the Work.

D. SUITS FOR INFRINGEMENT OF COPYRIGHT. The Author and the Publisher will notify one another in writing if either has reason to believe that any right granted to the Publisher by this Agreement has been infringed by any third party. In the event the parties proceed jointly, the Publisher shall select counsel with the Author's approval, not to be unreasonably withheld, and the expenses and any recoveries shall be shared equally. If after written notice either party declines to participate, the other may proceed independently and bear all expenses of the action and retain all proceeds that may be awarded; provided, further, that if the participating party is not the record copyright owner with respect to the Work in question, the other party shall permit the action to be brought in such party's name or names.

7. RELATED AND COMPETING WORKS

#7. The next clause states that the author cannot contract for his or her book until after delivery of the one under contract here. This seems draconian and may well need to be modified according to the author's work schedule and commitments.

The Author agrees that the Work shall be the Author's next book. The Author will not, without the Publisher's prior written consent, enter into an agreement to write another book before the Publisher has accepted the Work.

The Author, without obtaining the Publisher's prior written consent, shall not nor shall he or she permit anyone else to publish or otherwise reproduce or communicate in any media now known or later developed any portion of the Work or of any other version, revision, or other derivative work based thereon. The Author may, however, draw on and refer to material contained in the Work in preparing articles for publication in scholarly and professional journals and papers for delivery at professional meetings and the

Author may draw on and refer to material contained in the Work in personally presenting professional seminars and speeches.

The Author, without obtaining the Publisher's prior written consent, shall not prepare or assist in the preparation of any other work that might in the Publisher's judgment interfere with or injure the sale of the Work.

The Author shall not dispose of or grant any rights reserved to the Author in such a way as to substantially destroy, detract from or impair the value of any rights granted to the Publisher hereunder.

8. OPTION

> **#8. The following provision is very important. It's another of those "you've got to be kidding me" clauses. In case the book is as successful as everyone hopes it will be, the publishing house claims it should have an exclusive option to negotiate on the author's next book. Additionally, they want to wait until publication of the first book *before* considering the option work. There's no mention of whether the next work should be fiction or nonfiction. Such a distinction should be made. If fiction, it should include the phrase "synopsis and sample chapter for another book in *XXX*;" for nonfiction it should include the phrase "proposal for a full-length work of nonfiction on *XXX*." In both cases, *XXX* should be very narrowly defined as another book in the same style, genre, and general tone as the book currently under contract. The time period for exclusive consideration should be 30 days, not 60, following the acceptance of the current manuscript under contract. The phrase "solicit**

any third party offers, directly or indirectly" is too broad and should also be struck out if possible. "Reasonable period of exclusive negotiations" should be broadly defined as not longer than, say, a month after the initial indication of interest in the book.

The Author agrees to first submit to the Publisher for publication the Author's next full-length work. The Publisher shall have sixty (60) days from the date of submission to make a proposal for publication of said work, and the parties agree to negotiate in good faith in an effort to agree on mutually acceptable terms for publication. In no event shall the Publisher be required to exercise its option prior to sixty (60) days following the Publisher's acceptance of the Work which is the subject of this Agreement. If the parties are unable to agree on terms, the Author shall be free to submit the option work to other publishers, provided that the Author shall give the Publisher the right of last refusal, including the right to publish the option work on the same terms offered by any other publisher.

9. REVISIONS

If subsequent to publication of the Work the Publisher determines the Work requires revision the Publisher shall so inform the Author. If such notice is given and the Author is unable or unwilling to deliver a manuscript for such revision as requested by the Publisher, the Publisher may engage such person or persons competent in its opinion to perform the required work.

In such a case, the Author shall be consulted about the selection of the reviser and the content of the first such revision required, but acknowledges that the final decisions about these matters shall be made by the Publisher.

The Publisher shall have the right to reduce the royalties otherwise due to the Author pursuant to Appendix A hereto, with respect to the first such revision required, by up to fifty percent (50%) and, if a second such revision is required, by up to a total of seventy-five percent (75%). No royalties shall be paid to the Author with respect to third and additional revisions not prepared by the Author.

The Author understands and acknowledges that in any revised editions of the Work not prepared by Author, the Publisher may determine at its sole discretion whether the Work will be published under the same title or a different title; whether or not and in what form the Work will refer to the Author by name; and whether or not and in what form credit will be give to the revisers.

The royalties paid to the Author on any such revised editions will be based on the aggregate sales of all editions, unless agreed otherwise.

10. STATEMENTS TO AUTHOR

A. PAYMENTS. After publication, the Publisher will render semiannual statements of account for activity through June 30 and December 31, respectively, and such statements shall set forth the number of copies of the Work printed, sold, spoiled, returned, given away, and on hand. No later than ninety (90) days following the end of each reporting period, the Publisher shall send such reports to Author along with the net amount due hereunder. The Publisher shall have the right to withhold a reasonable reserve for returns of copies of the Work provided such reserve shall not be withheld for more than the first three (3) semiannual statements following publication of any edition. If the Author should at any time receive an overpayment of royalties as a result of returns, the Publisher may deduct such overpayment from any future earnings in the account for that Work. It is understood the term "overpayment" does not apply to an unearned advance.

(i) PROMOTIONAL COPIES. No royalty shall be paid on copies of the Work furnished gratis for review, advertising, promotion, sample, or like purposes, or on copies of the Work remaindered or otherwise sold at less than cost or on any returned or refunded copies, or on copies sold to the Author, or on destroyed or damaged copies.

(ii) AUTHOR'S CHARGES OR DEBTS. The Publisher may, in addition to any other remedies provided by law, deduct any charge provided for in this Agreement or other debt owed to the Publisher by the Author from any and all monies otherwise due the Author from the Publisher under this Agreement.

(iii) ANNUAL ACCOUNTING. If at any time after two (2) years from the date of publication the total amount due the Author is less than twenty-five dollars ($25) in any six-month payment period, the Publisher shall, after notification to the Author, be under no obligation to render any accounting to the Author until such time as the Author's earnings exceed twenty-five dollars ($25).

(iv) LICENSEES' INCOME STATEMENTS. The Publisher shall provide copies of statements from subsidiary rights licenses to the Author at the Author's request and expense.

B. VERIFICATION OF ACCOUNTING. The Author or the Author's representative, at the Author's expense, may examine the books of account of the Publisher as they relate to the Work as appropriate to verify the accuracy of the Publisher's records of account, provided that any examination is performed no more than once a year, after reasonable notice, during normal business hours. If errors in the total amount of the sums paid to the Author are found in the Publisher's favor and such errors concern an amount greater than $100 that represents no less than five percent (5%) of the total amount due to the Author with respect to the preceding reporting period, the reasonable expense incurred in examining the Publisher's records, up to an amount equal to that of the shortfall, shall be borne by the Publisher, provided that errors not objected to in writing within one (1) year shall be deemed waived by the Author.

11. DISCONTINUANCE OF PUBLICATION AND REVERSION OF RIGHTS

A. OUT OF PRINT. If at any time after the expiration of two years from the actual publication date, any of the following events occurs:

(i)   the Publisher notifies the Author in writing that the Publisher intends to discontinue publication of the Work in all media and does not intend to grant any future licenses for subsidiary rights, or

(ii) the Publisher allows all of its editions of the Work to become unavailable and does not contract for or place any edition on sale within six months after the Author has made a request therefor in writing, and if there is no licensed edition available or contracted for, then upon written notice by Author to the Publisher and upon repayment by the Author of any overpayment of royalties or other sums due, this Agreement shall terminate and all rights in the Work shall revert to the Author, with the exception that the Author and the Publisher shall each continue to have the right to receive their respective shares of sums due them from all licenses or contracts executed prior to such termination.

B. RIGHT TO BUY COPIES. In the event of such termination the Publisher may dispose of any copies remaining on hand as it deems best subject to the royalty provisions of Appendix A provided it first offers the Author by written notice to the Author's last known address the opportunity to purchase any remaining copies of the Work on hand and all plates therefor, if any, at their cost of production; provided, however, that Author must exercise such option within seven (7) days of said notice.

C. TERMINATION UPON BANKRUPTCY OR LIQUIDATION OF PUBLISHER. The Author shall have the right to buy back the rights of publication hereunder at fair market value to be determined promptly by mutual agreement of the parties or, if the parties cannot come to an agreement with respect to such value, by arbitration in accordance with the provisions of Section 14 hereof and to repurchase any plates or remaining copies of the Work, in the following circumstances:

(i)   if a voluntary or involuntary petition under the Bankruptcy Code is filed by or against Publisher and the petition is not challenged and rejected within a reasonable time;

(ii)   if a receiver is appointed for the business affairs of Publisher or Publisher makes an assignment for the benefit of creditors; or

(iii) if Publisher liquidates or ceases doing business as a going concern.

12. PROMOTION OF THE WORKS.

The Publisher shall use its reasonable efforts to promote the sale of the Work provided, however, that Publisher makes no warranty, representation or guarantee, implicit or otherwise, as to the amount of advertising and promotion to be devoted to the Work, to the length of the press run, to the length of the time the Work will be kept in print, or to the projected sale of the Work.

13. JOINT AUTHORS.

If the Author hereunder is more than one person or entity, any one (and an alternate) may be designated pursuant to this Section 13 of the Agreement to act on behalf of all such Authors jointly, and the Publisher may rely on the acts of the Author or the Author's alternate so designated as representative of and binding upon all the Authors hereunder, and in the absence of such designation, the Publisher may deal with any one of the Authors as the agent and representative of all, and may rely on the acts of such Author-representative as binding on all the Authors. If the Author hereunder is more than one person or entity, each of the Authors shall be jointly and severally liable with respect to all the duties, obligations and liabilities of the Author hereunder; provided, further, that Publisher may assume that all such Authors share equally in proceeds payable under this Agreement and may either issue separate checks in equal amounts payable to each Author severally or single checks payable jointly to all Authors.

14. RESOLUTION OF DISPUTES

Any controversy or claim arising out of, or relating to, any provisions of this Agreement or the breach thereof which cannot otherwise be resolved by good faith negotiations between the parties shall be resolved by final and binding arbitration under the rules of the American Arbitration Association then obtaining, subject to the following terms:

(a) The arbitrator shall announce the award in writing accompanied by written findings explaining the facts determined in support of the award, and any relevant conclusions of law.

(b) Any award rendered in such arbitration may be enforced by either party.

Notwithstanding the foregoing, nothing in this Section 14 shall be construed to waive any rights or timely performance of any obligations existing under this Agreement.

15. ASSIGNS

This Agreement shall be binding upon and for the benefit of the Author and the Author's heirs, executors, administrators, and assigns, and shall also bind and benefit the Publisher and its successors and assigns. The Publisher may assign this Agreement. The Author's obligations are personal and may not be assigned without the Publisher's written approval, except that the Author may by written request assign his royalties to a third party.

16. NOTICE

Any notice required under this Agreement shall be in writing and sent to the Author's address, stated above, or to the Publisher at *XXX* Street, *XXX, XXX XXXXX*, or such subsequent address as a party shall notify the other in writing. Unless otherwise specified, such notice may be sent by regular mail.

17. CONSTRUCTION AND VALIDITY

This Agreement constitutes the full understanding of the parties hereto, and no promises, representations, or undertakings involving the Work other than those incorporated herein shall be binding on either party. The parties shall have no obligations to each other except those specifically stated in this Agreement, and no modification or waiver of any provision shall be valid unless in writing and signed by both parties. This Agreement shall be governed by and construed in accordance with the laws of the United States of America. If any part of this Agreement is declared invalid or unenforceable by a court of competent jurisdiction, the remaining provisions shall continue in effect.

XXX Corporation

In the presence of

_____   By: _____
                                                  Publisher

In the presence of

_____   By: _____
                                                  Author

                                                 _____
                                                 Social Security Number

                                                 _____
                                                 Citizenship

APPENDIX A

AUTHOR'S COMPENSATION

As consideration for the Author's transfer of rights in the Work hereunder, the Publisher will pay the Author compensation, based on its exercise of those rights, as follows:

> **#1. This next paragraph details how much you'll get as an advance against royalties and how the company will pay it out. Traditionally it has been one-half on signing the contract and one-half on delivery by the author and acceptance by the editor of a completed manuscript. Publishers are trying to change this, particularly on higher advances, to include an on-publication payment. Resist it if you can.**

(1) ADVANCE. As an advance against and on account of all monies accruing to the Author under the terms of this Agreement, the Publisher shall pay the Author _____ as follows:

> **#2. Following is an important set of clauses to examine. They define what the royalty rates will be for the book under various circumstances. It's very hard to get publishers to alter these rates in any significant way, though in some circumstances there is a little flexibility. Note the phrase "upon sales less actual returns and less a reasonable reserve for returnable copies . . ." This means, in essence, that the publisher can hang onto money that you have earned until they deem that it is time to pay you**

everything you've earned. The fear is that they'll print too many copies, ship them out to booksellers who buy them on consignment, and then 6 months later find they can't move them off their shelves and so ship the copies back to the publisher, who is forced to issue a credit. This is a particularly onerous practice in publishing that agents and authors hate, but there isn't a great deal that can be done about it at present. You can try to change the amounts and timing more in the writer's favor.

You might try to get the publisher to add a "performance bonus" or "bestseller bonus." These bonuses are royalties paid if the book performs unexpectedly well to a certain level. Best-seller bonuses are tied to a particular list, for example, the *New York Times* list, and pay varying amounts for a fixed period, say, 10 weeks, according to the book's position on the list. A certain amount is paid for each week a book is in, say, positions 1 to 3, a little less for positions 4 to 7, and so on.

(2) ROYALTIES. The Publisher shall pay the Author royalties as follows:

(a) For copies of the Work published by the Publisher:

(i) For printed books, except as otherwise noted below, the royalty rate shall be _____ percent (_____ %) of the catalog retail price.

(ii)   For audio, video, film, Print-on-Demand and all electronic versions (as defined in paragraph 1 of the Author's Agreement), the royalty rate shall be five percent (5%) of the Net Amount Received.

(b) Where copies of the Work are sold within the Book Trade (as defined below) by the Publisher at a discount rate greater than fifty-five percent (55%), the royalty rate above shall be applied to the actual wholesale price received by the Publisher.

(c) Where copies of the Work are sold by the Publisher outside the United States, or within the United States but outside the Book Trade and at a discount rate greater than fifty percent (50%), the royalty rate above shall be applied to the actual wholesale price received by Publisher.

(d) No royalties shall be paid with respect to copies of the Work sold to the Author at a discount, or at a price less than or equal to the actual average manufacturing cost per copy.

(e) On the sale of reprint editions of the Work, which are defined as editions of the Work published at a less expensive price than the regular edition, the royalty rate above shall be applied to the actual Net Amount Received (as defined below) by the Publisher.

(f) On sales of the Work made directly from the Publisher to consumers through Publisher-owned book clubs, mail-order campaigns and other direct solicitation, including but not limited to television, radio, print, and electronic advertising, the royalty rate of five percent (5%) shall be applied to the Net Amount Received.

(g) On bulk sales and remainder sales at greater than the manufacturing cost of the Work to businesses and associations, not for the purpose of resale, the royalty rate of five percent (5%) shall be applied to the Net Amount Received.

(h) If the Publisher exploits any other rights other than those for which royalties are set forth elsewhere in this Appendix A, the royalty rate of five percent (5%) shall be applied to the Net Amount Received.

#2i. It is useful to ask for a "pass through" for monies earned through a sale of subsidiary rights within a fixed period, say, 30 days, if the publishing house is going to represent these rights. This means any money owed the author as the result of a subright sale will be passed through to the author within 30 days of the publisher receiving that money. They can make you wait for ages if you don't do this. You only get royalty statements every 6 months. What rights the author retains should be negotiated at the beginning of the deal. Even if the publishing house insists on keeping a right, it is possible to try and negotiate that the agent's subagents sell the subrights on behalf of the company and the author. Publishers don't much care for that, but it can be done. Also, the percentage split should be much closer to 80/20 in favor of the author; 75/25 is okay; 90/10 is great if you have to split the proceeds. Remember, every subrights sale that the publishing house makes on your behalf, if you've agreed to share the income, means that your share of the money will go toward paying off the royalty advance debt you incurred initially when the company gave you money up front on signing and delivery.

(i)   With respect to the licensing to third parties of any of the rights granted under this Agreement (but specifically excluding royalties for sales through third-party distributors as set forth in subparagraph 2(j), the royalty rate shall be fifty percent (50%) of the Net Amount Received.

(j) Sales through third parties to distribute, transmit, or deliver printed books or electronic versions (including "E-books" and Print-on-Demand editions) shall not be considered to be licenses for the purposes of this Agreement, and the royalties for sales through such arrangements shall be governed by sub-paragraphs 2(a) through 2(i).

For purposes of this Agreement:

The "Book Trade" shall mean those retail outlets for which the sale of books comprises fifty percent (50%) or more of gross sales, or wholesalers whose sales to such retail outlets and/or libraries constitutes fifty percent (50%) or more of gross sales.

"Electronic Book" or "E-book" shall mean a substantially verbatim version of the printed text in complete or abridged form, either with or without any or all of the illustrations that may appear in the printed text, that can be read on a computer terminal or other electronic device or medium. An Electronic Book may be contained on the same medium (such as a computer file or storage device) that contains other works. An Electronic Book may also include software that enables the reader to move from one place to another in the work and or to search or index the work for particular content.

"Interactive or multimedia version" means a version of the Work that includes all of or portions of the printed text, either with or without any or all illustrations that may appear in the printed text, together with substantial additional features, including without limitation additional text, additional illustrations, interactive software, video clips, animation, music, or interactive or game features. An interactive or multimedia version may also include software that enables the reader to move from one place to another in the work and or to search or index the work for particular content.

"Print-on-Demand Edition" shall mean a substantially verbatim version of the printed text, in complete or abridged form, either with or without any or all of the illustrations that may appear in the printed text, that is transmitted or distributed electronically to consumers or to third-party vendors who are authorized to download and/or print and sell individual copies of the Work in complete or abridged form.

"Net Amount Received" shall mean gross revenues actually received by Publisher for sales of the Work or licenses for use of the Work, less any of the following charges applicable to any such transaction: (i) allowances or rebates taken by the customer or rebated by the Publisher; (ii) foreign agents' commissions paid by the Publisher and expenses incurred in obtaining, where applicable, the necessary foreign language permissions, and, where applicable, foreign taxes on payments received from foreign countries; (iii) Publisher's reproduction, translation, material, and other costs in connection with any such foreign use; and (iv) reasonable reserves or deductions for returns.

If the Work is combined with any other material in any publication or product, the "Net Amount Received" shall be pro-rated according to the proportion that the Work bears to the publication or product as a whole.

CHAPTER 8

How Your Manuscript Becomes a Book

Presuming you've signed a contract for a book, you'll spend the next 6 months to a year (depending upon the delivery date specified in the contract) busily completing your manuscript. Deadlines are not really suggestions. It is the wise writer who always hands in his manuscript on time, or perhaps a little early if possible. If there's going to be a problem or a delay in hitting your deadline, *talk to both your agent and your editor* about it *ahead of time.* Don't wait to the last minute; it makes everyone's job twice as hard.

As stated previously, the editor is answerable to others from the art department to marketing, production, and so forth, all of whom need to be kept informed about a book's progress so that they can juggle and adjust their schedules if necessary. If you leave your editor dangling by missing your deadline and not letting him know in advance, you make him look unprofessional and incompetent in front of his colleagues. This is not a good way to go about nurturing a long-lasting business relationship. Usually, and within reason, he'll give you the extra time you need if you ask for it.

Handing It In

Whether it's fiction or nonfiction, you've now reached the stage in which you're ready to hand in a completed manuscript.

There are accepted formats that editors and production departments like. It's important to act like a professional at all times, and that includes handing in a professionally finished document that looks good and reads well. So don't handwrite anything or use single spacing, except in cover letters, and check all the grammar and spelling before you decide it's ready.

Quite often the publishing house will give you a style sheet when you sign the contract, explaining how they want the manuscript to look. In general, they will ask for either a double-spaced hard copy (i.e., a version printed out on paper) or an electronic version (a version saved to a disk).

If you can, you should use a modern, widely used word processing program like Microsoft Word or WordPerfect. Send one copy of your manuscript to the editor and another to your agent.

Save your files on a 3½-inch disk in either MSDOS/Windows or Mac formats, clearly labeling on the disk the operating system (i.e., Mac, Windows) as well as the word processing program used. It's better to save the files as individual chapters rather than in one long file, and you should *always, always, always back up* your material. *And never send an original of anything.* Guaranteed, it will get lost by somebody.

After the finished manuscript is delivered, you wait until the editor reads it. This could take a month or more. Remember, editors don't have just your book to work on; they may have to oversee more than ten books at any one time in various stages of the publishing process.

In your cover letter, when you deliver your manuscript, politely ask the editor to add a brief note of explanation for any change he might make.

When he's ready, he'll either call or write you about suggestions and changes that in his view will improve and tighten the book. Although it's clearly your talent and hard work that will carry things through, writing a book is a collaborative effort. Your editor can offer an objective opinion. If you feel he "gets" your book, he'll likely provide a great sounding board; you'll do well to listen to him.

If your editor starts asking for changes that you have real problems with, *don't* argue with him at this stage. Be noncommittal; say something like, "That's interesting. I hadn't thought of it like that. Let me think about that awhile." Then call your agent and say how you really feel and what your concerns are about these changes.

Your agent is experienced in dealing with these kinds of situations. She'll have read the book herself, and will be able to discuss the situation with you and the editor, reducing the possibility of unprofessional behavior. She almost certainly has a good personal relationship with the editor and will try to take advantage of that.

This kind of situation is occurring with increased frequency these days—as the dust settles from the latest round of publishing

Print It Out

Print your document in the following format, unless you've been asked to do something different by your editor:

- Use a deskjet or laser printer, not an old-fashioned dot matrix. Whatever you use, make sure there is a new ribbon or new cartridge or new toner if necessary; the words on every page must be clean, clear, and easy to read.
- Use a readable size font (e.g., a 12-point Courier or Elite typewriter face).
- Print on good, clean, white 8-1/2-by-11-inch paper.
- Along the top of each page, print a running head and page count something like the following: Your Name/ Book CatchWord Page (#)
- Make sure there is a 1-inch margin all around the page.
- Use double spacing.
- Indent each paragraph; do not use spaces between paragraphs unless you are introducing a break in the action, in which case a one-line space is common.
- Use ragged right text margins.
- Paper should be loose leafed and in a box, not bound.

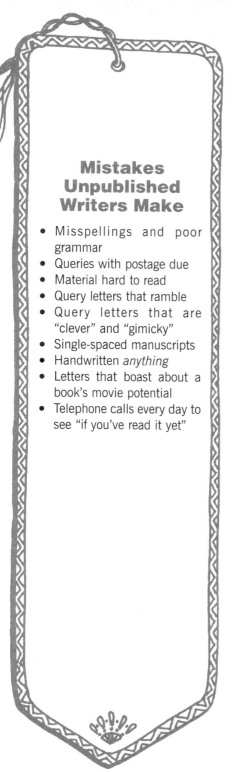

Mistakes Unpublished Writers Make

- Misspellings and poor grammar
- Queries with postage due
- Material hard to read
- Query letters that ramble
- Query letters that are "clever" and "gimicky"
- Single-spaced manuscripts
- Handwritten *anything*
- Letters that boast about a book's movie potential
- Telephone calls every day to see "if you've read it yet"

industry mergers and editors at various imprints find that they're out of a job, and the "musical chairs" of editors leaving one house for another takes place yet again. It can become particularly troubling when the original acquiring editor is no longer at the publishing house. One of "his" books is still going to be published, and a new editor steps forward to look after the "orphan."

Quite often, you'll get phone calls from people in the various departments involved with creating your book. Be kind and helpful to them, even if they ask a question that you've answered already, perhaps more than once. In other words, don't answer a question with an exasperated "I've already told my editor this." Gracefully tell the callers what they want to know. If someone wants something faxed to him or her, don't say, "My editor already has this." Fax it again. Cultivate a reputation for being easy to deal with. If necessary, develop a good-cop bad-cop act with your agent. If there's a problem that needs a tough stance, get your agent to take care of it.

If your book is nonfiction, it may well need illustrations of some sort. Getting permission for pictures and copyrighted material in general to use in your book is your responsibility, not that of your editor or agent.

Fill out any publicity forms you're asked to complete. The author questionnaire will ask about your background, influences, likes and dislikes and credentials, where you live, and your publishing history if any—anything that might help them promote you and your book and sell copies locally and nationally when the time comes.

When it's time for your editor to write catalog and flap copy for your book, ask if he'll fax you a copy. Editors and marketing people are pretty skilled at boiling down a book to a pithy, exciting nub—a sizzling one sentence that just "nails" the book. But you can still make a few suggestions for improvement if you're tactful. This is especially true if you've developed pamphlets, seminars, or brochures that have already done this job of selling you or your work to the public.

What Next?

After you return your manuscript, having made all the changes that were asked of you, about 6 weeks later, you'll get the copyedited manuscript. The book has moved from your editor's world to the world of the production editor or managing editor.

The managing editor is responsible for overseeing the rest of the stages of the manuscript's transformation into a book. The first of these stages is copyediting. The copy editor's main job is somewhat pedantic. She makes sure things are spelled correctly, grammar is correct, facts and figures are accurate, details are consistent within the book, and so forth.

Seeing the copyedited manuscript will come as a shock. The manuscript pages will be covered in indecipherable red pencil marks and bristle like a porcupine with yellow Post-Its asking some extremely nit-picking questions, particularly about names, dates, places, attributions, and correct spellings. If you're interested in learning more about this process and its signs and symbols, read *Words into Type* (Prentice Hall) or *Chicago Manual of Style* (Chicago); both are a production editor's bibles (if the publishing house hasn't developed its own style manual).

Answer all the questions directly on the copyedited manuscript as best you can, and make any changes that you feel have to be made. This is your last chance to make major alterations to your book.

Sometimes, copy editors can get overzealous. However, unlike when your editor line-edited your manuscript, if the copy editor's changes are more stylistic than technical, and you don't like them, consider writing *stet* in the margin opposite the change (*stet* is the term used to reinstate material marked as a deletion). It might be a good idea to discuss certain of these changes with your editor or the managing editor first. For example, a monologue at the end of a novel by an author of mine was written in dialect. As the editor, I saw the importance of leaving it the way it was written, but the copy editor took it upon herself to turn the whole speech into "proper" English and completely tore the guts out of the speech. So we had to laboriously fix the mistake.

Editors edit for three reasons: to improve clarity of meaning, promote brevity of language, and make the clumsy graceful. They also remove redundancies and smooth over inconsistencies in the text. They'll work on perfecting your book's structure, trimming

Assistant Editors

Your editor's assistant will be overseeing for the editor a lot of the day-to-day business of turning your manuscript into a book. It's likely that you will get to know each other quite well in the months your book is "in process."

Assistants help editors organize and are often more accessible than the editor, so you would be well advised to cultivate the friendship or at least the positive acquaintanceship of your editor's assistant and thank her occasionally for what she and your editor are doing for you. Not enough writers do this, and it's nice to know that your efforts are appreciated every once in awhile.

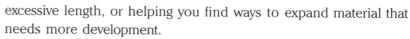

excessive length, or helping you find ways to expand material that needs more development.

It's worth considering that even if some poor decisions have been made in the editing of your book, it may well be because you have not explained yourself as clearly or explicitly as you could do. So rather than "stetting," perhaps you can find a way to say what you want to say in a way that overcomes the problem an editor thought was caused by clumsy or unfocused thought and language.

Pay attention to book titles and subtitles: Do they work together and give the essence of your book in a snappy, positive way? Is your title too long winded? Is your publisher's title too trite? Listen to what others have to say, but if your instincts tell you that your title is the way to go, don't compromise if you can help it. Make sure you know exactly who your core audience is, and then choose a title that will resonate with them.

Beyond Copyediting

Once you've been through the copyedited manuscript and returned it, you'll wait a couple of months before you are sent the page proofs, or galleys. There was a time when these were two different things, but these days the terms are becoming synonymous.

You will also, about this time, get to see some mock-up ideas of the cover of the book. Publishing houses will try to accommodate your ideas, but be prepared—they have the last word, even though it's your book. Nine times out of ten, with hindsight, they are usually right about how they've decided to market and present your book, but not always.

If you're not sure about your book cover, go to your local bookstores—you have made friends with the staff there already, haven't you?—and get their reaction to the cover art. Their reaction will certainly be more objective, and their point of sale perspectives may be very informative for you. Again, if you persist in having a problem, call your agent before you call anyone else to see if she can sort things out for you with the editor and the art department.

Again, go to a bookstore and study covers, taking note of the ones you thought most effective. Then send your editor a memo early on in the process detailing your thoughts on a cover design, mentioning the names of books that caught your attention, especially if they're successful and involve bold yet simple designs, colors, and motifs. Is there a particular illustration that you think is "just right" for your book cover? Mention it. But be prepared to be politely ignored.

Why do publishers insist on covers you don't like? That's a good question. They claim there is a certain science to what works and what doesn't on a book cover, a science they've learned in the "school of hard knocks" over the years of publishing books.

At the very least, you should be able to clearly read both the name of the book and the name of the author on the front cover. In many cases, disputes about the cover really involve disputes about how the book is going to be marketed, and again, that's an area the publishers feel they know better than anyone. In most cases they're right, but if you really know your core audience and what appeals to them, use every means available to make sure that the cover doesn't offend or put off people in this core group.

The book designer is responsible for the look of the pages and the inside of your book in general. Ask your editor's assistant to send you a couple of pages of page design when they're ready. Don't try to redesign them or feel you have to make suggestions. Few people do, and even fewer have a point that's worth making. However, if the design of the pages seems inappropriate and you really don't like it, call your agent and see if the two of you can get the editor to alter or remove the elements that are bothering you.

As well as being checked for accuracy by you, page proofs, which are quite literally a first pass print run of what the final pages of your book will look like, are reviewed by, among others, your editor, the managing editor, and the art director. There's usually at least one more pass, and sometimes two. During the second pass, all the changes are made and the "typos" corrected. The final

Think About This . . .

There's a philosophy that pervades publishing that the professionals in the industry know more about how to print and market a book than unpublished, or barely published, writers. Both writer and publisher should be prepared to listen to what the other has to say, because both, presumably, are experts when it comes to knowing the best way to exploit the commercial prospects of a particular book.

pass is checked by the proofreader just before the book is shipped to the printer.

The printer prepares your book, and this version of it is called the bluelines, which most people shorten to "blues." It's unlikely you'll see these.

About twice a year, sometimes three times, your publisher holds a large conference for the sales and editorial staffs. It's designed to let the sales reps know, through face-to-face contact with the book's editor, what that editor's coming book list looks like and which books are expected to perform well or exceptionally.

Sometimes your editor may ask for a photo, or even videotaped material by or about you that she can use to sell you and your book to the sales reps. If ever there was a time that your editor could be thought of as your "in house" agent, it's now.

Several months after you've turned in your manuscript and answered all the phone calls, and gotten to know the promotions person detailed to help push your book, read the galleys, and returned them, a padded manila envelope arrives in the mail.

You rip it open, and lo and behold, there's a pristine copy of your book, compliments of your editor. Set it prominently on a mantelpiece, and break out the champagne to celebrate. Your book—*this* book on your mantelpiece—will soon be for sale in the stores.

You thought your job was over? . . . only the writing part. The rest of it's really just beginning.

CHAPTER 9

Marketing and Publicity Swing into Action

S o, you've got one copy of your book. Where are the rest? Your agent will be sent twenty to thirty copies, depending on what's stipulated in the contract, and will send along your free copies, keeping hers for subrights submissions. Your editor will get a bunch delivered to her office, and so will the promotions, and marketing and sales people. The vast majority of copies will be in the warehouse. From there they will be shipped to bookstores across the country. But how many copies should each store get?

How Your Book Gets into the Stores

The bookstore buyers first learned about your book from the latest catalog put out by the publishing house. If your book is given a whole page rather than a half page, or two pages rather than one, the store's book buyer gets an immediate sense of how important, in commercial terms, the publisher considers the book.

Meanwhile, several times a year, sales reps for the company touch base with bookstore accounts. Some reps have large geographic areas, such as New England or the Pacific Northwest, and others have large volume clients such as Crown or Barnes & Noble. The larger publishing companies have full-time sales forces; the smaller houses use commissioned reps.

The problem with commissioned reps is that they often represent more than one publisher at a time and only earn money on the books they place. The inherent problems of the system are obvious. If the rep is selling your first novel at the same time he is promoting Tom Wolfe's new novel, guess who's going to get cheated?

There are two types of bookstores that book reps call on these days: the independent stores, and the chains retailers. The difference between them is obvious by their names: the chains, like Waldenbooks or Barnes and Noble, are made up of individual stores that buy merchandise from one buying unit at its corporate headquarters. The book buyers purchase books by category, and then assign different allotments to different stores, depending on past sales of like books. Books at independent stores are often chosen by the store's owner, based on his or her perception of what can sell in that particular store only.

Often, the comparative selecting process yields very different results, and there are pros and cons to each system. The chains usually stock many more titles, and tend to keep books on the shelves longer and stock more copies of individual titles. On the other hand, independent bookstores can always special order books they don't carry, and can act as a screening device, as they are forced to be more selective about the books they carry.

In either scenario, it is critical to get your book into both of these types of stores. The most important person at this point then becomes the sales rep, who calls on all of these accounts, and develops personal relationships with the buyers. A good sales rep will know how to "pitch" your book in such a way that he or she will get the buyer excited enough about your book to place an order. Ultimately, it is the rep's responsibility for taking the orders, and getting the books into the stores.

The Numbers Game

The meeting between buyer and rep in the case of independents usually takes place over coffee or lunch. Meetings with the chains can be somewhat distracted affairs held in a noisy office, with the phone ringing constantly and people bustling in and out.

The rep has about 2 minutes to present each of the new titles of the season and will often go through the catalog page by page for the buyer, discussing each book. If you'll recall, he learned about these books from the editor firsthand, at a sales conference not so long ago.

The rep basically discusses three things. Notice they're a version of the same items that you put in your book proposal when you first started shipping it around and that the editor then put to his editorial board and, ultimately, that are used in the sales conference. They are:

1. A description of the book
2. The publisher's plans to promote and sell the book
3. The author's credentials and past track record, including previous book sales

INFORMATION

Did You Know...

A *chain* usually refers to a store belonging to a nationwide bookstore like Barnes & Noble or Borders.

An *independent* is a store owned and operated by an individual store owner.

The question now becomes, How many copies of your book will the buyer take? Here we enter the Byzantine and rather cruel world of the "numbers game."

Bookstores track sales of inventory, that is, books, on their computers. A few years ago, a bookstore would buy, say, a month's worth of inventory; now, they take about 2 weeks' worth. If they need to restock, they'll get more copies from a book wholesaler. With less money tied up in inventory, the process becomes cheaper for the bookstore—at least that's the theory.

During their meeting, the rep and the book buyer may check the computer to look at sales for a particular author or for a particular book genre. Say, for instance, books about chess are not selling well at the moment. If your book is about chess, the number of copies the store takes will be affected by the perceived current popularity of that type of book.

Who knows better about what will sell? The publisher, who takes the gamble to create and promote the book because he believes it's a valuable addition to the genre or may even revitalize it? Or the guy who deals every day with the book-buying public?

One of the more insidious ways that bookstores make money these days is to charge publishers for premium display space in their stores. For several thousand dollars, publishers can buy prime placement, for a particular book, near the front of the store, say, to display their latest blockbusters. In many cases, bookstores also charge the publisher thousands of dollars to have their books included in the store's mail order or book club catalogs.

Again, the small guys are at an inherent disadvantage. The big publishers won't usually bother to spend this kind of money on a book unless the author is seen as a new Robert Parker or Joyce Carol Oates. You can ask all you want, but you have absolutely no control over what publishers decide to spend their money on, or if they will spend any money at all on a book, beyond publishing it.

Once all the advanced orders are in from the reps in the field, the publisher will have the warehouse ship the books to the stores. These days, publishers try to keep print runs low, perhaps three thousand to five thousand copies on average, and restock by going back to press more than once as demand comes in. Returns will also end up in the warehouse, so publishers may wait critical marketing periods if they think a book will return and then redistribute, rather than print more copies immediately.

This means, as happened to one of our agency clients, that, for example, a nonfiction book about vampires that was selling extremely well and should have been in the stores for Halloween, wasn't available to the public during a critical sales period because the publisher waited too long to go back to press. The author, meanwhile, was on an exhausting several-city promotional tour paid for by the publisher and found herself confounded at every turn by a dearth of books at precisely the time when the book was getting maximum public exposure and should have been at its most plentiful. Then the publisher had the gall to complain that the book didn't sell quite as well as they had hoped.

Publishing can often be a frustrating business.

What Your Publisher Will Do

What will your publisher do once your book is published and in the stores? The short answer is, "Not much." However, they will go where you lead.

"But they have publicity departments," I hear you cry. Yes, though they won't spend much time on your book unless it's a lead title. How can you tell if your book is one of the favored siblings? Find out how much space, compared to other titles, your book got in the sales catalog, and you'll have your answer.

Bear in mind that the publicity department is often small and overworked. They have limited and finite resources, and those resources are generally earmarked for the books that a committee (yes, another one!) has determined will benefit the company most.

The publicity department will get out copies of your book to reviewers and others who can help in the promotion of the book. They'll also work on getting you local signings and maybe limited tours. They'll also make follow-up calls and, if appropriate, arrange interviews.

INFORMATION

Did You Know...

A book's *placement* in a store refers to where in the store you can find it. Some stores charge publishers for preferred placement for their books.

Make a point of asking what the company's publicity and marketing plans for your book will be. Ask specifically if they intend to send you on a book tour. It's not likely, but you should be prepared in case they say yes. Find out who's going to pay for it, at least in terms of hotel and traveling expenses, and make sure it's them. If you do go on tour, make a space in your schedule to accommodate your publisher's plans. Again, if you have any problems, contact your agent.

Publishers won't advertise your book. Why? Because it's expensive and doesn't achieve anything. Advertisements for books work in only two ways: They boast of a book's success in prizes and sales, essentially telling its audience, "Don't miss out on this hot property everyone else has read!" And they tell the eager fans of famous authors that the author's next book is imminent. Clancy fans or King fans, for example, eagerly await the next novel, and the advertisements tell them it's on the way.

The publicity department will promote your book for about 3 months, before moving on to another author. If you ask nicely, they may give you a copy of their marketing plan and a copy of the press kit they used for the book. If you have a problem getting hold of these, ask your editor or your agent to get them for you. No marketing plan? There's an answer for you right there.

But don't get mad or fed up; you're experiencing the norm. The positive side of all this is that now you can take your own fate in your hands and show the so-called experts exactly how it should be done. If you're right, they'll applaud you and get the weight of the company behind you again. If you're wrong, well, that's a lesson or two learned, isn't it?

Yes, indeed, publishing can be a pretty brutal business, yet it is possible to load the dice more in your favor and get your publisher to work harder selling your book than he originally intended.

What You Can Do to Help Yourself

The simple answer to selling books is publicity—as much as you can get for yourself and your book. Start with local publicity, and then expand to regional and, finally, national.

How many people live in your town, your county, your state? What organizations are interested in your book's subject matter? How many members do they have?

If you can sell ten thousand copies regionally, you're already beating the odds big time and getting the system to work for you. Remember, even though all ten thousand were sold in the Barnes & Noble stores in and around your town in the north, a Barnes & Noble in Florida or Texas will consult the computer and see total figures nationwide. If a book looks like it's moving, they may well want to get on the bandwagon and provide a hot property for their customers—with some additional encouragement. How do you go about encouraging them, short of making them an offer "they can't refuse"? Read on.

Do You Have Famous Friends or Acquaintances Who'll Help Out?

It's almost never too soon to start working on publicity for your book—with this proviso: If you get people excited about the book before it's available, you will lose the momentum you began and will have to work twice as hard to get it back later on. Timing in publicity and public relations is always critical.

Once your manuscript is completed and handed in, draw up two lists. The first list should be of half a dozen people whom you can approach to ask for an endorsement once they've read the book. They should be both well known and relevant to your endeavors. The second list should be a wish list of famous people (obviously, they must all still be alive and approachable) whom your agent and/or editor might be able to help you reach. Both lists share the same objective: to get a quote. Your choices should be writers or experts in the field you've chosen to write about whose work you genuinely admire. With the backing of a publishing contract in particular, many people will say, "Send me something when it's ready."

It's your job to ask and their job to say yes or no. But it's business, so don't take rejection personally. Many authors have their own deadlines to meet, and many celebrities are simply burned out from the process of being asked for quotes.

The best letter to request an endorsement should be short and to the point and from someone who can write and who is clearly a fan. Include a brief synopsis of your book and a short bio. If you write from the heart, it will be hard to resist.

If you get a yes, send out the manuscript or galley promptly with a cover letter that says thank you. If you haven't heard anything after a month, politely get in touch by phone (presumably the number will be on the person's letterhead from when they responded to you) and ask whether the person received your manuscript. Check in once a month, no more. Be persistent and polite until you either get your response or you realize they're too busy to look at your book after all. Then drop it and move on to someone else.

If you're successful early enough in the publishing process, it's possible for your editor to get the art department to put the quote on the front cover of the book. Anything that will make you and your book stand out, that you're comfortable doing, is worth trying.

Publicity and Sales Hints and Tips

Some of what I'm going to discuss next should be going on in concert with your publisher's efforts to promote and sell your book. Keep in touch with your publisher's publicity department. When they ease back, start to pick up the slack, continuing the book's marketing momentum.

One of the first elements that I suggested you emphasize when writing your proposal was your ability to sell copies yourself. From the moment the editor read your proposal, and on down the line, the question everyone asked was, Does this author have a platform? A great deal of importance was placed on your claims to be able to promote your book. Now it's time to put your money where your mouth was.

Bear in mind that promoting a novel and promoting nonfiction are two different things. In general, promoting a novel is much tougher; you're focused much more specifically on who *you* are rather than what the novel is about, unless it won an award or prize. Few of the people you'll deal with will have the time to read it; conversations will be about what you went through to write the book, what inspired the story, and so forth.

With nonfiction you have an easier time of promoting both yourself and your subject. Sad but true, the book's success is far less tied to how well it's written.

In general, first, figure out your goal. It's not, as you might think, to sell as many copies as you can; that goal is too vague. You need something more concrete. Your plan should be to get as much positive publicity for yourself and your book as you can.

There are concrete steps you can take to achieve this goal. List the resources you can approach. Here are some basic ideas:

- Use your imagination. Think commercially; think practically.
- Talk to friends, friends of friends, and relatives in the PR or promotional fields who can give you advice or contacts.
- Approach newspapers, newsletters, and magazines who might be interested in knowing about your book's publication and for whom you can perhaps write articles.
- Buy advertisements in the newsletters of appropriate groups to let the membership know about your book.
- Think of places that might review your book.
- Come up with talks you can give in public or seminars you can be invited to as a guest speaker, at which you can promote yourself and your book
- Create a variety of press releases, fliers, and postcards that can be sent to newspapers, magazines, and specific groups interested in your book's topic or in knowing you have a new book out.
- Arrange author signings in bookstores, either organized or impromptu (i.e., wander into a bookstore, quietly make sure they're carrying your book, then introduce yourself to the manager and offer to sign copies if he would like you to).

Three Tips for Promoting Your Own Book

1. Don't promote your book ad hoc. Get a plan.

2. Be persistent but don't badger people. You want them on your side, not irritated at you.

3. Start publicity efforts early, but not too early. Timing is critical. Make sure you can follow through if you "strike gold."

- Give media interviews, especially radio and TV—as many as you can. People who listen to the radio often read books. And radio interviews can be done over the phone from home, so they're a relatively cheap way of reaching a wide audience.
- Join an organization such as Sisters in Crime or Romance Writers of America and become a part of the joint advertisements they put out at industry events such as Book Expo (formerly known as the ABA), Bouchercon for crime writers, or World Fantasy.
- Find a restaurant that's just about to open and ask if you can hold a book publishing party there. They'll often give you a special discounted rate, if they charge you at all. Invite as many "movers and shakers" as you can think of who might help promote and sell your book for you.
- Create a Web page and use the Internet to advertise and sell your book.

Let me repeat myself: Use your imagination. Make a point of studying how others have promoted their books.

If you're interested in radio and TV, go to the library and check out *Bacon's Media*, which lists radio stations across the country. (For a site that lists radio stations with Web pages, go to *http://www.ccnet.com/~suntzu/talk.htm.*) You should also check out *Radio-TV Interview Report* magazine, which goes out to about four thousand radio and television producers. *Radio-TV Interview Report* is published by Bradley Communications, 135 East Plumstead Avenue, Lansdowne, PA 19050-8206 800-989-1400 or 610-259-1070, ext. 408. If you ask, they might send you a free issue. It's worth looking at to see what other talk show guests are doing.

Should I Hire a Publicist?

Before you get a publicist, make sure you can take advantage of anything she or he puts in front of you. A good publicist is expensive; a bad or mediocre one probably can't do much more than you can do for yourself.

A great deal of publicity and promotion involves knocking on doors and getting them politely slammed in your face. What you get with a good publicist is her rolodex of sources, whom she knows personally and whom she can call up and often talk into giving you an interview. That means she will be picky about each book and author she takes on, because her credibility is riding on your ability to come across with "the goods" for her contact.

If you're going to do interviews, you have to learn how to get your point across quickly. Make sure that you know what it is about your book that's going to whet people's appetites to hear more. You need to get them to go out and pick up a copy of your book the next time they're in their local bookstores.

If you can take an evening class in media communications, do so. Media trainers are available, but they're expensive, although worth considering if you can find a good one. They can help you develop the ability to think fast on your feet.

Before you start doing interviews, jot down on a small index card what you want to get across. Come up with at least four major points of conversation. Always, if you're able, turn a question into something that will allow you to promote your book. ("Funny you should ask me about circuses, Jay. In my book, *Intelligent Supermice*, there's a story about a mouse who meets an elephant outside a circus big tent . . .")

Acquire a small library of witty stories and practice using them. Even if your topic is deadly serious, you can be a fun, energized guest.

If you can accomplish all this, then you'll help a potential publicist by giving him someone that TV and radio talk show hosts and their producers will want to have on their shows, regardless of the book you've written.

Think About This . . .

The organization Sisters in Crime—(SinC)—which includes Brothers in Crime, has an excellent pamphlet they put out about self-promotion. Contact:
Beth Wasson
Executive Secretary
Sisters in Crime
P.O. Box 442124
Lawrence, KS 66044-8933
(www.sinc-ic.org).

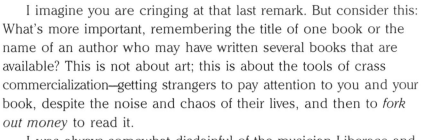

I imagine you are cringing at that last remark. But consider this: What's more important, remembering the title of one book or the name of an author who may have written several books that are available? This is not about art; this is about the tools of crass commercialization—getting strangers to pay attention to you and your book, despite the noise and chaos of their lives, and then to *fork out money* to read it.

I was always somewhat disdainful of the musician Liberace and his schmaltzy music, until I learned it was he who originated the phrase, "I'm doing what I love to do, and when people criticize me, I cry all the way to the bank!" You can't argue much with that.

No Fidgeting: What to Do and Not to Do on Local and National TV

Here's the horrible truth again, in case I haven't hit you over the head with it hard enough already: On TV in particular, nobody cares that you've written a book. I don't watch Arthur Schlesinger or John Le Carré to learn much about their latest books. I watch the interview because they are interesting *thinkers* who have written about their area of expertise and are witty raconteurs. They give a good *show*.

Talking-head programs often terrify TV producers because they don't provide much visual stimulation to the viewer. Take Jay Leno on the *Tonight* show. It's his guests you're interested in seeing. What will Robin Williams do next? What interesting, witty anecdote has Michael Caine got to spin for us? And along the way, they'll mention their new movies.

How do you get yourself on TV? Start locally and convince producers that you've got something interesting to say and that you'll make for an entertaining guest.

To achieve this you need to take lessons, listen to what experts say about your appearance, practice being interviewed, and study how to use the medium. Get a friend to videotape you and be pre-pared for a shock.

Study and research what works on camera and what doesn't. You need to learn how to sit and not fidget, how to dress, and how to make the camera like you, because the camera, you'll find, can be a pretty cruel instrument. What do your clothes say about you? What image do you want to present? Make sure your image doesn't detract from your ability to talk seriously about the topic you've been asked to discuss.

In much the same way that you got yourself an agent and a book deal, you need to sell yourself to TV producers when you contact them. Send them a photo to demonstrate how photogenic you are, plus a list of topics that they could base shows on and a suggested list of thought-provoking questions they might want to talk with you about. Is there something in the news, some current event, that you can tie into? Can you take questions from the audi-ence or your interviewer that test your knowledge of your subject in an entertaining way?

Oh, and include a copy of your book. But don't expect anyone (particularly the celebrity interviewer whose show you're trying to get on) other than maybe a research assistant to actually read it.

Use every opportunity to promote and sell your book, from on-air displays, if that's possible, to local bookstore signings (set up ahead of time for when you fly into a new town to give your interview). Make sure the bookstores know you're going to be a "celebrity" on local or regional or national TV. Milk it; sell books.

Radio Can Help

For a resource list of radio sta-tions with Web pages, visit *http://www.ccnet.com/~suntz u75/talk.htm*.

Or write *Radio-TV Interview Report,* Bradley Communica-tions, 135 East Plumstead Avenue, Lansdowne, PA 19050-8206 (800)-989-1400 or 610-259-1070, ext. 408.

CHAPTER 10

Subrights
and Royalties

As we saw in the chapter about contracts, selling a book creates a whole body of rights to the work, in addition to the publisher's right to print and publish it. Publishers always want as much as they can get, and they try hard to make you share as many rights as possible.

The more rights you license away, the less control you have over your work and the more money you should be paid as a result. Always be explicit about the rights that you're licensing. The more rights you keep for yourself, the more money you can potentially make through resale of a successful piece. The question is: Can I make more money keeping rights and selling them myself, or should I let a publisher take a share and have them sell the rights?

Book scouts, based mainly in New York, work on retainer for various foreign publishers (usually one per country) and keep an eye on new books published in the United States that might be of interest to their clients. It's a way for a foreign publisher to get an edge on its competitors and snag big books just as the buzz is starting. Many foreign publishers are already aware of big books or interesting books before they've even hit the bookshelves.

If a book's subrights are licensed to a publisher, they will be handled and sold by the subrights department. The subrights director will use subagents in various foreign countries, or she may travel to book fairs to meet international publishers—in places such as Frankfurt, Germany; Milan, Italy; and London, England—in an effort to interest them in her company's books.

If the rights are handled by the agent, she will also handle them through her subagents, in much the same way as the publisher's subrights department. In either case, the agents in the various foreign countries are considered the experts on the publishing industry in their locations. They know their markets as well as the agents in the United States know the North American market. If the U.S. agent doesn't attend one of the various international book fairs, one or other of her subagents almost certainly will on her behalf.

The agent will usually charge 20 percent for handling subrights if another agent is involved. The commission is generally split 50/50 between the agents.

I'm going to use the terms *owe* and *debt* very loosely in this chapter. In reality, if a book doesn't sell, the publisher is out of pocket the money advanced you, so you don't really *owe* anything in terms of having to pay any actual money back. The only way a publisher can recoup an advance against expected royalties paid to you is to sell books and/or licenses they've acquired to reprint the book in various formats and venues. Any money earned by you and divided between you and the publisher will go toward paying off the outstanding royalty advance *debt* that needs to be earned out or recouped before you start earning royalties.

If, for example, you were advanced $100,000, and the paperback rights were sold for $200,000, you'd think you'd see some of that money. But you'd be wrong. Given a 50/50 split between you and the publisher (the norm, in the case of a paperback sale), you'd get $100,000 and $100,000 will go to the publisher. However, because you need to earn out your royalty advance of $100,000 before you see any money, your share of the paperback deal would go toward paying off your royalty advance.

Consequently, of the $200,000 earned in the paperback deal, you would not see one cent. Any royalties earned by the book after this sale, however, you would receive. They would be detailed in your twice yearly royalty statement and accompanied by a check.

You can begin to see why your agent wants to retain and sell as many of these rights as possible for you. If he sells them, they generate an income for you that is not tied to your *debt* to the publisher.

Types of Rights

There are several types of rights that broadly fall into the following categories.

First Serial and Second Serial

Serial rights to publish excerpts from a book are offered to magazines and newspapers. *North America* is often added to specify a geographic limitation. When the excerpt comes from a book that has yet to be published, it is known as first serial. This is often split 90/10 in favor of the author; once the book has been published, the right to publish an excerpt is called second serial. This is usually split 50/50.

North American Rights

North American rights allow publication of a book in North America only. This includes the United States, Canada, and U.S. territories and dependencies.

World English Language

World English language rights allow publication of a book anywhere in the world where there is an English language market, such as the United Kingdom, Australia, and South Africa.

Translation and Foreign Rights

Some people rather clumsily refer to foreign rights when they mean translation. Foreign can include English language rights in other countries, so it is best to be specific. You can license world English language and retain translation but still not have all the foreign rights. Translation rights are the exclusive right to publish the book, in translation, into a country's native tongue (e.g., German rights published in German in Germany, French rights published in French in France).

Open Market

The open market is the *nonexclusive* right of a publisher to sell *its* version of a book in a foreign market regardless of whether or not publishers in that country have bought the right to publish their own version. So, for example, in Holland it may be possible to buy the Dutch version of Stephen King's *Bag of Bones* in translation (an *exclusive* right), as well as copies of the American edition and the British edition, both of which are shipped in, in small numbers, because the publishers have the right to sell their version of the book on the open market on a *nonexclusive* basis. Open market books are usually only shipped into a foreign market for big authors like Stephen King. They're aimed at an American audience stationed abroad (such as business men and women or serving members of the military) who would be interested in buying a copy.

World Rights

World rights allow the publisher to sell all foreign and translation rights to a book on behalf of an author and the company. There is an agreed-upon split, usually 80/20 or 75/25, in favor of the author.

Reprint Rights: Paperback

These rights are usually split 50/50. They relate mainly to hardcover sales, and publishers almost always retain them. Although publishing has been heading away from selling books in what was called horizontal publishing, or hardcover by one company and paperback by another, in favor of vertical publishing, in which the *same company* buys the right to publish both hardcover and paperback rights, it is still possible for successful small presses and mid-level publishing houses to have a hit hardcover and then sell the paperback. Walker's surprise hit *Longitude* by Dava Sobel, for example, was bought in paperback by Penguin USA.

Sometimes a house that has the license to publish a reprint in paperback decides to sell that right to another house to help recoup some of the money they have advanced on the book.

Book Clubs

The split here is usually 50/50. A book club has a specific consumer base and interest and will guarantee to sell a minimum number of copies because of its member base. The book may be acquired as a main selection or an alternate selection, depending on how successful it is seen to be. When club members join the book club, they guarantee to buy a set number of books over the course of their memberships, so the club, which may print up special club editions of the book and sell it at a special club discount, has a relatively known number of copies it will likely sell.

Other Book Publication

Other book publication rights include large-type editions, mail order, premium, and other special editions. These rights are usually split 50/50.

INFORMATION

Did You Know...

A book that's *in print* is still available from the publisher. A book that's *out of print* is no longer available from the publisher. The author can get his or her rights back from the publisher.

Performance or Dramatic Rights

Performance or dramatic rights include television, radio, theatrical (either dramatic and/or musical), motion picture, video rights and the like. Although it's not likely that anything more than an option will ever be made on your book, these rights are so potentially lucrative that authors should rarely give up any of them or even share them with a publisher, unless the publisher is willing to pay substantially for its share. The split then should be 90/10 in favor of the author, and the author's Hollywood agent usually handles the deal. Generally, "substantial" means in the very high six figures for a new writer and at least seven figures for a more established author.

Audio Recordings

Audio rights should be a part of dramatic, but they are treated separately these days. Audio rights can be split up into dramatized readings and nondramatic (i.e., one person reading the book's text into a microphone), and abridged (i.e., a condensed version) and unabridged (the whole book on tape). The most common version of an audio book will be nondramatic, abridged, but again, you should be specific about what you're licensing.

Commercial and Merchandising

Commercial and merchandising rights have to do with toys, games, calendars, T-shirts, greeting cards, and the like, based on characters and situations in a book. Again, they can be terrifically lucrative, so retain them for yourself unless the publisher is willing to pay handsomely to share in them.

Electronic Rights

I've left electronic rights until last because they are the most troublesome to resolve these days. This is a new frontier, and publishers and agents have been dueling over who should retain control of these rights and how, exactly, these rights should be defined. In general, there are two types: verbatim and adaptation.

Most agents and editors agree it's fair that publishers should have the right to reproduce electronically a verbatim version of the book they published. Such verbatim rights should cover text versions on the Internet, or on a CD-ROM or DVD—in effect, any version in any format that could be a substitute for the printed book itself.

Adaptation rights are something else. Publishers, particularly when they are part of a large media conglomerate that can create and market audio and electronic media as well as books, feel they have at the very least a right of first refusal to exploit the book electronically. For example, an adaptation could be a game based on a book or its characters. Whether or not a CD-ROM that includes extra film and illustrations and sound created especially for the electronic version, as well as the complete text of the book, could be considered verbatim or adaptation is a debatable question. In fact, there is some overlap between these two definitions, and that causes confusion and problems.

There is not as yet a standard license definition for electronic rights, and many agents and publishers are sidestepping the issue. Companies such as Random House are now claiming that not getting a share or at least first refusal on the resale of these rights can be a deal breaker in contract negotiations.

In many cases, a way out is to grant the publisher the right to do something with the property for a fixed period, say, 18 months. If nothing happens within that time, the author has the right to write to the publisher and demand back his electronic rights; the company may then hand them over or ask that they be given a further 6 months after receiving the letter to do something with the electronic rights before giving them up.

This solution is a clumsy but workable compromise in many contentious rights situations in which a publisher insists on getting a piece of a right that it'll probably never do anything with. A publisher retaining a share of such rights can put a crimp in an agent's efforts to sell the rights on his client's behalf.

INFORMATION

Did You Know...

A *list* is a publishing house's term for the books it is currently publishing or intending to publish. Backlists are lists of books already published. Frontlists are a list of books about to be published or currently published.

Royalty Checks and Statements

Royalty statements are sent out twice a year. While a contract may say that the statements will come in, say, July and December, the reality is that you probably won't see your copy until about 2 months after these dates. That's because it can take that long for the warehouse to complete its inventories and the royalty department to churn out statements for every author published by the publishing house. If the company owes you money, a check will accompany the statement; it is first sent to your agent. The agent takes her 15 percent and then forwards the rest to you.

Royalty statements are stunningly complicated things to read and vary greatly in form from publisher to publisher. Sometimes they contain accumulative figures of books sold; sometimes they only include figures for that 6-month period. The statements usually take into account sales to bookstores, retailers, wholesalers, book clubs, foreign rights sales (if applicable), discount premium sales, and so on.

The most inventive thing on the statement is a little column called Reserve Against Returns. This is one of the most insidious accounting tricks publishers pull. Here's how it works:

Publishing is perhaps the only retail industry that allows its customers to return the product, if they decide they don't want it or can't sell it, and exchange it for new and different items. What this practice means is that when your publisher sells, say, thirty thousand copies of your book, you can't be sure whether bookstores are going to hang on to them or send some of them back and ask for a refund. You could end up selling through only fifteen thousand to twenty thousand copies. So, for example, even though your July royalty statement says you've sold thirty thousand copies, the publisher won't pay you royalties on all those copies sold until the end of the forthcoming December period, or perhaps even the following July. Exactly when is up to them. They'll wait for the returns. And while they do, they hold back a certain percentage of the total money owed you, say, 1/3 (the actual amount is mentioned in your contract), as a reserve against returns, until they're certain of the actual sales.

The policy was devised several decades ago as mass market paperback books started to become big business to overcome booksellers' wariness about taking books by authors with whom they were unfamiliar. However, the practice of holding a reserve against returns is now applied to all authors, regardless of their fame or track record.

Today, it isn't uncommon for publishers to suffer returns of 50 percent or more. Paperback books return at a higher rate than hardcovers, as a rule.

As recessionary times gripped the industry, it dawned on bookstore owners and accountants that this was a system worth manipulating for their own ends. As times became financially trying, stores ordered books that were essentially on credit, sold a few copies, and then returned the rest, buying new titles with credits on books that didn't move quickly enough. After a while, it was possible for bookstores to order just enough and sell just enough that they didn't have to pay the publishing companies hardly anything in cold, hard cash. It all started to become a paper transaction. The publishing companies, of course, started to hemorrhage real money, and this contributed to the orgy of consolidations and mergers and the demise of small and mid-level publishing houses that we've witnessed in the past few years.

Needless to say, authors and agents get incensed about having their legitimate earnings "hijacked" this way; as a result, some royalty statements are deliberately designed to obfuscate exactly how many copies have been sold in any 6-month period.

In recessionary times in particular, in much the same way that booksellers manipulate publishers' bottom lines, publishers manipulate authors' royalties. If publishers need some ready cash, guess one of the places they go to get it? That's right, the "reserve against returns fund," which can be used to help relieve a liquidity problem or earn some extra interest for the company before the money has to be handed over.

At the stroke of a pen, by increasing the percentage of the reserve against returns from, say, 1/3 to 1/2, a publisher can find extra cash to pay a printer, distributor, or other creditor—at the author's expense.

Think About This . . .

The most obvious solution is for publishers to start selling books on a nonreturnable basis, print fewer copies, and, equally important, work out a system whereby both stores and authors make some sort of money on books that are remaindered. Will they do it? Will bookstores allow them to do it? Will authors stand for a solution that doesn't specifically address their needs and wants? Watch this space as "on demand" printing and electronic books enter the arena . . .

Remainders

On average, about 2 or more years after a book is published, depending on the sales rate, the author one day receives in the mail a letter from the publisher announcing that sales of his or her book have slowed to such a degree that they intend to "remainder" it prior to putting it "out of print."

If you want to purchase copies at a deeply discounted price, now's your chance to do so. Contact your editor, or the person named in the letter, and include a check.

If you sell books at seminars you run, or other events, it's probably worth your while to purchase as many copies as you can comfortably afford. You can sell them at a higher price to your audiences and end up making money.

Once all the returns have come back and the decision has been made by the publisher to remainder your book, the publisher will sell what it doesn't buy to a wholesaler who specializes in taking books off a publisher's hands on a "ten cents on the dollar" principle (the actual figure will vary, of course). He then sells them "job lot" for next to nothing back to the bookstore, who shovels them into large bins at the back of the store.

What happens next is torment for the author. His book sells like hotcakes at a dollar a time. And, as a final insult, he receives little or no royalty from the sales.

These factors form the nub of crucial publishing bottom-line questions that no one has yet managed to solve for all the parties concerned. How they are solved will determine the size, shape, and potency of twenty-first century publishing.

CHAPTER 11

Alternative Ways of Getting "Your Stuff" Out There

I f all else fails, there's always either self-publishing or electronic publishing. Until a few years ago, self-publishing was looked down upon by "legitimate" publishing. It was called Vanity Press, and the general philosophy was that if you had to pay to get your book published, it probably wasn't worth publishing in the first place.

However, recent self-published successes picked up later by major publishing houses, such as *The Celestine Prophecy, Mutant Message Down Under*, and *The Christmas Box* have made publishers look again at what individuals with determination, a focused message, and a demonstrable audience have to say. Numbers of books sold speak for themselves, and big publishers listen if the author's work speaks a loud enough commercial message.

Nontraditional Publishing

Nontraditional publishing breaks down into Vanity Press, self-published books, and electronic publishing, some of which is self-published, and some of which isn't, especially if it's issued on a CD-ROM, DVD, or floppy disk by a third party.

If you decide to self-publish, you should consider two things: It's expensive and it's a business project and should treated as such.

The big problem with book publishing, whether you're a conglomerate, a small press, or a self-publisher, is distribution. The professionals solved that problem ages ago, although they continually revisit it in an effort to refine and improve their distribution. As a beginner in the field, it is the number one obstacle to overcome. As I've said many times elsewhere, book publishing is about numbers of books sold. Nowhere will you be more starkly confronted with that fact than when you undertake to write, print, publish, and distribute your own book.

Successful self-publishers are entrepreneurs who look upon the creation and sale of their books as a business that needs their time and devotion. Actually, writing the book may be the smallest part of the process, so if that's what really interests you, self-publishing is probably not a good route to follow. To self-publish well, you need to have enough money to pay someone else to manage and market your book for you on a professional basis or to enjoy doing masses of that work yourself. You also need to figure out exactly who your target audience for the book is and aggressively market to them.

Self-published authors use a variety of techniques for distributing their books: the Internet, direct mail, specialty stores, conferences, seminars, advertisements in trade magazines and newsletters, and the like. Bookstores often are low on the list. Authors have been known to rack up significant sales figures by selling books out of the trunk of their cars, for example, after giving a lecture.

All sales should be accounted for and documented. One day, if you're successful, one of the major companies may well make you an offer, and you'll need to document your sales figures so that you can ask for that seven-figure advance!

The advantages of self-publishing, in whatever form you decide, are that you can control exactly what goes into your book and how it will look. These are not small things, as we've seen; authors fight with publishers about such things all the time.

From a traditional publishing perspective, one of the best reasons to self-publish is to have written material to sell at the end of seminars and lectures that you give routinely. You can also get out the product much faster than a traditional house, and you can make money faster because you're taking all the profit, once your expenses are taken care of.

The economics of self-publishing are interesting. The following math is obviously very generic, but it will give you some idea of what your income and expenses could be.

You have to figure that publishing three thousand copies of a 200-to 250-page hardcover book will cost about $30,000. The more copies you print, the cheaper things become, proportionally. However, you will also have to figure out the cost of how many you can store and for how long.

If you sell three thousand books at $10 per book, you've made back your initial costs, and everything after that is gravy. And in the world of publishing, three thousand hardcover copies sold is a reasonable number. If you sell ten thousand books . . . well, you do the math. Again, ten thousand copies of a book sold is a modest but respectable number.

Think About This . . .

If you're interested in self-publishing, read *The Publish-It-Yourself Handbook* by Bill Henderson,(Pushcart Press and W. W. Norton) the owner and publisher of the prestigious Pushcart Press.

Also read *How to Publish, Promote, and Sell Your Own Book* by Robert Lawrence Holt (St Martin's Press).

On the other hand, if a mainstream publisher publishes this book, and you earn on average, say, $3 per book, to earn back a $30,000 royalty advance, you will have to sell at least ten thousand books, or more than three times as many as if you published it yourself.

If a publishing company makes you an offer for this book based on successful sales, you know how much you will be advanced because you know and can substantiate how many copies you've sold and how much money you've made from those sales.

If a book looks and reads like it has been professionally produced, most people won't turn to the spine and say, "John Doe Press? Never heard of them. Are they an imprint of Random House?" The exception will probably be reviewers, who are inundated with books and are usually forced to be highly selective about what they review, even among the "legitimate" books they're sent.

However, if you want to catch the attention of an agent with your next book, a self-published book that sold five thousand to ten thousand copies or more is impressive and will almost certainly get you noticed, and probably picked up.

The Difference Between Vanity Press and Self-Publishing

Many "Publish Your Book" ads look alike. Yet some are for subsidy publishers or Vanity Presses, and others are for printing companies that help authors self-publish their work. How do you tell the difference?

A commercial publisher purchases manuscripts from authors and handles the cost of producing those manuscripts: cover and interior design, typesetting, printing, marketing, distribution, and so forth. The author is not expected to pay any of these costs. The books are owned by the publisher and remain in the publisher's possession until sold; the author receives a portion of sales in the form of royalties.

A subsidy publisher or Vanity Press does not purchase manuscripts; instead, it asks authors to pay for the cost of publication. With the exception of certain types of publishers, such as university or scholarly presses, any publisher that requests a fee from the author is a subsidy publisher.

Self-Publishing: What to Know Beforehand

Before signing a contract make sure you know the following:

1. Who owns the book? Subsidy houses not only charge for design, printing, and distribution services but also claim various rights to your book. Printers and book producers charge only for their services. All rights to your book remain with you.

2. If you are told you receive "royalties," you're dealing with a subsidy house. Subsidy publishers pay authors a standard royalty of around 10 to 15 percent. When you self-publish, you receive all sales proceeds.

3. A subsidy publisher will retain all books except for a few "author copies." A printer or book producer will give you the option of storing the books yourself or paying for warehousing. In either case, the books belong to you.

4. With subsidy publishers, the author's input usually ends with the delivery of the manuscript. A book producer will offer you a menu of services; you pay only for those you need. You should be able to review and approve any suggested designs, layouts, fonts, and so forth.

5. If you self-publish, sending out review copies is entirely your responsibility, but since the books already belong to you, you won't pay anything "extra" for those copies.

6. Subsidy publishing and self-publishing both require that you market the book. Subsidy publishers may include "marketing" as one of the services you're paying for but generally do little beyond placing a small ad in a major newspaper. A key question to ask yourself is whether the benefits of a marketing campaign outweigh the costs of self-publishing.

Here's the key: As with commercial publishers, the books are owned by the publisher and remain in the publisher's possession; authors receive royalties.

A self-publisher is an author who pays a printer to help professionally design, print, and distribute his or her book. The author often invents and registers a publishing "imprint."

This part is important: Self-published books are the property of the author and usually remain in the author's possession; all sales proceeds belong to the author.

The printer or "book producer" is a company that works with self-publishing authors to produce professional-quality books. Some printers may call themselves "publishers," but they're not publishers in the traditional sense of the word. Instead, they offer a range of book production services (such as design, typesetting, and printing); they may also offer marketing, distribution, warehousing, and fulfillment services such as order processing, book shipping, and customer invoicing.

If you decide to go this route with your book, make sure you know what services you're paying for.

Book Packagers and Work for Hire

We've talked about thinking up an idea for a book and then enticing an agent and then a publisher to publish your book. There are, however, other ways to get published.

There exists in the world of books a strange hybrid creature that is neither agent nor publisher but has some of the qualities of both. These are called *book packagers* or producers, and they have a professional organization called the American Book Producers Association (ABPA).

Packagers are entrepreneurs who think up ideas for books and hire writers to work on a "for hire" basis. This usually entails a flat fee for the work, with no share of royalties once the book is published. They then sell the finished product to a publisher.

Many projects that packagers develop are design intensive. Kids' books with merchandising attached to the book might be an example, or a line of books connected to a single entity such as the Smithsonian Museum in Washington, D.C.

Many packagers are well versed in the production and technical sides of publishing and deliver to the publisher books the publisher could not afford to do under normal circumstances. The books are almost always much too time intensive for a publishing house staff to bother with.

A packager might, for example, approach an institution like the Smithsonian, enter into a license agreement to use their imprimatur, and then craft a book proposal based on the idea of, say, the Smithsonian Twenty-First Century Encyclopedia.

Having got the go-ahead, they will assemble a panel of experts, give each one a series of articles to write for the book, and then find a freelance writer/editor who will be able to oversee the editorial process. All the people on the team work as employees to the packager, either as freelancers or on staff. In the end, packagers deliver to the publisher either finished books or film for the printer to use.

Packagers do many different types of books, from cookbooks to dictionaries. Parachute Press, for example, specializes in children's books, and the Stonesong Press specializes in dictionaries and encyclopedias. Byron Press Visuals is more of a generalist, tending toward fiction and nonfiction based on successful copyrighted characters created in the comics world (e.g., Marvel's Daredevil) or other copyrighted material that they license from the creators (such as books based on the show *Battlestar Gallactica*).

If you think you can write something "for hire" knowing that once you've handed in the manuscript your part in the project is probably over, then you might want to try and connect with some packagers.

Working for a packager is not for everyone; it demands a great deal of discipline. But if you can do it, it's a good way to break into book publishing. Your name often goes on the book cover, and it's a way of making ready cash between book projects.

Be warned: It's not worthwhile approaching a packager with an idea; thinking up ideas is what they do. If your idea is any good, market it yourself.

Packagers look for writers that are experienced and professional, so craft a cover letter and resume that emphasizes that. You need to be able to write quickly and well, be flexible and roll with punches, and meet deadlines. Include in the resume your hobbies and interests; a lot of packagers do nonfiction books and are drawn to writers who have an existing knowledge or interest in a subject.

Book Packagers

Here are five questions to think about if you want to try to get work from a packager:

1. Can you work as part of a team and put your ego aside?

2. Can you work in someone else's world while he or she looks over your shoulder?

3. Can you work from someone else's outlines?

4. Can you accept someone else having the final say about what you're writing?

5. Can you deal with earning no royalties for writing something that someone else thought up?

Electronic Publishing

The Internet is the Wild West of the book world at present. It's in its pioneering infancy, filled with both good and bad cowboys, and it's changing almost daily. Sites go up and sites go down; finding stability and dependability is a challenge.

Electronic publishing is developing in ways that are starting to leave behind traditional notions of publishing. Is this the death knell of the book as we know it? I don't believe so, but some would have you think otherwise. Despite electronic publishing's ardent supporters, will it ever be more than an intriguing fringe for a literary *avant garde* and those who just can't make it in traditional publishing?

At present, the harsh fact is that relatively few people read books on their computer screens. It's awkward, inconvenient, and strains the eyes. None of the so-called electronic books, such as RocketBooks, Palm Pilot, or Psion, make reading on screen a viable or even pleasant option for enough readers—and that's if you can find a book "published" in a format that will work on your computer.

But all that may change. A community of writers and publishers, called E-publishers, is betting that these problems and trends can be resolved in their favor.

Something else to consider when selling the electronic rights of a book to an electronic publisher is that it solves one important problem for the writer of a traditional book: It takes off the table the contentious question of whether or not a traditional book publisher should share in electronic rights. They can't, because the rights have already been sold to someone else. Will this be a hindrance to selling your book in traditional book markets? Not at present, but who's to say down the road?

What Is E-Publishing?

Electronic publishing, or e-publishing, produces and stores books electronically. E-books are distributed in a variety of ways such as on-line, on disk, or on CD-ROM or DVD, usually as a file or series of files. These files can be downloaded directly to a handheld electronic reader, or via the Internet to a personal computer.

E-publishers create and distribute original books (even the term *book* begins to become an anachronism here) that are appearing for the first time in an electronic format.

E-publishing is a separate entity from EText projects, such as Project Gutenberg, for example, which reproduces public domain and noncopyrighted material for ready access by anyone who has a computer and a modem.

E-publishing does not offer an electronic version of a book that is simultaneously being produced in print (e.g., by making an edition available for a handheld e-reader).

Three Types of E-Publishing

Like traditional publishing, electronic publishing can be divided into three basic categories: commercial, subsidy, and self-publishing.

Commercial e-publishers work like traditional publishers. Manuscripts are accepted on the basis of quality and marketability and go through a similar process of review, editing, and proofreading before publication. Writers pay no fee for publication and receive royalties.

Commercially published e-books are sold primarily through the publisher's Web site but are also available from on-line bookstores (including Amazon.com and Barnes & Noble). Some are beginning to be available through stores in the form of handheld readers, such as Rocket Editions downloadable for the RocketBook e-reader. As all e-books have ISBNs, they can be ordered through any bookstore.

Subsidy e-publishers produce and distribute books for a fee, usually about $500 per manuscript, but authors receive a royalty comparable to that offered by commercial e-publishers.

Unlike commercial e-publishers, however, subsidy publishers provide little screening (except for offensive content such as pornography or hate material) and usually accept any manuscript, regardless of quality. Most subsidy publishers provide no editorial services or proofreading (though some offer these services for an extra fee), and books are posted exactly as submitted.

Like commercially published e-books, subsidy-published e-books are available through most on-line bookstores. They are less likely to be available in a downloadable RocketBook edition, however, and are

The ABPA

The American Book Producers Association
160 Fifth Avenue, Suite 625
New York, NY 10010
Phone: 212-645-2368 (800-209-4575)
Fax: 212-989-7542
E-mail: 4164812@mcimail.com
Managing Agent: SKP Associates
Sandra K. Paul, President
Established in 1980
http://lcweb.loc.gov/loc/cfbook/coborg/abp.html

rarely found in traditional bookstores. Like commercially published e-books, they also have ISBNs and can be ordered from any bookstore.

Similar again to traditional publishing, *self-published* e-books are produced entirely by the author. These are usually posted on and sold through the author's Web site, rather than that of a publisher. All the expenses of publication and distribution are handled by the author, who also receives all revenues, rather than royalties, from book sales.

E-Books Pros and Cons

One of the big problem with e-books, neatly sidestepped by EText producers such as Project Gutenberg, is the wide range of formats the text can be created in. This, of course, affects the distribution of the e-book. E-books are available in rich text, html for Windows and Windows CE, AportisDoc for Palm Pilots, RocketBooks, and Librius books, as well as PDF files, which can be read by Adobe Acrobat.

E-publishers have moved slowly from proprietary formats (which meant readers needed special software to read each publisher's books) to more generic formats such as Adobe Acrobat's PDF. Some publishers still only offer Windows-compatible formats, and while powerMac users should be able to read such disks, it's not likely people are going to go out and buy the latest technology just to read a book on screen. In fact, one of the problems with e-books is that not many people are willing to go out and spend $500 or more to buy a device just to read an electronic handheld version of a book.

E-books' fiction compares in price to a paperback's (i.e., between $7 and $12) though shorter works, such as Diana Gabaldon's novella *Hellfire* (Dreams Unlimited), can be as cheap as $2. Nonfiction titles, however, particularly self-published, can range up to $30 or more.

E-publishers often pay 30 percent royalties, usually sent on a quarterly basis. The royalty statements also often breaks down sales by how many titles were sold on disk, by download, and so forth.

However, e-books pay no royalty advance, sell significantly less than traditional books, and sell much slower. It can take years for a book to become a "best-seller," and sales of five hundred copies are considered good.

The lack of a royalty advance can create other problems for authors. Several genre organizations consider a book "commercially published" only if an advance is paid, so an e-book may not qualify an author for membership or for an industry award.

Offbeat genre fiction, particularly cross-genre and nontraditional romance, science fiction, and fantasy, does well in the e-publishing market. The general philosophy of commercial e-publishing is that it fills the "holes" that traditional publishing is leaving in its wake. They're the publishers to go to when traditional publishers tell you your book is great but are not willing to publish it.

Unlike print publishing, length is far less important in e-publishing. Best-selling author Diana Gabaldon told Moira Allen—who writes regularly on e-publishing on the Inkspot Web site—that she offered her story, *Hellfire* (previously anthologized in Britain), to Dreams Unlimited because, as she put it, "care to guess how many paying markets there are for 11,000-word historical mystery stories?" The answer is, Barely any.

Most e-publishers also only ask for electronic rights, leaving the author free to market print rights and subsidiary rights elsewhere. Most reputable e-publishers post their contracts on-line. Be cautious of any publisher that posts an incomplete contract, such as a contract that omits key details about royalties or rights or states that such rights are "negotiable."

The concern of piracy stops many authors from considering e-publishing. The truth is that there's not much to stop someone from making and distributing copies of your book.

Choosing an E-Publisher

Do substantial research before committing to anything. Does the publisher offer books you like to read? Have you read any of them? If not, do so. Visit each publisher to get a feel for what they publish. Read some of their books, their guidelines, and their contract before submitting.

Electronic Publishing Resources

Association of Electronic Publishers
http://welcome.to/AEP

Electronically Published Internet Connection (EPIC)
http://www.eclectics.com/epic

AcqWeb's Directory for On-Line Information Vendors and Electronic Publishers
http://www.library,vanderbilt. edu/law/acqs/pubr/online.html

Inkspot—The Writer's Resource
http://www.inkspot.com
(If you're interested in day-to-day news and features about e-publishing, this site is well worth visiting.)

Hard Shell Word Factory
http://www.hardshell.com

David Reilly's Electronic Publishing Guide
http://www.davidreilly.com/ epublishing/

For links to additional e-publishers, check out romance writer Mary Wolf's Guide to Electronic Publishers,
http://www.coredcs.com/~ mermaid/epub.html

Project Gutenberg

Project Gutenberg was born after Michael Hart was given a grant of $1 million for research on a computer project. What he came up with was an idea he called "Replicator Technology." The concept of Replicator Technology is simple: Once a book or any other item such as pictures or sounds is stored in a computer, then any number of copies can and will be available. Everyone in the world can have a copy of any document that has been entered into a computer.

Project Gutenberg ETexts are made available in "Plain Vanilla ASCII," meaning the low set of the American Standard Code for Information Interchange, so that italics, underlines, and bolds are replaced by capitalization. The reason for this is that 99 percent of the hardware and software a person is likely to run into can read and search these files.

Here are the questions to ask:

- Does the publisher have a good Web site?
- Have they won awards or praise from worthwhile organizations?
- Is the publisher asking for money up front? If so, be on your guard.
- Who have they published? What do they consider a sales success to be?
- Does the publisher use a proprietary format, or do they port the book to different formats (such as Internet download using Acrobat's PDF format, print-on-demand, RocketBooks, or Palm Pilot)? Do they offer only downloads, or disks as well?
- Does the publisher get reviews for their e-books, and where?
- Do they advertise, and where?
- What are the marketing plans for your book?
- Is the publisher a member of the Association of Electronic Publishers (AEP) or the Electronically Published Internet Connection (EPIC)?
- Will you feel proud of the finished product?

Beware of a binding or demanding contract. Most e-publishers use time-limited contracts that enable either party to terminate the agreement easily after a period of 1 or 2 years. Reputable subsidy publishers do the same. Be very careful of anything else, and take advice before committing yourself. Watch out for a contract that asks for other rights (e.g., print, translation, dramatic, etc.). Give these away and you leave yourself open to sharing with a publisher a percentage of any money you earn from selling those rights later on.

E-Book Resources

The following are AEP approved companies who are not members:

The Book Nook: a mail-order romance bookstore that carries e-books *www.thebooknook.com*

eBookShoppe: a mail-order bookstore specializing in electronic books *www.ebookshoppe.com*

Novelon: a virtual library service for book publishers and book readers *www.novelon.com*

The following sites specialize in Web-based e-readers:

Net Library.com*: http://www.netlibrary.com/*

Electronic Ink: *http://www.electronicink.com*

E-Ink Corp: *http://www.eink.com*

Xerox PARC:
http://www.parc.xerox.com/dhl/projects/epaper/
Hardware-based e-readers:

Nuvomedia Rocket eBook *http://www.rocket-ebooks.com*

Softbook Press *http://www.softbooks.com*

Gembook *http://www.gemtronicsinc.com/gembook.html*

Softwarebased e-readers

Glassbook *http://www.glassbook.com*

Librius Millennium *http://www.librius.com*

Everybook *http://www.everybk.com*

Peanut Press *http://www.peanut.press*

AEP Resources

The following publishers are members of AEP (Association of Electronic Publishers):

Awe-Struck E-Books
Kathryn Struck and Dick Claassen, publishers
2458 Cherry Street
Dubuque, Iowa 52001

or
109 NW Scott
Ankeny, Iowa 50021
URL: *www.awe-struck.net*
E-mail: kathrynd@mwci.net
Genres Published: romance—sci-fi, paranormal, new age, contemporary, historical, suspense, and mystery; sci-fi—soft sci-fi, sci-fi romance, sci-fi fantasy; historical fiction; Ennoble Series—fiction featuring heroes/heroines who are disabled
Guidelines: author guidelines
AEP member since May 1999

Boson Books
3905 Meadow Field Lane
Raleigh, NC 27606
URL: *www.cmonline.com/boson*
E-mail: cm@cmonline.com
Genres Published: fiction, nonfiction, drama, poetry, out-of-print works
Guidelines: author guidelines
AEP member since May 1999

Dreams Unlimited
P.O. Box 543
Northford, CT 06472-0543
or: 21 Drummond Gardens
Epsom
Surrey
KT19 8RP, UK
URL: *www.dreams-unlimited.com*
Email: info@dreams-unlimited.com
Genres Published: fantasy romance, futuristic romance, paranormal romance, erotic romance, gay romance, lesbian romance
Guidelines: author guidelines
AEP member since May 1998

Diskus Publishing
P.O. Box 43
Albany, IN 47320
URL: *www.diskuspublishing.com*
E-mail: editor@diskuspublishing.com
Genres Published: fiction, nonfiction, romance (all categories) science fiction, fantasy, horror, mystery and suspense, western, action and adventure, mainstream, children's and young adult novels. May also be interested in poetry if you have enough to fill a book.
Guidelines: author guidelines
AEP member since December 1998

The Fiction Works
P.O. Box 5363
Lake Tahoe, NV 89449
URL: *www.fictionworks.com*
E-mail: cyberquill@nanosecond.com
Genres Published: fiction—fiction/adventure, children's books, fantasy, historical fiction, horror, inspirational, mainstream, mystery, romance, science fiction, western, young adult; nonfiction—business titles, how-to, self-help
Guidelines: *www.fictionworks.com/ebookguidelines.htm*
AEP member since December 1998

GLB Publishers
P.O. Box 78212
San Francisco, CA 94107
URL: *www.glbpubs.com*
Email: warner@glbpubs.com
Genres Published: fiction (explicit and nonexplicit), nonfiction (e.g., history), and poetry by and for gays, lesbians, and bisexuals; transgender also okay.
Guidelines: author guidelines
AEP member since May 1999

MountainView Publishing
1022 NE O'Leary Street
Oak Harbor, WA 98277
URL: *http://www.whidbey.com/mountainview*
Email: junebug@whidbey.net
Genres Published: Christian fiction, inspirational romance, traditional (sweet) romance
Guidelines: author guidelines
AEP member since December 1998

New Concepts Publishing
4729 Humphreys Road
Lake Park, GA 31636
URL: *www.newconceptspublishing.com*
Email: ncp@newconceptspublishing.com
Genres Published: romance (all sub-genres), mystery, science fiction, fantasy, mainstream, horror, young adult
Guidelines: author guidelines
AEP member since June 1998

Petals of Life Publishing
231 Oil Well Road, Suite C
Jackson, TN 38305
URL: *www.petalsoflife.com*
Email: petals@petalsoflife.com
Genres Published: metaphysical and new thought fiction and nonfiction
Guidelines: author guidelines
AEP member since May 1998

AEP Membership Rules

The following is a copy of the AEP membership rules as posted on their Web site *http://www.welcome.to/AEP:*

1. AEP Membership can only be granted to companies who are in the business of publishing electronic books.
   A. Distributors, Resellers, etc., cannot hold AEP membership, but may apply for AEP approval.
   B. AEP approval means that an AEP approved company is a legitimate business involved in either distributing or reselling electronic books for a period of 6 months or more.
   C. AEP cannot govern AEP approved companies but will advise if grievances against any approved company come to light so that they can be resolved.
2. Full AEP membership status, along with voting rights, will only be granted to publishers in the business of selling electronic books for twelve (12) months or longer.
   A. Associate AEP membership—nonvoting—will be granted to publishers in the business of selling electronic books for at least six (6) months if all other criteria are fulfilled.
   B. Once the twelve (12) month period has been met, the Associate AEP membership will be transferred to full membership status.
   C. No associate AEP member can hold an official role within AEP or act in an official capacity.
   D. Neither of these memberships will be granted unless the publisher also complies with the balance of this application.
3. No more than 5% of a AEP member publisher's catalog can be self-published works by the owner of the company.
4. AEP member publishers must pay royalties of at least 20% on electronically published works.
5. AEP member publishers may not charge any up-front fees for publication of an author's work. This excludes the right to request an author to pay for his or her own copyright.
   A. AEP member publishers agree that authors can be expected to pay for any extraordinary expenses such as special art, manuscript typing, and anything else that is not considered "standard" publishing expenses ordinarily incurred by the publisher.

6. Authors published by an AEP member publisher retain sole copyright of their material after expiration of contract.

7. All AEP member publishers' books must have ISBN numbers for each book published.

8. AEP members agree not to disclose any confidential information about authors, customers, applicants, or members. This includes addresses, phone numbers, financial information, etc.

9. Members shall be held to a high standard of ethical behavior when dealing with customers, staff, and authors. This ethical behavior shall include and extend not only to the rules that AEP has set forth in their regulations, but also to the standards they have set forth in their own contracts.

10. Applicants must provide a sample contract for AEP review.
    A. AEP contracts must state an end date ("Out Of Print Date")
    B. No AEP member will hold electronic rights indefinitely.

11. AEP members must display the "AEP MEMBER" button provided by AEP on their Web site, linked to the member page, so that customers and authors can check that the member is legitimate.

12. AEP provides its members with a private facility (mailing list) to discuss member issues.
    A. No member may discuss issues raised within the AEP mailing list with third parties except if requested to do so by AEP.
    B. All topics within the mailing list remain strictly confidential.
    C. No member may forward any post made to the mailing list, except to another member.

13. AEP maintains a Web site, providing member information.
    A. A named AEP member acts as Web master for the AEP Web site and is responsible for maintenance.
    B. New members must be added within a week of acceptance.
    C. New members must provide their details (address, contact, URL, e-mail contact, etc.) upon request for inclusion on the member page.
    D. Members will provide changes of address or similar details if and when they change to allow member information to be up to date.

    E. All original correspondence addressed to AEP and received by a member must be forwarded to the AEP mailing list unedited.

14. AEP provides a "grievance committee" comprised of three full members to take complaints about any member or company.

    A. The grievance committee will investigate and substantiate claims and bring non-complying members before the board for review, dismissal, or warning, whatever the case may warrant.

    B. The grievance committee will not disclose any details of a grievance to any member, the board, or any uninvolved third party until it is fully substantiated.

15. AEP has a spokesperson, and this is established through voting by all (full) AEP members.

    A. No spokesperson may hold the post for more than six (6) months.

    B. The spokesperson is responsible for determining eligibility of membership of new applicants.

    C. A substitute spokesperson must be named if the elected spokesperson is absent for a considerable length of time.

    D. If there are grievances against the spokesperson, said spokesperson cannot act in this capacity and must be replaced by a substitute spokesperson elected through voting.

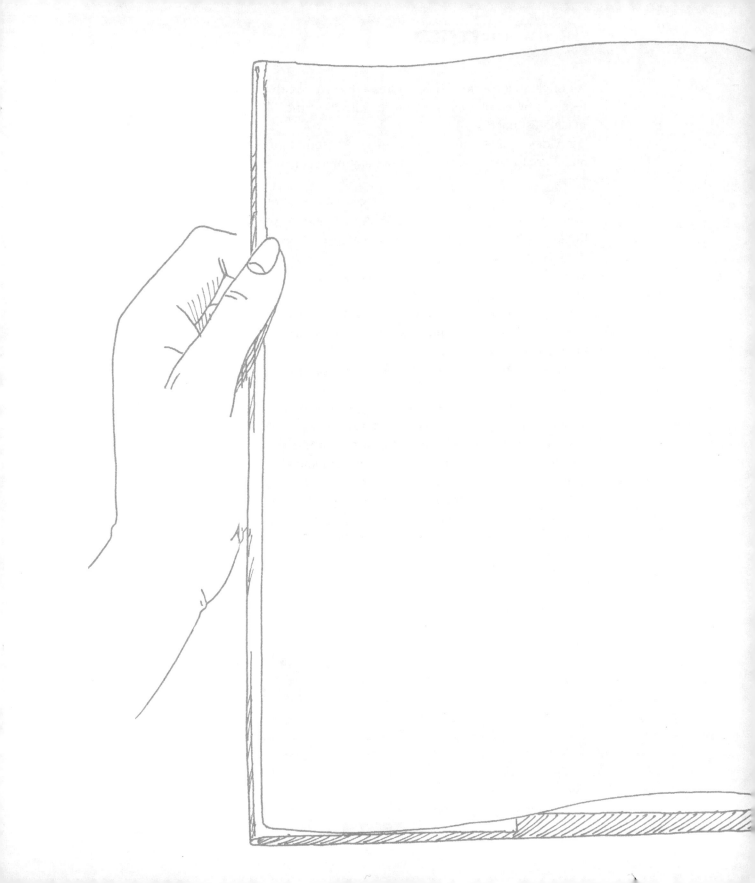

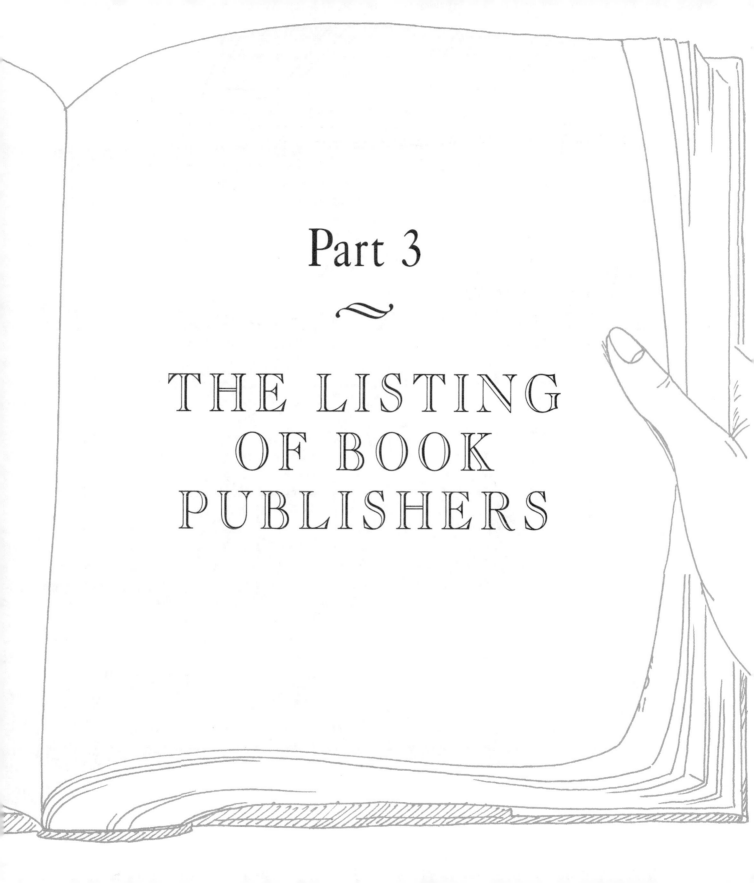

Part 3

THE LISTING OF BOOK PUBLISHERS

CHAPTER 12

Where to Find Book Publishers in North America

Conglomerates

This section provides a listing of large and small presses that you may find useful. It is not exhaustive, but covers most of the places you're likely to want to approach the first time you want to submit something for publication. For the most comprehensive professional listing, go to your local library and use R.R. Bowker's Literary Marketplace (known in the trade as the LMP). It's a thick book, though, heavy, and upgraded every year, costing between $300-400 per edition.

The listings are broken into mid-sized and conglomerate publishing houses and their imprints (companies who publish over 50 books or so a year), and small press and university press publishers, defined broadly as companies who publish 50 or fewer books a year.

As you examine the conglomerate and imprint chart, you'll see how compressed and compacted things are becoming at the commercial end of publishing. As major publishers concentrate more and more on "winners" (whatever that means), more small presses (including University Presses) are moving in and arising to fill in the diversity gap that has been left by the decision by larger publishers to focus on more homogenous bottom line projects. This is a good thing for writers and is a dynamic aspect of the modern publishing scene. In many ways, the larger publishers are happy to let the smaller develop talent that they hope to adopt as their own at the appropriate time.

If you have an agent, the listings can be a helpful discussion tool between you and your agent, providing leads or a reminder to contact a particular house on your behalf.

While they claim to not take unsolicited manuscripts, most publishing house editors, approached professionally, will usually entertain a well crafted query letter and proposal. However, if a listing says "Agented Submission Only" don't be upset if no one takes your call or you get a recorded message. Where possible I've included an editor's name, but editors move so don't rely on the lead as gospel.

The listings contain brief tips that characterize what the company is known to publish, and wishes to publish, and other information that may help you in your submission to that company.

Before the early 1980s there were probably between 20-30 mid- to large-sized publishing houses. Since that time the houses have gobbled each other up and merged with one another to such an extent that there are really only about 6 major groups now. The former independent houses are either defunct (such as Dodd Mead), morphed into another entity (such as Harper & Row, which is now HarperCollins), or imprints of larger groups, (such as Avon and Morrow, now part of HarperCollins).

These imprints still publish books, and you can still submit to them, but in general the various imprints don't like to compete with each other for the same books.

It is useful to know, for example, that while Holzbrinck is a financial umbrella grouping, Farrar, Straus & Giroux, St. Martin's Press, and Henry Holt (all part of that group) still consider themselves independent of one another.

This is less true for imprints under the Penguin Putnam, or Random House umbrellas.

The amassing of imprints under one roof has slowed down and extended the submission process, making it harder for agents, for example, to submit multiple manuscripts and proposals as they have done over the years, and allowing publishers to take longer to pay authors. It is a means for publishers to try to control the costs of producing and selling books.

It is almost a certainty that by the time you read this, the larger groups will have made some sort of adjustment yet again. With such continuous activity, this grouping, for the curious writer, offers a guide to who owns whom and under which umbrella. The conglomerates chart below tries to give you a graphic picture of how modern publishing has evolved, and is continuing to evolve.

Bertelsmann Book Groups
Random House, Inc.

Bantam Dell Group
Bantam Classics
Bantam Crime Line
Bantam Fanfare
Bantam Spectra
Delacorte Press
Dell Books
Delta Books
Dial Press
DTP
Island Books
Laurel Books

Doubleday Broadway Group
Broadway Books
Currency
Doubleday
Doubleday Religious Publishing
Image Books
Main Street Books
Nan A. Talese
WaterBrook Press
Doubleday Books for Young Readers

The Ballantine Publishing Group
Ballantine Books
Columbine
Del Rey
Fawcett (Crest, Gold Medal, Juniper)
House of Collectibles
Ivy
Library of Contemporary Thought
One World

The Crown Publishing Group
Bell Tower
Clarkson Potter
Crown Publishers Inc.
Custom Publishing
Harmony Books
Living Language
Park Lane Press
Three Rivers Press

Fodor's Travel Publications

Random House New Media
Knopf Publishing Group
Everyman's Library

Alfred A. Knopf Inc.
Pantheon Books
Schocken Books
Vintage Anchor Books
Vintage
Anchor

Random House AudioBooks Group
BDD House Audio Publishing
Random House Audio Publishing

Random House Trade Group
The Modern Library
Random House Adult Trade Books
Villard Books

Random House Information Group
Discovery Books
Princeton Review
Random House Reference & Information Publishing
Sierra Club Adult Books
Times Books
Times Business Books

Random House Children's Publishing
Bantam Books for Young Readers
Crown Books for Young Readers
CTW Publishing
Delacourt Books for Young Readers
Doubleday Books for Young Readers
Dragonfly Books
First Choice Chapter Books
Knopf Books for Young Readers
Knopf Paperbacks
Laurel Leaf
Picture Yearling
Random House Children's Media
Random House Children's Publishing
Random House Entertainment
Skylark
Starfire
Yearling

Random House Diversified Publishing Group
Children's Classics
Crescent Books
Derrydale
Gramercy Books
Gramercy Park Gift & Stationery
JellyBean Press
Random House Large Print Publishing
Wings Books

Random House International
Bantam Doubleday Dell of Canada
Knopf
Knopf Canada
Random House of Canada
Random House UK

Pearson Publishing Groups
Penguin Putnam, Inc.

Penguin USA
Viking Penguin
Penguin Studio
Viking

Dutton Signet
DAW Books
Dutton
Marian Wood Books
Mentor
Meridian
NAL (New American Library)
Obelisk
Onyx
Pelham
Plume
ROC
Signet
Topaz

The Putnam Berkley Group
Ace
Berkley Books
Berkley Prime Crime
Boulevard
HP Books
Jove
Perigee
Price Stern Sloan, Inc.
G.P. Putnam's Sons
Riverhead
Jeremy P. Tarcher

Penguin Putnam Books For Young Readers Group
Dial Books for Young Readers
Dutton Children's Books
Phyllis Fogelman Books
Grosset & Dunlap
Philomel Books
Planet Dexter

Price Stern Sloan, Inc.
Puffin
PaperStar
G.P. Putnam's Sons
Viking Children's Books
Frederick Warne
Wee Sing

Viacom, Inc Publishing Group

Simon & Schuster
Pocket Books
Archway Paperbacks
Minstrel Books
MTV Books
Pocket Books Hardcover
Pocket Books Trade Paperbacks
Sonnet
Washington Square Press

Simon & Schuster Children's Publishing
Aladdin Paperbacks
Atheneum Books for Young Readers
Little Simon
Margaret K. McElderry Books
Simon & Schuster Books for Young Readers
Simon Spotlight
Simon & Schuster Interactive

Simon & Schuster Audio

Simon & Schuster Trade
Fireside
The Free Press
Scribner
Lisa Drew Books
Rawson Associates
Simon & Schuster
Simon & Schuster Editions
Simon & Schuster Libros en Espanol
Touchstone

Rupert Murdoch Publishing Group

HarperCollins Group
Cliff Street Books
HarperAudio
HarperBusiness
HarperCollins
HarperCollins Children's Books
HarperEdge
HarperEntertainment
HarperEntertainment Children's Books

HarperFlamingo
HarperHorizon
HarperPaperbacks
HarperPerennial
HarperPrism
HarperResource
HarperSanFrancisco
HarperTaste
HarperTrophy
HarperVoyager
Regan Books
Zondervan Publishing House

HarperInternational Group
HarperCollinsAustralia
HarperCollinsCanada
HarperCollinsUK

Avon Morrow Group
Avon
Avon Books
Avon Eos
Avon Flare
Bard
Camelot
Mass Market
Spike
Tempest
Trade Paperback
Twilight
WholeCare

William Morrow Group
Beech Tree Books
Eagle Brook
Greenwillow Books
Lothrop, Lee & Shepard Books
William Morrow Books
Morrow Junior Books
Mulberry Books
Quill Trade Paperbacks
Tupelo Books

Holtzbrinck Publishing Group

St. Martin's Press
Bedford Books
Buzz Books
Dead Letter
Tom Doherty Associates, Inc.
Tor
Forge
Tom Dunne Books
Griffin

Let's Go
Picador
St. Martin's Paperbacks
St. Martin's Press
St. Martin's Scholarly & Reference
Stonewall Inn
Truman Talley Books

Farrar Straus & Giroux
Faber & Faber Inc.
Farrar Straus & Giroux
Farrar Straus & Giroux Books for Young Readers
Aerial Fiction
Frances Foster Books
Mirasol/Libros Juveniles
R and S Books
Sunburst Paperbcks
Hill and Wang
Noonday Press
Northpoint Press
Sunburst Paperbacks

Henry Holt & Co.
Henry Holt & Co. Books for Young Readers
Edge Books
Red Feather Books
Henry Holt Books
Henry Holt Reference Books
John Macrae Books
Bill Martin Jr. Books
Metropolitan Books
Owl Books

Time Warner Publishing Group

Warner Books
Mysterious Press
Warner Aspect
Warner Romance
Warner Vision
Warner Books

Time Life Inc.

Time Warner Audiobooks

Little, Brown and Company
Back Bay Books
Bulfinch Press
Little, Brown Books for Children and Young Adults
Little Brown

Mid-Level Publishers

The following are details and requirements of mid-sized and major houses and their imprints.

ACE SCIENCE FICTION AND FANTASY

The Berkley Publishing Group
Penguin Putnam Inc.
375 Hudson Street
New York, NY 10014
Phone: 212-366-2000
Web site: *http://www.penguinputnam.com*
Acquisitions: Anne Sowards, editor. Estab. 1953. Publishes hardcover, paperback and trade paperback originals and reprints. **Publishes 75 titles/year.** Reports in 6 months. Manuscript guidelines for #10 SASE.
Tips: Ace publishes exclusively science fiction and fantasy. *Agented submissions only.* Query first with SASE.

ADAMS MEDIA CORPORATION

57 Littlefield Street
Avon, MA 02322
Phone: 508-427-7100
Fax: 508-427-6790
Web site: *http://www.adamsmedia.com*
Director of Editorial: Gary M. Krebs. Acquisitions: Jill Alexander, Tracy Quinn McLennan, Bethany Brown, Eric Hall, Kate Epstein. Estab. 1980. Publishes trade paperback originals and some hardcover originals. **Publishes 160 plus titles/year. Receives 1,500 queries and 500 manuscripts/year. 35% of books from first-time authors; 40% from unagented writers. Pays standard royalty or makes outright purchase. Offers variable advance.** Publishes book approximately 1 year after acceptance of manuscript. Accepts simultaneous submissions. Reports in 3 months.
Tips: Adams Media publishes commercial nonfiction, not scholarly or literary material, including career titles, innovative business, self-help books, and many other nonfiction categories.

ALFRED A. KNOPF, INC.

Knopf Publishing Group
Random House, Inc.
201 East 50th Street
New York, NY 10022
Phone: 212-751-2600
Web site: *http://www.randomhouse.com/knopf/aak*
Acquisitions: Senior Editors: Jane Garrett; Robin Desser Estab. 1915. **Publishes hardcover and paperback originals. Publishes 200 titles/yearly. 15% of books from first-time authors; 30% from unagented writers. Royalty and advance vary.** Publishes book 1 year after acceptance of manuscript. Accepts simultaneous submissions, if so noted. Reports in 3 months.
Tips: Knopf is a general publisher of quality nonfiction and fiction.

ALFRED A. KNOPF AND CROWN BOOKS FOR YOUNG READERS

Random House, Inc.
201 East 50th Street
New York, NY 10022
Phone: 212-782-5623
Web site: *http://www.randomhouse.com/kids*
Vice President/Publishing Director: Simon Boughton. Associate Publishing Director: Andrea Cascardi. Executive Editor: Nancy Siscoe. **Acquisitions**: Send manuscripts to Crown/Knopf Editorial Department. Publishes hardcover originals, trade paperback reprints. **Publishes 60 titles/year. 10% of books from first-time authors; 40% from unagented writers. Pays 4-10% royalty on retail price. Offers advance of $3,000 and up.** Publishes book 1-2 years after acceptance of manuscript. Accepts simultaneous submissions. Reports in 3 months on manuscripts. Manuscript guidelines free.
Tips: *Knopf* is known for high-quality literary fiction and is willing to take risks with writing styles. It publishes for children ages 4 and up. *Crown* is known for books young children immediately use and relate to. It focuses on children ages 2-6.
Imprint(s): Alfred A. Knopf Books for Young Readers, Crown Books for Young Readers, Knopf Paperbacks, Dragonfly.

AMACOM BOOKS

American Management Association
1601 Broadway
New York, NY 10019-7406
Phone: 212-903-8081
Fax: 212-903-8083
Web site: *http://www.amanet.org*
Managing Director: Weldon P. Rackley. Publisher: Hank Kennedy.
Acquisitions: Adrienne Hickey, executive editor (management, human resources development, training); Ellen Kadin, senior acquisitions editor (marketing, sales, customer service, personal development); Ray O'Connell, senior acquisitions editor (manufacturing, finance, project management); William Hicks, senior acquisitions editor (management, organization development); Jacquie Flynn, acquisitions editor (information technology, training). Estab. 1923. Publishes hardcover and trade paperback originals, professional books in various formats, multimedia, and self-study courses. **Publishes 75 titles/year. Receives 500 submissions/year. 40% of books from first-time authors; 70% from unagented writers. Pays 10-15% royalty on net receipts by the publisher.** Publishes book 9 months after acceptance. Reports in 2 months. Proposal guidelines free.
Tips: Amacom is the publishing arm of the American Management Association, the world's largest training organization for managers and executives. Amacom publishes books on business issues, strategies,a and tasks to enhance organizational and individual effectiveness.

ANDREWS McMEEL UNIVERSAL

4520 Main Street
Kansas City, MO 64111-7701
Phone: 816-932-6700
Web site: *http://www.nexpress.com*
Acquisitions: Christine Schillig, vice president/editorial director. Estab. 1973. Publishes hardcover and paperback originals. **Publishes 300 titles/year. Pays royalty on retail price. Offers advance.**
Tips: Andrews McMeel publishes general trade books, humor books, miniature gift books, calendars, greeting cards, and stationery products. *Agented submissions only.*

ARABESQUE, BET Books

850 Third Avenue, 16th Floor
New York, NY 10022
Phone: 212-407-1500
Web site: *http://www.arabesque.com*
Acquisitions: Karen Thomas, senior editor. Publishes mass market paperback originals. **Publishes 60 titles/year. 30-50% of books from first-time authors; 50% from unagented writers. Pays royalty on retail price, varies by author. Advance varies by author.**
Publishes book 18 months after acceptance of manuscript. Accepts simultaneous submissions. Reports in 3 months on manuscripts.
Tips: Arabesque publishes contemporary romances about African-American couples.

ARCADE PUBLISHING

141 Fifth Avenue
New York, NY 10010
Phone: 212-475-2633
E-mail: arcadepub@aol.com
Acquisitions: Cal Barksdale, senior editor; Richard Seaver, publisher/editor in chief; Jeannette Seaver, publisher/executive editor. Estab. 1988. Publishes hardcover originals, trade paperback originals and reprints. **Publishes 40 titles/year. 5% of books from first-time authors. Pays royalty on retail price. Offers $3,000-50,000 advance.** Publishes book within 18 months after acceptance of manuscript. Reports in 3 months on queries.
Tips: Arcade prides itself on publishing top-notch commercial nonfiction and literary fiction, with an emphasis on foreign writers.

ARCADIA PUBLISHING

Tempus Publishing
2-A Cumberland Street
Charleston, SC 29401
Phone: 843-853-2070
Fax: 843-853-0044
E-mail: arcadia@charleston.net
Web site: *http://www.arcadiaimages.com*
Acquisitions: Mark Berry, Christine Riley, Katie White (southern subjects); Allison Carpenter (Western subjects); Patrick Catel, Tessa Hellbusch (Midwestern subjects); Heather Gunsalas, Pamela O'Neil, Amy Sutton

(Northeastern subjects). Query with SASE. Publishes mass-market paperback originals. **Publishes 800 titles/year; imprint publishes 350 titles/year. Receives 100 queries and 20 manuscripts/year. 80% of books from first-time authors; 95% from unagented writers. Pays 10% royalty.** Accepts simultaneous submissions. Reports in 1 month on queries. Book catalog on Web site. Manuscript guidelines for #10 SASE.
Tips: Arcadia is the publisher of the Images of America series, which chronicles the history of diverse communities across the United States.

ARCHWAY PAPERBACKS

pocket Books for Young Readers
Simon & Schuster
1230 Avenue of the Americas
New York, NY 10020
Phone: 212-698-7669
Web site: *http://www.simonsayskids.com*
Vice President/Editorial Director: Patricia MacDonald. **Acquisitions**: Send all submissions Attn: Manuscript Proposals. Publishes mass-market paperback originals and reprints. **Publishes approximately 100 titles/year. Receives over 1,000 submissions/year. Pays 6-8% royalty on retail price.** Publishes book 2 years after acceptance. Reports in 3 months.
Tips: Archway Paperbacks publishes fiction and current nonfiction for young adult readers ages 12-18.

ATHENEUM BOOKS FOR YOUNG READERS

Simon & Schuster
1230 Avenue of the Americas
New York, NY 10020
Phone: 212-698-2715
Web site: *http://www.randomhouse.com*
Associate Publisher/Vice President/Editorial Director: Jonathan J. Lanman. **Acquisitions**: Marcia Marshall, executive editor (nonfiction, fantasy); Anne Schwartz, editorial director, Anne Schwartz Books; Caitlyn Dlouhy, senior editor. Estab. 1960. Publishes hardcover originals. **Publishes 70 titles/year. Receives 15,000 submissions/year. 8-12% of books from first-time authors; 50% from unagented writers. Pays 10% royalty on retail price. Offers $2,000-3,000 average advance.** Publishes book 18 months after acceptance. Reports within 3 months. Manuscript guidelines for #10 SASE.
Tips: Atheneum Books for Young Readers publishes books aimed at children from preschool age through high school.

AVALON BOOKS

160 Madison Ave.
New York, NY 10016
Phone: (212) 598-0222
Web site: *http://www.avalonbooks.com*
Acquisitions: Veronica Mixon, executive editor. Estab. 1950. **Publishes 60 titles/year. 10% of books from unagented writers. Pays royalty; contracts negotiated on an individual basis.** Publishes book

6 months after acceptance. Reports in 6 months. Manuscript guidelines for #10 SASE.

Tips: Considers themselves the "Family Channel" of publishing. Currently de-emphasizing romantic suspense.

AVON BOOKS.

1350 Avenue of the Americas
New York, NY 10019
Phone: 212-207-7000
Web site: *http://www.avonbooks.com*
Editor in Chief: Jennifer Hersche.
Acquisitions: Editorial Submissions. Estab. 1941. Publishes hardcover, trade and mass market paperback originals and reprints. **Publishes 400 titles/year. Royalty and advance negotiable.** Publishes manuscript 2 years after acceptance of manuscript. Accepts simultaneous submissions. Reports in 3 months. Guidelines for SASE.
Imprint(s): Avon Eos, Avon Flare, Avon Twilight, Bard, Camelot, post Road Press, Spike, WholeCare.
Tips: Avon publishes high quality, genre-based mass market books.

AVON EOS, Avon Books

1350 Avenue of the Americas
New York, NY 10019
Phone: 212-207-7000
Web site: *http://www.avonbooks.com*
Acquisitions: Jennifer Brehl, executive editor; Diana Gill, associate editor. Publishes hardcover originals, trade and mass market paperback originals and reprints. **Publishes 55-60 titles/year. Receives 2,500 queries and 800 manuscripts/year. 25% of books from first-time authors; 5% from unagented writers. Pays royalty on retail price, range varies.** Publishes book 18-24 months after acceptance of manuscript. Accepts simultaneous submissions, if so noted. Reports in 6 months. Manuscript guidelines for #10 SASE.
Tips: Cutting-edge, literary, science fiction/fantasy line.

AVON FLARE BOOKS, Avon Books

1350 Avenue of the Americas
New York, NY 10019
Phone: 212-207-7000
Web site: *http://www.avonbooks.com*
Acquisitions: Elise Howard, editor in chief; Ruth Katcher, senior editor. Publishes mass market paperback originals and reprints for young adults. **Publishes 24 new titles/year. 25% of books from first-time authors; 15% from unagented writers. Pays 6-8% royalty. Offers $2,500 minimum advance.** Publishes book 2 years after acceptance. Accepts simultaneous submissions. Reports in 4 months. Manuscript guidelines for 8x10 SASE with 5 first-class stamps.
Tips: Avon Flare publishes young adult books, primarily fiction.

AVON TWILIGHT, Avon Books

1350 Avenue of the Americas
New York, NY 10019
Phone: 212-207-7000
Web site: *http://www.avonbooks.com*
Acquisitions: Jennifer Sawyer Fisher, senior editor (series detective mysteries). Publishes hardcover originals, trade paperback reprints, mass market paperback originals and reprints. **Publishes 60 titles/year. Pays 7 1/2-15% royalty on retail price, depending on format.** Accepts simultaneous submissions.
Tips: Avon Twilight publishes mainstream mystery novel series.

BAEN PUBLISHING ENTERPRISES

P.O. Box 1403
Riverdale, NY 10471-0671
Phone: 718-548-3100
Web site: *http://www.baen.com*
Acquisitions: Jim Baen, editor in chief; Toni Weisskopf, executive editor. Estab. 1983. Publishes hardcover, trade paperback and mass market paperback originals and reprints. **Publishes 120 titles/year. Receives 5,000 submissions/year. 5% of books from first-time authors; 50% from unagented writers. Pays royalty on retail price.** Reports in 6-8 months on queries and proposals, 9-12 months on complete manuscripts. Manuscript guidelines for #10 SASE.
Tips: Science fiction and fantasy. Submit outline/synopsis and sample chapters or complete manuscript by email to tweisskopf@mindspring.net.

BALLANTINE BOOKS, Random House, Inc.

201 East 50th Street
New York, NY 10022
Phone: 212-572-4910
Fax: 212-940-7580
Web site: *http://www.randomhouse.com*
President: Gina Centrello. Editorial Coordinator: Betsy Flagler.
Acquisitions: Leona Nevler, editor (all kinds of fiction and nonfiction); Peter Borland, executive editor (commercial fiction, pop culture); Elisa Wares, executive editor (romance, health, parenting, mystery); Joe Blades, associate publisher (mystery); Elizabeth Zack, editor (motivational, inspirational, women's sports, career, seasonal tie-ins); Joanne Wyckoff, senior editor (religion, spirituality, nature/pets, psychology); Andrea Schulz, editor (literary fiction, travel, women's studies, narrative nonfiction); Shauna Summers, senior editor (historical and contemporary romance, commercial women's fiction, general fiction, thrillers/suspense); Ginny Faber, senior editor (health, psychology, spirituality, travel, general nonfiction); Sarah Glazer, assistant editor (historical fiction, commercial fiction, arm-chair travel, animals). Estab. 1952. Publishes hardcover, trade paperback, mass market paperback originals.
Tips: Ballantine Books publishes a wide variety of nonfiction and fiction.

BANTAM BOOKS

Bantam Dell Publishing Group
Random House, Inc.
1540 Broadway
New York, NY 10036
Phone: 212-354-6500
Web site: *http://www.randomhouse.com*
Senior Vice President/Deputy Publisher: Nita Taublib. **Acquisitions**: Toni Burbank, Ann Harris, executive editors. Estab. 1945. Publishes hardcover, trade paperback and mass market paperback originals, mass-market paperback reprints and audio. **Publishes 350 titles/year.** Publishes book an average of 1 year after manuscript is accepted. Accepts simultaneous submissions from agents.
Imprint(s): Bantam Classics (reprints); Crime Line (Kate Miciak, associate publisher); **Fanfare** (Beth DeGuzman, Wendy McCurdy), **Spectra** (Pat LoBrutto, Anne Groell).

BANTAM DOUBLEDAY DELL BOOKS FOR YOUNG READERS

Random House Children's Publishing
Random House, Inc.
1540 Broadway
New York, NY 10036
Phone: 212-782-9000
Fax: 212-782-9452
Web site: *http://www.randomhouse.com/kids*
Vice President/Associate Publisher/Editor in Chief: Beverly Horowitz. Editorial Director: Michelle poploff. **Acquisitions**: Wendy Lamb, executive editor; Francoise Bui, executive editor; Lauri Hornik, senior editor; Karen Wojtyla, editor; Wendy Loggia, editor. Publishes hardcover, trade paperback and mass market paperback series originals, trade paperback reprints. **Publishes 300 titles/year. Receives thousands of queries/year. 10% of books from first-time authors; few from unagented writers. Pays royalty. Advance varies.** Publishes book 2 years after acceptance of manuscript. Reports in 2 months.
Tips: Bantam Doubleday Dell Books for Young Readers publishes award-winning books by distinguished authors and the most promising new writers.
Imprint(s): Delacorte Press Books for Young Readers, Doubleday Books for Young Readers, Laurel Leaf, Picture Yearling, Skylark, Starfire, Yearling.

BASIC BOOKS

10 East 53rd Street
New York NY 10022
Phone: 212-207-7600
Fax: 212-207-7703
Web site: *http://www.perseusbooksgroup.com*
Executive Editor: Jo Ann Miller
Part of the Perseus book group distributed by HarperCollins.
Publisher: John Donatich
Tips: High-quality science and commercial academic.

BEACON PRESS

25 Beacon Street
Boston, MA 02108-2892
Phone: 617-742-2110
Fax: 617-723-3097
E-mail: kdaneman@beacon.org
Web site: *http://www.beacon.org/Beacon*
Director: Helene Atwan.
Acquisitions: Deborah Chasman, editorial director (African-American, Asian American, Latino, Native American, Jewish, and gay and lesbian studies, anthropology); Deanne Urmy, executive editor, (child and family issues, environmental concerns); Micah Kleit, editor (education, current affairs, philosophy, religion); Tisha Hooks, associate editor (cultural studies, Asian and Caribbean studies, women and spirituality); Amy Caldwell, assistant editor (poetry, gender studies, gay/lesbian studies, and Cuban studies). Estab. 1854. Publishes hardcover originals and paperback reprints. **Publishes 60 titles/year. Receives 4,000 submissions/year. 10% of books from first-time authors. Pays royalty. Advance varies.** Accepts simultaneous submissions. Reports in 3 months.
Tips: Beacon Press publishes general interest books that promote the inherent worth and dignity of every person; justice, equity, and compassion in human relations; acceptance of one another; a free and responsible search for truth and meaning; the goal of world community with peace, liberty, and justice for all; respect for the interdependent web of all existence. Currently emphasizing innovative nonfiction writing by people of all colors. De-emphasizing poetry, children's stories, art books, self-help.
Imprint(s): Bluestreak Series (contact Deb Chasman, editor, innovative literary writing by women of color).

THE BERKLEY PUBLISHING GROUP

Penguin Putnam, Inc.
375 Hudson Street
New York, NY 10014
Phone: 212-366-2000
Web site: *http://www.penguinputnam.com*
Acquisitions: Denise Silvestro, senior editor (general nonfiction, business); Judith Stern Palais, senior editor (women's general, literary, and romance fiction); Tom Colgan, senior editor (history, business, inspiration, biography, suspense/thriller, mystery, adventure); Gail Fortune, senior editor (women's fiction, romance, mystery); Martha Bushko, assistant editor (nonfiction, mystery, health); Kimberly Waltemyer, editor (adult Western, romance, mystery); Lisa Considine, senior editor (nonfiction, literary fiction). Estab. 1954. Publishes paperback and mass-market originals and reprints. **Publishes approximately 800 titles/year. Few books from first- time authors; 1% from unagented writers. Pays 4-15% royalty on retail price. Offers advance.** Publishes book 2 years after acceptance of manuscript. Reports in 6 weeks on queries.
Tips: The Berkley Publishing Group publishes a variety of general nonfiction and fiction including the traditional categories of romance, mystery, and science fiction.
Imprint(s): Ace Science Fiction, Berkley, Boulevard, Jove, Prime Crime.

BOYDS MILLS PRESS

Highlights for Children
815 Church Street
Honesdale, PA 18431-1895
Phone: 570-253-1164
Web site: *http://www.boydsmillspress.com*
Publisher: Kent L. Brown.
Acquisitions: Beth Troop, manuscript coordinator; Larry Rosler, editorial director. Estab. 1990. Publishes hardcover originals and trade paperback originals and reprints. **Publishes 50 titles/year; imprint publishes 2-6 titles/year. Receives 10,000 queries and manuscripts/year. 20% of books are from first-time authors; 20% from unagented writers. Pays 8-15% royalty on retail price. Advance varies.** Accepts simultaneous submissions. Reports in 1 month. Book catalog and manuscript guidelines for $2 postage and SASE.
Tips: Boyds Mill Press, the book publishing arm of *Highlights for Children*, publishes a wide range of children's books of literary merit, from preschool to young adult. Currently emphasizing preschool picture books, *not* board books.
Imprint(s): Wordsong (poetry).

BROADWAY BOOKS

Doubleday Broadway Publishing Group
Random House, Inc.
1540 Broadway
New York, NY 10036
Phone: 800-223-6834
Web site: *http://www.broadwaybooks.com*
Publisher/Editor in Chief: Robert Asahina. **Acquisitions**: Harriet Bell, executive editor (cookbooks); Lauren Marino, editor (pop culture, entertainment, spirituality); Suzanne Oaks, senior editor (business); Tracy Behar, associate publisher/senior editor (psychology/self-help, parenting, health); Charles Conrad, vice president and executive editor (general nonfiction). Estab. 1995. Publishes hardcover and trade paperback originals and reprints.
Tips: Broadway publishes general interest nonfiction and fiction for adults. *Agented submissions only.*

BULFINCH PRESS

Little, Brown & Co.
3 Center Plaza
Boston, MA 02108
Phone: 617-263-2797
Fax: 617-263-2857
Web site: *http://www.littlebrown.com*
Publisher: Carol Judy Leslie.
Acquisitions: Stacy Botelho, department assistant. Publishes hardcover and trade paperback originals. **Publishes 60-70 titles/year. Receives 500 queries/year. Pays variable royalty on wholesale price. Advance varies.** Publishes book 18 months after acceptance of manuscript. Accepts simultaneous submissions. Reports in 2 months on proposals.
Tips: Bulfinch Press publishes large format art books.

BUSINESS McGRAW-HILL

The McGraw Hill Companies
11 West 19th Street
New York, NY 10011
Phone: 212-337-4098
Fax: 212-337-5999
Web site: *http://www.mcgraw-hill.com*
Publisher: Philip Ruppel.
Acquisitions: Susan Barry, editorial director; Barbara Gilson (Schaum's Outline Series); Nancy Mikhail (trade reference); Betsy Brown, senior editor (self-help, communications). **Publishes 100 titles/year. Receives 1,200 queries and 1,200 manuscripts/year. 30% of books from first-time authors; 60% from unagented writers. Pays 10-15% royalty on net price. Offers $5,000 advance and up.** Publishes book 6 months after acceptance of manuscript. Accepts simultaneous submissions. Reports in 3 months. Manuscript guidelines free on request with SASE.
Tips: McGraw Hill's business division and trade reference is the world's largest business publisher, offering nonfiction trade and paperback originals in more than ten areas, including management, sales and marketing, careers, trade reference, self-help, training, finance, and science.

CAMELOT BOOKS

Avon Books
1350 Avenue of the Americas
New York, NY 10019
Phone: 212-261-6800
Fax: 212-261-6895
Web Site: *http://www.avonbooks.com*
Acquisitions: Elise Howard, editor in chief; Ruth Katcher, senior editor. Publishes hardcover and paperback originals and reprints. **Publishes 80 titles/year. Pays 6-8% royalty on retail price. Offers $2,000 minimum advance.** Publishes book 2 years after acceptance. Reports back in 4 months. Manuscript guidelines for 8x10 SASE with 5 first-class stamps.
Tips: Camelot publishes fiction for children ages 8-12.

CANDLEWICK PRESS

Walker Books Ltd. (London)
2067 Massachusetts Avenue
Cambridge, MA 02140
Phone: 617-661-3330
Fax: 617-661-0565
Web site: *http://www.toydirerectory.com/CandlewickPress*
Acquisitions: Liz Bicknell, editor in chief (poetry, picture books, fiction); Mary Lee Donovan, senior editor (nonfiction/fiction); Gale Pryor, editor (nonfiction/fiction); Amy Ehrlich, editor-at-large (picture books); Kara LaReau, assistant editor; Cynthia Platt, assistant editor. Estab. 1991. Publishes hardcover originals, trade paperback originals and reprints. **Publishes 200 titles/year. Receives 1,000 queries and 1,000 manuscripts/year. 5% of books from first-time authors; 20% from unagented writers. Pays 10% royalty on retail price. Advance varies.** Publishes book 3 years after acceptance of manuscript

for illustrated books, 1 year for others. Accepts simultaneous submissions, if so noted. Reports in 10 weeks on manuscripts.

Tips: Candlewick Press publishes high-quality, illustrated children's books for infant through young adult.

CARROLL & GRAF PUBLISHERS INC.

Avalon Publishing Group
19 West 21st Street, Suite 601
New York, NY 10010
Phone: 212-627-8590
Fax: 212-627-8490
Web site: *http://www.carrollandgraf.com*
Acquisitions: Kent Carroll, publisher/executive editor. Estab. 1983. Publishes hardcover and trade paperback originals. **Publishes 120 titles/year. 10% of books from first-time authors. Pays 10-15% royalty on retail price for hardcover, 7½% for paperback. Offers $5,000 plus advance.** Publishes book 9 months after acceptance of manuscript. Reports in 1 month on queries.

Tips: Quality fiction and nonfiction for a general readership. Carroll and Graf is one of the few remaining independent trade publishers and is therefore able to publish successfully and work with first-time authors and novelists.

CARTWHEEL BOOKS

Scholastic, Inc.
555 Broadway
New York, NY 10012
Phone: 212-343-6100
Fax: 212-343-4444
Web site: *http://www.scholastic.com*
Vice President/Editorial Director: Bernette Ford. **Acquisitions**: Grace Maccarone, executive editor; Sonia Black, editor; Kimberly Weinberger, editor; Liza Baker, acquisitions editor. Estab. 1991. Publishes hardcover originals. **Publishes 85-100 titles/year. Receives 250 queries/year; 1,200 manuscripts/year. 1% of books from first-time authors; 50% from unagented writers. Pays royalty on retail price. Offers advance.** Publishes book 2 years after acceptance of manuscript. Accepts simultaneous submissions. Reports in 2 months on queries; 3 months on proposals; 6 months on manuscripts. Manuscript guidelines free.

Tips: Cartwheel Books publishes innovative books for children, ages 3-9. They look for "novelties" that are books first, play objects second.

CHRONICLE BOOKS

Chronicle Publishing Co.
85 Second Street, 6th Floor
San Francisco, CA 94105
Phone: 415-537-3730
Fax: 415-537-4440
E-mail: frontdesk@chronbooks.com
Web site: *http://www.chronbooks.com*
President: Nion McEvoy.

Acquisitions: Jay Schaefer, editor (fiction); Bill LeBlond, editor (cookbooks); Victoria Rock, editor (children's); Debra Lande, editor (ancillary products); Leslie Jonath, editor (lifestyle); Alan Rapp (art and design); Sarah Malarky (popular culture). Estab. 1966. Publishes hardcover and trade paperback originals. **Publishes 250 titles/year. Receives 22,500 submissions/year. 20% of books from first-time authors. 15% from unagented writers.** Publishes book 18 months after acceptance. Accepts simultaneous submissions. Reports in 3 months on queries. Guidelines available on Web site.

Tips: High-quality, reasonably priced illustrated books for adults and children.

Imprint(s): Chronicle Books for Children, GiftWorks (ancillary products, such as stationery, gift books).

CHRONICLE BOOKS FOR CHILDREN

Chronicle Books
85 Second Street, 6th Floor
San Francisco, CA 94105
Phone: 415-537-3730
Fax: 415-537-4420
E-mail: frontdesk@chronbooks.com
Web site: *http://www.chroniclebooks.com/kids*
Acquisitions: Victoria Rock, director of Children's Books (nonfiction/fiction); Amy Novesky, assistant managing editor (nonfiction/fiction plus middle grade and young adult). Publishes hardcover and trade paperback originals. **Publishes 40-50 titles/year. Receives 20,000 submissions/year. 5% of books from first-time authors; 25% from unagented writers. Pays 8% royalty. Advance varies.** Publishes book 18 months after acceptance of manuscript. Accepts simultaneous submissions if so noted. Reports in 2-18 weeks on queries; 5 months on manuscripts. Manuscript guidelines for #10 SASE.

Tips: Chronicle Books for Children publishes an eclectic mixture of traditional and innovative children's books.

DAW BOOKS, INC.

Penguin Putnam Inc.
375 Hudson Street, 3rd Floor
New York, NY 10014-3658
Phone: 212-366-2096
Fax: 212-366-2090
Web site: *http://www.dawbooks.com*
Publishers: Elizabeth Wollheim and Sheila Gilbert. Estab. 1971. Publishes hardcover and paperback originals and reprints. **Publishes 60-80 titles/year. Pays in royalties with an advance negotiable on a book-by-book basis.** Sends galleys to author. Simultaneous submissions "returned unread at once, unless prior arrangements are made by agent." Reports in 6 weeks "or longer, if a second reading is required."

Tips: DAW Books publishes science fiction and fantasy.

DEL REY BOOKS

Ballantine Publishing Group
Random House, Inc.
201 East 50th Street
New York, NY 10022-7703
Phone: 212-572-2677
E-mail: delrey@randomhouse.com
Web site: *http://www.randomhouse.com/delrey/*
Acquisitions: Shelley Shapiro, editorial director (science fiction). Estab. 1977. Publishes hardcover, trade paperback, and mass market originals and mass market paperback reprints. **Publishes 70 titles/year. Receives 1,900 submissions/year. 10% of books from first-time authors; 0% from unagented writers. Pays royalty on retail price. Offers competitive advance.** Publishes book 1 year after acceptance. Reports in 6 months, occasionally longer. Writer's guidelines for #10 SASE.
Tips: Del Rey publishes top-level fantasy and science fiction.

DELACORTE PRESS

Bantam Dell Publishing Group
Random House, Inc.
1540 Broadway
New York, NY 10036
Phone: 212-354-6500
Web site: *http://www.randomhouse.com*
Editor in Chief: Leslie Schnur.
Acquisitions: (Ms.) Jackie Cantor (women's fiction); Tom Spain (commercial nonfiction and fiction). Publishes hardcover and trade paperback originals. **Publishes 36 titles/year.**
Tips: Nonfiction and Fiction: *Agented submissions only.*

DELL PUBLISHING ISLAND

Bantam Dell Publishing Group
Random House, Inc.
1540 Broadway
New York, NY 10036
Phone: 212-354-6500
Web site: *http://www.randomhouse.com*
Acquisitions: Maggie Crawford, editorial director. Publishes mass market paperback originals and reprints. Publishes bestseller fiction and nonfiction. **Publishes 12 titles/year.**
Tips: Publishes commercial massmarket genre material. Study the list.

DELL TRADE PAPERBACKS

Bantam Dell Publishing Group
Random House, Inc.
1540 Broadway
New York, NY 10036
Phone: 212-354-6500
Web site: *http://www.randomhouse.com*
Acquisitions: Tom Spain, editorial director. Publishes trade paperback originals. **Publishes 36 titles/year.**
Tips: Dell Trade Paperbacks publishes light, humorous material and books on pop culture. Nonfiction: Humor, self-help, pop culture. *Agented submissions only.*

DELTA TRADE PAPERBACKS Bantam Dell Publishing Group, Random House, Inc.

1540 Broadway
New York, NY 10036
Phone: 212-354-6500
Acquisitions: Tom Spain, editorial director. **Publishes 36 titles/year.**
Tips: Delta Trade Paperbacks publishes serious nonfiction and literary fiction. **Nonfiction**: Biography, memoir. Subjects include ethnic, health/medicine, music. *Agented submissions only.*

DIAL BOOKS FOR YOUNG READERS

Penguin Putnam Inc.
345 Hudson Street, 3rd Floor
New York, NY 10014
Phone: 212-366-2800
Web site: *http://www.penguinputnam.com*
President/Publisher: Nancy Paulsen. Assistant Editor: Jocelyn Wright.
Acquisitions: Submissions Editor. Publishes hardcover originals.
Publishes 50 titles/year. Receives 5,000 queries and submissions/year. 10% of books from first-time authors. Pays variable royalty and advance. Reports in 4 months.
Tips: Dial Books for Young Readers publishes quality picture books for ages 18 months to 8 years, lively, believable novels for middle readers and young adults, and well-researched manuscripts for young adults and middle readers.
Imprint(s): Phyllis Fogelman Books.

DIAL PRESS

Bantam Dell Publishing Group
Random House, Inc.
1540 Broadway
New York, NY 10036
Phone: 212-354-6500
Fax: 212-782-9698
Web site: *http://www.randomhouse.com*
Acquisitions: Susan Kamil, vice president, editorial director. Estab. 1924. **Publishes 6-12 titles/year. Receives 200 queries and 450 manuscripts/year. 75% of books from first-time authors. Pays royalty**

on retail price. **Offers advance**. Publishes book 18 months after acceptance of manuscript. Accepts simultaneous submissions.

Tips: Dial Press publishes quality fiction and nonfiction. *Agented submissions only;* query with SASE.

DORCHESTER PUBLISHING CO., INC.

276 Fifth Avenue, Suite 1008
New York, NY 10001-0112
Phone: 212-725-8811
Fax: 212-532-1054
E-mail: dorchedit@dorchesterpub.com
Web site: *http://www.dorchesterpub.com*
Imprint(s): Love Spell (romance), Leisure Books.

DOUBLEDAY ADULT TRADE

Random House, Inc.
1540 Broadway
New York, NY 10036
Phone: 212-782-9911
Fax: 212-782-9700
Web site: *http://www.randomhouse.com*
Vice President/Editor in Chief: William Thomas. Estab. 1897. Publishes hardcover and trade paperback originals and reprints. **Publishes 200 titles/year. Receives thousands of queries and manuscripts/year. 30% of books from first-time authors. Pays royalty on retail price. Advance varies.** Publishes book 1 year after acceptance of manuscript. Reports in 6 months on queries.

Tips: Doubleday publishes high-quality fiction and nonfiction.

Imprint(s): Anchor Books; **Currency; Doubleday Religious Division; Image Books; Main Street; Nan A. Talese.**

DOUBLEDAY RELIGIOUS DIVISION

Doubleday Broadway Publishing Group
Random House, Inc.
1540 Broadway
New York, NY 10036
Phone: 212-354-6500
Fax: 212-782-8911
Web site: *http://www.randomhouse.com*
Acquisitions: Eric Major, vice president, religious division; Mark Fretz, senior editor; Trace Murphy, editor. Estab. 1897. Publishes hardcover originals and reprints, trade paperback originals and reprints. **Publishes 45-50 titles/year; each imprint publishes 12 titles/year. Receives 1,000 queries/year; receives 500 manuscripts/year. 30% of books are from first-time authors; 3% from unagented writers. Pays 7 1/2-15% royalty. Advance varies.** Publishes book 1 year after acceptance of manuscript. Accepts simultaneous submissions. Reports in 3 months on proposals.

Imprint(s): Image Books, Anchor Bible Commentary, Anchor Bible Reference, Galilee, New Jerusalem Bible.

Tips: Nonfiction: *Agented submissions only.* **Fiction:** *Agented submissions only.* Publishes only religious and spiritual material.

DOVER PUBLICATIONS, INC.

31 East 2nd Street
Mineola, NY 11501
Phone: 516-294-7000
Acquisitions: Paul Negri, editor in chief; John Grafton (math/science reprints). Estab. 1941. Publishes trade paperback originals and reprints. **Publishes 500 titles/year. Makes outright purchase.**
Nonfiction: Biography, children's/juvenile, coffee table book, cookbook, how-to, humor, illustrated book, textbook. Subjects include agriculture/horticulture, Americana, animals, anthropology/archaeology, art/architecture, cooking/food/nutrition, health/medicine, history, hobbies, language/literature, music/dance, nature/environment, philosophy, photography, religion, science, sports, translation, travel. Publishes mostly reprints. Accepts original paper doll collections, game books, coloring books (juvenile). Query. Reviews artwork/photos as part of manuscript package.
Tips: Specializes in art and illustrated books.

DUMMIES TRADE PRESS

IDG Books Worldwide
645 North Michigan Avenue
Chicago, IL 60611
Phone: 312-482-8460
Fax: 312-482-8561
E-mail: kwelton@idgbooks.com
Web site: *http://www.dummies.com*
Acquisitions: Kathleen A. Welton, vice president/publisher. Publishes trade paperback originals. **Pays 10-15% royalty. Offers $0-25,000 advance.** Publishes book 3 months after acceptance of manuscript. Reports in 2 months. Manuscript guidelines free.
Tips: Dummies Trade Press dedicates itself to publishing innovative, high-quality "For Dummies" titles on the most popular business, self-help, and general reference topics.

DUTTON PLUME

Penguin Putnam Inc.
375 Hudson Street
New York, NY 10014
Phone: 212-366-2000
Web site: *http://www.penguinputnam.com*
President: Clare Ferraro.
Acquisitions: Lori Lipsky, publisher (business, mainstream fiction); Brian Tart, editor in chief (commercial fiction, self-help/spirituality); Rosemary Ahern, senior editor (literary fiction, narrative nonfiction); Deb Brody, senior editor (narrative nonfiction, memoir, health, parenting, history, psychology, Judaica); Laurie Chittenden, senior editor (multicultural and women's fiction, narrative nonfiction); Jennifer Dickerson, associate editor (women's commercial fiction, literary fiction, spirituality, self-help); Jennifer Moore, associate editor (narrative nonfiction, African-American history/politics/culture, memoir, self-help, pop culture, women's fiction); Kimberly Perdue, assistant editor (Gen-X fiction, humor, self-help). Estab. 1852. **Publishes 60 titles/year. Receives 20,000 queries and 10,000**

manuscripts/year. 30-40% of books from first-time authors; 2% from unagented writers. Advance negotiable. Publishes book 18 months after acceptance. Reports in 6 months.

Tips: Dutton publishes hardcover, original, mainstream, and contemporary fiction and nonfiction in the areas of biography, self-help, politics, psychology, and science for a general readership.

DUTTON CHILDREN'S BOOKS

Penguin Putnam Inc.
345 Hudson Street
New York, NY 10014
Phone: 212-414-3700
Web site: *http://www.penguinputnam.com*

Acquisitions: Lucia Monfried, editor in chief. Estab. 1852. Publishes hardcover originals. **Publishes 80 titles/year. 15% from first-time authors. Pays royalty on retail price.**

Tips: Dutton Children's Books publishes fiction and nonfiction for readers ranging from preschoolers to young adults on a variety of subjects.

FACTS ON FILE, INC.

11 Penn Plaza
New York, NY 10001
Phone: 212-967-8800
Fax: 212-967-9196
E-mail: pkatzman.factsonfile.com
Web site: *http://www.factsonfile.com*

Acquisitions: Laurie Likoff, editorial director (science, music, history); Eleanora Von Dehsen (science, nature, multi-volume reference); Nicole Bowen, senior editor (American history, women's studies, young adult reference); James Chambers, trade editor (health, pop culture, sports); Pam Katzman, editorial assistant. Estab. 1941. Publishes hardcover originals and reprints. **Publishes 135 titles/year. Receives approximately 2,000 submissions/year. 25% of books from unagented writers. Pays 10-15% royalty on retail price. Offers $10,000 average advance.** Accepts simultaneous submissions. Reports in 2 months on queries.

Tips: Facts on File produces high-quality reference materials on a broad range of subjects for the school library market and the general nonfiction trade.

Imprint(s): Checkmark Books.

FALCON PUBLISHING, INC., Landmark Communications

P.O. Box 1718
Helena, MT 59624
Phone: 406-442-6597
Fax: 406-442-0384
E-mail: falcon@falconguide.com
Web site: *http://www.FalconOutdoors.com*

Acquisitions: Glenn Law, editorial director; Charlene Patterson, editorial assistant (Two Dot Books: regional and western history, western Americana). Estab. 1978. Publishes hardcover and trade paperback originals. **Publishes 80 titles/year. Receives 350 queries and 30 man-**

uscripts/year. 20% of books from first-time authors; 95% from unagented writers. Pays royalty on net sales. Publishes book 1-2 years after acceptance of manuscript. Accepts simultaneous submissions. Reports in 2 months on queries.

Tips: Falcon Press is primarily interested in ideas for recreational guidebooks and books on regional outdoor subjects.

Imprint(s): Chockstone, Falcon Guide, Insiders', Sky House, **Two Dot.**

FANFARE

Bantam Dell Publishing Group
Random House, Inc.
1540 Broadway
New York, NY 10036
Phone: 212-354-6500
Fax: 212-782-9523
Web site: *http://www.bdd.com*

Acquisition: Beth de Guzman, senior editor; Wendy McCurdy, senior editor; Stephanie Kip, editor. **Published 30 titles/year. 10-15% of books from first-time authors; less than 5% from unagented writers. Royalty and advance negotiable.** Publishes book 18 months after acceptance of manuscript. Accepts simultaneous submissions. Reports in 3 months on queries; 4 months on requested proposals and manuscripts.

Tips: Fanfare publishes a range of the best voices in women's fiction from brand new to established authors.

FARRAR STRAUS & GIROUX BOOKS FOR YOUNG READERS

Farrar Straus Giroux, Inc.
19 Union Square West
New York, NY 10003
Phone: 212-741-6900
Fax: 212-633-2427
Web site: *http://www.fsbassociates.com/fsg*

Acquisitions: Margaret Ferguson, editor in chief. Estab. 1946. Publishes hardcover and trade paperback originals. **Publishes 50 titles/year. Receives 6,000 queries and manuscripts/year. 10% of books from first-time authors; 50% from unagented writers. Pays 6% royalty on retail price for paperbacks, up to 10% for hardcovers. Offers $3,000-15,000 advance.** Publishes book 18 months after acceptance of manuscript. Accepts simultaneous submissions, if informed. Reports in 2 months on queries, 3 months on manuscripts. Manuscript guidelines for #10 SASE.

Tips: Original and well-written material for all ages.

Imprint(s): Aerial Fiction, Frances Foster Books, Mirasol/Libros Juveniles, R&S Books, Sunburst Paperbacks.

FARRAR, STRAUS & GIROUX, INC.

19 Union Square West
New York, NY 10003
Phone: 212-741-6900
Fax: 212-633-2427
Web site: *http://www.fsbassociates.com/fsg*
Estab. 1946. **Publishes 120 titles/year. Receives 5,000 submissions/year. Pays variable royalty. Offers advance. Publishes book 18 months after acceptance.**
Tips: Farrar, Straus & Giroux is one of the most respected publishers of top-notch commercial-literary fiction and specialized nonfiction, as well as cutting-edge poetry. Publishes hardcover originals.
Imprint(s): Faber & Faber Inc., **Farrar Straus & Giroux Books for Young Readers, Hill & Wang, Noonday Press, North point Press,** Sunburst Books.
Nonfiction and Fiction: Query.

FAWCETT JUNIPER

Ballantine Books
201 East 50th Street
New York, NY 10022
Phone: 212-751-2600
Web site: *http://www.randomhouse.com*
Acquisitions: Leona Nevler, editor. **Publishes 24 titles/year. Pays royalty. Offers advance.** Publishes book 1 year after acceptance of manuscript. Accepts simultaneous submissions. Reports in 6 months on queries.
Tips: Adult books in paperback.

FORGE

Tom Doherty Associates, LLC
175 Fifth Avenue, 14th Floor
New York, NY 10010
Phone: 212-388-0100
Fax: 212-388-0191
Web site: *http://www.tor.com*
Acquisitions: Melissa Ann Singer, senior editor (Western/historical, medical, or biotechnological thriller, mysteries, contemporary women's fiction, historical, women's or health issues, horror/occult); Natalia Aponte, editor (Western/historical, Women of the West, contemporary mystery, women's fiction, suspense/thriller, historical); Claire Eddy, editor (science fiction and fantasy, contemporary and historical mystery, historical suspense). Publishes hardcover, trade paperback, and mass market paperback originals, trade and mass market paperback reprints. **Receives 5,000 manuscripts/year. 2% of books from first-time authors; a few from unagented writers. Royalties: paperback, 6-8% first-time authors, 8-10% established authors; hardcover, 10% first 5,000, 12 1/2% second 5,000, 15% thereafter. Offers advance.** Reports in 4 months on proposals.
Tips: The best of past, present, and future—meaning they cover all ground in fiction from historicals set in prehistory to the sharpest contemporary fiction to the acknowledged best in science fiction and fantasy.

FOUR WALLS EIGHT WINDOWS

39 West 14th Street, Room 503
New York, NY 10011
Phone: 212-206-8965
Fax: 212-206-8799
E-mail: edit@fourwallseightwindows.com
Web site: *http://www.fourwallseightwindows.com*
Estab. 1987. Publisher: John Oakes.
Acquisitions: Jill Ellyn Riley, Senior Editor. Estab. 1987. Publishes hardcover originals, trade paperback originals, and reprints. **Publishes 20 titles/year. Receives 3,000 submissions/year. 15% of books from first-time authors; 50% from unagented writers. Pays royalty on retail price. Advance varies widely.** Publishes book 1-2 years after acceptance. Reports in 2 months on queries.
Tips: Emphasizes fine literature and quality nonfiction.
Imprint(s): No Exit.

FRANKLIN WATTS

Grolier Publishing
90 Sherman Turnpike
Danbury, CT 06816
Phone: 203-797-6802
Web site: *http://publishing.grolier.com/publishing.html*
Publisher: John Selfridge.
Acquisitions: Mark Friedman, executive editor; Melissa Stewart, senior editor (science); Douglas Hill, senior editor (reference). Estab. 1942. Publishes hardcover and softcover originals. **Publishes 150 titles/year. 5% of books from first-time authors; 95% from unagented writers. Advance varies.** Publishes book 18 months after acceptance of manuscript. Accepts simultaneous submissions. Reports in 4 months on queries.
Tips: Franklin Watts publishes nonfiction books for the library market (K-12) to supplement textbooks.

THE FREE PRESS

Simon & Schuster
1230 Avenue of the Americas
New York, NY 10020
Phone: 212-698-7000
Fax: 212-632-4989
Web site: *http://www.simonsays.com*
Acquisitions: Liz Maguire, editorial director; Paul Golob, associate editor; Chad Conway, associate editor; Robert Wallace, senior editor (business); Bruce Nichols, senior editor (history); Paul Golob (current events/politics); Philip Rapapport, editor (psychology/social work/self-help); Steven Morrow, editor (science, math, literature, art). Estab. 1947. **Publishes 120 titles/year. Receives 3,000 submissions/year. 15% of books from first-time authors; 50% of books from unagented writers. Pays variable royalty.** Publishes book 1 year after acceptance of manuscript. Reports in 2 months.
Tips: The Free Press publishes serious adult nonfiction.

THE GLOBE PEQUOT PRESS, INC.

P.O. Box 833
Old Saybrook, CT 06475-0833
Phone: 860-395-0440
Fax: 203-395-1418
Web site: *http://www.globe-pequot.com*
President/Publisher: Linda Kennedy.
Acquisitions: Shelly Wolf, submissions editor. Estab. 1947. Publishes hardcover originals, paperback originals and reprints. **Publishes 150 titles/year. Receives 1,500 submissions/year. 30% of books from first-time authors; 70% from unagented writers. Average print order for a first book is 4,000-7,500. Makes outright purchase or pays 10% royalty on net price. Offers advance.** Publishes book 1 year after acceptance of manuscript. Accepts simultaneous submissions. Reports in 3 months.
Tips: Globe Pequot is among the top sources for travel books in the United States and offers the broadest selection of travel titles of any vendor in this market.

G.P. PUTNAM'S SONS (Adult Trade)

Penguin Putnam, Inc.
375 Hudson
New York, NY 10014
Phone: 212-366-2000
Fax: 212-366-2666
Web site: *http://www.penguinputnam.com*
Acquisitions: Acquisitions Editor. Publishes hardcover and trade paperback originals. **5% of books from first-time authors; none from unagented writers. Pays variable advance on retail price.** Accepts simultaneous submissions. Reports in 6 months on queries. Manuscript guidelines free.
Imprint(s): Perigee, Price Stern Sloan, Putnam (children's), **Jeremy P. Tarcher.**
Tips: Trade books of high commercial quality.

GREENWILLOW BOOKS

William Morrow & Co.
1350 Avenue of the Americas
New York, NY 10019
Phone: 212-261-6500
Web site: *http://www.williammorrow.com*
Senior Editor: Elizabeth Shub.
Acquisitions: Editorial Department, Greenwillow Books. Estab. 1974. Publishes hardcover originals and reprints. **Publishes 60-70 titles/year. 1% of books from first-time authors; 30% from unagented writers. Pays 10% royalty on wholesale price for first-time authors. Advance varies.** Publishes manuscript 2 years after acceptance of manuscript. Accepts simultaneous submissions, if so noted. Reports in 3 months on manuscripts. Manuscript guidelines for #10 SASE.
Tips: Greenwillow Books publishes quality picture books and fiction for young readers of all ages, and nonfiction primarily for children under 7.

GREENWOOD PUBLISHING GROUP

Reed-Elsevier (USA) Inc.
88 post Road West
Westport, CT 06881
Phone: 203-226-3571
Fax: 203-222-1502
Web site: *http://www.greenwood.com*
Executive Vice President: Jim Sabin.
Acquisitions: Reference Publishing: Academic Reference—Cynthia Harris (history and economics, ext. 460, charris@greenwood.com); George Butler (anthropology, education, literature, drama and sociology, ext. 461, gbutler@greenwood.com); Alicia Merritt (art and architecture, music and dance, philosophy and religion, popular culture, ext. 443, amerritt@greenwood.com); Nita Romer (multicultural and women's studies, gerontology, media, political science and law, psychology, ext. 445, nromer@greenwood.com); interdisciplinary studies, such as African-American studies, are handled by all editors (contact js@greenwood.com). Secondary School Reference—Barbara Rader (literature, history, women's studies, school librarianship, ext. 442, brader@greenwood.com); Emily Birch (sociology, psychology, arts, religion, sports and recreation, ext. 448, ebirch@greenwood.com). Academic and Trade: Alan Sturmer (economics, business, law, ext. 475, asturmer@greenwood.com); Dan Eades (history and military studies, ext. 479, deades@greenwood.com); Jane Garry (library science, pregnancy, parenting, alternative medicine, education, and anthropology, ext. 480, jgarry@greenwood.com). Professional Publishing: Eric Valentine (Quorum Books, ext. 471, evalentine@greenwood.com). Publishes hardcover and trade paperback originals. **Publishes 700 titles/year. Pays royalty on net price. Offers advance rarely.** Publishes book 1 year after acceptance of manuscript. Accepts simultaneous submissions. Manuscript guidelines online.
Tips: The Greenwood Publishing Group consists of five distinguished imprints with one unifying purpose: to provide the best possible reference, professional, text, and scholarly resources in the humanities and the social and behavioral sciences.
Imprint(s): Auburn House, Bergin & Garvey, Greenwood Press, Praeger Publishers, Quorum Books.

GROLIER PUBLISHING

Grolier Inc.
90 Sherman Turnpike
Danbury, CT 06816
Phone: 203-797-3500
Fax: 203-797-3197
Web site: *http://www.publishing.grolier.com*
Executive Editor: Mark Friedman. Estab. 1895. Publishes hardcover and trade paperback originals.
Tips: A leading publisher of reference, educational, and children's books.
Imprint(s): Children's Press, Grolier Educational, **Orchard Books, Franklin Watts.**

GROSSET & DUNLAP PUBLISHERS

Penguin Putnam Inc.
345 Hudson Street
New York, NY 10014
Phone: 212-366-2000
Web site: *http://www.penguinputnam.com*
Associate Publisher: Ronnie Ann Herman. **Acquisitions**: Jane O'Connor, president. Estab. 1898. Publishes hardcover (few) and paperback originals. **Publishes 175 titles/year.** Publishes book 18 months after acceptance. Reports in 2 months.
Tips: Grosset & Dunlap publishes children's books that examine new ways of looking at the world of a child.
Imprint(s): Planet Dexter, Price Stern Sloan.
Nonfiction: *Agented submissions only.*
Fiction: *Agented submissions only.*

GROVE/ATLANTIC, INC.

841 Broadway
New York, NY 10003
Phone: 212-614-7850
Fax: 212-614-7886
Publisher: Morgan Entrekin.
Acquisitions: Joan Bingham, executive editor. Elizabeth Schmitz, senior editor/director of subsidiary rights. Estab. 1952. Publishes hardcover originals, trade paperback originals and reprints. **Publishes 60-70 titles/year. Receives 1000s queries/year. 10-15% of books from first-time authors; "very few" from unagented writers. Pays 7 1/2-15% royalty on retail price. Advance varies considerably.** Publishes book 1 year after acceptance of manuscript. Accepts simultaneous submissions. Because of volume of queries, Grove/Atlantic can only respond when interested—though SASE might generate a response.
Tips: Grove/Atlantic publishes serious nonfiction and literary fiction.

HARCOURT INC.

(formerly Harcourt Brace & Company)
Trade Division
525 B Street, Suite 1900
San Diego, CA 92101
Phone: 619-699-6560
Fax: 619-699-5555
Web site: *http://www.harcourtbooks.com*
Acquisitions: David Hough, managing editor; Jane Isay, editor-in- chief (science, math, history, language); Drenka Willen, senior editor (poetry, fiction in translation, history); Walter Bode, editor (history, geography, American fiction). Publishes hardcover and trade paperback originals and trade paperback reprints. **Publishes 120 titles/year. 5% of books from first-time authors; 5% from unagented writers. Pays 6-15% royalty on retail price. Offers $2,000 minimum advance.** Accepts simultaneous manuscripts.
Tips: Harcourt Inc. owns some of the world's most prestigious publishing imprints—imprints that distinguish quality products for the juvenile, educa-

tional, scientific, technical, medical, professional, and trade markets worldwide. Currently emphasizing science and math.
Imprint(s): Harvest (contact Andre Bernard).

HARCOURT INC.

(formerly Harcourt Brace & Company)
Children's Books Division
525 B Street, Suite 1900
San Diego, CA 92101
Phone: 619-261-6616
Fax: 619-699-6777
Web site: *http://www.harcourtbooks.com/Childrens/childrn.html*
Publisher: Louise Pelan. Estab. 1919. Publishes hardcover originals and trade paperback reprints.
Tips: Harcourt Inc. owns some of the world's most prestigious publishing imprints—imprints that distinguish quality products for the juvenile, educational, scientific, technical, medical, professional, and trade markets worldwide.
Imprint(s): Browndeer Press, Gulliver Books, Gulliver Green, Magic Carpet, Red Wagon, Silver Whistle, Voyager Paperbacks.

HARPERCOLLINS PUBLISHERS

10 E. 53rd Street
New York, NY 10022
Phone: 212-207-7000
Web site: *http://www.harpercollins.com*
Publishes hardcover fiction and nonfiction. **Publishes 120-150 titles a year.** Reports on solicited queries in 6 weeks. *Agented submissions only.*
Tips: HarperCollins, one of the largest English language publishers in the world, is a broad-based publisher with strengths in serious nonfiction and quality fiction, commercial fiction, business and professional, children's, educational, general interest, religious and spiritual books, self-help books, as well as multimedia titles.
Imprint(s): Cliff Street Books (contact Diane Reverand), **Ecco Press**, Harper Adult Trade, HarperAudio, **HarperBusiness**, **HarperCollins**, **HarperCollins Children's Books**, HarperEdge, **HarperEntertainment**, HarperFlamingo (contact Susan Weinberg), HarperHorizon, **HarperLibros**, HarperPaperbacks, **HarperPerennial**, HarperPrism, HarperResource, **HarperSanFrancisco**, HarperTrophy, HarperVoyager, **Regan Books**, **Zondervan Publishing House**.

HARPERBUSINESS, HarperCollins Publishers

10 E. 53rd St.
New York, NY 10036
Phone: 212-207-7006
Web site: *http://www.harpercollins.com*
Acquisitions: Adrian Zackheim, senior vice president/publisher; David Conti, executive editor; Laureen Rowland, senior editor. Estab. 1991. Publishes hardcover, trade paperback and mass market paperback originals, hardcover and trade paperback reprints. **Publishes 50-55 titles/year. Receives 500 queries and manuscripts/year. 1% of books from first-time authors; 10% from unagented writers.**

Pays royalty on retail price; varies. Offers advance. Accepts simultaneous submissions. Reports in 2 months on proposals and manuscripts.

Tips: HarperBusiness publishes the inside story on ideas that will shape business practices and thinking well into the next millennium, with cutting-edge information and visionary concepts. Currently emphasizing finance, motivation, technology.

HARPERCOLLINS CHILDREN'S BOOKS

HarperCollins Publishers
1350 Sixth Avenue
New York, NY 10022
Phone: 212-207-7000
Web site: *http://www.harpercollins.com*
Editor in Chief: Kate Morgan Jackson. **Acquisitions**: Alix Reid, executive editor; Robert Warren, editorial director; Phoebe Yeh, executive editor. Publishes hardcover originals. **Publishes 350 titles/year. Receives 200 queries and 5,000 manuscripts/year. 5% of books from first-time authors; 25% from unagented writers. Pays 10-12½% royalty on retail price. Advance varies.** Publishes novel 1 year and picture books 2 years after acceptance of manuscript. Accepts simultaneous submissions. Reports in 1 month on queries and proposals, 4 months on manuscripts. Ms guidelines for #10 SASE.

Tips: "We have no rules for subject matter, length or vocabulary, but look instead for ideas that are fresh and imaginative, good writing that involves the reader is essential."

Imprint(s): Joanna Cotler Books (Joanna Cotler, editorial director); Michael DiCapua Books (Michael DiCapua, editorial director); **Laura Geringer Books** (Laura Geringer, editorial director); HarperFestival (Mary Alice Moore, editorial director); HarperTrophy (Ginee Seo, editorial director).

HARPERENTERTAINMENT (formerly HarperActive)

HarperCollins Publishers
10 East 53rd Street
New York, NY 10022
Phone: 212-207-7000
Web site: *http://www.harpercollins.com/imprints/harper_entertainment*
Editorial Director/Vice President: John Silbersacki. **Acquisitions**: Lara Comstock, editor. Caitlin Blasdell editor. Estab. 1997. **20% of books from first-time authors. Writer-for- hire arrangements mostly. Fees vary.** Reports in 3-12 months on manuscripts. Manuscripts guidelines not available.

Tips: HarperEntertainment is dedicated to publishing sports, movie and TV tie-ins, celebrity bios, and books reflecting trends in popular culture.

HARPERLIBROS, HarperCollins Publishers

10 East 53rd Street
New York, NY 10022
Phone: 212-207-7000
Fax: 212-207-7145

Web site: *http://www.harpercollins.com*
Acquisitions: Terry Karten, editorial director. Estab. 1994. Publishes hardcover and trade paperback originals. **Publishes 10 titles/year. Receives 250 queries/year. 30% of books from first-time authors. Pays variable royalty on net price. Advance varies.** Publishes book 1 year after acceptance of manuscript.

Tips: Harper Libros offers Spanish language editions of selected HarperCollins titles, sometimes reprints, and sometimes new books that are published simultaneously in English and Spanish.

HARPERPERENNIAL, HarperCollins Publishers

10 East 53rd Street
New York, NY 10036
Phone: 212-207-7000
Web site: *http://www.harpercollins.com*
Acquisitions: Acquisitions Editor. Estab. 1963. Publishes trade paperback originals and reprints. **Publishes 100 titles/year. Receives 500 queries/year. 5% of books from first-time authors; 2% from unagented writers. Pays 5-7 1/2% royalty. Advance varies.** Publishes book 6 months after acceptance of manuscript. Reports in 2 weeks on queries, 1 month on manuscripts.

Tips: Harper Perennial publishes a broad range of adult literary fiction and nonfiction paperbacks.

HARPERSANFRANCISCO, HarperCollins Publishers

353 Sacramento Street, Suite 500
San Francisco, CA 94111-3653
Phone: 415-477-4400
Fax: 415-477-4444
E-mail: hcsanfrancisco@harpercollins.com
Web site: *http://www.harpercollins.com*
Senior Vice President: Diane Gedymin. **Acquisitions**: Liz Perle, editor-at-large (women's studies, psychology, personal growth, inspiration); Douglas Adams, senior editor (Hebrew Bible, Judaism, religion, health, sexuality); John Loudon, executive editor (religious studies, biblical studies, psychology/personal growth, Eastern religions). Estab. 1977. Publishes hardcover originals, trade paperback originals and reprints. **Publishes 75 titles/year. Receives about 10,000 submissions/year. 5% of books from first-time authors. Pays royalty.** Publishes book within 18 months after acceptance.

Tips: HarperSanFrancisco publishes books that nurture the mind, body, and spirit.

HARRY N. ABRAMS, INC.

La Martiniere Groupe
100 Fifth Avenue
New York, NY 10011
Phone: 212-206-7715
Web site: *http://www.abramsbooks.com*
President/Publisher/Editor in Chief: Paul Gottlieb. Executive Editor: Susan Randol.

Acquisitions: Margaret Chace, managing editor. Estab. 1949. Publishes hardcover and "a few" paperback originals. **Publishes 100 titles/year. Pays royalty. Offers variable advance.** Publishes book 2 years after acceptance of manuscript. Reports in 3 months.

Tips: Abrams publishes *only* high-quality illustrated art books, i.e., art, art history, and museum exhibition catalogs, written by specialists and scholars in the field.

HAZELDEN PUBLISHING

P.O. Box 176
Center City, MN 55012
Phone: 651-257-4010
Web site: *http://www.hazelden.org*

Acquisitions: Rebecca post, executive editor. Estab. 1954. Publishes hardcover and trade paperback originals and trade paperback reprints. **Publishes 80 titles/year. Receives 2,500 queries and 1,000 manuscripts/year. 30% of books from first-time authors; 50% from unagented writers. Pays 8% royalty on retail price. Offers advance based on first-year sales projections.** Publishes book 1 year after acceptance of manuscript. Accepts simultaneous submissions. Reports in 6 months. Manuscript guidelines free.

Tips: Hazelden specializes in psychology, self-help, and spiritual books that help enhance the quality of people's lives. Products include gift books, curriculum, workbooks, audio and video, computer-based products, and wellness products.

HEINEMANN, Reed Elsevier (USA) Inc.

361 Hanover Street
Portsmouth, NH 03801
Phone: 603-431-7894
Fax: 603-431-7840
Web site: *http://www.heinemann.com*

Acquisitions: Leigh Peake, executive editor (education); Lisa Barnett, senior editor (performing arts); William Varner, acquisitions editor (literacy); Lisa Luedeke, acquisitions editor (Boynton/Cook). Estab. 1977. Publishes hardcover and trade paperback originals. **Publishes 80-100 titles/year. 50% of books from first-time authors; 75% from unagented writers. Pays royalty on wholesale price. Advance varies widely.** Publishes book 9 months after acceptance of manuscript. Accepts simultaneous submissions. Reports in 3 months on proposals. Manuscript guidelines for #10 SASE.

Tips: Heinemann specializes in theater and education titles. Their goal is to offer a wide selection of books that satisfy the needs and interests of educators from kindergarten to college. Currently emphasizing literacy education, K-12 education through technology.

Imprint(s): Boynton/Cook Publishers, Beeline Books.

HENRY HOLT & COMPANY, INC.

115 West 18th Street
New York, NY 10011
Phone: 212-886-9200
Web site: *http://www.henryholt.com*

President: John Sterling. Executive Director, Owl Books: Wendy Sherman. **Acquisitions**: Sara Bershtel, editorial director of Metropolitan Books (literary fiction, politics, history); Elizabeth Stein, adult trade editor; Elizabeth Crossman, editor (cooking); David Sobel, senior editor (science, culture, history, health); (Mr.) Tracy Brown, executive editor (adult literary fiction, culture, popular music, biography); Amelia Sheldon, editor, Owl Books (lifestyle, health, self-help, women's studies). Query before submitting.

Tips: Holt is a general interest publisher of quality fiction and nonfiction.

Imprint(s): John Macrae Books, Metropolitan Books, Owl Books, Henry Holt & Company Books for Young Readers (Books by Michael Hague, Books by Bill Martin Jr. and John Archambault, Owlet Paperbacks, Redfeather Books, W-5 Reference).

HENRY HOLT & COMPANY BOOKS FOR YOUNG READERS

Henry Holt & Co., Inc.
115 West 18th Street
New York, NY 10011
Phone: 212-886-9200
Web site: *http://www.henryholt.com*

Associate Publisher: Laura Godwin (picture books, chapter books and middle grade). Senior Editor: Marc Aronson (young adult). Senior Editor: Christy Ottaviano (picture books, chapter books and middle grade). Associate Editor: Margaret Garrou. Acquisitions: BYR Submissions. Estab. 1866 (Holt). Publishes hardcover originals. **Publishes 70-80 titles/year. 5% of books from first-time authors; 50% from unagented writers. Pays royalty on retail price. Offers $3,000 and up advance.** Publishes book 18 months after acceptance of manuscript. Reports in 5 months on queries and manuscripts. Manuscript guidelines free with SASE.

Tips: Highly original and cutting-edge fiction and nonfiction for all ages, from the very young to the young adult.

Imprint(s): Books by Michael Hague; Books by Bill Martin Jr. and John Archambault; Edge Books (cutting-edge young adult books); Owlet Paperbacks; Redfeather Books (chapter books for ages 7-10), W-5 Reference.

HERITAGE BOOKS, INC.

1540-E pointer Ridge Place
Bowie, MD 20716-1859
Phone: 301-390-7708
Fax: 301-390-7193
Web site: *http://www.heritagebooks.com*

Acquisitions: Karen Ackerman, editorial supervisor. Estab. 1978. Publishes hardcover and paperback originals and reprints. **Publishes 100 titles/year. Receives 300 submissions/year. 25% of books from first-time authors; 100% from unagented writers. Pays 10% royalty on list price.** Accepts simultaneous submissions. Reports in 1 month. Allow 2 months for reply.

Tips: Nonfiction dealing with history and genealogy.

HILL AND WANG, Farrar Straus & Giroux, Inc.

19 Union Square West
New York, NY 10003
Phone: 212-741-6900
Fax: 212-633-9385
Acquisitions: Elisabeth Sifton, publisher; Lauren Osborne, senior editor.
Estab. 1956. Publishes hardcover and trade paperback originals.
Publishes 12 titles/year. Receives 1,500 queries/year. 5% of books from first-time authors; 50% from unagented writers. Pays 7 1/2% royalty on retail price. Advances "vary widely from a few hundred to several thousand dollars." Publishes book 1 year after acceptance of manuscript. Accepts simultaneous submissions. Reports in 2 months.
Tips: Hill and Wang publishes serious nonfiction books, primarily in history and the social sciences.

HIPPOCRENE BOOKS INC.

171 Madison Avenue
New York, NY 10016
Phone: 212-685-4371
Fax: 212-779-9338
E-mail: hippocre@ix.netcom.com
Web site: *http://www.hippocrenebooks.com*
President/Publisher: George Blagowidow. **Acquisitions**: Carol Chitnis, managing editor (cooking, classic poetry, travel, polish interest); Nadia Hassani, associate editor (foreign language dictionaries, leaning guides); Kara Migliorelli, associate editor (illustrated histories, weddings, proverbs). Estab. 1971. Publishes hardcover and trade paperback originals. **Publishes 100 titles/year. Receives 250 submissions/year. 10% of books from first-time authors; 95% from unagented writers. Pays 6-10% royalty on retail price. Offers $2,000 advance.** Publishes book 16 months after acceptance of manuscript. Accepts simultaneous submissions. Reports in 2 months. Manuscript guidelines for #10 SASE.
Tips: Reference books of international interest, often bilingual, in the fields of cookery, travel, language, and literature. It specializes in foreign language dictionaries and learning guides and also publishes ethnic cuisine cookbooks, travel, and history titles. Currently emphasizing cookery, history, and foreign language. De-emphasizing military history and travel.

HOUGHTON MIFFLIN BOOKS FOR CHILDREN

Houghton Mifflin Company
222 Berkeley Street
Boston, MA 02116
Phone: 617-351-5959
Fax: 617-351-1111
Web site: *http://www.hmco.com*
Acquisitions: Amanda Sullivan, submissions coordinator. Publishes hardcover and trade paperback originals and reprints. **Publishes 100 titles/year. Receives 5,000 queries and 12,000 manuscripts/year. 10% of books from first-time authors; 70% from unagented writers. Pays 5-10% royalty on retail price. Advance dependent on many factors.** Publishes book 18 months after acceptance of manu-

script. Accepts simultaneous submissions. Reports in 4 months. Manuscript guidelines for #10 SASE.
Tips: Houghton Mifflin gives shape to ideas that educate, inform, and, above all, delight.
Imprint(s): Sandpiper Paperback Books (Eden Edwards, editor).

HOUGHTON MIFFLIN COMPANY

222 Berkeley Street
Boston, MA 02116
Phone: 617-351-5000
Fax: 617-351-1202
Web site: *http://www.hmco.com*
Vice President: Arthur S. Battle Jr. Senior Editor: Anton Mueller. Executive Editor: Janet Silver. **Acquisitions**: Submissions Editor. Estab. 1832. Publishes hardcover and trade paperback originals and reprints.
Publishes 60 hardcovers, 30-40 paperbacks/year. 10% of books from first-time authors; 20% from unagented writers. Hardcover: pays 10-15% royalty on retail price, sliding scale or flat rate based on sales; paperback: 7 1/2% flat fee, but negotiable. Advance varies. Publishes book 1-2 years after acceptance of manuscript. Accepts simultaneous submissions. Reports in 3 months. Manuscript guidelines free.
Tips: Houghton Mifflin gives shape to ideas that educate, inform, and delight.
Imprint(s): Chapters Publishing Ltd., Clarion Books, Peter Davison Books, Walter Lorraine Books, **Houghton Mifflin Books for Children**, Mariner Paperbacks, Sandpiper Paperbacks, Frances Tenenbaum Books.

HOWELL BOOK HOUSE

Macmillan General Reference
1633 Broadway
New York, NY 10019
Phone: 212-654-8500
Acquisitions: Dominique DeVito, editor in chief; Don Stevens, associate publisher; Seymour Weiss, executive editor (dogs, birds); Beth Adelman, editor (dogs, cats, birds); Amanda Pisani, editor (dogs, cats, fish, reptiles). Publishes hardcover originals, trade paperback originals and reprints.
Publishes 60- 100 titles/year. Receives 3,000 queries/year. 15% of books from first-time authors; 40% from unagented writers. Pays royalty on retail price or net sales, or makes outright purchase or work-for-hire assignments. Offers variable advance. Publishes book 1 year after acceptance of manuscript. Accepts simultaneous submissions. Reports in 2 months on queries and manuscripts, 1 month on proposals.
Tips: Howell Book House is a publisher of reference books for owners of companion animals: horses, dogs, cats, fish, birds, reptiles, small mammals, and exotics. Currently emphasizing dogs.

HUMAN KINETICS PUBLISHERS, INC.

P.O. Box 5076
Champaign, IL 61825-5076
Phone: 217-351-5076
Fax: 217-351-2674
Web site: *http://www.humankinetics.com*
Acquisitions: Ted Miller, director (trade); Loarn Robertson, director (academic); Martin Barnard, trade senior acquisitions editor (fitness, running, golf, tennis, cycling, fishing); Scott Wikgren, academic director (physical education, youth fitness and physical activity, recreation); Mike Bahrke, academic acquisitions editor (exercise physiology, strength and conditioning, health-fitness leadership, personal training, nutrition, supplements); Loarn Robertson, academic acquisitions editor (biomechanics, anatomy, athletic training, cardiac rehab, test/measurement); Judy Wright, academic acquisitions editor (dance, motor, learning/behavior/performance/development, gymnastics, adapted physical education, older adults); Steve pope, academic acquisitions editor (sport psychology, sport history, sport sociology, sport management, women and sport, recreation and leisure); Dale Lloyd, American fitness alliance director (youth fitness, fitness testing). Publisher: Rainer Martens. Estab. 1974. Publishes hardcover and paperback text and reference books, trade paperback originals, software and audiovisual.
Publishes 120 titles/year. Receives 300 submissions/year. 30% of books from first-time authors; 90% of books from unagented writers. Pays 10-15% royalty on net income. Publishes book an average of 18 months after acceptance. Accepts simultaneous submissions. Reports in 2 months.
Tips: Human Kinetics publishes books that accurately interpret sport and fitness training and techniques, physical education, sports sciences and sports medicine for coaches, athletes and fitness enthusiasts, and professionals in the physical action field.
Imprint(s): HK Trade, HK Academic.

HUNTER PUBLISHING, INC.

130 Campus Drive
Edison, NJ 08818
Phone: 561-546-7986
Fax: 561-546-8040
E-mail: hunterp@bellsouth.net
Web site: *http://www.hunterpublishing.com*
Acquisitions: Kim Andre, editor; Lissa Dailey. President: Michael Hunter. Estab. 1985. **Publishes 100 titles/year. Receives 300 submissions/year. 10% of books from first-time authors; 75% from unagented writers. Pays royalty. Offers negotiable advance.** Publishes book 5 months after acceptance of manuscript. Accepts simultaneous submissions. Reports in 3 weeks on queries, 1 month on manuscript. Allow 2 months for reply.
Tips: Hunter Publishing publishes practical guides for travelers going to the Caribbean, United States, Europe, South America, and the far reaches of the globe.
Imprint(s): Adventure Guides, Romantic Weekends Guides, Alive Guides.

HYPE RIAN BOOKS

77 W. 66th Street 11th Floor
New York, NY 10023
(212) 456-6298
Publisher: Martha Levin
Part of the Disney group. **Publishes 100 books per year apprximately**. No unagented submissions.

INTERLINK PUBLISHING GROUP, INC.

46 Crosby Street
Northampton, MA 01060
Phone: 413-582-7054
Fax: 413-582-7057
E-mail: interpg@aol.com
Web site: *http://www.interlinkbooks.com*
Acquisitions: Michel Moushabeck, publisher. Estab. 1987. Publishes hardcover and trade paperback originals. **Publishes 50 titles/year. Receives 600 submissions/year. 30% of books from first-time authors; 50% from unagented writers. Pays 6-8% royalty on retail price.** Publishes book 18 months after acceptance. Accepts simultaneous submissions. Reports in 1 month on queries. Allow 2 months for reply. Manuscript guidelines free.
Tips: Interlink publishes a general trade list of adult fiction and nonfiction with an emphasis on books that have a wide appeal while also meeting high intellectual and literary standards.
Imprint(s): Crocodile Books, USA; Interlink Books; Olive Branch Press.

KENSINGTON

850 Third Avenue, 16th Floor
New York, NY 10022
Phone: 212-407-1500
Fax: 212-935-0699
Web site: *http://www.kensingtonbooks.com*
Acquisitions: Ann LaFarge, executive editor (romance, fiction); Tracy Bernstein, editorial director (pop culture, spiritual, new age, parenting, health); Paul Dinas, editor in chief (nonfiction, true crime thrillers); Kate Duffy, editorial director (historical, regency, romance); John Scognamiglio, editorial director (romance, mystery thrillers, gay fiction); Hillary Sares, editor (Precious Gem romances); Karen Thomas, senior editor (Arabesque multicultural romances); Diane Stockwell, editor (Encanto, Hispanic romances). Estab. 1975. Publishes hardcover originals, trade paperback originals and reprints. **Kensington publishes 300 titles/year; Pinnacle 60; Zebra 140-170; Arabesque 48. Receives 6,000 queries/year. 3-5% of books from first-time authors. Pays royalty on retail price, varies by author and type of book. Advance varies by author and type of book.** Publishes book 18 months after acceptance of manuscript. Accepts simultaneous submissions. Reports in 1 month on queries; 3 months on manuscripts. Manuscript guidelines for SASE or on Web site.
Tips: Kensington focuses on profitable niches and uses aggressive marketing techniques to support its books.
Imprint(s): Arabesque, Bouquet, Encanto, Kensington, Pinnacle, Precious Gems, Zebra.

LAUREL BOOKS

Bantam Dell Publishing Group
Random House, Inc.
1540 Broadway
New York, NY 10036
Phone: 212-354-6500
Web site: *http://www.randomhouse.com*
Acquisitions: Maggie Crawford, editorial director. Publishes trade paperback and mass market originals. **Publishes 4 titles/year.**
Fiction: Literary anthologies. *Agented submissions only.*
Tips: High quality, literary material only.

LEISURE BOOKS

276 Fifth Avenue, Suite 1008
New York, NY 10001-0112
Phone: 212-725-8811
Fax: 212-532-1054
E-mail: dorchedit@dorchesterpub.com
Web site: *http://www.dorchesterpub.com*
Acquisitions: Jennifer Bonnell, editorial assistant; Kate Seaver, editorial assistant; Alicia Condon, editorial director; Don D'Auria, senior editor (Westerns, technothrillers, horror); Christopher Keeslar, editor. Estab. 1970. Publishes mass market paperback originals and reprints. **Publishes 160 titles/year. Receives thousands of manuscripts/year. 20% of books from first-time authors; 20% from unagented writers. Pays royalty on retail price. Advance negotiable.** Publishes book 18 months after acceptance of manuscript. Reports in 6 months on queries.
Tips: Leisure Books is seeking historical romances, Westerns, horror, and technothrillers.
Imprint(s): **Love Spell** (romance), **Leisure** (romance, Western, techno, horror).

LERNER PUBLISHING GROUP

241 First Avenue North
Minneapolis, MN 55401
Phone: 612-332-3344
Web site: *http://www.lernerbooks.com*
Editor in Chief: Mary Rodgers.
Acquisitions: Jennifer Martin, editor. Estab. 1959. Publishes hardcover originals, trade paperback originals and reprints. **Publishes 150-175 titles/year; First Avenue Edition, 30; Carolrhoda, 50-60; Runestone Press, 3. Receives 1,000 queries and 300 manuscripts/year. 20% of books from first-time authors; 95% from unagented writers. Pays 3-8% royalty on net price (approximately 60% of books) or makes outright purchase of $1,000-3,000 (for series and work-for-hire). Offers $1,000-3,000 advance.** Publishes book 2 years after acceptance of manuscript. Submissions accepted March 1 to March 31 and October 1 to October 31, only. Accepts simultaneous submissions. Reports in 4 months on

proposals. Manuscript guidelines for #10 SASE. Requests for submissions guidelines must be clearly addressed as such on envelope.
Tips: Books that educate, stimulate and stretch the imagination, foster global awareness, encourage critical thinking and inform, inspire, and entertain. Currently emphasizing biographies. De-emphasizing fiction.
Imprint(s): **Carolrhoda Books**; First Avenue Editions (paperback reprints for hard/soft deals only); Lerner Publications; Runestone Press.

LISA DREW BOOKS

Simon & Schuster
1230 Avenue of the Americas
New York, NY 10020
Phone: 212-698-7000
Web site: *http://www.simonandschuster.com*
Acquisitions: Lisa Drew, publisher. Publishes hardcover originals. **Publishes 10-14 titles/year. Receives 600 queries/year. 10% of books from first-time authors. Pays royalty on retail price, varies by author and project. Advance varies.** Publishes book 1 year after acceptance of manuscript. Accepts simultaneous submissions, if so noted. Reports in 1 month on queries.
Tips: Nonfiction that tell a story, not "14 ways to improve your marriage." *Agented submissions only.*

LITTLE, BROWN AND CO., INC.

Time Warner Inc.
1271 Avenue of the Americas
New York, NY 10020
Phone: 212-522-8700
Web site: *http://www.littlebrown.com*
Editor in Chief: Michael Pietsch.
Acquisitions: Editorial Department, Trade Division. Estab. 1837. Publishes hardcover originals and paperback originals and reprints. **Publishes 100 titles/year. "Royalty and advance agreements vary from book to book and are discussed with the author at the time an offer is made."**
Tips: High quality and the promise of commercial success as always the first considerations.
Imprint(s): Back Bay Books; **Bulfinch Press**; **Little, Brown and Co. Children's Books.**

LITTLE SIMON

Simon & Schuster Children's Publishing Division
Simon & Schuster
1230 Avenue of the Americas
New York, NY 10020
Phone: 212-698-7200
Web site: *http://www.simonandschuster.com*
Vice President/Publisher: Robin Corey. Acquisitions: Alison Weir, editorial director; Laura Hunt, senior editor. Publishes novelty books only. **Publishes 75 titles/year. 5% of books from first-time authors; 5% from unagented writers. Pays 2-5% royalty on retail price for original, nonlicensed manuscripts.** Publishes book 6 months after acceptance of manuscript. Reports on queries in 8 months.
Tips: Fresh material in an innovative format for preschool to age 8. Our books are often, if not exclusively, illustrator driven.

LITTLE, BROWN AND CO., CHILDREN'S BOOKS

3 Center Plaza
Boston, MA 02108
Phone: 617-227-0730
Web site: *http://www.littlebrown.com*
Editorial Director/Associate Publisher: Maria Modugno. Executive Editor: Megan Tingley. **Acquisitions**: Leila Little. Estab. 1837. Publishes hardcover originals, trade paperback originals and reprints. **Firm publishes 60-70 titles/year. Pays royalty on retail price. Offers advance to be negotiated individually.** Publishes book 2 years after acceptance of manuscript. Accepts simultaneous submissions, if so noted. Reports in 1 month on queries, 2 months on proposals and manuscripts.
Tips: Little, Brown and Co. publishes books on a wide variety of nonfiction topics that may be of interest to children and is looking for strong writing and presentation, but no predetermined topics.

LLEWELLYN PUBLICATIONS

Llewellyn Worldwide, Ltd.
P.O. Box 64383
Street Paul, MN 55164-0383
Phone: 612-291-1970
Fax: 612-291-1908
E-mail: lwlpc@llewellyn.com
Web site: *http://www.llewellyn.com*
Acquisitions: Nancy J. Mostad, acquisitions manager (new age, metaphysical, occult, self-help, how-to books); Barbara Wright, acquisitions editor (kits and decks). Estab. 1901. Publishes trade and mass market paperback originals. **Publishes 100 titles/year. Receives 2,000 submissions/year. 30% of books from first-time authors; 90% from unagented writers. Pays 10% royalty on moneys received both wholesale and retail.** Accepts simultaneous submissions. Reports in 3 months. Manuscript guidelines for SASE.

Tips: Llewellyn publishes new age fiction and nonfiction exploring new worlds of mind and spirit. Currently emphasizing astrology, wicca, alternative health and healing, tarot. De-emphasizing fiction, channeling.

LONELY PLANET PUBLICATIONS

150 Linden Street
Oakland, CA 94607-2538
Phone: 510-893-8555
Fax: 510-893-8563
E-mail: info@lonelyplanet.com
Web site: *http://www.lonelyplanet.com*
Acquisitions: Mariah Bear, publishing manager (travel guide books); Roslyn Bullas, publishing manager (Pisces). Estab. 1973. Publishes trade paperback originals. **Publishes 60 titles/year. Receives 500 queries and 100 manuscripts/year. 5% of books from first-time authors; 50% from unagented writers. Makes outright purchase or negotiated fee—1/3 on contract, 1/3 on submission, 1/3 on approval.** Publishes book 2 years after acceptance of manuscript. Accepts simultaneous submissions. Reports in 3 months on queries. Manuscript guidelines for #10 SASE.
Tips: Lonely Planet publishes travel guides, atlases, travel literature, diving, and snorkeling guides.

LOWELL HOUSE, NTC/Contemporary

2020 Avenue of the Stars, Suite 300
Los Angeles, CA 90067
Phone: 310-552-7555
Web site: *http://www.ntc-cb.com*
Executive Editor: Linda Grey.
Acquisitions: Bud Sperry, senior editor (trade health, nonfiction, mental health, cookbooks); Peter Hoffman, senior editor (natural and alternative trade titles); Michael Artenstein, editor in chief (fiction, nonfiction); Brenda pope-Ostron, editorial director (juvenile, educational titles). Publishes hardcover originals, trade paperback originals and reprints. **Publishes 120 titles/year. 60% of books from first-time authors; 75% from unagented writers. Pays royalty on retail price.** Publishes book 20 months after acceptance of manuscript. Accepts simultaneous submissions. Reports in 3 months on proposals.
Tips: Lowell House publishes reference titles in health, parenting, and adult education that emphasize alternative, natural health. Currently emphasizing health.
Imprint(s): Anodyne, Draw Science, Extension Press, 50 Nifty, Classics, Gifted & Talented, Legacy Press, Woman to Woman.

MACMILLAN BRANDS

Macmillan General Reference
1633 Broadway
New York, NY 10019
Phone: 212-654-8500
Fax: 212-654-4822

Web site: *http://www.mgr.com*

Acquisitions: Susan Clarey, publisher; Anne Ficklen, executive editor (Weight Watchers, Betty Crocker); Jim Willhite, editor (Burpee gardening); Emily Nolan, editor (Weight Watchers, Betty Crocker). Publishes hardcover originals, trade paperback originals and reprints. **Publishes 60-100 titles/year. Receives 3,000 queries/year. 15% of books from first-time authors; 5% from unagented writers. Pays royalty on retail price or net sales, or makes outright purchase or work-for-hire assignments. Offers variable advance.** Publishes book 1 year after acceptance of manuscript. Accepts simultaneous submissions. Reports in 2 months on queries and manuscripts, 1 month on proposals.

Tips: Macmillan Brands publishes cooking and gardening reference titles.

MACMILLAN GENERAL REFERENCE

1633 Broadway
New York, NY 10019
Phone: 212-654-8500
Fax: 212-654-4822
Web site: *http://www.mgr.com*

Acquisitions: Gary Krebs, managing editor. Publishes hardcover originals, trade paperback originals and reprints. **Publishes 400- 500 titles/year. Receives 10,000 queries/year. 15% of books from first-time authors; 5% from unagented writers. Pays royalty on retail price or net sales or makes outright purchase or work-for-hire assignments. Offers $1,000-1,000,000 advance depending on imprint.** Publishes book 1 year after acceptance of manuscript. Accepts simultaneous submissions. Reports in 2 months on queries and manuscripts, 1 month on proposals.

Tips: Macmillan General Reference publishes popular reference in travel, pet books, consumer information, careers, test preparation, tax guides, cooking, gardening, sports, health, history, psychology, parenting, writing guides, atlases, dictionaries, music, the arts, business, parenting, science, religion.

Imprint(s): **Arco** (contact Marie Butler, publisher); **Howell Book House** (contact Kelly Nebenhaus, publisher); **Macmillan Brands and Cookbooks** (contact Susan Clarey, publisher), Macmillan Lifestyle Guides (contact Kathy Nebenhaus, publisher); **Macmillan Travel** (contact Mike Spring, publisher).

MACMILLAN TRAVEL

Macmillan General Reference
1633 Broadway
New York, NY 10019
Phone: 212-654-8500
Fax: 212-654-4822
Web site: *http://www.frommers.com*

Acquisitions: Michael Spring, publisher. Publishes trade paperback originals and reprints. **Publishes 60-100 titles/year. Receives 3,000 queries/year. 15% of books from first-time authors. Pays royalty on retail price or net sales, or makes outright purchase or work-for-hire assignments. Offers variable advance.** Publishes book 1 year after acceptance of manuscript. Accepts simultaneous submis-

sions. Reports in 2 months on queries and manuscripts, 1 month on proposals.

Tips: Macmillan Travel publishes regional travel guides that fit destination-specific formats or series.

MAIN STREET BOOKS

Doubleday Broadway Publishing Group
Random House, Inc.
1540 Broadway
New York, NY 10036
Phone: 212-354-6500
Web site: *http://www.randomhouse.com*

Acquisitions: Gerald Howard, editor in chief; Jennifer Griffen, senior editor. Estab. 1992. Publishes hardcover originals, trade paperback originals and reprints. **Publishes 20-30 titles/year. Receives 600 queries, 200 manuscripts/year. 25% of books from first-time authors. Offers advance and royalties.** Publishes book 18 months after acceptance of manuscript. Accepts simultaneous submissions, if so noted. Reports in 1 month on queries, 6 months on manuscripts. Manuscript guidelines free.

Tips: Main Street Books publishes backlist books, but also "up front" big sellers in the areas of self-help, fitness, and popular culture.

MASQUERADE BOOKS

Crescent Publishing
801 Second Avenue
New York, NY 10017
Phone: 212-661-7878
Fax: 212-983-2548
E-mail: masqbks@aol.com

Acquisitions: Marti Hohmann, editor in chief (upscale erotica). Estab. 1989. Publishes trade paperback and mass market paperback originals and reprints. **Publishes 40 titles/year. Receives 500 queries and 1,000 manuscripts/year. 10% of books from first-time authors; 95% from unagented writers. Pays 5% royalty on retail price. Offers $1,200 advance.** Publishes book 1 year after acceptance of manuscript. Reports in 1 month on queries and proposals, 3 months on manuscripts. Manuscript guidelines free.

Tips: Masquerade publishes upscale, literary erotica.

MBI PUBLISHING

Chronicle Publishing
729 Prospect Avenue
P.O. Box 1
Osceola, WI 54020-0001
Phone: 715-294-3345
Fax: 715-294-4448
E-mail: mbibks@motorbooks.com
Web site: *http://www.motorbooks.com*
Publishing Director: Zack Miller.

Acquisitions: Lee Klancher, senior acquisitions editor (tractors, stock car racing, motorcycles); Mike Haenggi, acquisitions editor (aviation, military history); Keith Mathiowetz, acquisitions editor (American cars, Americana, railroading collectibles); Paul Johnson, acquisitions editor (automotive how-to, boating); Christopher Batio, acquisitions editor (Americana, collectibles); John Adams-Graf, acquisitions editor (foreign cars, vintage racing). Estab. 1973. Publishes hardcover and paperback originals. **Publishes 125 titles/year. Receives 200 queries and 50 manuscripts/year. 95% of books from unagented writers. Pays 12% royalty on net receipts. Offers $5,000 average advance.** Publishes book 1 year after acceptance. Accepts simultaneous submissions. Reports in 3 months. Manuscript guidelines for #10 SASE.

Tips: MBI is a transportation-related publisher: cars, motorcycles, racing, trucks, tractors, boats, bicycles—also Americana, aviation, and military history.

Imprint(s): Bay View, Bicycle Books, Crestline, Zenith Books.

MINOTAUR BOOKS, St. Martin's Press

175 5th Avenue
New York, NY 10010
(212) 674-5151
Web site: www.minotaurbooks.com
Aquisitions: Senior Editor. Joe Veltre. Mystery imprint of St. Martin's Press.
Publishes 175 books per year, the largest number of mysteries of any US Publisher.
Tips: Looking for mysteries of all types, from cozy to hardboiled.

MINSTREL BOOKS, pocket Books for Young Readers

Simon & Schuster
1230 Avenue of the Americas
New York, NY 10020
Phone: 212-698-7669
Web site: *http://www.simonsayskids.com*
Editorial Director: Patricia MacDonald.
Acquisitions: Attn: Manuscript proposals. Estab. 1986. Publishes hardcover originals and reprints, trade paperback originals. **Publishes 125 titles/year. Receives 1,200 queries/year. Less than 25% from first-time authors; less than 25% from unagented writers. Pays 6-8% royalty on retail price. Advance varies.** Publishes book 2 years after acceptance of manuscript. Accepts simultaneous submissions. Reports in 3 months on queries. Manuscript guidelines free.
Tips: Fun, kid-oriented books, the kinds kids pick for themselves, for middle grade readers, ages 8-12.

WILLIAM MORROW AND CO.

10 E. 53rd Street
New York, NY 10022
Phone: 212-207-7000
Web site: *http://www.williammorrow.com*
Acquisitions: Pam Hoenig, associate publisher (Hearst Books, Hearst Marine Books); David Reuther, editor in chief (Beech Tree Books, Morrow Junior Books, Mulberry Books); Susan Pearson, editor in chief (Lothrop, Lee & Shepard Books); Toni Sciarra, editor (Quill Trade Paperbacks); Susan Hirschman (Greenwillow Books). Estab. 1926. **Publishes 200**

titles/year. Receives 10,000 submissions/year. 30% of books from first-time authors; 5% from unagented writers. Pays standard royalty on retail price. Advance varies.** Publishes book 2 years after acceptance of manuscript. Reports in 3 months.
Tips: Recently aquired by HarperCollins. William Morrow publishes a wide range of titles that receive much recognition and prestige. A most selective house.
Imprint(s): Beech Tree Books (juvenile); **Greenwillow Books** (juvenile); Hearst Books; Hearst Marine Books; **Lothrop, Lee & Shepard Books** (juvenile); **Morrow Junior Books** (juvenile); Mulberry Books (juvenile); Quill Trade Paperbacks; Tupelo Books; Rob Weisbach Books.

MORROW JUNIOR BOOKS

William Morrow and Co., The Hearst Corp.
1350 Avenue of the Americas
New York, NY 10019
Phone: 212-261-6691
Web site: *http://www.williammorrow.com*
Publisher: Barbara Lalicki.
Acquisitions: Meredith Carpenter, executive editor; Rosemary Brosnan, executive editor; Andrea Curley, senior editor; Marisa Miller, assistant editor. Publishes hardcover originals. **Publishes 50 titles/year. All contracts negotiated individually. Offers variable advance.**
Tips: Morrow Junior Books is one of the nation's leading publishers of books for children, including bestselling fiction and nonfiction.

JOHN MUIR PUBLICATIONS, Agora Inc.

P.O. Box 613
Santa Fe, NM 87504
Phone: 505-982-4078
Fax: 505-988-1680
Acquisitions: Cassandra Conyers, acquisitions manager. Estab. 1969. Publishes trade paperback originals. **Publishes 60-70 titles/year. Receives 1,000 queries and 50 manuscripts/year. 60% of books from first-time authors; 90% from unagented writers. Pays 10% average royalty on wholesale price or makes outright purchase occasionally. Offers $3,500 average advance.** Publishes book 1 year after acceptance of manuscript. Accepts simultaneous submissions if noted in cover letter. Reports in 6 weeks on queries, 4 months on proposals. Manuscript guidelines for #10 SASE.
Tips: Muir authors sort through time-sapping and money-wasting alternatives of life to offer readers the best information for decision-making. Currently emphasizing natural health and special-interest travel.

THE MYSTERIOUS PRESS, Warner Books

1271 Avenue of the Americas
New York, NY 10020
Phone: 212-522-5144
Fax: 212-522-7990
Web site: *http://www.warnerbooks.com*
Acquisitions: William Malloy, editor in chief; Sara Ann Freed, executive editor; Susanna Einstein, associate editor. Estab. 1976. Publishes hardcover

and mass market editions. **Publishes 36 titles/year. No agented writers. Pays standard, but negotiable, royalty on retail price. Amount of advance varies widely.** Publishes book an average of 1 year after acceptance of manuscript. Reports in 2 months.

Tips: The Mysterious Press publishes well-written crime/mystery/suspense fiction.

NAN A. TALESE

Doubleday Broadway Publishing Group
Random House, Inc.
1540 Broadway
New York, NY 10036
Phone: 212-782-8918
Fax: 212-782-9261
Web site: *http://www.nantalese.com*

Acquisitions: Nan A. Talese, editorial director. Publishes hardcover originals. **Publishes 15 titles/year. Receives 400 queries and manuscripts/year. Pays variable royalty on retail price. Advance varies.** Publishes book 8 months after acceptance of manuscript. Accepts simultaneous submissions. Reports in 1 week on queries, 2 months on proposals and manuscripts.

Tips: Nan A. Talese publishes nonfiction with a powerful guiding narrative and relevance to larger cultural trends and interests and literary fiction of the highest quality.

NAVAL INSTITUTE PRESS, US Naval Institute

291 Wood Avenue
Annapolis, MD 21402-5035
Phone: 410-268-6110
Fax: 410-269-7940
E-mail: esecunda@usni.org
Web site: *http://www.usni.org*
Press Director: Ronald Chambers.

Acquisitions: Paul Wilderson, executive editor; Mark Gatlin, senior acquisitions editor; Eric Mills, acquisitions editor. Estab. 1873. **Publishes 80 titles/year. Receives 700-800 submissions/year. 50% of books from first-time authors; 85% from unagented writers. Pays 5-10% royalty on net sales.** Publishes book 1 year after acceptance. Manuscript guidelines for #10 SASE.

Tips: The U.S. Naval Institute Press publishes general and scholarly books of professional, scientific, historical, and literary interest to the naval and maritime community.

Imprint(s): Bluejacket Books (paperback reprints).

NEW AMERICAN LIBRARY

Penguin Putnam Inc.
375 Hudson Street
New York, NY 10014
Phone: 212-366-2000
Web site: *http://www.penguin.com*
Executive Editor: Carolyn Nichols.

Acquisitions: Ellen Edwards, executive editor (commercial women's fiction—mainstream novels and contemporary romances; mysteries in a series and single title suspense; nonfiction of all types for a general audience); Laura Anne Gilman, executive editor (science fiction/fantasy/horror, mystery series, New Age); Audrey LaFehr, executive editor (contemporary and historical romance, women's suspense, multicultural fiction); Hilary Ross, associate executive editor (romances, Regencies); Doug Grad, senior editor (thrillers, suspense novels, international intrigue, technothrillers, military fiction and nonfiction, adventure nonfiction); Joe Pittman, senior editor (mysteries, suspense, thrillers, horror, commerical fiction); Dan Slater, editor (historical fiction, adult westerns, thrillers, military fiction and nonfiction, true crime, media tie-ins); Don Hymans, associate editor (classics, adventure/exploration); Cecilia Oh, associate editor (romance, Regency, commercial women's fiction, inspirational nonfiction); Genny Ostertag, associate editor (suspense, multicultural commercial fiction, women's fiction). Publishes mass market paperback originals and reprints. **Publishes 500 titles/year. Receives 20,000 queries and 10,000 manuscripts/year. 30-40% of books from first-time authors; 5% from unagented writers. Advance and royalty negotiable.** Publishes book 2 years after acceptance of manuscript. Reports in 6 months.

Tips: NAL publishes commercial fiction and nonfiction for the popular audience.

Imprint(s): Mentor, Onyx, **ROC**, Signet, Signet Classic, Signet Reference, Topaz.

NEW YORK UNIVERSITY PRESS

70 Washington Square South
New York, NY 10012
Phone: 212-998-2575
Fax: 212-995-3833
Web site: *http://www.nyupress.nyu.edu*

Acquisitions: Eric Zinner (cultural studies, literature, media, anthropology); Jennifer Hammer (Jewish studies, psychology, religion, women's studies); Niko Pfund (business, history, law); Stephen Magro (social sciences). Estab. 1916. Hardcover and trade paperback originals. **Publishes 150 titles/year. Receives 800- 1,000 queries/year. 30% of books from first-time authors; 90% from unagented writers. Advance and royalty on net receipts varies by project.** Publishes book 8 months after acceptance of manuscript. Accepts simultaneous submissions. Reports in 1 month on proposals (peer reviewed).

Tips: New York University Press embraces ideological diversity. Often publishes books on the same issue from different poles to generate dialogue, engender and resist pat categorizations.

W.W. NORTON CO., INC.

500 Fifth Avenue
New York, NY 10110
Phone: 212-354-5500
Fax: 212-869-0856
Web site: *http://www.wwnorton.com*

Acquisitions: Robert Weil, executive editor; Edwin Barber, vice chairman; Jill Bialosky (literary fiction, biography, memoirs); Amy Cherry (history, biography, women's issues, African-American, health); Carol Houck-Smith (literary fiction, travel memoirs, behavioral sciences, nature); Starling Lawrence, editor in chief; Angela von der Leppe (trade nonfiction, behavioral sciences, earth sciences, astronomy, neuroscience, education); Jim Mairs (history, biography, illustrated books); Alane Mason (serious nonfiction cultural and intellectual history, illustrated books, literary fiction, and memoir); W. Drake McFeely, president (nonfiction, particularly science and social science). Estab. 1923. Publishes hardcover and paperback originals and reprints. **Publishes 300 titles/year. Pays royalty.** Reports in 2 months.

Tips: General trade publisher of fiction, poetry, and nonfiction educational and professional books. W.W. Norton Co. strives to carry out the imperative of its founder to publish books not for a single season, but for the years, in the areas of fiction, nonfiction, and poetry.

Imprint(s): Backcountry Publications, Countryman Press, Foul Play Press, W.W. Norton.

NTC/CONTEMPORARY PUBLISHING GROUP

4255 West Touhy Avenue
Lincolnwood, IL 60646-1975
Phone: 847-679-5500
Fax: 847-679-2494
E-mail: ntcpub2@aol.com
Web site: *http://www.ntc-cb.com*
Editorial Director: John T. Nolan.

Acquisitions: Danielle Egan- Miller, business editor; Rob Taylor, associate editor; Denise Betts, assistant editor; Betsy Lancefield, senior editor; Anne Knudsen, executive editor. Estab. 1947. Publishes hardcover originals and trade paperback originals and reprints. **Publishes 850 titles/year. Receives 9,000 submissions/year. 10% of books from first-time authors; 25% of books from unagented writers. Pays 6-15% royalty on retail price.** Publishes book 1 year after acceptance. Accepts simultaneous submissions. Reports in 2 months. Manuscript guidelines for SASE.

Tips: "We are a midsize, niche-oriented, backlist-
oriented publisher. We publish exclusively nonfiction in general interest trade categories plus travel, reference and quilting books."

Imprint(s): Contemporary Books, Country Roads Press, Keats Publishing, Lowell House, Masters Press, NTC Business Books, NTC Publishing Group, National Textbook Company, Passport Books, Peter Bedrick Books, The Quilt Digest Press, VGM Career Horizons.

ONE WORLD

Ballantine Publishing Group
Random House, Inc.
201 East 50th Street
New York, NY 10022
Phone: 212-572-2620
Fax: 212-940-7539
Web site: *http://www.randomhouse.com*

Acquisitions: Cheryl Woodruff, publisher (multicultural fiction and nonfiction, spirituality, and health); Gary Brozek, editor (multicultural and general fiction and nonfiction). Estab. 1991. Publishes hardcover, trade paperback and mass market, originals, trade and mass market paperback reprints.

Publishes 8-10 titles/year. Receives 1,200 queries and manuscripts/year. 25% of books from first-time authors; 5% from unagented writers. Pays 8-12% royalty on retail price, varies from hardcover to mass market. Advance varies. Publishes book 18 months after acceptance of manuscript. Accepts simultaneous submissions, if so noted. Reports in 6 months. Manuscript guidelines for #10 SASE.

Tips: One World's list includes books written by and focused on African Americans, Native Americans, Asian Americans, and Latino Americans. Concentrates on *American* multicultural experiences. Currently looking for high-quality commercial fiction. No romance. Query with synopsis, 3 sample chapters (100 pages), and SASE.

ORCHARD BOOKS

Grolier Publishing
95 Madison Avenue
New York, NY 10016
Phone: 212-951-2650
Web site: *http://www.publishing.grolier.com*
President/Publisher: Judy V. Wilson.

Acquisitions: Sarah Caguiat, editor; Ana Cerro, editor. Estab. 1987. Publishes hardcover and trade paperback originals. **Publishes 60-70 titles/year. Receives 1,600 queries/year. 25% of books from first-time authors; 50% from unagented writers. Pays 6-10% royalty on retail price. Advance varies.** Publishes book 1 year after acceptance of manuscript. Reports in 3 months on queries.

Tips: Orchard specializes in children's picture books.

OSBORNE/MCGRAW-HILL

The McGraw-Hill Companies
2600 10th Street
Berkeley, CA 94710
Phone: 510-548-2805
Web site: *http://www.osborne.com*

Acquisitions: Scott Rogers, editor in chief. Estab. 1979. Publishes computer trade paperback originals. **Publishes 100 titles/year. Receives 120 submissions/year. 30% of books from first-time authors. Pays 8-12% royalty on wholesale price. Offers $5,000 average advance.** Publishes book an average of 6 months after acceptance. Accepts simultaneous submissions. Reports in 2 months.

Tips: Osborne publishes technical computer books and software.

OSPREY PUBLISHING LIMITED, SBM Inc.

443 Park Avenue South, #801
New York, NY 10016
Phone: 212-685-5560
Fax: 212-685-5836
E-mail: ospreyusa@aol.com
Web site: *http://www.osprey-publishing.co.uk*

Acquisitions: Lee Johnson, managing editor (military, uniforms, battles); Shaun Barrington, managing editor (aviation, automotive). Publishes hardcover and trade paperback originals. **Publishes 78 titles/year. Receives hundreds of queries/year. 25% of books from first-**

time authors; 100% from unagented writers. Makes outright purchases of $1,000-5,000. Offers advance. Publishes book 6 months after acceptance of manuscript. Reports in 2 months.

Tips: Osprey Publishing produces high-quality nonfiction series in the areas of military and aviation history and automotive titles. Lines include Air Combat, Aircraft of the Aces, Campaign, Elite, Men at Arms, New Vanguard, Warrior.

OWL BOOKS, Henry Holt & Co., Inc.

115 West 18th Street
New York, NY 10011
Phone: 212-886-9200
Web site: *http://www.hholt.com*
Acquisitions: David Sobel, senior editor. Estab. 1996. Publishes trade paperback originals. **Firm publishes 135-140 titles/year; imprint publishes 50-60 titles/year. 30% of books from first-time authors; 5% from unagented writers. Pays 6-7 1/2% royalty on retail price. Advance varies.** Publishes book 1 year after acceptance of manuscript. Accepts simultaneous submissions. Reports in 3 months on proposals.
Tips: Original, great ideas that have commercial appeal.

OXFORD UNIVERSITY PRESS

198 Madison Avenue
New York, NY 10016
Phone: 212-726-6000
Web site: *http://www.oup-usa.org/*
Acquisitions: Joan Bossert, vice president/editorial director; Laura Brown, director (trade publishing). Estab. 1896. Publishes hardcover and trade paperback originals and reprints. **Publishes 1,500 titles/year. 40% of books from first-time authors; 80% from unagented writers. Pays 0-15% royalty on wholesale price or retail price. Offers $0-40,000 advance.** Publishes book 10 months after acceptance of manuscript. Accepts simultaneous submissions. Reports in 3 months on proposals.
Tips: Books that make a significant contribution to the literature and research in a number of disciplines that reflect the departments at the University of Oxford.

PANTHEON BOOKS

Knopf Publishing Group
Random House, Inc.
201 East 50th Street, 25th Floor
New York, NY 10022
Phone: 212-751-2600
Fax: 212-572-6030
Web site: *http://www.randomhouse.com*
Editorial Director: Dan Frank. Senior Editor: Shelley Wagner. Executive Editor: Erroll McDonald. **Acquisitions**: Adult Editorial Department. Estab. 1942. **Pays royalty. Offers advance.**
Tips: Pantheon Books publishes authors of literary fiction and important nonfiction.

PERIGEE BOOKS

Penguin Putnam Inc.
375 Hudson Street
New York, NY 10014
Phone: 212-366-2000
Web site: *http://www.penguinputnam.com*
Acquisitions: John Duff, editor, Sheila Curry, editor. Publishes trade paperback originals and reprints. **Publishes 12-15 titles/year. Receives hundreds of queries/year; 30 proposals/year. 30% first-time authors; 10% unagented writers. Pays 7 1/2-15% royalty. Offers $5,000-150,000 advance.** Publishes book 18 months after acceptance of manuscript. Reports in 2 months. Catalog free. Manuscript guidelines given on acceptance of manuscript.
Nonfiction: Prescriptive books. Subjects include health/fitness, child care, spirituality. Query with outline. Prefers agented manuscripts but accepts unsolicited queries.

PICADOR USA, St. Martin's Press

175 Fifth Avenue
New York, NY 10010
Phone: 212-674-5151
Web site: *http://www.stmartins.com*
Acquisitions: George Witte. Estab. 1994. Publishes hardcover originals and trade paperback originals and reprints. **Publishes 70-80 titles/year. 30% of books from first-time authors. Publishes few unagented writers. Pays 7 1/2-12½% royalty on retail price. Advance varies.** Publishes book 18 months after acceptance of manuscript. Accepts simultaneous submissions. Reports in 2 months on queries. Manuscript guidelines for #10 SASE.
Tips: High-quality literary fiction and nonfiction written by authoritative authors.

PLATINUM PRESS INC.

311 Crossways Park Drive
Woodbury, NY 11797
Phone: 516-364-1800
Fax: 516-364-1899
Acquisitions: Herbert Cohen. Estab. 1990. Publishes hardcover originals and reprints. **Publishes 100 titles/year; each imprint publishes 30 titles/year. 25% of books from first-time authors; 25% from unagented writers. Pays 5-10% royalty on retail price. Offers $500-750 advance.** Accepts simultaneous submissions.
Tips: Platinum Press publishes nonfiction gardening, history, religion, and military and mystery fiction.
Imprint(s): Detective Book Club, Home Craftsman Book Club, Outdoor Sportsman Library, Platinum Press.
Nonfiction: Gardening, history, military/war, religion subjects. Query with SASE.
Fiction: Mystery, suspense. Query with SASE.

PRICE STERN SLOAN, INC.
Penguin Putnam Inc.
345 Hudson
New York, NY 10014
Phone: 212-951-8700
Fax: 212-951-8694
Web site: http://www.penguinputnam.com
Editorial Director: Jon Anderson.
Acquisitions: Submissions Editor (juvenile submissions); Calendars Editor (calendar submissions). Estab. 1963. **Publishes 80 titles/year (95% children's). Makes outright purchase. Offers advance.** Reports in 3 months. Manuscript guidelines for SASE. Address to Manuscript Guidelines.
Tips: Price Stern Sloan publishes quirky mass-market novelty series for children and adult page-a-day calendars.
Imprint(s): Doodle Art, I Can Read Comics, Mad Libs, Mad Mysteries, Mr. Men & Little Miss, Plugged In, Serendipity, Travel Games to Go, Troubador Press, Wee Sing.

PRIMA PUBLISHING
3875 Atherton Rd
Rocklin, CA 95677-1260
Phone: 916-632-4400
Web site: http://www.primapublishing.com
President/Founder: Ben Dominitz.
Acquisitions: *Lifestyles Division:* Steven Martin, editorial director; Susan Silva, acquisitions editor; Jamie Miller, acquisitions editor; Denise Sternad, acquisitions; Lorna Dolley, acquisitions; Julie McDonald, acquisitions. *Prima Games Division:* Debra Kempker, publisher; Stacy DeFoe, product manager; Amy Raynor, product manager. *PrimaTech Division:* Matthew Carleson, publisher; Dan J. Foster, managing editor; Deborah F. Abshier, acquisitions editor; Jenny Watson, acquisitions editor. Estab. 1984. Publishes hardcover originals and trade paperback originals and reprints. **Publishes 300 titles/year. Receives 750 queries/year. 10% of books from first-time authors; 30% from unagented writers. Pays 15-20% royalty on wholesale price. Advance varies.** Publishes book 18 months after acceptance. Accepts simultaneous submissions. Reports in 3 months. Writer's guidelines for #10 SASE.
Tips: Books for the way we live, work, and play.

PUFFIN BOOKS
Penguin Putnam Inc.
345 Hudson Street
New York, NY 10014-3657
Phone: 212-366-2000
Web site: http://www.penguin.com/childrens
President/Publisher: Tracy Tang.
Acquisitions: Sharyn November, senior editor; Kristin Gilson, executive editor; Joy Peskin, assistant editor. Publishes trade paperback originals and reprints. Publishes 175-200 titles/year. Receives 300 queries and manuscripts/year. 1% of books by first-time authors; 5% from unagented writers. Royalty and advance vary. Publishes book 1 year after acceptance of manuscript. Accepts simultaneous submissions, if so noted. Reports in 1 month on manuscripts.
Tips: Puffin Books publishes high-end trade paperbacks and paperback reprints for preschool children, beginning and middle readers, and young adults.
Imprint(s): PaperStar.

QUE, Macmillan Computer Publishing USA
201 West 103rd Street
Indianapolis, IN 46290
Phone: 317-581-3500
Web site: http://www.mcp.com/que/
Vice President/Publisher: James Price.
Acquisitions: Holly Allender, acquisitions editor (Linut/Unity networking, programming, ERP); Gretchen Ganser, acquisitions editor (Linut/Unity networking, programming, ERP); Karen Whitehouse, acquisitions editor (applications, web, graphics, MacIntosh); Jamie Milazzo, acquisitions editor (applications, Web, graphics, MacIntosh); Stephanie McComb, acquisitions editor (Idiot's Guides, Easy Series, Quick Reference Series); Jiri Byus, acquisitions editor (Windows 2000, hardware, certification); Tracy Williams, acquisitions editor (Windows 2000, hardware, certification). Publishes hardcover, trade paperback and mass market paperback originals and reprints. **Publishes 200 titles/year. 85% of books from unagented writers. Pays variable royalty on wholesale price or makes work-for-hire arrangements. Advance varies.** Accepts simultaneous submissions. Reports in 1 month on proposals. Manuscript guidelines free.
Nonfiction: Computer books.
Tips: Specializes in computer books. Study the catalog before submitting.

RANDOM HOUSE CHILDREN'S PUBLISHING
Random House, Inc.
201 East 50th Street
New York, NY 10022
Phone: 212-751-2600
Fax: 212-940-7685
Web site: http://www.randomhouse/com/kids
Vice President/Publishing Director: Kate Klimo. **Acquisitions**: Ruth Koeppel, senior editor/licensing director (Stepping Stones); Heidi Kilgras, editor (Step into Reading); Stephanie Street Pierre, senior editor (Picturebacks). Estab. 1935. Publishes hardcover, trade paperback, and mass market paperback originals and reprints. **Publishes 200 titles/year. Receives 1,000 queries/year. Pays 1-6% royalty or makes outright purchase. Advance varies.** Publishes book 1 year after acceptance of manuscript. Accepts simultaneous submissions. Reports in 3 weeks-6 months.
Tips: Random House Books aim to create books that nurture the hearts and minds of children, providing and promoting quality books and a rich variety of media that entertain and educate readers from 6 months to 12 years.
Imprint(s): Random House Books for Young Readers, **Alfred A. Knopf and Crown Children's Books**, Dragonfly.

REGAN BOOKS, HarperCollins

10 East 53rd Street
New York, NY 10022
Phone: 212-207-7400
Fax: 212-207-6951
Web site: *http://www.harpercollins.com*
Acquisitions: Judith Regan, president/publisher. Estab. 1994. Publishes hardcover and trade paperback originals. **Publishes 30 titles/year. Receives 7,500 queries and 5,000 manuscripts/year. Pays royalty on retail price. Advance varies.** Publishes book 1 year after acceptance of manuscript. Accepts simultaneous submissions. Reports in 3 months on proposals.
Tips: Regan Books publishes general fiction and nonfiction and is known for contemporary topics and controversial authors and titles.

ROC BOOKS, Penguin Putnam Inc.

375 Hudson Street
New York, NY 10014
Phone: 212-366-2000
Web site: *http://www.penguinputnam.com*
Acquisitions: Laura Anne Gilman, executive editor; Jennifer Heddle, assistant editor. Publishes mass market, trade and hardcover originals.
Publishes 36 titles/year. Receives 500 queries/year. Pays royalty. Advance negotiable. Accepts simultaneous submissions. Report in 2-3 months on queries.
Tips: Books that are a good read, that people will want to pick up time and time again.

RODALE BOOKS, Rodale Press, Inc.

400 Sout Tenth Street
Emmaus, PA 18098
Phone: 610-967-5171
Web site: *http://www.rodalepress.com*
Vice President, Active Living Books: Neil Wertheimer. Editorial Director for Health and Fitness Books: Deborah Yost.
Acquisitions: Sally Reith, acquisitions editor. Estab. 1932. Publishes hardcover originals, trade paperback originals and reprints. **Publishes 75-100 titles/year; imprints publish 10-15 titles/year. Pays 6-15% royalty on retail price.** Publishes book 18 months after acceptance of manuscript. Accepts simultaneous submissions. Reports in 1 month on queries, 2 months on proposals and manuscripts. Manuscript guidelines free.
Tips: How people can use the power of their bodies and minds to make their lives better.

RUNNING PRESS BOOK PUBLISHERS

125 South 22nd Street
Philadelphia, PA 19103
Phone: 215-567-5080
Fax: 215-568-2919
Web site: *http://www.runningpress.com*
President/Publisher: Stuart Teacher.

Acquisitions: Nancy Steele, director of acquisitions; Maryellen Lewis, assistant to the editorial director; Brian Perrin, associate publisher; Jennifer Worick; Mary McGuire Ruggiero, acquiring editor (cookbooks); Patty Smith, acquiring editor (children's projects); Greg Jones, acquiring editor (photography and general nonfiction); Jason Rekulak, acquiring editor (novelty and general nonfiction). Estab. 1972. Publishes hardcover originals, trade paperback originals and reprints. **Publishes 150 titles/year. Receives 600 queries/year. 50% of books from first-time authors; 30% from unagented writers. Payment varies. Advances varies.** Publishes book 6-18 months after acceptance of manuscript. Accepts simultaneous submissions. Reports in 6 weeks on queries. Manuscript guidelines for #10 SASE.
Tips: Running Press and Courage Books publish nonfiction trade and promotional titles, including pop culture books, cookbooks, quote books, children's learning kits, photo-essay books.
Imprint(s): Courage Books.

RUTLEDGE HILL PRESS

211 Seventh Avenue North
Nashville, TN 37219-1823
Phone: 615-244-2700
Fax: 615-244-2978
Web site: *http://www.rutledgehillpress.com*
Acquisitions: Mike Towle, executive editor. Estab. 1982. Publishes hardcover and trade paperback originals and reprints. **Publishes 60 titles/year. Receives 1,500 submissions/year. 25% of books from first-time authors; 60% from unagented writers. Pays 10-20% royalty on net price.** Publishes book 1 year after acceptance. Reports in 2 months.
Tips: Market-specific books, focusing on particular genres or regions.

SAMS, Macmillan Computer Publishing USA

201 West 103rd Street
Indianapolis, IN 46290
Phone: 317-581-3500
Web site: *http://www.mcp.com/sams/*
Publisher/Vice President: James Price.
Acquisitions: Angela Kozlowski, acquisitions editor (unleashed series, Pine North Guides); Steve Anglin, acquisitions editor (operating systems, certification, professional programming); Randi Roger, acquisitions editor (applications, Web); Chris Webb, acquisitions editor (programming); Sharon Cox, acquisitions editor (programming). Estab. 1951. Publishes trade paperback originals. **Publishes 160 titles/year. 30% of books from first-time authors; 95% from unagented writers. Pays royalty on wholesale price, negotiable. Advance negotiable.** Publishes book 1 year after acceptance of manuscript. Accepts simultaneous submissions if noted; however, once contract is signed, Sams Publishing retains first option rights on future works on same subject. Reports in 6 weeks on queries. Manuscript guidelines free.
Tips: Sams has made a major commitment to publishing books that meet the needs of computer users, programmers, administrative and support personnel, and managers.

SCHIRMER BOOKS, Macmillan Reference

1633 Broadway
New York, NY 10019-6785
Phone: 212-654-8414
Fax: 212-654-4745
Acquisitions: Richard Carlin, executive editor. Publishes hardcover and paperback originals, related CDs, CD-Roms, audiocassettes. **Publishes 50 books/year. Receives 250 submissions/year. 25% of books from first-time authors; 75% of books from unagented writers.** Publishes book 1 year after acceptance of manuscript. Reports in 4 months. Manuscript guidelines for SASE.
Tips: Schirmer publishes scholarly and reference books on the performing arts. Currently emphasizing popular music, including rock and jazz.

SCHOLASTIC PRESS, Scholastic Inc.

555 Broadway
New York, NY 10012
Phone: 212-343-6100
Web site: *http://www.scholastic.com*
Acquisitions: Elizabeth Szabla, editorial director. Publishes hardcover originals. **Publishes 50 titles/year. Receives 2,500 queries/year. 5% of books from first-time authors. Pays royalty on retail price. Royalty and advance vary.** Publishes book 18-24 months after acceptance of manuscript. Reports in 6 months on queries.
Tips: Scholastic Press publishes a range of picture books, middle grade, and young adult novels.

SCRIBNER, Simon & Schuster

1230 Avenue of the Americas
New York, NY 10020
Phone: 212-698-7000
West site: *http://www.simonandschuster.com*
Acquisitions: Jillian Blake, editor. Publishes hardcover originals. **Publishes 70-75 titles/year. Receives thousands of queries/year. 20% of books from first-time authors; none from unagented writers. Pays 7 1/2-12 1/2% royalty on wholesale price. Advance varies.** Publishes book 9 months after acceptance of manuscript. Accepts simultaneous submissions. Reports in 3 months on queries.
Imprint(s): Rawson Associates; Lisa Drew Books ; Scribner Classics (reprints only); Scribner poetry (by invitation only).
Tips: Publishes highquality, and proven commercially successful books.

SILHOUETTE BOOKS

300 East 42nd Street
New York, NY 10017
Phone: 212-682-6080
Fax: 212-682-4539
Web site: *http://www.romance.net*
Editorial Director, Silhouette Books, Harlequin Historicals: Tara Gavin.
Acquisitions: Mary Theresa Hussey, senior editor (Silhouette Romance); Karen Taylor Richman, senior editor (Silhouette Special Editions); Joan

Marlow Golan, senior editor (Silhouette Desires); Leslie Wainger, executive senior editor/editorial coordinator (Silhouette Intimate Moments); Tracy Farrell, senior editor/editorial coordinator (Harlequin Historicals). Estab. 1979. Publishes mass market paperback originals. **Publishes 350 titles/year. Receives 4,000 submissions/year. 10% of books from first-time authors; 50% from unagented writers. Pays royalty.** Publishes book 1-3 years after acceptance. Manuscript guidelines for #10 SASE.
Tips: Silhouette publishes contemporary adult romances.
Imprint(s): *Silhouette Romances* (contemporary adult romances, 53,000-58,000 words); *Silhouette Desires* (contemporary adult romances, 55,000-60,000 words); *Silhouette Intimate Moments* (contemporary adult romances, 80,000-85,000 words); *Silhouette Yours Truly* (contemporary adult romances, 53,000-58,000 words); *Harlequin Historicals* (adult historical romances, 95,000-105,000 words).

SIMON & SCHUSTER BOOKS FOR YOUNG READERS

Simon & Schuster Children's Publishing Division
1230 Avenue of the Americas
New York, NY 10020
Phone: 212-698-2851
Web site: *http://www.simonandschuster.com* or *http://www.simonsayskids.com.*
Acquisitions: Stephanie Owens Lurie, editorial director, vice president/associate publisher (humorous picture books, fiction, nonfiction); Kevin Lewis, editor (African-American/multicultural picture books, humorous picture books, middle-grade); David Gale, senior editor (young adult/middle grade novels); Michele Coppola, editor (toddler books, middle-grade fiction); Rebecca Davis, editor (character-centered picture books and poetry). Publishes hardcover originals. **Publishes 80-90 titles/year. Receives 2,500 queries and 10,000 manuscripts/year. 5-10% of books from first-time authors; 40% from unagented writers. Pays 4-12% royalty on retail price. Advance varies.** Publishes book 1-3 years after acceptance of manuscript. Accepts simultaneous submissions. Reports in 2 months on queries. Manuscript guidelines for #10 SASE.
Tips: The three adjectives S&S use are fresh, family oriented, and accessible. Currently emphasizing middle grade humor/adventure stories. De-emphasizing nonfiction.

SOURCEBOOKS, INC.

P.O. Box 372
Naperville, IL 60566
Phone: 630-961-3900
Fax: 630-961-2168
Web site: *http://www.sourcebooks.com*
Publisher: Dominique Raccah.
Acquisitions: Todd Stocke, managing editor (nonfiction trade); Mark Warda (Legal Survival Guides self-help/law series); Deborah Werksman (Hysteria Publications). Estab. 1987. Publishes hardcover and trade paperback originals. **Publishes 70 titles/year. 50% of books from first-time authors; 75% from unagented writers. Pays 6-15% royalty**

on wholesale price. Publishes book 1 year after acceptance. Accepts simultaneous submissions. Reports in 3 months on queries.

Tips: Sourcebooks publishes in the how-to and reference areas, including books on parenting, self-help/psychology, business and health. Focus is on practical, useful information and skills. It also continues to publish in the reference, new age, history, current affairs, and travel categories. Currently emphasizing humor, gift, women's interest, new age.

Imprint(s): Casablanca Press, Legal Survival Guides, Sphinx Publishing (self-help legal), Hysteria Publications (women's humor/gift book).

SOUTHERN ILLINOIS UNIVERSITY PRESS

P.O. Box 3697
Carbondale, IL 62902-3697
Phone: 618-453-2680
Fax: 618-453-1221
Web site: *http://www.siu.edu/siupress*

Acquisitions: Jim Simmons, editorial director (film, theater, aviation, American history); Karl Kageff, sponsoring editor (composition, rhetoric, criminology); Rick Stetter, director (military history, criminology, trade non-fiction). Estab. 1956. Publishes hardcover and trade paperback originals and reprints. **Publishes 50-60 titles/year; imprint publishes 4-6 titles/year. Receives 800 queries and 300 manuscripts/year. 45% of books from first-time authors; 100% from unagented writers. Pays 5-10% royalty on wholesale price. Rarely offers advance.** Publishes book 1 year after receipt of a final manuscript. Reports in 3 months. Manuscript guidelines free.

Tips: Serves the academy and serious readers of the Mississippi Valley. Currently emphasizing theater, film, baseball. De-emphasizing literary criticism, philosophy.

SPECTRA, Bantam Dell Publishing Group

Random House, Inc.
1540 Broadway
New York, NY 10036
Phone: 212-782-9418
Fax: 212-782-9523
Web site: *http://www.bdd.com*

Acquisitions: Anne Lesley Groell, editor, Pat LoBruto, editor. Estab. 1984. Publishes hardcover, trade and mass market paperback originals and reprints. **Receives hundreds of queries and 500 manuscripts/year. 20% of books from first-time authors. Pays 8-10% royalty on wholesale price. Pays $5,000 and up advance.** Publishes book 1 year after acceptance of manuscript. Accepts simultaneous submissions, if so noted. Reports in 8 months. Manuscript guidelines for #10 SASE.

Tips: Spectra has a high-quality list of fantasy and science fiction.

ST. MARTIN'S PRESS SCHOLARLY & REFERENCE DIVISION

St. Martin's Press
175 Fifth Avenue
New York, NY 10010
Phone: 212-982-3900
Fax: 212-777-6359

Web site: *http://www.stmartins.com*

Acquisitions: Michael Flamini, senior editor (history, politics, education, religion); Karen Wolny, editor (politics); Kirsti Long, editor (literature, cultural studies, anthropology). Publishes hardcover and trade paperback originals. **Firm publishes 700 titles/year. Receives 500 queries and 600 manuscripts/year. 25% of books from first-time authors; 75% from unagented writers. Pays royalty: trade, 7-10% list; other, 7-10% net. Advance varies.** Publishes book 7 months after acceptance of manuscript. Accepts simultaneous submissions. Reports in 1 month on proposals. Manuscript guidelines free.

Tips: Publishes as a scholarly press.

SYRACUSE UNIVERSITY PRESS

1600 Jamesville Avenue
Syracuse, NY 13244-5160
Phone: 315-443-5534
Fax: 315-443-5545
Web site: *http://www.syr.edu/www-syr/aboutsu/supress/index*

Acquisitions: Robert A. Mandel, director. Estab. 1943. **Averages 80 titles/year. Receives 600-700 submissions/year. 25% of books from first-time authors; 75% from unagented writers. Nonauthor subsidy publishes 20% of books.** Pays royalty on net sales. Publishes book an average of 15 months after acceptance of manuscript. Simultaneous submissions discouraged.

Tips: Currently emphasizing television, Jewish studies, Middle East topics. De-emphasizing peace studies.

JEREMY P. TARCHER, INC.

Penguin Putnam, Inc.
375 Hudson Street
New York, NY 10014
Phone: 212-366-2000
Web site: *http://www.penguinputnam.com*

Publisher: Joel Fotinos.

Acquisitions: Mitch Horowitz, senior editor; Wendy Hubbert, senior editor; David Groff, editor; Joel Fotinos, publisher (nonfiction). Estab. 1965. Publishes hardcover and trade paperback originals and reprints. **Publishes 30-40 titles/year. Receives 500 queries and 500 manuscripts/year. 10% of books from first-time authors; 5% from unagented writers. Pays 5-8% royalty on retail price. Offers advance.** Accepts simultaneous submissions.

Tips: Although Tarcher is not a religion imprint per se, Jeremy Tarcher's vision was to publish ideas and works about human consciousness that were large enough to include matters of spirit and religion.

TEN SPEED PRESS

P.O. Box 7123
Berkeley, CA 94707
Phone: 510-559-1600
Fax: 510-524-1052
E-mail: info@tenspeed.com
Web site: *http://www.tenspeed.com*
Publisher: Kirsty Melville. Publisher/Editorial Director: Phillip Wood.

Acquisitions: Address submissions to Acquisitions Department. Estab. 1971. Publishes trade paperback originals and reprints. **Firm publishes 100 titles/year; imprints average 70 titles/year. 25% of books from first-time authors; 50% from unagented writers. Pays 8-12% royalty on retail price. Offers $2,500 average advance.** Publishes book 1 year after acceptance. Accepts simultaneous submissions. Reports in 3 months on queries.Manuscript guidelines for #10 SASE.
Tips: Ten Speed Press publishes authoritative books for an audience interested in innovative, proven ideas.
Imprint(s): Celestial Arts, Tricycle Press.

THOMAS DUNNE BOOKS

St. Martin's Press
175 Fifth Avenue
New York, NY 10010
Phone: 212-674-5151
Web site: *http://www.stmartins.com*
Acquisitions: Tom Dunne, publisher; Peter J. Wolverton, associate publisher; Ruth Cavin, associate publisher (mysteries). Publishes hardcover originals, trade paperback originals and reprints. **Publishes 90 titles/year. Receives 1,000 queries/year. 20% of books from first-time authors; less than 5% from unagented writers. Pays 10-15% royalty on retail price for hardcover, 7 1/2% for paperback. Advance varies with project.** Publishes book 1 year after acceptance of manuscript. Accepts simultaneous submissions. Reports in 2 months on queries. Ms guidelines for #10 SASE.
Tips: Thomas Dunne publishes a wide range of fiction and nonfiction.

THOMAS NELSON PUBLISHERS

NelsonWord Publishing Group
P.O. Box 141000
Nashville, TN 37214-1000
Web site: *http://www.thomasnelson.com*
(Corporate address does not accept unsolicited manuscripts; no phone queries.)
Acquisitions: Janet Thoma (Janet Thoma Books, 1157 Molokai, Tega Cay SC 29715, fax: 803/548-2684); Victor Oliver (Oliver-Nelson Books, 1360 Center Dr., Suite 102-B, Atlanta GA 30338, fax: 770/391-9784); Mark Roberts (religious, reference, academic, or professional only, P.O. Box 141000, Nashville TN 37214, fax: 615/391-5225). Estab. 1984. **Publishes 150-200 titles/year. Pays royalty on net sales with rates negotiated for each project.** Publishes books 1-2 years after acceptance. Reports in 3 months. Accepts simultaneous submissions, if so noted.
Tips: Thomas Nelson publishes Christian lifestyle nonfiction and fiction.
Imprint(s): Janet Thoma Books, Oliver-Nelson Books, **Tommy Nelson**.
Nonfiction: Adult inspirational, motivational, devotional, self-help, Christian living, prayer and evangelism, reference/Bible study. Query with SASE, then send brief, prosaic resume, 1-page synopsis, and 1 sample chapter to one of the acquisitions editors at the above locations with SASE.
Fiction: Seeking successfully published commercial fiction authors who write for adults from a Christian perspective. Send brief, prosaic resume, 1-page synopsis, and 1 sample chapter to one of the acquisitions editors at the above locations with SASE.

TIMES BUSINESS

Random House, Inc.
201 East 50th Street
New York, NY 10022
Phone: 212-572-2275
Fax: 212-572-4949
Web site: *http://www.randomhouse.com*
Acquisitions: John Mahaney, executive editor. Estab. 1995. Publishes hardcover and trade paperback originals. **Publishes 20- 25 titles/year. 50% of books from first-time authors; 15% from unagented writers. Pays negotiable royalty on list price; hardcover on invoice price. Advance negotiable.** Publishes book 9 months after acceptance of manuscript. Accepts simultaneous submissions. Reports in 1 month on proposals. Manuscript guidelines for #10 SASE.
Nonfiction: Subjects include business/economic, money/finance, management, technology, and business. Query with proposal package including outline, 1-2 sample chapters, market analysis, and SASE.
Tips: Publishes high quality narrative nonfiction, particularly science and business books.

TOR BOOKS, Tom Doherty Associates, LLC

175 Fifth Avenue
New York, NY 10010
Phone: 212-388-0100
Web site: *http://www.stmartins.com*
Acquisitions: Patrick Nielsen Hayden, senior editor. Estab. 1980. Publishes hardcover originals and trade and mass market paperback originals and reprints. **Publishes 150-200 books/year. 2-3% of books from first-time authors; 3-5% from unagented writers. Pays royalty on retail price.** Publishes book 1-2 years after acceptance. No simultaneous submissions. "No queries please." Reports in 2-6 months on proposals and manuscripts. Manuscript guidelines for SASE.
Tips: Tor Books publishes what is arguably the largest and most diverse line of science fiction and fantasy.

TOTLINE PUBLICATIONS

Frank Schaffer Publications, Inc.
P.O. Box 2250
Everett, WA 98203-0250
Phone: 206-353-3100
E-mail: totline@gte.net
Web site: *http://www.frankschaffer.com/totline.html*
Acquisitions: Mina McMullin, managing editor (book manuscripts); Submissions Editor (single activity ideas). Estab. 1975. Publishes educational activity books and parenting books for teachers and parents of 2 to 6-year-olds. **Publishes 50-60 titles/year. 100% from unagented writers. Makes outright purchase plus copies of book/newsletter author's material appears in.** Book catalog and manuscript guidelines free on written request.
Tips: Totline publishes educationally and developmentally appropriate books for 2-, 3- to 5-, and 6-year-olds.

TRANS-ATLANTIC PUBLICATIONS, INC.

311 Bainbridge Street
Philadelphia, PA 19147
Phone: 215-925-5083
Fax: 215-925-7412
E-mail: rsmolin@lx.netcom.com
Web site: *http://www.transatlanticpub.com.*

Acquisitions: Ron Smolin. Estab. 1984. Publishes hardcover, trade paperback and mass market paperback originals. **Publishes 100 titles/year. Imprint publishes 20 titles/year. Receives 500 queries and 500 manuscripts/year. 15% of books from first-time authors; 20% from unagented writers. Pays 7 1/2-12% royalty on retail price. Offers $2,000-10,000 advance.** Publishes book 11 months after acceptance of manuscript. Accepts simultaneous submissions.

Tips: Trans-Atlantic publishes a wide variety of nonfiction and fiction and distributes a wide variety of business books published in England.

CHARLES E. TUTTLE CO.

153 Milk Street, 5th Floor
Boston, MA 02109
Phone: 802-773-8930
Web site: *http://www.tuttle-periplus.com*

Acquisitions: Michael Lewis, acquisitions editor. Estab. 1832. Publishes hardcover and trade paperback originals and reprints. **Publishes 60 titles/year. Receives over 1,000 queries/year. 20% of books from first-time authors; 60% from unagented writers. Pays 5-10% royalty on net or retail price, depending on format and kind of book.** Publishes book 18 months after acceptance of manuscript. Accepts simultaneous submissions. Reports in 3 months on proposals.

Tips: Tuttle is America's leading publisher of books on Japan and Asia.

TWENTY-FIRST CENTURY BOOKS

Millbrook Press
2 Old New Milford Road
Brookfield, CT 06804
Phone: 203-740-2220
Web site: *http://www.millbrookpress.com*

Publisher: Pat Culleton. Editor: Dominic Barth. **Acquisitions**: Editorial Department. Publishes hardcover originals. **Publishes 40 titles/year. Receives 200 queries and 50 manuscripts/year. 20% of books from first-time writers; 75% from unagented writers. Pays 5-8% royalty on net price.** Publishes book 18 months after acceptance of manuscript. Accepts simultaneous submissions. Reports in 3 months on proposals.

Tips: Twenty-First Century Books publishes nonfiction science, technology, and social issues titles for children and young adults.

UNIVERSITY OF GEORGIA PRESS

330 Research Drive
Athens, GA 30602-4901
Phone: 706-369-6130
Fax: 706-369-6131

E-mail: ugapress@uga.edu
Executive Editor/Director: Karen Orchard. **Acquisitions**: David Des Jardines, acquisition editor. Estab. 1938. Publishes hardcover originals, trade paperback originals and reprints. **Publishes 85 titles/year; imprint publishes 10-15 titles/year. Receives 600 queries/year. 33% of books from first-time authors; 66% from unagented writers. Pays 7-10% royalty on net price. Rarely offers advance; amount varies.** Publishes book 1 year after acceptance of manuscript. Reports in 2 months on queries. Manuscript guidelines for #10 SASE.

Imprint(s): Brown Thrasher Books, David Des Jardines, acquisition editor (paperback originals and reprints, Southern history, literature and culture).

Tips: Literary fiction and nonfiction, Americana, regional bias. Query or submit outline with 1 sample chapter, author's bio with SASE.

UNIVERSITY OF ILLINOIS PRESS

1325 South Oak Street
Champaign, IL 61820-6903
Phone: 217-333-0950
Fax: 217-244-8082
E-mail: uipress@uiuc.edu
Web site: *http://www.press.uillinois.edu*

Acquisitions: Willis Regier, director/editor in chief. Estab. 1918. Publishes hardcover and trade paperback originals and reprints. **Publishes 100-110 titles/year. 50% of books from first-time authors; 95% from unagented writers. Nonauthor-subsidy publishes 10% of books. Pays 0-10% royalty on net sales. Offers $1,000-1,500 advance (rarely).** Publishes book 1 year after acceptance. Reports in 1 month.

Tips: Scholarly books and serious nonfiction with a wide range of study interests.

UNIVERSITY OF NEW MEXICO PRESS

1720 Lomas Boulevard NE
Albuquerque, NM 87131-1591
Phone: 505-277-2346
E-mail: unmpress@unm.edu
Director: Elizabeth Hadas.

Acquisitions: Barbara Guth, managing editor (women's studies, Chicano/a studies); Dana Asbury, editor (art, photography); Larry Durwood Ball, editor (western Americana, anthropology); David V. Holby, editor (Latin American studies, history). Estab. 1929. Publishes hardcover originals and trade paperback originals and reprints. **Publishes 70 titles/year. Receives 600 submissions/year. 12% of books from first-time authors; 90% from unagented writers. Royalty varies.** Allow 2 months for reply.

Tips: Well known as a publisher in the fields of anthropology, archaeology, Latin American studies, photography, architecture and the history and culture of the American West, fiction, some poetry, Chicano/a studies, and works by and about American Indians.

UNIVERSITY OF TEXAS PRESS

P.O. Box 7819
Austin, TX 78713-7819
Phone: 512-471-7233
Fax: 512-320-0668
E-mail: castiron@mail.utexas.edu
Web site: *http://www.utexas.edu/utpress/*
Acquisitions: Theresa May, assistant director/executive editor (social sciences, Latin American studies); James Burr, acquisition editor (humanities, classics); Sheri Englund, acquisitions editor (science). Estab. 1952.
Publishes 80 titles/year. Receives 1,000 submissions/year. 50% of books from first-time authors; 99% from unagented writers. Pays royalty usually based on net income. Offers advance occasionally. Publishes book 18 months after acceptance of manuscript. Reports in up to 3 months. Manuscript guidelines free.
Tips: In addition to publishing the results of advanced research for scholars worldwide, UT Press has a special obligation to the people of its state to publish authoritative books on Texas.

UNIVERSITY PRESS OF KANSAS

2501 West 15th Street
Lawrence, KS 66049-3905
Phone: 785-864-4154
Fax: 785-864-4586
E-mail: mail@newpress.upress.ukans.edu
Acquisitions: Michael J. Briggs, editor in chief (military history, political science, law); Nancy Scott Jackson, acquisitions editor (Western history, American studies, environmental studies, women's studies, philosophy); Fred M. Woodward, director (political science, presidency, regional). Estab. 1946. Publishes hardcover originals, trade paperback originals and reprints. **Publishes 50 titles/year. Receives 600 queries/year. 20% of books from first-time authors; 98% from unagented writers. Pays 5-15% royalty on net price.** Publishes book 10 months after acceptance of manuscript. Reports in 1 month on proposals. Manuscript guidelines free.
Tips: The University Press of Kansas publishes scholarly books that advance knowledge and regional books that contribute to the understanding of Kansas, the Great Plains, and the Midwest.

UNIVERSITY PRESS OF MISSISSIPPI

3825 Ridgewood Road
Jackson, MS 39211-6492
Phone: 601-982-6205
Fax: 601-982-6217
E-mail: press@ihl.state.ms.us
Web site: *http://www.upress.state.ms.us*
Director/Editor in Chief: Seetha Srinivasan. **Acquisitions**: Acquisitions Editor Craig Gill, senior editor (regional studies, anthropology, military history); Anne Stascavage, editor (performance art, literature). Estab. 1970. Publishes hardcover and paperback originals and reprints. **Publishes 55 titles/year. Receives 750 submissions/year. 20% of books from first-time authors; 90% from unagented writers. "Competitive

royalties and terms."** Publishes book 1 year after acceptance. Reports in 3 months.
Tips: Scholarly and trade titles, as well as special series.
Imprint(s): Muscadine Books (regional trade), Banner Books (literary reprints).

VERSO

180 Varick Street, 10th Floor
New York, NY 10014
Phone: 212-807-9680
Fax: 212-807-9152
E-mail: versoinc@aol.com
Web site: *http://www.verso-nlr.com*
Acquisitions: Colin Robinson, managing director. Estab. 1970. Publishes hardcover and trade paperback originals. **Publishes 40-60 titles/year. Receives 300 queries and 150 manuscripts/year. 10% of manuscripts from first-time authors, 95% from unagented writers. Pays royalty.** Publishes book 1 year after acceptance of manuscript. Accepts simultaneous submissions. Reports in 5 months.
Tips: Books cover politics, culture, and history (among other topics), but all from a critical, leftist viewpoint, on the border between trade and academic.

VIKING

Penguin Putnam Inc.
375 Hudson Street
New York, NY 10014
Phone: 212-366-2000
Web site: *http://www.penguinputnam.com*
Acquisitions: Barbara Grossman, publisher. Publishes hardcover and trade paperback originals. **Pays 10-15% royalty on retail price. Advance negotiable.** Publishes book 1 year after acceptance of manuscript. Accepts simultaneous submissions. Reports in 6 months on queries.
Tips: Viking publishes a mix of academic and popular fiction and nonfiction.

VIKING CHILDREN'S BOOKS

Penguin Putnam Inc.
375 Hudson Street
New York, NY 10014
Phone: 212-366-2000
Web site: *http://www.penguinputnam.com*
Editor in Chief: Elizabeth Law. **Acquisitions**: Submissions Editors. Publishes hardcover originals. Publishes 80 books/year. **Receives 7500 queries/year. 25% of books from first-time authors; 33% from unagented writers. Pays 10% royalty on retail price. Advance negotiable.** Publishes book 1 year after acceptance of manuscript. Report in 4 months on queries.
Tips: Viking Children's Books publishes high-quality trade books for children including fiction, nonfiction, and novelty books for preschoolers through young adults.

VILLARD BOOKS
Random House Inc.
201 East 50th Street
New York, NY 10022
Phone: 212-572-2878
Web site: *http://www.randomhouse.com*
Publisher: Ann Godoff. Estab. 1983. Publishes hardcover and trade paper-back originals. **Publishes 55-60 titles/year. 95% of books are agented submissions. Advances and royalties; negotiated separately.** Accepts simultaneous submissions.
Tips: Savvy and sometimes quirky bestseller hardcovers and trade paper-backs.

VINTAGE, Knopf Publishing Group
Random House Inc.
201 East 50th Street
New York, NY 10020
Phone: 212-751-2600
Web site: *http://www.randomhouse.com*
Vice President: LuAnn Walther. Editor in Chief: Martin Asher.
Acquisitions: Submissions Department; publishes trade paperback originals and reprints. **Publishes 200 titles/year. Receives 600- 700 manuscripts/year. 5% of books from first time-authors; less than 1% from unagented writers. Pays 4-8% on retail price. Offers $2,500 and up advance.** Publishes book 1 year after acceptance of manuscript. Accepts simultaneous submissions. Reports in 6 months. Nonfiction: Subjects include anthropology/archaeology, biography, business/economics, child guidance/parenting, education, ethnic, gay/lesbian, government/politics, health/medicine, history, language/literature, military/war, nature/environment, philosophy, psychology, regional, science, sociology, translation, travel, women's issues/studies. Submit outline and 2-3 sample chapters. Reviews artwork as part of manuscript package. Send photocopies.
Fiction: Literary, mainstream/contemporary, short story collections. Submit synopsis with 2-3 sample chapters.
Tips: Specializes in high quality, literary material.

WALKER AND CO.
Walker Publishing Co.
435 Hudson Street
New York, NY 10014
Phone: 212-727-8300
Fax: 212-727-0984
Publisher: George Gibson. Editors: Jacqueline Johnson, Michael Seidman. Juvenile Publisher: Emily Easton. Juvenile Editor: Soyung Pak.
Acquisitions: Submissions Editor or Submissions Editor-Juvenile. Estab. 1959. Publishes hardcover and trade paperback originals. **Publishes 70 titles/year. Receives 3,500 submissions/year. Pays royalty on retail price, 7 1/2-12% on paperback, 10-15% on hardcover. Offers competitive advances.** Material without SASE will not be returned. Reports in 3 months. Manuscript guidelines for 9x12 SASE with 3 first-class stamps.

Tips: Walker publishes general nonfiction on a variety of subjects as well as mysteries, children's books, and large print religious reprints. Currently emphasizing science, history, technology, math. De-emphasizing music, bio, self-help, sports.

WARNER ASPECT, Warner Books
1271 Avenue of the Americas
New York, NY 10020
Phone: 212-522-7200
Web site: *http://www.twbookmark.com*
Editor in Chief: Betsy Mitchell. Publishes hardcover, trade paperback, mass market paperback originals and mass market paperback reprints.
Publishes 30 titles/year. Receives 500 queries and 350 manuscripts/year. 5-10% of books from first-time authors; 1% from unagented writers. Pays royalty on retail price. Offers $5,000-up advance. Publishes book 1 year after acceptance of manuscript. Reports in 3 months on manuscripts.
Tips: Looking for "epic" stories in both fantasy and science fiction.

WARNER BOOKS, Time & Life Building
1271 Avenue of the Americas
New York, NY 10020
Phone: 212-522-7200
Web site: *http://www.twbookmark.com*
President, Maureen Egen.
Acquisitions: (Ms.) Jamie Raab, senior vice president/publisher (general nonfiction, commercial fiction); Rick Horgan, vice president/executive editor, (pop culture, general nonfiction, thriller fiction); Amy Einhorn, executive editor, trade paperback (popular culture, business, fitness, self-help); Claire Zion, executive editor, mass market (women's fiction, spirituality and human potential); Rick Wolff, executive editor (business, humor, sports); Betsy Mitchell, executive editor (science fiction); Caryn Karmatz Rudy, senior editor (fiction, general nonfiction, popular culture); Rob McMahon (fiction, business, sports); Diana Baroni, editor (health, fitness, general nonfiction); Jessica Papin, associate editor (commercial fiction, general nonfiction); John Aherne, associate editor (popular culture, fiction, general nonfiction); William Malloy, editor in chief, Mysterious Press (mysteries, cookbooks); Sara Ann Freed, executive editor (mysteries, suspense); Susanna Einstein, associate editor (mysteries, literary fiction). Estab. 1961. Publishes hardcover, trade paperback and mass market paperback originals and reprints. **Publishes 350 titles/year. Pays variable royalty. Advance varies.** Publishes book 2 years after acceptance of manuscript. Responds in 4 months.
Tips: Warner publishes general interest fiction and nonfiction.
Imprint(s): **Mysterious Press** (mystery/suspense), **Warner Aspect** (science fiction and fantasy), Warner Vision.

JOHN WILEY & SONS, INC.
605 Third Avenue
New York, NY 10158
Phone: 212-850-6000
Web site: *http://www.wiley.com*

Editor in Chief/Senior Editor of African-American Books: Carole Hall.
Acquisitions: Editorial Department. Estab. 1807. Publishes hardcover originals, trade paperback originals and reprints. **Pays "competitive royalty rates."** Accepts simultaneous submissions. Manuscript guidelines free with #10 SASE.
Tips: The General Interest group publishes books for the consumer market.

WRITER'S DIGEST BOOKS

F&W Publications
1507 Dana Avenue
Cincinnati, OH 45207
Phone: 513-531-2690
Fax: 513-531-7107
Web site: *http://www.writersdigest.com*
Editor: Jack Heffron.
Acquisitions: Acquisitions Coordinator. Estab. 1920. Publishes hardcover and paperback originals. **Publishes 28 titles/year. Receives 500 queries and 50 manuscripts/year. No books from first-time authors; 40% unagented writers. Pays 10-20% royalty on net receipts. Offers average advance of $5,000 and up.** Accepts simultaneous submissions, if so noted. Publishes book 18 months after acceptance of manuscript. Reports in 2 months.
Tips: Writer's Digest Books is the premiere source for books about writing, publishing instructional and reference books for writers that concentrate on the creative technique and craft of writing rather than the marketing of writing.

YALE UNIVERSITY PRESS

302 Temple Street
New Haven, CT 06520
Phone: 203-432-0960
Fax: 203-432-0948
Web site: *http://www.yale.edu/yup*
Acquisitions: Jonathan Brent, editorial director (humanities, cold war studies, annuals of communism, philosophy); Charles Grench, editor in chief (anthropology, history, Judaic studies, religion, women's studies); Jean E. Thomson Black, editor (science, medicine); John S. Covell, senior editor (economics, law, political science); Harry Haskell, editor (music, classics, archaeology, performing arts); Richard Miller, assistant editor, (poetry); Judy Metro, senior editor (art, art history, architecture, geography); Susan Arellano, senior editor (education, psychiatry, psychology, sociology). Estab. 1908. Publishes hardcover and trade paperback originals. **Publishes 225 titles/year. Receives 8,000 queries and 400 manuscripts/year. 15% of books from first-time authors; 85% from unagented writers. Pays 0-15% royalty on net price. Offers $500-50,000 advance (based on expected sales).** Publishes book 1 year after acceptance of manuscript. Accepts simultaneous submissions, if so noted. Reports in 1 month on queries, 2 months on proposals, 3 months on manuscripts. Manuscript guidelines for #10 SASE.
Tips: Yale University Press publishes scholarly and general interest books.

ZEBRA BOOKS, Kensington

850 Third Avenue, 16th Floor
New York, NY 10022
Phone: 212-407-1500
Web site: *http://www.kensingtonbooks.com*
Acquisitions: Ann Lafarge, editor; Kate Duffy, senior editor (historical, regency, romance); John Scognamiglio, senior editor (romance, mystery, thrillers, pop culture); Hillary Sares (Precious Gem romances). Publishes hardcover originals, trade paperback and mass market paperback originals and reprints. **Publishes 140-170 titles/year. 5% of books from first-time authors; 30% from unagented writers. Pays variable royalty and advance.** Publishes book 18 months after acceptance of manuscript. Accepts simultaneous submissions. Reports in 1 month on queries, in 3 months on manuscripts.
Tips: Zebra Books is dedicated to women's fiction, which includes, but is not limited to romance.

ZONDERVAN PUBLISHING HOUSE

HarperCollins Publishers
5300 Patterson Avenue SE
Grand Rapids, MI 49530-0002
Phone: 616-698-6900
E-mail: zpub@zph.com
Web site: *http://www.zondervan.com*
Publisher: Scott Bolinder. Editors: David Lambert, Sandy Vander Zicht.
Acquisitions: Manuscript Review Editor. Estab. 1931. Publishes hardcover and trade paperback originals and reprints. **Publishes 120 titles/year. Receives 3,000 submissions/year. 20% of books from first-time authors; 80% from unagented writers. Pays 14% royalty on net amount received on sales of cloth and softcover trade editions; 12% royalty on net amount received on sales of mass market paperbacks. Offers variable advance.** Reports in 3 months on proposals. SASE required. Guidelines for #10 SASE. To receive a recording about submissions, call 616-698-6900, ext. 344.
Tips: Aims to be the leading Christian communications company meeting the needs of people with resources that glorify Jesus Christ and promote biblical principles.

Small Presses and University Presses

These small presses and imprints each publish up to fifty books a year, accept unagented submissions, and pay royalty advances.

A&B PUBLISHERS GROUP

1000 Atlantic Avenue
Brooklyn, NY 11238
Phone: 718-783-7808

Acquisitions: Maxwell Taylor, editor. Estab. 1992. Publishes hardcover originals and trade paperback originals and reprints. **Publishes 12 titles/year. Receives 120 queries and 150 manuscripts/year. 30% of books from first-time authors; 30% from unagented writers. Pays 5-12% royalty on net price. Offers $500-2,500 advance.** Publishes book 12-18 months after acceptance of manuscript. Accepts simultaneous submissions. Reports in 2 months on queries and proposals, 5 months on manuscripts.

Tips: The audience for A&B Publishers Group is children and adult African-Americans.

A.K. PETERS, LTD.

63 South Avenue
Natick, MA 01760
Phone: 781-235-2210
Fax: 781-235-2404
E-mail: editorial@akpeters.com
Web site: *http://www.akpeters.com*

Acquisitions: Alice and Klaus Peters, publishers. Publishes hardcover originals and reprints. **Publishes 20 titles/year. Receives 50 queries and 30 manuscripts/year. 75% of books from first-time authors; 100% from unagented writers. Pays 15-20% royalty on net price.** Publishes book 4 months after acceptance of manuscript. Accepts simultaneous submissions. Reports in 3 months. Manuscript guidelines free.

Tips: A. K. Peters, Ltd. publishes scientific/technical/medical books and popular nonfiction titles related to science and technology. Stories of people behind the science are also of interest. They are the predominant publisher of mathematics and computer science, and are expanding our list in robotics and health/medicine as well.

ABC-CLIO, INC.

501 South Cherry Street, Suite 350
Denver, CO 80246
Phone: 303-333-3003
Fax: 303-333-4037
Web site: *http://www.abc-clio.com*
Subsidiaries include ABC-CLIO Ltd.

Acquisitions: Gary Kuris, editorial director; Alicia Merritt, senior acquisitions editor (history, law, mythology); Todd Hallman, senior acquisitions editor (social sciences, folklore, multicultural studies); Kristi Ward, senior acquisitions editor (science, literature); Marie Ellen Larcada, senior acquisitions editor (history, environment, education). Estab. 1955. Publishes hardcover originals. **Publishes 45 titles/year. Receives 500 submissions/year. 20% of books from first-time authors; 95% from unagented writers. Pays royalty on net receipts. Offers advance.** Publishes manuscript 10 months after acceptance. Reports in 2 months on queries. Manuscript guidelines free.

Tips: ABC-CLIO publishes easy-to-use, authoritative sources on high-interest topics for the high school, undergraduate and public library audience. Currently emphasizing social sciences, science and folklore. Query or submit outline and sample chapters.

ABSEY & CO.

5706 Root Road, Suite #5
Spring, TX 77389
Phone: 281-257-2340
E-mail: abseyandco@aol.com
Web site: *http://www.absey.com*

Acquisitions: Trey Hall, editor in chief. Publishes hardcover, trade paperback and mass market paperback originals. **Publishes 6- 10 titles/year. 50% of books from first-time authors; 50% from unagented writers. Royalty and advance vary.** Publishes book 1 year after acceptance of manuscript. No e-mail submissions. Reports in 3 months on queries, 9 months on manuscripts. Manuscript guidelines for #10 SASE or on Web site.

Tips: Works of literary merit. Currently emphasizing educational, young adult literature. Query with SASE.

ACADA BOOKS

1850 Union Street, Suite 1236
San Francisco, CA 94123
Phone: 415-776-2325

Acquisitions: President: Brian Romer. Publishes college textbooks. **Publishes 3 titles/year. Receives 50 queries/year; 20 manuscripts/year. 33% of books from first-time authors; 100% from unagented writers. Royalty varies.** Publishes book 4 months after acceptance of manuscript. Accepts simultaneous submissions. Reports in 2 months on proposals. Manuscript guidelines free.

Nonfiction: Textbook. Subjects include business, criminal justice, communications, politics, history, nature/environment, psychology, sociology.

Tips: Works of technical interest to those in the legal and business worlds.

ACCENT BOOKS, Cheever Publishing, Inc.

P.O. Box 700
Bloomington, IL 61702
Phone: 309-**378-2961**
Fax: (309)378-4420

Acquisitions: Betty Garee, editor. **Publishes 2 titles/year. Receives 50 queries and 150 manuscripts/year. 90% of books from first-time authors; 90% from unagented writers.** Makes outright purchase. Publishes book 3 months after acceptance of manuscript. Accepts simultaneous submissions. Reports on queries in 1 month. Manuscript guidelines for #10 SASE.

Tips: Nonfiction Books pertaining to people with physical disabilities who are trying to live an independent life.

ADDICUS BOOKS, INC.

P.O. Box 45327
Omaha, NE 68145
Phone: 402-330-7493
E-mail: addicusbks@aol.com
Web site: *http://www.AddicusBooks.com*

Acquisitions: Rod Colvin, president. Estab. 1994. Publishes trade paperback originals. **Publishes 8-10 titles/year. 70% of books from first-time authors; 60% from unagented writers. Pays royalty on retail price.** Publishes book 9 months after acceptance of manuscript. Accepts simultaneous submissions. Reports in 1 month on proposals. Guidelines for #10 SASE.

Nonfiction: How-to, self-help. Subjects include Americana, business/economics, health/medicine, psychology, regional, true-crime. Query with outline and 3-4 sample chapters.

ALBERT WHITMAN AND CO.

6340 Oakton Street
Morton Grove, IL 60053-2723
Phone: 847-581-0033
Acquisitions: Kathleen Tucker, editor in chief. Estab. 1919. Publishes hardcover originals and paperback reprints. **Publishes 30 titles/year. Receives 5,000 submissions/year. 20% of books from first-time authors; 70% from unagented writers. Pays 10% royalty for novels; 5% for picture books.** Publishes book an average of 18 months after acceptance of manuscript. Accepts simultaneous submissions. Reports in 5 months. Manuscript guidelines for #10 SASE.
Tips: Good books for children ages 2-12.

ALEF DESIGN GROUP

Torah Aura Productions
4423 Fruitland Avenue
Los Angeles, CA 90058
Phone: 213-585-7312
Web site: *http://www.torahaura.com*
Acquisitions: Jane Golub. Estab. 1990. Publishes hardcover and trade paperback originals. **Publishes 25 titles/year; imprint publishes 10 titles/year. Receives 30 queries and 30 manuscripts/year. 80% of books from first-time authors; 100% from unagented writers. Pays 10% royalty.** Publishes book 3 years after acceptance of manuscript. Accepts simultaneous submissions. Reports in 6 months on manuscripts.
Tips: The Alef Design Group publishes books of Judaic interest only. Currently de-emphasizing picture books.

ALYSON PUBLICATIONS, INC.

6922 Hollywood Boulevard, Suite 1000
Los Angeles, CA 90028
Phone: 323-860-6065
Fax: 323-467-0152
Web site: *http://www.alyson.com*
Acquisitions: Attn. Editorial Department; Scott Brassart, associate publisher (fiction, science); Angela Brown, associate editor (women's fiction, arts). Estab. 1979. Publishes trade paperback originals and reprints. **Publishes 40 titles/year. Receives 1,500 submissions/year. 40% of books from first-time authors; 70% from unagented writers. Pays 8-15% royalty on net price. Offers $1,500-15,000 advance.**

Publishes book 18 months after acceptance. Reports in 2 months. Manuscript guidelines for 6x9 SASE with 3 first-class stamps.
Tips: Alyson Publications publishes books for and about gay men and lesbians. They also consider bisexual and transgender material. Emphasizing medical, legal, and financial nonfiction titles. De-emphasizing first fiction.
Imprint(s): Alyson Wonderland, Alyson Classics Library.

AMERICA WEST PUBLISHERS

P.O. Box 2208
Carson City, NV 89702-2208
Phone: 775-585-0700
Fax: 877-726-2632
E-mail: global@hidlink.com
Acquisitions: George Green, president. Estab. 1985. Publishes hardcover and trade paperback originals and reprints. **Publishes 20 titles/year. Receives 150 submissions/year. 90% of books from first-time authors; 90% from unagented writers. Pays 10% on wholesale price. Offers $300 average advance.** Publishes book 6 months after acceptance. Accepts simultaneous submissions. Reports in 1 month. Manuscript guidelines free.
Tips: America West seeks the "other side of picture," political cover-ups, and new health alternatives.
Imprint(s): Bridger House Publishers, Inc.

AMERICAN EAGLE PUBLICATIONS INC.

P.O. Box 1507
Show Low, AZ 85901
Phone: 520-537-5512
Fax: 520-537-5512
E-mail: ameagle@whitemtns.com
Web site: *http://www.logoplex.com/resources/ameagle*
Acquisitions: Mark Ludwig, publisher. Estab. 1988. Publishes scholarly hardcover and trade paperback originals and reprints. **Publishes 8 titles/year. 50% of books from first-time authors; 100% from unagented writers. Pays 7-15% royalty on retail price. Offers $1,000 average advance.** Publishes book 6 months after acceptance of manuscript. Accepts simultaneous submissions. Reports in 2 months. NO military or other autobiographies.
Nonfiction: Historical biography, technical. Subjects include computers/electronics (security), military/war and science (computers, artificial intelligence). Query. Reviews artwork/photos as part of freelance manuscript package. Send photocopies.
Tips: Audience is very technical, very international.

AMERICAN FEDERATION OF ASTROLOGERS

P.O. Box 22040
Tempe, AZ 85285
Phone: 480-838-1751
Fax: 480-838-8293
E-mail: afa@msn.com

Web site: *http://www.astrologers.com*
Acquisitions: Kris Brandt Riske, publications manager. Estab. 1938. Publishes trade paperback originals and reprints. **Publishes 10-15 titles/year. Receives 10 queries and 20 manuscripts/year. 50% of books from first-time authors; 100% from unagented writers. Pays 10% royalty.** Publishes book 10 months after acceptance of manuscript. Accepts simultaneous submissions. Reports in 6 months on manuscripts. Manuscript guidelines free.
Tips: American Federation of Astrologers publishes only astrology books, calendars, charts, and related aids.

AMHERST MEDIA, INC.

155 Rano Street, Suite 300
Buffalo, NY 14207
Phone: 716-874-4450
Fax: 716-874-4508
E-mail: amherstmed@aol.com
Web site: *http://www.members.aol.com/photobook/index*
Acquisitions: Craig Alesse, publisher. Estab. 1974. Publishes trade paperback originals and reprints. **Publishes 30 titles/year. Receives 50 submissions/year. 80% of books from first-time authors; 100% from unagented writers. Pays 6-8% royalty on retail price.** Publishes book 1 year after acceptance. Accepts simultaneous submissions. Reports in 2 months. Manuscript guidelines free.
Tips: Amherst Media publishes how-to photography books.
Nonfiction: Photography how-to. Query with outline, 2 sample chapters, and SASE. Reviews artwork/photos as part of manuscript package.

ANCHORAGE PRESS, INC.

P.O. Box 8067
New Orleans, LA 70182-8067
Phone: 504-283-8868
Fax: 504-866-0502
Acquisitions: Orlin Corey, editor. Publishes hardcover originals. Estab. 1935. **Publishes 10 titles/year. Receives 450-900 submissions/year. 50% of books from first-time authors; 80% from unagented writers. Pays 10-15% royalty on retail price. Playwrights also receive 50-75% royalties.** Publishes book 1-2 years after acceptance. Reports in 1 month on queries, 4 months on manuscripts. Manuscript guidelines free.
Tips: Plays for young people.
Nonfiction: Textbook, plays. Subjects include education, language/literature, plays, play anthologies, and texts for teachers of drama/theater (middle school and high school.) Query. Reviews artwork/photos.

APPALACHIAN MOUNTAIN CLUB BOOKS

5 Joy Street
Boston, MA 02108
Phone: 617-523-0636
Fax: 617-523-0722
Web site: *http://www.outdoors.org*

Acquisitions: Mark Russell, acquisitions. Estab. 1897. Publishes trade paperback originals. **Publishes 6-10 titles/year. Receives 200 queries and 20 manuscripts/year. 30% of books from first-time authors; 90% from unagented writers. Pays 6-10% royalty on retail price. Offers modest advance.** Publishes book 10 months after acceptance of manuscript. Accepts simultaneous submissions. Reports in 3 months on proposals. Manuscript guidelines for #10 SASE.
Tips: Appalachian Mountain Club publishes hiking guides, water-recreation guides (non-motorized), nature, conservation and mountain-subject guides for America's Northeast. Query. Reviews artwork/photos as part of manuscript package.

ARDEN PRESS INC.

P.O. Box 418
Denver, CO 80201-0418
Phone: 303-697-6766
Web site: *http://www.libertynet.org/ardenpop/*
Acquisitions: Susan Conley, publisher. Estab. 1980. Publishes hardcover and trade paperback originals and reprints. 95% of books are originals; 5% are reprints. **Publishes 4-6 titles/year. Receives 600 submissions/year. 20% of books from first-time authors; 80% from unagented writers. Pays 8-15% royalty on wholesale price. Offers $2,000 average advance.** Publishes book 6 months after acceptance. Accepts simultaneous submissions. Reports in 2 months on queries. Manuscript guidelines free.
Tips: Nonfiction on women's history and women's issues. Query with outline/synopsis and sample chapters.

ARTE PUBLICO PRESS

University of Houston
Houston, TX 77204-2174
Phone: 713-743-2841
Fax: 713-743-2847
Web site: *http://www.arte.uh.edu*
Acquisitions: Nicolas Kanellos, editor. Estab. 1979. Publishes hardcover originals, trade paperback originals and reprints. **Publishes 36 titles/year. Receives 1,000 queries and 500 manuscripts/year. 50% of books from first-time authors; 80% from unagented writers. Pays 10% royalty on wholesale price. Offers $1,000-3,000 advance.** Publishes book 2 years after acceptance of manuscript. Accepts simultaneous submissions. Reports in 1 month on queries and proposals; 4 months on manuscripts. Manuscript guidelines for #10 SASE.
Tips: Considers itself a showcase for Hispanic literary creativity, arts, and culture.
Imprint(s): Pinata Books.

ASTRO COMMUNICATIONS SERVICES

5521 Ruffin Road
San Diego, CA 92123
Phone: 619-492-9919
Fax: 619-492-9917
E-mail: maritha@astrocom.com

Web site: *http://www.astrocom.com*

Acquisitions: Maritha pottenger, editorial director. Publishes trade paperback originals and reprints and mass market paperback originals and reprints. **Publishes 4-5 titles/year. Receives 100 queries and 15 manuscripts/year. 20% of books from first-time authors; 95% from unagented writers. Pays 10-15% royalty.** Publishes book 1 year after acceptance of manuscript. Accepts simultaneous submissions. Reports in 3 months on queries and proposals, 6 months on manuscripts. Manuscript guidelines for 9x12 SASE with threee first-class stamps.

Tips: Nonfiction astrology titles for professionals.

AVANYU PUBLISHING INC.

P.O. Box 27134
Albuquerque, NM 87125
Phone: 505-266-6128
E-mail: brentric@aol.com

Acquisitions: J. Brent Ricks, president. Estab. 1984. Publishes hardcover and trade paperback originals and reprints. **Publishes 4 titles/year. Receives 40 submissions/year. 30% of books from first-time authors; 90% from unagented writers. Pays 8% maximum royalty on wholesale price.** Publishes book 1 year after acceptance. Reports in 2 months.

Tips: Highly illustrated, history-oriented books and contemporary American Indian/Western art. Query with SASE. Reviews artwork/photos as part of manuscript package.

AVERY PUBLISHING GROUP, INC.

120 Old Broadway
Garden City Park, NY 11040
Phone: 516-741-2155
Fax: 516-742-1892
Web site: *http://www.averypublishing.com*

Acquisitions: Rudy Shur, publisher; Norman Goldfind, vice president, marketing and product development (health, alternative medicine). Estab. 1976. Publishes trade paperback originals. **Publishes 50 titles/year. Receives 3,000 queries and 1,000 manuscripts/year. 70% of books from first-time authors; 90% from unagented writers. Pays royalty. Conservative advances offered.** Publishes book 1 year after acceptance of manuscript. Accepts simultaneous submissions. Reports in 2 weeks on queries, 3 weeks on proposals and manuscripts. Allow 2 months for reply. Manuscript guidelines free.

Tips: Avery specializes in alternative medicine, natural medicine, health, healthy cooking, health reference, child care, and childbirth. Currently emphasizing health. De-emphasizing gardening.

AVISSON PRESS, INC.

3007 Taliaferro Road
Greensboro, NC 27408
Phone: 336-288-6989

Acquisitions: M. L. Hester, editor. Estab. 1994. Publishes hardcover originals and trade paperback originals and reprints. **Publishes 9-10 titles/year. Receives 600 queries and 400 manuscripts/year. 5%** of books from first-time authors; 90% from unagented writers. **Pays 8-10% royalty on wholesale price. Offers occasional small advance.** Publishes book 15 months after acceptance of manuscript. Accepts simultaneous submissions, if so noted. Reports in 1 week on queries and proposals, 3 months on manuscripts.

Tips: Avisson Press publishes helpful nonfiction for senior citizens, minority topics, and young adult biographies (African-American, women).

B&B PUBLISHING, INC.

P.O. Box 96
Walworth, WI 53184
Fax: 414-275-9530

Acquisitions: N. Kirchschlager. Publishes hardcover and trade paperback originals. **Publishes 5-10 titles/year. Receives 1,000 queries and 100 manuscripts/year. 10% of books from first-time authors; 90% from unagented writers. Usually contracts authors as work-for-hire.** Publishes book 1 year after acceptance. Accepts simultaneous submissions. Any submissions or queries without SASE will not be acknowledged. No unsolicited manuscripts. Reports in 3 months. Manuscript guidelines free.

Tips: B&B Publishing seeks innovative supplementary educational materials, especially geography-based materials, for grades K-12. Also publishes a Southeastern Wisconsin quarterly tourism publication. Query with SASE. Reviews artwork/photos as part of manuscript package. Send photocopies.

BACKCOUNTRY PUBLICATIONS

The Countryman Press
P.O. Box 748
Woodstock, VT 05091-0748
Phone: 802-457-4826
Fax: 802-457-1678
E-mail: countrymanpress@wwnorton.com
Web site: *http://www.countrymanpress.com*

Acquisitions: Ann Kraybill, managing editor. Estab. 1996. Publishes trade paperback originals. **Publishes 15 titles/year. Receives 1,000 queries and a few manuscripts/year. 25% of books from first-time authors; 75% from unagented writers. Pays 7-10% royalty on retail price. Offers $1,500-2,500 advance.** Publishes book 18 months after acceptance of manuscript. Accepts simultaneous submissions. Returns submissions only with SASE. Reports in 2 months on proposals. Ms guidelines for #10 SASE.

Tips: Guidebooks that encourage physical fitness and appreciation for and understanding of the natural world, self-sufficiency, and adventure.

BANDANNA BOOKS

319-B Anacapa Street
Santa Barbara, CA 93101
Phone: 805-564-3559
Fax: 805-564-3278
E-mail: bandana@bandanabooks.com.25
Web site: *http://www.bandannabooks.com*

Publisher: Sasha Newborn. Editor: Joan Blake. Publishes trade paperback originals and reprints. **Publishes 3 titles/year. Receives 300 queries and 100 manuscripts/year. 25% of books from first-time authors; 100% from unagented writers. Pays negotiable royalty on net receipts. Offers up to $1,000 advance.** Accepts simultaneous submissions. Reports in 4 months on proposals.

Tips: Textbooks for college students, some illustrated. Bandanna Books seeks to humanize the classics, history, language in non-sexist, modernized translations, using direct and plain language. Submit query letter, table of contents, and first chapter. Include a SASE for reply. Reviews artwork/photos as part of manuscript package. Send photocopies.

BARNEGAT LIGHT PRESS

P.O. Box 607
Chatsworth, NJ 08019-0607
Phone: 609-894-4415
Fax: 609-894-2350

Acquisitions: R. Marilyn Schmidt, publisher. Publishes trade paperback originals. **Publishes 8 titles/year. Receives 12 queries and 10 manuscripts/year. 0% of books from first-time authors; 100% from unagented writers. Makes outright purchase.** Publishes book 6 months after acceptance of manuscript. Reports in 1 month.

Tips: Emphasizes gardening and cooking in the mid-Atlantic region. Query.

BATSFORD BRASSEY INC., (formerly Brassey's, Inc.)

4380 MacArthur Boulevard, NW, 2nd Floor
Washington, D.C. 20007
Phone: 202-333-2500
Fax: 202-333-5100
E-mail: brasseys@aol.com
Web site: *http://www.batsford.com*

Acquisitions: Don McKeon, editorial director. Estab. 1984. Publishes hardcover and trade paperback originals and reprints. **Publishes 30 titles/year. Receives 900 queries/year. 30% of books from first-time authors; 80% from unagented writers. Pays 6-12% royalty on wholesale price. Offers $50,000 maximum advance.** Publishes book 1 year after acceptance of manuscript. Accepts simultaneous submissions. Reports in 2 months on proposals. Manuscript guidelines for 9x12 SASE.

Tips: Batsford Brassey specializes in national and international affairs, military history, biography, intelligence, foreign policy, defense and sports. The audience consists of military personnel, government policymakers, and general readers with an interest in military history, biography, national/international affairs, defense issues, intelligence studies, and sports. No fiction.

BEAVER POND PUBLISHING

P.O. Box 224
Greenville, PA 16125
Phone: 724-588-3492

Acquisitions: Rich Faler, publications director. Estab. 1990. Publishes trade paperback originals and reprints. **Publishes 4 titles/year. Receives 30 queries and 20 manuscripts/year. 50% of books from first-time authors; 100% from unagented writers. Pays 8% royalty on net sales or makes outright purchase.** Publishes book 1 year after acceptance of manuscript. Accepts simultaneous submissions. Reports in 1 month. Manuscript guidelines free.

Nonfiction: Outdoor how-to. Subjects include photography (outdoor), hunting, fishing. Seeks shorter length manuscripts suitable for 20-40 page booklets, in addition to longer length books. Query or submit outline and 2 sample chapters with SASE. Reviews artwork/photos as part of manuscript package.

Easy to read information for those interested in outdoors subjects.

BERKSHIRE HOUSE PUBLISHERS, INC.

480 Pleasant Street, Suite #5
Lee, MA 01238
Phone: 413-243-0303
Fax: 413-243-4737
Web site: *http://www.berkshirehouse.com*
President: Jean J. Rousseau.

Acquisitions: Philip Rich, editorial director. Estab. 1989. **Publishes 12-15 titles/year. Receives 100 queries and 6 manuscripts/year. 50% of books from first-time authors; 80% from unagented writers. Pays 5-10% royalty on retail price. Offers $500-5,000 advance.** Publishes book 18 months after acceptance. Accepts simultaneous submissions. Reports in 1 month on proposals.

Tips: Travel guides (the Great Destinations Series), about specific U.S. destinations, guides to appeal to upscale visitors, specialize in books about the Berkshires in western Massachusetts, especially recreational activities in the area. Currently emphasizing guides to U.S. destinations of cultural interest. De-emphasizing cookbooks, except those related to New England or country living and country inns.

BICK PUBLISHING HOUSE

307 Neck Road
Madison, CT 06443
Phone: 203-245-0073
Fax: 203-245-5990
E-mail: bickpubhse@aol.com
Web site: *http://pma-online.org/list/2882.html*

Acquisitions: Dale Carlson, president (psychology); Hannah Carlson (special needs, disabilities); Irene Ruth (wildlife). Estab. 1994. Publishes trade paperback originals. **Publishes 4 titles/year. Receives 6-12 queries and manuscripts/year. 55% of books from first-time authors; 55% from unagented writers. Pays 10% royalty on retail price. Offers $500-1,000 advance.** Publishes book 1 year after acceptance of manuscript. Reports in 1 month on queries, 2 months on proposals, 3 months on manuscripts. Manuscript guidelines for #10 SASE.

Tips: Step-by-step, easy-to-read professional information for the general adult public about physical, psychological and emotional disabilities or special needs, teenage psychology, and also about wildlife rehabilitation.

BIRCH BROOK PRESS

P.O. Box 81
Delhi, NY 13753
Phone: 212-353-3326
Acquisitions: Tom Tolnay, editor. Estab. 1982. Publishes hardcover and trade paperback originals. **Publishes 4-6 titles/year. Receives hundreds of queries and manuscripts/year. 95% of books from unagented writers. Royalty varies. Offers modest advance.** Publishes book 1 year after acceptance of manuscript. Accepts simultaneous submission, if informed. Reports in 1 month on queries, 2 months on manuscripts. Manuscript guidelines for #10 SASE.
Tips: Birch Brook Press is a popular culture and literary publisher of handcrafted books and art, featuring letterpress editions produced at its own printing, typesetting, and binding facility. Currently emphasizing anthologies. Recently took over the poetry publishing company Persephone Press.

BLACKBIRCH PRESS, INC.

P.O. Box 3573
Woodbridge, CT 06525
Phone: 203-387-7525
E-mail: staff@blackbirch.com
Web site: *http://www.blackbirch.com*
Acquisitions: Bruce Glassman, editorial director. Estab. 1990. Publishes hardcover and trade paperback originals. **Publishes 30- 40 titles/year. Receives 400 queries and 75 manuscripts/year. 100% of books from unagented writers. Pays 4-8% royalty on wholesale price or makes outright purchase. Offers $1,000-5,000 advance.** Publishes book 1 year after acceptance of manuscript. Accepts simultaneous submissions. Replies only if interested. Manuscript guidelines free. "We cannot return submissions or send guidelines/replies without an enclosed SASE."
Tips: Blackbirch Press publishes juvenile and young adult nonfiction and fiction titles.

BLOOMBERG PRESS, Bloomberg L.P.

100 Business Park Drive
P.O. Box 888
Princeton, NJ 08542-0888
Phone: 609-279-4670
Web site: *http://www.bloomberg.com*
Acquisitions: Jared Kieling, editorial director; Jacqueline Murphy, senior acquisitions editor (Bloomberg Professional Library). Estab. 1995. Publishes hardcover and trade paperback originals. **Publishes 12-18 titles/year. Receives 90 queries and 17 manuscripts/year. 45% of books from unagented writers. Pays negotiable, competitive royalty. Offers negotiable advance.** Publishes book 9 months after acceptance of manuscript. Accepts simultaneous submissions. Reports in 1 month on queries.
Tips: Bloomberg Press publishes professional books for practitioners in the financial markets and finance and investing for informed personal investors, entrepreneurs, and consumers.

BOA EDITIONS, LTD.

260 East Avenue
Rochester, NY 14604
Phone: 716-546-3410
Fax: 716-546-3913
E-mail: boaedit@frontiernet.net
Web site: *http://www.boaeditions.org*
Acquisitions: Steven Huff, publisher/managing editor; Tom Ward, editor. Estab. 1976. Publishes hardcover and trade paperback originals. **Publishes 10 titles/year. Receives 1,000 queries and 700 manuscripts/year. 15% of books from first-time authors; 90% from unagented writers. Pays 7 1/2-10% royalty on retail price. Advance varies, usually $500.** Publishes book 18 months after acceptance of manuscript. Accepts simultaneous submissions. Reports in 1 month on queries, 4 months on manuscripts. Manuscript guidelines free.
Tips: Distinguished collections of poetry and poetry in translation.

BONUS BOOKS, INC., Precept Press

160 East Illinois Street
Chicago, IL 60611
Phone: 312-467-0580
Fax: 312-467-9271
Web site: *http://www.bonus-books.com*
Managing Editor: Andrea Rackel.
Acquisitions: Jean Kang and Benjamin Strong, assistant editors. Estab. 1985. Publishes hardcover and trade paperback originals and reprints. **Publishes 30 titles/year. Receives 400-500 submissions/year. 40% of books from first-time authors; 60% from unagented writers. Royalties vary. Rarely offers advance.** Publishes book 8 months after acceptance. Accepts simultaneous submissions, if so noted. Reports in 2 months on queries. Manuscript guidelines for #10 SASE.
Tips: Bonus Books is a publishing and audio/video company featuring subjects ranging from human interest to sports to gambling.

BOOKHOME PUBLISHING

P.O. Box 5900
Navarre, FL 32566
Phone: 850-936-4050
Fax: 850-939-4953
E-mail: bookhome@gte.net
Web site: *http://www.bookhome.com*
Acquisitions: Scott Gregory, publisher (small business, relationships, lifestyles, self-help). Publishes hardcover and trade paperback originals. **Publishes 5 titles/year. Receives 100 queries and 100 manuscripts/year. 50% of books from first-time authors; 50% from unagented writers. Pays 7-12% royalty on wholesale price. Offers $0-1,000 advance.** Publishes book 1 year after acceptance of manuscript. Accepts simultaneous submissions. Reports in 2 months on proposals. Manuscript guidelines for #10 SASE.

Nonfiction: How-to, self-help. Subjects include business/economics, child guidance/parenting, creative nonfiction, lifestyles, career. Submit proposal package, including outline, marketing plan, 2 sample chapters, and SASE. **Tips**: Focuses on small business books, and lifestyle material.

BREWERS PUBLICATIONS, Association of Brewers

736 Pearl Street
Boulder, CO 80302
Phone: 303-447-0816
Fax: 303-447-2825
E-mail: bp@aob.org
Web site: *http://www.beertown.org*
Acquisitions: Toni Knapp, publisher. Estab. 1986. Publishes hardcover and trade paperback originals. **Publishes 8 titles/year. 50% of books from first-time authors; 50% from unagented writers. Pays royalty on net receipts. Advance negotiated.** Publishes book within 18 months of acceptance of manuscript. Accepts simultaneous submissions. Reports in 3 months.
Nonfiction: Books on history, art, culture, literature, brewing and science of beer. In a broad sense, this also includes biographies, humor, cooking, and suspense/mystery fiction. Query first with brief proposal and SASE.
Fiction: Suspense/mystery with a beer theme. Query.
Tips: Only interested in beer related material.

BRIDGE WORKS PUBLISHING CO.

Box 1798, Bridge Lane
Bridgehampton, NY 11932
Phone: 516-537-3418
Fax: 516-537-5092
Acquisitions: Barbara Phillips, editor/publisher. Estab. 1992. Publishes hardcover originals and reprints. **Publishes 4-6 titles/year. Receives 1,000 queries and manuscripts/year. 50% of books from first-time authors; 80% from unagented writers. Pays 10% royalty on retail price. Offers $1,000 advance.** Publishes book 1 year after acceptance of manuscript. Reports in 1 month on queries and proposals, 2 months on manuscripts. Manuscript guidelines for #10 SASE.
Tips: Dedicated to quality fiction and nonfiction. No mass market material.
Nonfiction: Biography, history, language/literature, philosophy, psychology, sociology. No multiple submissions. Query or submit outline and proposal package with SASE. Reviews artwork/photos as part of manuscript package. Send photocopies.
Fiction: Historical, literary, mystery, short story collections. Query or submit synopsis and 2 sample chapters with SASE.

BRYANT & DILLON PUBLISHERS, INC.

P.O. Box 39
Orange, NJ 07050
Phone: 973-763-1470
Fax: 973-675-8443
Acquisitions: (Ms.) Gerri Dillon, editor (women's issues, film, photography). Estab. 1993. Publishes hardcover and trade paperback originals.

Publishes 8-10 titles/year. Receives 500 queries and 700 manuscripts/year. 100% of books from first-time authors; 90% from unagented writers. Pays 6-10% royalty on retail price. Publishes book 1 year after acceptance of manuscript. Accepts simultaneous submissions. Reports in 3 months on proposals.
Tips: Bryant & Dillon publishes books that speak to an African-American audience and others interested in the African-American experience.

BUTTE PUBLICATIONS, INC.

P.O. Box 1328
Hillsboro, OR 97123-1328
Phone: 503-648-9791
Fax: 503-693-9526
Acquisitions: M. Brink, president. Estab. 1992. **Publishes 6-8 titles/year. Receives 30 queries and 20 manuscripts/year. 50% of books from first-time authors; 100% from unagented writers. Pays 8-12% royalty on net receipts.** Publishes book 1 year after acceptance of manuscript. Accepts simultaneous submissions. Reports in 1 month on queries, 4 months on proposals, 6 months on manuscripts. Manuscript guidelines free.
Tips: Children's/juvenile, nonfiction and fiction all related to field of deafness and education. Submit proposal package, including author bio, synopsis, market survey, and complete manuscript, if completed. Reviews artwork/photos as part of manuscript package (if essential to the educational value of the work). Send photocopies.

CARDOZA PUBLISHING

132 Hastings Street
Brooklyn, NY 11235
Phone: 800-577-9467
Web site: *http://www.cardozapub.com*
Acquisitions: Rose Swann, acquisitions editor. Estab. 1981. Publishes trade paperback originals, mass market paperback originals and reprints. **Publishes 15 titles/year. Receives 175 queries and 70 manuscripts/year. 50% of books from first-time authors; 90% from unagented writers. Pays 5% royalty on retail price. Offers $500-2,000 advance.** Publishes book 6 months after acceptance of manuscript. Accepts simultaneous submissions. Reports in 2 months on queries.
Imprint(s): Gambling Research Institute, Word Reference Library.
Nonfiction: How-to, reference. Subjects include gaming, gambling, health/fitness, publishing, reference/word, travel. Travel guides for sister company Open Road Publishing (32 Turkey Lane, Cold Spring Harbor, NY 11724) and multimedia and software titles on all subjects for sister company, Cardoza Entertainment. Submit outline, table of contents, and 2 sample chapters.
Tips: Only interested in gambling related material.

CARSTENS PUBLICATIONS, INC., Hobby Book Division

P.O. Box 700
Newton, NJ 07860-0700
Phone: 973-383-3355

Fax: 973-383-4064

Web site: *http://www.carstens-publications.com*

Acquisitions: Harold H. Carstens, publisher. Estab. 1933. Publishes paperback originals. **Averages 8 titles/year. 100% of books from unagented writers. Pays 10% royalty on retail price. Offers advance. Publishes book 1 year after acceptance.**

Nonfiction: Model railroading, toy trains, model aviation, railroads, and model hobbies. Railroad books are presently primarily photographic essays on specific railroads. Query. Reviews artwork/photos as part of manuscript package.

Tips: Interested on books about models and modeling.

CASSANDRA PRESS

P.O. Box 868

San Rafael, CA 94915

Phone: 415-382-8507

President: Gurudas. Estab. 1985. Publishes trade paperback originals. **Publishes 3 titles/year. Receives 200 submissions/year. 50% of books from first-time authors; 50% from unagented writers. Pays 6-8% maximum royalty on retail price. Advance rarely offered.** Publishes book 1 year after acceptance. Accepts simultaneous submissions. Reports in 3 weeks on queries, 3 months on manuscripts. Manuscript guidelines free.

Nonfiction: new age, how-to, self-help. Subjects include cooking/foods/nutrition, health/medicine (holistic health), philosophy, psychology, religion (new age), metaphysical, political tyranny. Submit outline and sample chapters.

Tips: Interested in New Age material in valuing materials.

CATBIRD PRESS

16 Windsor Road

North Haven, CT 06473-3015

Phone: 203-230-2391

Web site: *http://www.catbirdpress.com*

Acquisitions: Robert Wechsler, publisher. Estab. 1987. Publishes hardcover and trade paperback originals and trade paperback reprints. **Publishes 4-5 titles/year. Receives 1,000 submissions/year. 5% of books from first-time authors; 90% from unagented writers. Pays 2½-10% royalty on retail price. Offers $2,000 average advance.** Publishes book 1 year after acceptance. Accepts simultaneous submissions, if so noted. Reports in 1 month on queries if SASE is included. Manuscript guidelines for #10 SASE.

Tips: Fiction and nonfiction. Up-market prose humorists. No joke or other small gift books. Also interested in very well-written general nonfiction that takes fresh, sophisticated approaches. Submit outline, sample chapters, and SASE.

CATO INSTITUTE

1000 Massachusetts Avenue NW

Washington, D.C. 20001

Phone: 202-842-0200

Acquisitions: David Boaz, executive vice president. Estab. 1977. Publishes hardcover originals, trade paperback originals and reprints. **Publishes 12 titles/year. Receives 50 submissions/year. 25% of books from first-time authors; 90% from unagented writers. Makes outright purchase of $1,000-10,000.** Publishes book 9 months after acceptance. Accepts simultaneous submissions. Reports in 3 months.

Tips: Cato Institute publishes books on public policy issues from a free-market or libertarian perspective.

CAXTON PRESS, (formerly The Caxton Printers, Ltd.)

312 Main Street

Caldwell, ID 83605-3299

Phone: 208-459-7421

Fax: 208-459-7450

Web site: *http://www.caxtonprinters.com*

President: Gordon Gipson.

Acquisitions: Wayne Cornell, managing acquisitions editor. Estab. 1907. Publishes hardcover and trade paperback originals. **Publishes 6-10 titles/year. Receives 250 submissions/year. 50% of books from first-time authors; 60% from unagented writers. Pays royalty. Offers advance.** Publishes book 18 months after acceptance. Accepts simultaneous submissions. Reports in 3 months.

Nonfiction: Americana, Western Americana. Serious, narrative nonfiction. Query. Reviews artwork/photos as part of manuscript package.

Tips: Wants books on Americana.

CCC PUBLICATIONS

9725 Lurline Avenue

Chatsworth, CA 91311

Phone: 818-718-0507

Acquisitions: Cliff Carle, editorial director. Estab. 1983. Publishes trade paperback and mass market paperback originals. **Publishes 40-50 titles/year. Receives 1,000 manuscripts/year. 25% of books from first-time authors; 25% of books from unagented writers. Pays 8-12% royalty on wholesale price.** Publishes book 6 months after acceptance. Accepts simultaneous submissions. Reports in 3 months.

Tips: CCC publishes humor that is "today" and will appeal to a wide demographic. Currently emphasizing short, punchy pieces with *lots* of cartoon illustrations, or very well-written text if long form.

CELESTIAL ARTS, Ten Speed Press

999 Harrison Street

Berkeley, CA 94710

Phone: 510-559-1600

Fax: 510-524-1052

Acquisitions: Veronica Randall, managing editor/interim publisher. Estab. 1966. Publishes hardcover and trade paperback originals, trade paperback reprints. **Publishes 40 titles/year. Receives 500 queries and 200 manuscripts/year. 30% of books from first-time authors; 10% from unagented writers. Pays 15% royalty on wholesale price.**

Offers modest advance. Publishes book 9 months after acceptance of manuscript. Accepts simultaneous submissions. Reports in 6 weeks. manuscript guidelines free.
Tips: Celestial Arts publishes nonfiction for a forward-thinking, open-minded audience interested in psychology, self-help, spirituality, health, and parenting.

CENTENNIAL PUBLICATIONS
256 Nashua Court
Grand Junction, CO 81503
Phone: 970-243-8780
Web site: *http://www.gorp.com/ci_angle/bookcat.htm*
Acquisitions: Dick Spurr, publisher. Estab. 1990. Publishes hardcover and trade paperback originals and reprints. **Publishes 4-5 titles/year. Receives 20 queries and 10 manuscripts/year. 80% of books from first-time authors; 100% from unagented writers. Pays 8-10% royalty on retail price. Offers $1,000 average advance.** Publishes book 8 months after acceptance of manuscript. Reports in 1 week on queries, 2 weeks on proposals, 1 month on manuscripts.
Nonfiction: Biography, how-to. Subjects include Americana, history, hobbies, fishing. Submit proposal package, including outline and sample chapters. Reviews artwork/photos as part of the manuscript package. Send photocopies.
Tips: Interested in books on Americana.

CHANDLER HOUSE PRESS
Rainbow New England Corp.
335 Chandler Street
Worcester, MA 01602
Phone: 508-756-7644
Fax: 508-756-9425
E-mail: databooks@tatnuck.com
Web site: *http://www.tatnuck.com*
President: Lawrence J. Abramoff.
Acquisitions: Richard J. Staron, publisher. Estab. 1993. Publishes hardcover and trade paperback originals and reprints. **Publishes 25 titles/year. Receives 200 queries and 50 manuscripts/year. 50% of books from first-time authors; 70% from unagented writers. Pays royalty on net sales.** Publishes book 6-12 months after acceptance of manuscript. Accepts simultaneous submissions. Reports in 1 month. Allow 2 months for reply. Manuscript guidelines free.
Tips: Chandler House Press is a general interest nonfiction publisher. Timely books that are tools for living better personal and professional lives.

CHICAGO REVIEW PRESS
814 North Franklin
Chicago, IL 60610-3109
Phone: 312-337-0747
Fax: 312-337-5985
E-mail: ipgbook@mcs.com
Web site: *http://www.ipgbook.com*

Acquisitions: Cynthia Sherry, executive editor (general nonfiction, children's); Yuval Taylor, editor (African, African-American). Estab. 1973. Publishes hardcover and trade paperback originals and trade paperback reprints. **Publishes 30-35 titles/year. Receives 200 queries and 600 manuscripts/year. 50% of books from first-time authors; 50% from unagented writers. Pays 7-12½% royalty. Offers $1,500-3,000 average advance.** Publishes book 15 months after acceptance. Accepts simultaneous submissions. Reports in 3 months. Book catalog for $3.50. Manuscript guidelines for #10 SASE or on Web site.
Tips: Chicago Review Press publishes intelligent nonfiction on timely subjects for educated readers with special interests.
Imprint(s): Lawrence Hill Books, A Capella Books (contact Yuval Taylor).

CHINA BOOKS & PERIODICALS, INC.
2929 24th Street
San Francisco, CA 94110-4126
Phone: 415-282-2994
Fax: 415-282-0994
Web site: *http://www.chinabooks.com*
Acquisitions: Greg Jones, editor (language study, health, history); Baolin Ma, senior editor (music, language study); Michael Rice, editor (language study, poetry, history). Estab. 1960. Publishes hardcover and trade paperback originals. **Averages 5 titles/year. Receives 300 submissions/year. 10% of books from first-time authors; 95% from unagented writers. Pays 6-8% royalty on net receipts. Offers $1,000 average advance.** Publishes book 1 year after acceptance. Accepts simultaneous submissions. Reports in 3 months on queries. Manuscript guidelines for #10 SASE or on Web site.
Nonfiction: *All* books *must* be on topics related to China or East Asia, or Chinese Americans. Books on China's history, politics, environment, women; language textbooks, acupuncture and folklore. Query with outline and sample chapters. Reviews artwork/photos as part of manuscript package.
Tips: Interested in books on and about China and East Asia.

CIRCLET PRESS INC.
1770 Massachusetts Avenue, #278
Cambridge, MA 02140
Phone: 617-864-0492
Fax: 617-864-0663
E-mail: circlet-info@circlet.com
Web site: *http://www.circlet.com*
Acquisitions: Cecilia Tan, publisher/editor. Estab. 1992. Publishes hardcover and trade paperback originals. **Publishes 6-10 titles/year. Receives 50-100 queries and 500 manuscripts/year. 50% of stories from first-time authors; 90% from unagented writers. Pays 4-12% royalty on retail price or makes outright purchase (depending on rights); also pays in books if author prefers.** Publishes stories 12-18 months after acceptance of manuscript. Accepts simultaneous submissions. Reports in 1 month on queries, 6-18 months on manuscripts. Manuscript guidelines for #10 SASE.
Tips: Science fiction/fantasy that is too erotic for the mainstream. The audience is adults who enjoy science fiction and fantasy, especially the

works of Anne Rice, Storm Constantine, Samuel Delany, who enjoy vivid storytelling and erotic content.

Fiction: Erotic science fiction and fantasy short stories only. Gay/lesbian stories needed but all persuasions welcome. Submit full short stories up to 10,000 words between April 15 and August 31. Manuscripts received outside this reading period are discarded. Queries only via e-mail.

CITY & COMPANY

22 West 23rd Street
New York, NY 10010
Phone: 212-366-1988
Fax: 212-242-0412
E-mail: cityco@bway.net
Web site: *http://newyork.citysearch.com/E/V/NYCNY/0017/33/59/1.html*
Acquisitions: Helene Silver, publisher. Estab. 1994. Publishes hardcover and trade paperback originals. **Publishes 10 titles/year. Receives 75 queries and 10 manuscripts/year. 50% of books from first-time authors; 75% from unagented writers. Pays 5-10% royalty on wholesale price. Offers advance.** Publishes book 6 months after acceptance of manuscript. Accepts simultaneous submissions. Reports in 3 months on queries. Manuscript guidelines free.
Tips: City & Company specializes in single subject city guide books.

CLEIS PRESS

P.O. Box 14684
San Francisco, CA 94114-0684
Fax: 415-864-3385
Web site: *http://www.cleispress.com*
Acquisitions: Frederique Delacoste. Estab. 1980. Publishes trade paperback originals and reprints. **Publishes 17 titles/year. 10% of books are from first-time authors; 90% from unagented writers. Pays variable royalty on retail price.** Publishes book 2 years after acceptance of manuscript. Accepts simultaneous submissions "only if accompanied by an original letter stating where and when manuscript was sent." Reports in 1 month.
Tips: Cleis Press specializes in gay/lesbian fiction and nonfiction.

COACHES CHOICE, Sagamore Publishing, Inc.

804 North Neil
Champaign, IL 61820
Phone: 217-359-5940
Fax: 217-359-5975
E-mail: soutlaw@sagamorepub.com
Web site: *http://www.coacheschoice-pub.com*
Acquisitions: Holly Kondras, general manager (sports); Tom Bast, director of acquisitions (sports); Sue Outlaw, director of operations (football, baseball, basketball). Publishes trade paperback originals and reprints. **Publishes 40 titles/year. Receives 100 queries and 60 manuscripts/year. 50% of books from first-time authors; 95% from unagented writers. Pays 10-15% royalty. Offers $500-1,000 advance.** Publishes book 1 year after receipt of manuscript. Accepts simultaneous submissions. Reports in 2 months. Manuscript guidelines free.

Tips: Books for anyone who coaches a sport or has an interest in coaching a sport—all levels of competition.

COMMUNE-A-KEY PUBLISHING

P.O. Box 58637
Salt Lake City, UT 84158
Phone: 801-581-9191
Fax: 801-581-9196
E-mail: keypublish@lgcy.com
Acquisitions: Caryn Summers, editor in chief. Estab. 1992. Publishes trade paperback originals. **Publishes 4-6 titles/year. 40% of books from first-time authors; 75% from unagented writers. Pays 7-8% royalty on retail price.** Publishes book 1 year after acceptance of manuscript. Accepts simultaneous submissions. Reports in 1 month on queries and proposals, 2 months on manuscripts. Manuscript guidelines with SASE.
Nonfiction: Gift book/inspirational, humor, self-help/psychology, spiritual. Subjects include health/medicine, psychology, men's or women's issues/studies, recovery, Native American. Query with SASE. Reviews artwork/photos as part of manuscript package. Send photocopies.
Tips: Gift books about Americana.

COMPANION PRESS

P.O. Box 2575
Laguna Hills, CA 92654
Phone: 949-362-9726
Fax: 949-362-4489
E-mail: sstewart@companionpress.com
Web site: *http://www.companionpress.com*
Acquisitions: Steve Stewart, publisher. Publishes trade paperback originals. **Publishes 6 titles/year. Receives 50 queries and 25 manuscripts/year. 50% of books from first-time authors; 100% from unagented writers. Pays 6-8% royalty on retail price or makes outright purchase. Offers $500-750 advance.** Publishes book 9 months after acceptance of manuscript. Reports in 1 month. Manuscript guidelines for #10 SASE.
Nonfiction and Fiction: Biographies, anthologies, photobooks, video guidebooks. Subjects niche: gay adult entertainment. Query. Reviews artwork/photos as part of manuscript package. Send photocopies.
Tips: Interested in books appealing to gay adults.

CONARI PRESS

2550 Ninth Street, Suite 101
Berkeley, CA 94710
Phone: 510-649-7175
Fax: 510-649-7190
E-mail: conari@conari.com
Web site: *http://www.conari.com*
Acquisitions: Claudia Schaab, managing editor. Estab. 1987. Publishes hardcover and trade paperback originals. **Publishes 30 titles/year. Receives 1,000 submissions/year. 50% of books from first-time authors; 50% from unagented writers. Pays 12-16% royalty on**

net price. **Offers $5,000 average advance.** Publishes book 1-3 years after acceptance. Accepts simultaneous submissions. Reports in 3 months. Manuscript guidelines for 6x9 SASE.

Tips: Conari Press seeks to be a catalyst for profound change by providing enlightening books on topics ranging from relationships, personal growth, and parenting to women's history and issues, social issues, and spirituality.

CONFLUENCE PRESS, INC.

Lewis-Clark State College
500 Eighth Avenue
Lewiston, ID 83501-1698
Phone: 208-799-2336
Fax: 208-799-2324

Acquisitions: James R. Hepworth, publisher. Estab. 1975. Publishes hardcover originals and trade paperback originals and reprints. **Publishes 4-5 titles/year. Receives 500 queries and 150 manuscripts/year. 50% of books from first-time authors; 50% from unagented writers. Pays 10-15% royalty on net sales price. Offers $100-2,000 advance.** Publishes book 18 months after acceptance of manuscript. Accepts simultaneous submissions. Reports in 2 months on queries, 1 month on proposals, 3 months on manuscripts. Manuscript guidelines free.

Tips: Regional fiction and nonfiction books by regional authors and rarely publish writers from outside the western United States.

CONSUMER PRESS

13326 SW 28 Street, Suite 102
Ft. Lauderdale, FL 33330
954-370-9153

Acquisitions: Joseph Pappas, editorial director. Estab. 1989. Publishes trade paperback originals. **Publishes 2-5 titles/year. Receives 1,000 queries and 700 manuscripts/year. 50% of books from first-time authors; 70% from unagented writers. Pays royalty on wholesale price or on retail price, as per agreement.** Publishes book 6 months after acceptance of manuscript. Accepts simultaneous submissions.

Imprint(s): Women's Publications.

Nonfiction: How-to, self-help. Subjects include homeowner guides, building/remodeling, child guidance/parenting, health/medicine, money/finance, women's issues/studies. Query by mail with SASE.

CORNELL MARITIME PRESS, INC.

P.O. Box 456
Centreville, MD 21617-0456
Phone: 410-758-1075
Fax: 410-758-6849

Acquisitions: Charlotte Kurst, managing editor. Estab. 1938. Publishes hardcover originals and quality paperbacks for professional mariners and yachtsmen. **Publishes 7-9 titles/year. Receives 150 submissions/year. 41% of books from first-time authors; 99% from unagented writers. "Payment is negotiable but royalties do not exceed 10% for first 5,000 copies, 12½% for second 5,000 copies, 15% on all additional. Royalties for original paper-**backs are invariably lower. Revised editions revert to original royalty schedule."** Publishes book 1 year after acceptance. Reports in 2 months.

Imprint: **Tidewater** (regional history, folklore, and wildlife of the Chesapeake Bay and the Delmarva Peninsula).

Nonfiction: Marine subjects (highly technical), manuals, how-to books on maritime subjects. Query first, with writing samples and outlines of book ideas.

Tips: Interested in books on the Chesapeake Bay area and the sea.

COTTONWOOD PRESS, INC.

305 West Magnolia, Suite 398
Fort Collins, CO 80521
Phone: 800-864-4297
Fax: 970-204-0761
E-mail: cottonwood@cottonwoodpress.com
Web site: *http://www.verinet.com/cottonwood*

Acquisitions: Cheryl Thurston, editor. Estab. 1965. Publishes trade paperback originals. **Publishes 2-8 titles/year. Receives 50 queries and 400 manuscripts/year. 50% of books from first-time authors; 100% from unagented writers. Pays 10-12% royalty on net sales**. Publishes book 1 year after acceptance. Accepts simultaneous submissions, if so noted. Reports in 1 month on queries and proposals, 3 months on manuscripts. Manuscript guidelines for #10 SASE.

Nonfiction: Textbook. Subjects include education, language/literature. Query with outline and 1-3 sample chapters.

Tips: *Only* supplemental textbooks for English/language arts teachers, grades 5-12, with an emphasis upon middle school and junior high materials.

COUNTERPOINT, Perseus Books Group

1627 I Street NW, Suite 500
Washington, D.C. 20006
Phone: 202-887-0363
Fax: 202-887-0562
Web site: www.perseusbooksgroup.com

Acquisitions: Jack Shoemaker, editor in chief. Estab. 1994. Publishes hardcover and trade paperback originals and reprints. **Publishes 20-25 titles/year. Receives 50 queries/week, 250 manuscripts/year. 2% of books from first-time authors; 2% from unagented writers. Pays 7½-15% royalty on retail price.** Publishes book 18 months after acceptance of manuscript. Accepts simultaneous submissions. Reports in 3 months.

Tips: Counterpoint publishes serious literary work, with particular emphasis on natural history, science, philosophy and contemporary thought, history, art, poetry, and fiction.

THE COUNTRYMAN PRESS, W.W. Norton, Inc.

P.O. Box 748
Woodstock, VT 05091-0748
Phone: 802-457-4826
Fax: 802-457-1678
E-mail: countrymanpress@wwnorton.com
Web site: *http://www.countrymanpress.com*
Editor in Chief: Helen Whybrow.
Acquisitions: Ann Kraybill, managing editor. Estab. 1973. Publishes hardcover originals, trade paperback originals and reprints. **Publishes 25 titles/year. Receives 1,000 queries/year. 30% of books from first-time authors; 70% from unagented writers. Pays 5-15% royalty on retail price. Offers $1,000-5,000 advance.** Publishes book 18 months after acceptance of manuscript. Accepts simultaneous submissions. Reports in 2 months on proposals. Manuscript guidelines for #10 SASE.
Tips: Countryman Press publishes books that encourage physical fitness and appreciation for and understanding of the natural world, self-sufficiency, and adventure.
Imprint(s): Backcountry Publications.

CQ PRESS, Congressional Quarterly, Inc.

1414 22nd Street NW
Washington, D.C. 20037
Phone: 202-887-8500
Fax: 202-822-6583
E-mail: dtarr@cq.com
Web site: *http://www.books.cq.com*
Acquisitions: David Tarr; Paul McClure (library/reference); Carrie Hutchisson (college/political science); Debra Mayberry (directory); Brenda Carter (CQ Press); acquisitions editors. Estab. 1945. **Publishes 50-70 hardcover and paperback titles/year. 95% of books from unagented writers. Pays college or reference royalties or fees. Sometimes offers advance.** Publishes book an average of 1 year after acceptance. Accepts simultaneous submissions. Reports in 3 months.
Tips: Authoritative works on American and international government and politics.
Imprint(s): CQ Press; College/political Science, Library/Reference, Directory.

CRICKET BOOKS

Carus Publishing
332 South Michigan Avenue, #1100
Chicago, IL 60604
Phone: 312-939-1500
E-mail: cricketbooks@caruspub.com
Web site: *http://www.cricketmag.com*
Acquisitions: Laura Tillotson, associate editor. Estab. 1999. Publishes hardcover originals. **Publishes 12 titles/year. Receives 300 queries and 600 manuscripts/year. 33% of books from first-time authors; 33% from unagented writers. Pays 8-12½% royalty on retail price. Offers advance of $2,000-5,000.** Publishes book 18 months after acceptance. Accepts simultaneous submissions. Reports in 1 month on queries and proposals, 2 months on manuscripts. Manuscript guidelines for #10 SASE.
Tips: Cricket Books publishes chapter books and middle-grade novels for children ages 7 to 12.

THE CROSSING PRESS

97 Hangar Way
Watsonville, CA 95019
Phone: 408-722-0711
Fax: 408-772-2749
Web site: *http://www.crossingpress.com*
Acquisitions: Caryle Hirshberg, acquisitions editor; Elaine Goldman Gill, publisher. Estab. 1967. Publishes trade paperback originals. **Publishes 40-50 titles/year. Receives 2,000 submissions/year. 10% of books from first-time authors; 75% from unagented writers. Pays royalty.** Publishes book 18 months after acceptance of manuscript. Accepts simultaneous submissions. Reports in 2 months on queries.
Tips: The Crossing Press publishes titles on a theme of "tools for personal change," with an emphasis on health, spiritual growth, healing, and empowerment.

CUMBERLAND HOUSE PUBLISHING

431 Harding Industrial Drive
Nashville, TN 37211
Phone: 615-832-1171
Fax: 615-832-0633
E-mail: cumbhouse@aol.com
Web site: *http://www.cumberlandhouse.com*
Acquisitions: Ron Pitkin, president; Julia M. Pitkin (cooking/lifestyle). Estab. 1996. Publishes hardcover and trade paperback originals, and hardcover and trade paperback reprints. **Publishes 35 titles/year; imprint publishes 5 titles/year. Receives 1,000 queries and 400 manuscripts/year. 30% of books from first-time authors; 80% from unagented writers. Pays 10-20% royalty on wholesale price. Offers $1,000-10,000 advance.** Publishes book an average of 8 months after acceptance. Accepts simultaneous submissions. Reports in 6 months on queries and proposals, 4 months on manuscripts. Manuscript guidelines free.
Imprint(s): Cumberland House Hearthside (contact Julia M. Pitkin, editor in chief).
Nonfiction: Cookbook, gift book, how-to, humor, illustrated book, reference. Subjects include Americana, cooking/foods/nutrition, government/politics, history, military/war, recreation, regional, sports, travel. Query or submit outline. Reviews artwork/photos as part of manuscript package. Send photocopies.
Fiction: Mystery. Very few books. Query.
Tips: Books about cooking and travel.

DANTE UNIVERSITY OF AMERICA PRESS, INC.

P.O. Box 843
Brookline Village, MA 02147-0843
Fax: 617-734-2046
E-mail: danteu@usa1.com
Web site: *http://www.danteuniversity.org/dpress.html*
Acquisitions: Adolph Caso, president. Estab. 1975. Publishes hardcover and trade paperback originals and reprints. **Publishes 5 titles/year. Receives 50 submissions/year. 50% of books from first-time authors; 50% from unagented writers. Pays royalty. Negotiable advance.** Publishes book 10 months after acceptance of manuscript. Reports in 2 months.
Tips: Quality, educational books about Italian heritage as well as Italian and Italian American historical and political studies of America.
Fiction: Translations from Italian and Latin. Query first with SASE.

DAWN PUBLICATIONS

14618 Tyler Foote Road
Nevada City, CA 95959
Phone: 800-545-7475
Fax: 530-478-7541
E-mail: Dawnpub@oro.net
Web site: *http://www.dawnpub.com*
Acquisitions: Victoria Covell, submissions editor. Estab. 1979. Publishes hardcover and trade paperback originals. **Publishes 6 titles/year. Receives 550 queries and 2,500 manuscripts/year. 35% of books from first-time authors; 100% from unagented writers. Pays royalty on wholesale price.** Publishes book 2 years after acceptance of manuscript. Accepts simultaneous submissions. Reports in 2 months. Manuscript guidelines for #10 SASE.
Nonfiction: Children's/juvenile. Nature awareness and inspiration. Query with SASE.
Tips: All animals and art should appear as realistically as in nature.

THE DENALI PRESS

P.O. Box 021535
Juneau, AK 99802-1535
Phone: 907-586-6014
Fax: 907-463-6780
E-mail: denalipr@alaska.net
Web site: *http://www.alaska.net/~denalipr/index.html*
Acquisitions: Alan Schorr, editorial director; Sally Silvas- Ottumwa, editorial associate. Estab. 1986. Publishes trade paperback originals. **Publishes 5 titles/year. Receives 120 submissions/year. 50% of books from first-time authors; 80% from unagented writers. Pays 10% royalty on wholesale price or makes outright purchase.** Publishes book 1 year after acceptance of manuscript. Accepts simultaneous submissions. Reports in 1 month.
Nonfiction: Reference. Subjects include Americana, Alaskana, anthropology, ethnic, government/politics, history, recreation. Query with outline and sample chapters. All unsolicited manuscripts are tossed. Author must contact prior to sending manuscript.
Tips: Books about Americana.

THE DESIGN IMAGE GROUP INC.

231 South Frontage Road, Suite 17
Burr Ridge, IL 60521
Phone: 630-789-8991
Fax: 630-789-9013
E-mail: dig1956@aol.com
Web site: *http://www.designimagegroup.com*
Acquisitions: Thomas J. Strauch, president (horror). Estab. 1984. Publishes trade paperback originals. **Publishes 6 titles/year. Receives 400 queries and 1,200 manuscripts/year. 100% of books from first-time authors; 90% of books from unagented writers. Pays 7½-12% royalty on wholesale price. Offers $2,400-3,600 advance.** Accepts simultaneous submissions. Reports in 1 month on queries; 2 months on manuscripts. Manuscript guidelines for #10 SASE.
Fiction: Traditional supernatural, human form, monster-based horror fiction. Query. Submit 3 sample chapters and SASE.
Tips: Send for guidelines before querying.

DORAL PUBLISHING, INC.

8560 SW Salish Lane, #300
Wilsonville, OR 97070-9612
Phone: 503-682-3307
Fax: 503-682-2648
E-mail: doralpub@easystreet.com
Web site: *http://www.doralpubl.com*
Acquisitions: Alvin Grossman, publisher; Luana Luther, editor in chief (pure bred dogs); Mark Anderson, editor (general dog books). Estab. 1986. Publishes hardcover and trade paperback originals. **Publishes 7 titles/year. Receives 30 queries and 15 manuscripts/year. 60% of manuscripts from first-time authors, 85% from unagented writers. Pays 10% royalty on wholesale price.** Publishes book 6 months after acceptance of manuscript. Manuscript guidelines for #10 SASE.
Tips: Nonfiction and fiction. How-to, children's/juvenile, reference. Subjects must be dog related (showing, training, agility, search and rescue, health, nutrition, etc.). Query first or submit outline and 2 sample chapters with SASE. Reviews artwork/photos as part of the manuscript package. Send photocopies.

DUFOUR EDITIONS

P.O. Box 7
Chester Springs, PA 19425
Phone: 610-458-5005
Acquisitions: Thomas Lavoie, associate publisher. Estab. 1948. Publishes hardcover originals, trade paperback originals and reprints. **Publishes 5-6 titles/year. Receives 100 queries and 15 manuscripts/year. 20-30% of books from first-time authors; 50% from unagented writers. Pays 6-10% royalty on net receipts. Offers $500-1,000 advance.** Publishes book 18 months after acceptance of manuscript. Accepts simultaneous submissions. Reports in 3 months on queries and proposals, 6 months on manuscripts. Manuscript guidelines free.

Nonfiction: Biography. Subjects include history, translation. Query with SASE. Reviews artwork/photos as part of manuscript package. Send photocopies.

Fiction: Ethnic, historical, literary, short story collections. Query with SASE.

poetry: Query.

EAGLE'S VIEW PUBLISHING

6756 North Fork Road
Liberty, UT 84310
Fax: 801-745-0903
E-mail: eglcrafts@aol.com
Acquisitions: Denise Knight, editor in chief. Estab. 1982. Publishes trade paperback originals. **Publishes 4-6 titles/year. Receives 40 queries and 20 manuscripts/year. 90% of books from first-time authors; 100% from unagented writers. Pays 8-10% royalty on net selling price.** Publishes book 1 year or more after acceptance of manuscript. Accepts simultaneous submissions. Reports in 1 year on proposals. Manuscript guidelines for $3.
Nonfiction: How-to, Indian, mountain man, and American frontier (history and craft). Subjects include anthropology/archaeology (Native American crafts), ethnic (Native American), history (American frontier historical patterns and books), hobbies (crafts, especially beadwork, earrings). Submit outline and 1-2 sample chapters. Reviews artwork/photos as part of manuscript package. Send photocopies or sample illustrations.
Tips: How—to and Americana.

EASTLAND PRESS

P.O. Box 99749
Seattle, WA 98199
Phone: 206-217-0204
Fax: 206-217-0205
Web site: *http://www.eastlandpress.com*
Acquisitions: John O'Connor, managing editor. Estab. 1981. Publishes hardcover and trade paperback originals. **Publishes 4-6 titles/year. Receives 25 queries/year. 30% of books from first-time authors; 90% from unagented writers. Pays 10-15% royalty on receipts. Offers $500-1,500 advance.** Publishes book 18 months after acceptance of manuscript. Accepts simultaneous submissions. Reports in 1 month.
Nonfiction: Reference, textbook, alternative medicine (Chinese and physical therapies and related body work). Manuscript must be completed or close to completion before being considered for publication. Submit outline and 2-3 sample chapters. Reviews artwork/photos as part of manuscript package. Send photocopies.
Tips: Reference book an alternate medicine.

ENCOUNTER BOOKS

116 New Montgomery Street, Suite 206
San Francisco, CA 94105-3640
Phone: 415-538-1460
Fax: 415-538-1461
E-mail: read@encounterbooks.com
Web site: *http://www.encounterbooks.com*
Acquisitions: Peter Collier, publisher; Judy Hardin, operations manager. Hardcover originals and trade paperback reprints. **Publishes 12-20 titles/year. Receives 200 queries and 100 manuscripts/year. 40% of books from first-time authors; 60% from unagented writers. Pays 7-10% royalty on retail price. Offers $2,000-25,000 advance.** Publishes book 14 months after acceptance of manuscript. Accepts simultaneous submissions. Reports in 1 month on queries, 2 months on proposals and manuscripts. Manuscript guidelines free or on Web site.
Tips: Serious nonfiction—books that can alter our society, challenge our morality, stimulate our imaginations. Currently emphasizing history, culture, social criticism, and politics.

FIREBRAND BOOKS

141 The Commons
Ithaca, NY 14850
Phone: 607-272-0000
Web site: *http://wwwfirebrandbooks.com*
Acquisitions: Nancy K. Bereano, publisher. Estab. 1985. Publishes hardcover and trade paperback originals. **Publishes 6-8 titles/year. Receives 400-500 submissions/year. 50% of books from first-time authors; 90% from unagented writers. Pays 7-9% royalty on retail price, or makes outright purchase.** Publishes book 18 months after acceptance. Accepts simultaneous submissions, if so noted. Reports in 1 month on queries.
Nonfiction: Personal narratives, essays. Subjects include feminism, lesbianism. Submit complete manuscript.
Fiction: Considers all types of feminist and lesbian fiction.
Tips: Books on feminism and lesbian interests.

FLORICANTO PRESS, Inter American Corp.

650 Castro Street, Suite 120-331
Mountain View, CA 94041
Phone: 415-552-1879
Fax: 415-793-2662
E-mail: floricanto@msn.com
Web site: *http://www.floricantopress.com*
Publishes hardcover and trade paperback originals and reprints.
Publishes 6 titles/year. Receives 200 queries/year. 60% of books from first-time authors; 5% from unagented writers. Pays 5% royalty on wholesale price. Offers $500-1,500 advance. Rejected manuscripts destroyed. Reports in 3 months on queries, 7 months on manuscripts.
Tips: Fiction and nonfiction for a general public interested in Hispanic culture.

FOGHORN PRESS

P.O. Box 2036
Santa Rosa, CA 95405-0036
Phone: 707-521-3300
Fax: 707-521-3361
Web site: *http://www.foghorn.com*

Acquisitions: Dave Morgan, publisher; Kyle Morgan, editor-in- chief. Estab. 1985. Publishes trade paperback originals and reprints. **Publishes 30 titles/year. Receives 500 queries and 200 manuscripts/year. 10% of books from first-time authors; 98% from unagented writers. Pays 12% royalty on wholesale price; occasional work-for-hire.** Publishes book 18 months after acceptance of manuscript. Accepts simultaneous submissions. Reports in 1 month on queries, 2 months on proposals and manuscripts.

Tips: Publishes outdoor recreation guidebooks.

FORUM, Prima Publishing

3875 Atherton Road
Rocklin, CA 95765
Phone: 916-632-4400
Fax: 916-632-4403
Web site: *http://www.primapublishing.com*

Acquisitions: Steven Martin, editorial director. Publishes hardcover and trade paperback originals and reprints. **Publishes 10-15 titles/year. 25% of books from first-time authors; 5% from unagented writers. Pays variable advance and royalty.** Publishes book 1 year after acceptance of manuscript. Accepts simultaneous submissions. Reports in 1 month on queries and proposals, 2 months on manuscripts.

Tips: Business books that contribute to the marketplace of ideas.

FREDERIC C. BEIL, PUBLISHER, INC.

609 Whitaker Street
Savannah, GA 31401
Phone: 912-233-2446
Fax: 912-233-2446
E-mail: beilbook@beil.com
Web site: *http://www.beil.com*

Acquisitions: Mary Ann Bowman, editor. Estab. 1982. Publishes hardcover originals and reprints. **Publishes 7 titles/year. Receives 1,500 queries and 7 manuscripts/year. 80% of books from first-time authors; 100% from unagented writers. Pays 7 1/2% royalty on retail price.** Publishes book 20 months after acceptance. Accepts simultaneous submissions. Reports in 1 month on queries.

Imprint(s): The Sandstone Press.

Nonfiction: Biography, general trade, illustrated book, juvenile, reference. Subjects include art/architecture, history, language/literature, book arts. Query. Reviews artwork/photos as part of manuscript package. Send photocopies.

Fiction: Historical and literary. Query.

Tips: General submissions on history and literature.

GEM GUIDES BOOK COMPANY

315 Cloverleaf Drive, Suite F
Baldwin Park, CA 91706-6510
Phone: 626-855-1611
Fax: 626-855-1610
Email: gembooks@aol.com

Acquisitions: Kathy Mayerski, editor. Estab. 1965. **Publishes 6-8 titles/year. Receives 40 submissions/year. 30% of books from first-time authors; 100% from unagented writers. Pays 6-10% royalty on retail price.** Estab. 1965. Publishes book 1 year after acceptance. Accepts simultaneous submissions. Reports in 3 months.

Imprint(s): Gembooks.

Nonfiction: Gem Guides specializes in books on earth sciences, lapidary and jewelry-making, nature books, also travel/local interest titles for the Western United States. Subjects include hobbies, Western history, nature/environment, recreation, travel. Query with outline/synopsis and sample chapters with SASE. Reviews artwork/photos as part of manuscript package.

Tips: Books on and about gems.

GIFTED EDUCATION PRESS

10201 Yuma Court
P.O. Box 1586
Manassas, VA 20109
Phone: 703-369-5017

Acquisitions: Maurice Fisher, publisher. Estab. 1981. Publishes mass market paperback originals. **Publishes 10 titles/year. Receives 75 queries and 25 manuscripts/year. 90% of books from first-time authors; 100% from unagented writers. Pays 10-12% royalty on retail price.** Publishes book 3 months after acceptance of manuscript. Accepts simultaneous submissions. Reports in 1 month. Manuscript guidelines for #10 SASE.

Tips: Gifted Education Press publishes books on multiple intelligences, humanities education for gifted children and how to parent gifted children. Currently emphasizing multiple intelligences. De-emphasizing humanities.

GIFTED PSYCHOLOGY PRESS, INC., Anodyne, Inc.

P.O. Box 5057
Scottsdale, AZ 85261
Phone: 602-954-4200
Fax: 602-954-0185
E-mail: giftedbook@earthlink.net
Web site: *http://www.GiftedPsychologyPress.com*

Acquisitions: James T. Webb, president. Estab. 1986. Publishes trade paperback originals. **Publishes 4-5 titles/year. Receives 10 queries and 10 manuscripts/year. 25% of books from first-time authors; 100% from unagented writers. Pays 9-15% royalty on retail price. Offers $0-750 advance.** Publishes book 6 months after acceptance of manuscript. Accepts simultaneous submissions. Reports in 2 months on queries, 3 months on proposals, 4 months on manuscripts. Manuscript guidelines free or on Web site.

Tips: Gifted Psychology Press publishes books on the social/emotional/interpersonal needs of gifted and talented children and adults for parents and teachers of gifted and talented youngsters.

GREENE BARK PRESS

P.O. Box 1108
Bridgeport, CT 06601

Phone: 203-372-4861

Fax: 203-371-5856

Web site: *http://www.bookworld.com/greenebark*

Acquisitions: Thomas J. Greene, publisher; Michele Hofbauer, associate publisher. Estab. 1991. Publishes hardcover originals. **Publishes 5 titles/year. Receives 100 queries and 6,000 manuscripts/year. 60% of books from first-time authors; 100% from unagented writers. Pays 10-15% royalty on wholesale price.** Publishes book 1 year after acceptance of manuscript. Accepts simultaneous submissions. Reports in 3 months on manuscripts. Manuscript guidelines with SASE.

Tips: Greene Bark Press only publishes books for children and young adults, mainly picture and read-to books.

HARVARD BUSINESS SCHOOL PRESS

Harvard Business School Publishing Corp.

60 Harvard Way

Boston, MA 02163

Phone: 617-495-6700

Fax: 617-496-8066

Web site: *http://www.hbsp.harvard.edu*

Director: Carol Franco.

Acquisitions: Nikki Sabin, acquisitions editor; Marjorie Williams, executive editor; Kirsten Sandberg, senior editor; Hollis Heimbouch, senior editor. Estab. 1984. Publishes hardcover originals. **Publishes 35-45 titles/year. Receives 500 queries and 300 manuscripts/year. 20% of books from first-time authors; 10% from unagented writers. Pays escalating royalty on retail price. Advances vary widely depending on author and market for the book.** Publishes book 9 months after acceptance of manuscript. Accepts simultaneous submissions. Reports in 1 month on proposals and manuscripts. Manuscript guidelines free.

Tips: The Harvard Business School Press publishes books for an audience of senior and general managers and business scholars. HBS Press is the source of the most influential ideas and conversation that shape business worldwide.

THE HARVARD COMMON PRESS

535 Albany Street

Boston, MA 02118-2500

Phone: 617-423-5803

Fax: 617-423-0679 or 617-695-9794

Acquisitions: Bruce P. Shaw, president/publisher. Associate Publisher: Dan Rosenberg. Estab. 1976. Publishes hardcover and trade paperback originals and reprints. **Publishes 12 titles/year. Receives 1,000 submissions/year. 20% of books from first-time authors; 40% of books from unagented writers. Pays royalty. Offers average $4,000 advance.** Publishes book 1 year after acceptance of manuscript. Accepts simultaneous submissions. Reports in 2 months. Manuscript guidelines for SASE.

Tips: Strong, practical books that help people gain control over a particular area of their lives. Currently emphasizing cooking, child care/parenting, health. De-emphasizing general instructional books, travel. Imprint(s): Gambit Books.

HEALTH COMMUNICATIONS, INC.

3201 SW 15th Street

Deerfield Beach, FL 33442

Phone: 954-360-0909

Web site: *http://www.hci-online.com*

Acquisitions: Christine Belleris, editorial codirector; Matthew Diener, editorial codirector; Allison Janse, associate editor; Lisa Drucker, associate editor. Publishes hardcover and trade paperback originals. Estab. 1976. **Publishes 40 titles/year. 20% of books from first-time authors; 90% from unagented writers. Pays 15% royalty on net price.** Publishes book 9 months after acceptance of manuscript. Accepts simultaneous submissions. Reports in 1 month on queries, 3 months on proposals and manuscripts. Manuscript guidelines for #10 SASE.

Tips: Publisher of *Chicken Soup for the Soul* series. Publish books that help people grow and improve their lives from physical and emotional health to finances and interpersonal relationships. Currently emphasizing visionary fiction–fiction with a message.

HEALTH INFORMATION PRESS (HIP)

PMIC (Practice Management Information Corp.)

4727 Wilshire Boulevard

Los Angeles, CA 90010

Phone: 213-954-0224

Fax: 213-954-0253

E-mail: pmiceditor@aol.com

Web site: *http://medicalbookstore.com*

Acquisitions: Kathryn Swanson, managing editor. Publishes hardcover originals, trade paperback originals and reprints. **Publishes 8-10 titles/year. Receives 100 queries and 50 manuscripts/year. 10% of books from first-time authors; 90% from unagented writers. Pays 10-15% royalty on net receipts. Offers $1,500-5,000 average advance.** Publishes books 18 months after acceptance of manuscript. Reports in 6 months. Manuscript guidelines for #10 SASE.

Nonfiction: How-to, illustrated book, reference, self-help. Subjects include health/medicine, psychology, science. Submit proposal package, including outline, 3 to 5 sample chapters. Reviews artwork/photos as part of the manuscript package.

Tips: Health books for consumers, and professionals.

HEALTH PRESS

P.O. Box 1388

Santa Fe, NM 87504

Phone: 505-982-9373

Fax: 505-983-1733

E-mail: hthprs@trail.com

Web site: *http://www.healthpress.com*

Acquisitions: Corie Conwell, editor. Estab. 1988. Publishes hardcover and trade paperback originals. **Publishes 4 titles/year. 90% of books from first-time authors; 90% from unagented writers. Pays standard royalty on wholesale price.** Publishes book 1 year after acceptance of manuscript. Accepts simultaneous submissions. Reports in 2 months on proposals.

Tips: Health Press publishes books by health care professionals on cutting-edge patient education topics.

HELIX BOOKS, Perseus Books Group

One Jacob Way
Reading, MA 01867
Phone: 781-944-3700, ext. 285
Fax: 781-944-8243
Web site: *http://www.aw.com*

Acquisitions: Jeffrey Robbins, executive editor (physics, astronomy, complexity); Amanda Cook, editor (biology, evolution, complexity). Estab. 1992. Publishes hardcover and trade paperback originals and reprints. **Publishes 30 titles/year. Receives 160 queries/year. 50% of books from first-time authors; 60% from unagented writers. Pays 7 1/2-15% royalty on retail price "sliding scale based on number of copies sold." Offers $5,000 and up advance.** Publishes book 6 months after acceptance of manuscript. Accepts simultaneous submissions but prefers exclusive. Reports in 1 month on queries.

Tips: Helix Books presents the world's top scientists and science writers sharing with the general public the latest discoveries and their human implications, across the full range of scientific disciplines. Currently emphasizing physics/astronomy, biology, evolution, complexity. De-emphasizing earth sciences, philosophy of science, neuroscience.

HENDRICK-LONG PUBLISHING CO., INC.

P.O. Box 25123
Dallas, TX 75225-1123
Phone: 214-358-4677
Fax: 214-352-4768
E-mail: hendrick-long@worldnet.att.net

Acquisitions: Joann Long. Estab. 1969. Publishes hardcover and trade paperback originals and hardcover reprints. **Publishes 8 titles/year. Receives 500 submissions/year. 90% of books from unagented writers. Pays royalty on selling price.** Publishes book 18 months after acceptance. Reports in 1 month on queries, 2 months if more than query sent. Manuscript guidelines for #10 SASE.

Tips: Hendrick-Long publishes historical fiction and nonfiction primarily about Texas and the Southwest for children and young adults.

HEYDAY BOOKS

P.O. Box 9145
Berkeley, CA 94709-9145
Fax: 510-549-1889
E-mail: heyday@heydaybooks.com
Web site: *http://www.heydaybooks.com*

Acquisitions: Malcolm Margolin, publisher. Estab. 1974. Publishes hardcover originals, trade paperback originals and reprints. **Publishes 8-10 titles/year. Receives 200 submissions/year. 50% of books from first-time authors; 90% of books from unagented writers. Pays 8-10% royalty on net price.** Publishes book 8 months after acceptance of manuscript. Reports in 1 week on queries, 5 weeks on manuscripts.

Tips: Books about Native Americans, natural history, history, and recreation, with a strong California focus.
Query with outline and synopsis. Reviews artwork/photos.

HIGH PLAINS PRESS

P.O. Box 123
539 Cassa Road
Glendo, WY 82213
Fax: 307-735-4590

Acquisitions: Nancy Curtis, publisher. Estab. 1986. Publishes hardcover and trade paperback originals. **Publishes 4 titles/year. Receives 300 queries and 200 manuscripts/year. 80% of books from first-time authors; 95% from unagented writers. Pays 10% royalty on wholesale price. Offers $100-600 advance.** Publishes book 2 years after acceptance of manuscript. Accepts simultaneous submissions. Reports in 1 month on queries and proposals, 3 months on manuscripts. Manuscript guidelines for 8 1/2 x 10 SASE.

Tips: History of the Old West, particularly things relating to Wyoming.

HOLLIS PUBLISHING COMPANY

Puritan Press, Inc.
95 Runnells Bridge Road
Hollis, NH 03049
Phone: 603-889-4500
Fax: 603-889-6551
E-mail: books@hollispublishing.com
Web site: *http://www.hollispublishing.com*

Acquisitions: Rebecca Shannon, editor. Publishes hardcover and trade paperback originals. **Publishes 5 titles/year. Receives 25 queries and 15 manuscripts/year. 50% of books from first-time authors; 100% from unagented writers. Pays 5-10% royalty on retail price.** Publishes book within 6 months of acceptance of manuscript. Reports in 1 month on queries and proposals, 2 months on manuscripts.Manuscript guidelines for #10 SASE.

Tips: Hollis publishes books on social policy, U.S. government and politics, current events and recent events, intended for use by professors and their students, college and university libraries, and the general reader. Currently emphasizing works about education, the Internet, government, history-in-the-making, social values, and politics.

HOWELLS HOUSE

P.O. Box 9546
Washington, D.C. 20016-9546
Phone: 202-333-2182

Acquisitions: W. D. Howells, publisher. Estab. 1988. Publishes hardcover and trade paperback originals and reprints. **Publishes 4 titles/year; each imprint publishes 2-3 titles/year. Receives 2,000 queries and 300 manuscripts/year. 50% of books from first-time authors; 60% from unagented writers. Pays 15% net royalty or makes outright purchase. May offer advance.** Publishes book 8 months after manuscript development completed. Reports in 2 months on proposals.

Tips: Institutions and institutional change.
Imprint(s): The Compass Press, Whalesback Books.

HUNGRY MIND PRESS
1648 Grand Avenue
Street Paul, MN 55105
Phone: 651-699-0587
Fax: 651-699-7190
E-mail: hmindpress@aol.com
Web site: *http://www.hungrymind.com*
Acquisitions: Pearl Kilbride. Publishes hardcover originals, trade paperback originals and reprints. **Publishes 8-10 titles/year. Receives 200 queries and 300 manuscripts/year. 25% of books from unagented writers. Royalties and advances vary.** Publishes book 10 months after acceptance of manuscript. Accepts simultaneous submissions. Reports in 2 months on proposals. Manuscript guidelines for #10 SASE.
Tips: Literary fiction and nonfiction.

HUNTER HOUSE
P.O. Box 2914
Alameda, CA 94501
Phone: 510-865-5282
Fax: 510-865-4295
Web site: *http://www.hunterhouse.com*
Publisher: Kiran S. Rana.
Acquisitions: Jeanne Brondino, acquisitions coordinator. Estab. 1978. Publishes hardcover and trade paperback originals and reprints. **Publishes 12 titles/year. Receives 200-300 queries and 100 manuscripts/year. 50% of books from first-time authors; 80% from unagented writers. Pays 12-15% royalty on net receipts, defined as selling price. Offers $250-2,500 advance.** Publishes book 1-2 years after acceptance of final manuscript. Accepts simultaneous submissions. Reports in 2 months on queries, 3 months on proposals, 6 months on manuscripts. Manuscript guidelines for 8 1/2 x 11 SASE with 3 first-class stamps.
Tips: Hunter House publishes health books (especially women's health), self-help health, sexuality and couple relationships, violence prevention and intervention. Currently de-emphasizing human rights.

ICON EDITIONS
Westview Press, Perseus Books Group
10 East 53rd Street
New York, NY 10036
Phone: 212-207-7282
www.perseusbooksgroup.com
Acquisitions: Cass Canfield, editor. Estab. 1973. Publishes hardcover and trade paperback originals and reprints. **Publishes 6 titles/year. Receives hundreds of queries/year. 25% of books from first-time authors; 80% from unagented writers. Royalty and advance vary.** Publishes book 18 months after acceptance of manuscript. Accepts simultaneous submissions, if so noted. Returns submissions with SASE if author requests.

Tips: Books on architecture, art history, and art criticism for the academic and semi-academic market, college and university market.

IDYLL ARBOR, INC.
P.O. Box 720
Ravensdale, WA 98051
Phone: 425-432-3231
Fax: 425-432-3726
E-mail: editors@idyllarbor.com
Web site: http://*www.idyllarbor.com*
Acquisitions: Tom Blaschko. Publishes hardcover and trade paperback originals and trade paperback reprints. **Publishes 6 titles/year. 50% of books from first-time authors; 100% from unagented writers. Pays 8-15% royalty on wholesale price or retail price.** Publishes book 1 year after acceptance of manuscript. Accepts simultaneous submissions. Reports in 1 month on queries, 2 months on proposals, 4 months on manuscripts. Manuscript guidelines free.
Tips: Health care practice. Currently emphasizing therapies (recreational, occupational, music, horticultural), activity directors in long term care facilities, and social service professionals. Books must be useful for the health practitioner who meets face to face with patients or the books must be useful for teaching undergraduate and graduate level classes.

IMPACT PUBLISHERS, INC.
P.O. Box 910
Atascadero, CA 93423
Phone: 805-466-3917
Web site: *http://www.impactpublishers.com*
Acquisitions: Freeman porter, acquisitions editor. Estab. 1970. Publishes trade paperback originals. **Publishes 6 titles/year. Receives 250 queries and 250 manuscripts/year. 40% of books from first-time authors; 60% from unagented writers. Pays 10% royalty on net receipts.** Publishes book 12-18 months after acceptance of manuscript. Accepts simultaneous submissions. Reports in 5 months on proposals. Manuscript guidelines free.
Tips: Books on human services expertise. Currently emphasizing professional resources for "The Practical Therapist Series." De-emphasizing children's books. Only popular psychology and self-help materials written in "everyday language" by professionals with advanced degrees and significant experience in the human services.
Imprint(s): American Source Books, Little Imp Books.

INFO NET PUBLISHING
34188 Coast Highway, Suite C
Dana point, CA 92629
Phone: 949-489-9292
Fax: 949-489-9549
E-mail: infonetpub@aol.com
Web site: *http://www.infonetpublishing.com*
Acquisitions: Herb Wetenkamp, president. Estab. 1987. Publishes hardcover and trade paperback originals. **Publishes 6 titles/year. Receives 50 queries and 20 manuscripts/year. 80% of books from first-**

time authors; **85% from unagented writers. Pays 7-10% royalty on wholesale price or makes outright purchase of $1,000-10,000. Offers $1,000-2,000 advance in some cases.** Publishes book 10 months after acceptance of manuscript. Accepts simultaneous submissions. Reports in 2 months. Manuscript guidelines for #10 SASE.

Tips: Info Net publishes for easily identified niche markets; specific markets with some sort of special interest, hobby, avocation, profession, sport, or lifestyle.

INNISFREE PRESS

136 Roumfort Road
Philadelphia, PA 19119
Phone: 215-247-4085
Fax: 215-247-2343
E-mail: InnisfreeP@aol.com
Web site: *http://www.innisfreepress.com*

Acquisitions: Marcia Broucek, publisher. Estab. 1996. Publishes trade paperback originals. **Publishes 6-8 titles/year. Receives 500 queries and 300 manuscripts/year. 50% of books from first-time authors; 90% from unagented writers. Pays 10-15% royalty on wholesale price.** Publishes book 1 year after acceptance of manuscript. Accepts simultaneous submissions. Reports in 1 month on queries; 2 months on proposals; 3 months on manuscripts. Manuscript guidelines free.

Tips: Innisfree publishes books that nourish individuals both emotionally and spiritually. Currently emphasizing women's issues, spirituality. De-emphasizing child guidance/parenting.

ITALICA PRESS

595 Main Street, Suite 605
New York, NY 10044-0047
Phone: 212-935-4230
Fax: 212-838-7812
E-mail: inquiries@italicapress.com
Web site: *http://www.italicapress.com*

Acquisitions: Ronald G. Musto and Eileen Gardiner, publishers. Estab. 1985. Publishes trade paperback originals. **Publishes 6 titles/year. Receives 75 queries and 20 manuscripts/year. 50% of books from first-time authors; 100% from unagented writers. Pays 7-15% royalty on wholesale price.** Publishes book 1 year after acceptance of manuscript. Accepts simultaneous submissions. Reports in 1 month on queries. Guidelines on Web site.

Tips: Italica Press publishes English translations of modern Italian fiction and medieval and Renaissance nonfiction.

JAIN PUBLISHING CO.

P.O. Box 3523
Fremont, CA 94539
Phone: 510-659-8272
Fax: 510-659-0501
E-mail: mail@jainpub.com
Web site: *http://www.jainpub.com*

Acquisitions: M.K. Jain, editor in chief. Estab. 1989. Publishes hardcover and trade paperback originals and reprints. **Publishes 6 titles/year. Receives 300 queries/year. 100% from unagented writers. Pays up to 15% royalty on net sales. Offers occasional advance.** Publishes book 1-2 years after acceptance of manuscript. Reports in 3 months on manuscripts, if interested. Manuscript guidelines available on Web site.

Tips: Jain Publishing Company is a general trade and college textbook publisher with a diversified list in subjects such as business/management, computers/internet, health/healing and religions/philosophies. Also publish fine pocket-size motivational/inspirational gift books and vegetarian cookbooks. Submit proposal package, including cv and list of prior publications. Reviews artwork/photos as part of manuscript package. Send photocopies. Does not return submissions.

JAMES RUSSELL

P.O. Box 10121, Suite 2098
Eugene, OR 97440
Phone: 775-348-8711
Fax: 775-348-8711
E-mail: scrnplay@powernet.net
Web site: *http://www.powernet.net/~scrnplay*

Acquisitions: James Russell, publisher. Publishes trade paperback originals. **Publishes 2 titles/year. Receives 10 queries and 2 manuscripts/year. 90% of books from first-time authors; 90% from unagented writers. Pays 5-7% royalty on wholesale price.** Publishes book 1 year after acceptance of manuscript. Accepts simultaneous submissions. Reports in 1 month. Manuscript guidelines on Web site.

Nonfiction: How-to, technical. Subjects include sports (including gambling, shooting), screenwriting, theatrical, movies, TV. Query with SASE. *All unsolicited manuscripts returned unopened.* Reviews artwork/photos as part of manuscript package. Send simple line art illustrations. Wants less photos, more illustrations, at least 40/ms.

Fiction: Historical (Nevada), humor, plays (script format), regional (Nevada), religious (Christian), sports (competitive), Western (Nevada). Books are 150-200 pages long. Query with SASE. *All unsolicited manuscripts returned unopened.*

Tips: Books focusing on Nevada and spirituality.

JOSSEY-BASS/PFEIFFER

350 Sansome Street
San Francisco, CA 94104
Phone: 415-433-1740
Fax: 415-433-1711
E-mail: mholt@jbp.com
Web site: *http://www.pfeiffer.com.*

Acquisitions: Matthew Holt, editor. **Publishes 25-50 titles/year. 25% of books from first-time authors; 95% of books from unagented writers. Pays 10% average royalty.** Publishes book 1 year after acceptance of manuscript. Accepts simultaneous submissions. Reports in 2 months on queries

Tips: Jossey-Bass/Pfeiffer specializes in human resource development titles in the fields of business, management, and training.

KAR-BEN COPIES, INC.

6800 Tildenwood Lane
Rockville, MD 20852
Phone: 800-452-7236
Fax: 301-881-9195
E-mail: karben@aol.com
Web site: *http://www.karben.com*
Acquisitions: Madeline Wikler, editor (juvenile Judaica). Estab. 1976. Publishes hardcover and trade paperback originals. **Publishes 8-10 titles/year. Receives 50-100 queries and 300-400 manuscripts/year. 5% of books from first-time authors; 100% from unagented writers. Pays 5-8% royalty of net sales. Offers $500-2,500 advance.** Publishes book 10 months after acceptance of manuscript. Accepts simultaneous submissions. Reports in 1 month. Manuscript guidelines for 9x12 SASE with 2 first-class stamps.
Tips: Kar-Ben Copies publishes Jewish books, calendars and cassettes, fiction and nonfiction, for preschool and primary children interested in Jewish holidays and traditions.

KNOWLEDGE, IDEAS & TRENDS, INC. (KIT)

1131-0 Tolland Turnpike, Suite 175
Manchester, CT 06040
Phone: 860-646-0745
Acquisitions: Ruth Kimball-Bailey, editor. Publishes hardcover and trade paperback originals. **Publishes 4-5 titles/year. 80% of books from first-time authors; 100% from unagented writers. Pays royalty on wholesale price or advance against royalty. Advance varies.** Publishes book 18 months after acceptance of manuscript. Accepts simultaneous submissions. Reports in 3 months on manuscripts. Manuscript guidelines free.
Nonfiction: Biography, humor, reference, self-help. Subjects include anthropology/archaeology, history, psychology, sociology, women's issues/studies. Send outline and 3 sample chapters. Reviews artwork/photos as part of manuscript package. Send photocopies.
Tips: Books on lifestyle issues.

KODANSHA AMERICA, INC.

114 Fifth Ave
New York, NY 10011
Phone: 212-727-6460
Fax: 212-935-6929
Web site: *http://www.kodansha.co.jp*
Acquisitions: Editorial Department. Estab. 1989 (in United States). Publishes 70% hardcover and trade paperback originals; 30% trade paperback reprints in Kodansha Globe series. **Publishes 25-30 titles/year. Receives 3,000 submissions/year. 20% of books from first-time authors; 10% from unagented writers. Pays 6-15% royalty on retail price. Offers $2,000 (reprints), $10,000 (original) average**

advances. Publishes book 9 months after acceptance of manuscript. Accepts simultaneous submissions. Reports in up to 3 months.
Tips: Nonfiction titles of a cross-cultural nature, well- researched, written with authority, bringing something of a world view and a fresh eye to the general reading public.

LAKE VIEW PRESS

P.O. Box 578279
Chicago, IL 60657
Acquisitions: Paul Elitzik, director. Publishes hardcover and trade paperback originals. **Publishes 5 titles/year. Receives 100 queries and 10 manuscripts/year. 100% of books from unagented writers. Pays 6-10% royalty on wholesale price.** Publishes book 1 year after acceptance of manuscript. Reports in 1 month on queries. Query with toc, cv, and SASE. No sample chapters.
Tips: Lake View Press publishes scholarly nonfiction on sociology, criminology, and film written in a manner accessible to a nonprofessional reader.

LIFETIME BOOKS, INC.

2131 Hollywood Boulevard, Suite 305
Hollywood, FL 33073
Phone: 954-925-5242
Fax: 954-925-5244
E-mail: lifetime@shadow.net
Web site: *http://www.lifetimebooks.com*
Acquisitions: Callie Rucker, senior editor. Estab. 1943. Publishes hardcover and trade paperback originals. **Publishes 20- 25 titles/year. Receives 1,500-2,00 queries and 1,000 manuscripts/year. 95% of books from first-time authors; 95% from unagented writers. Pays negotiable royalty on retail price. Offers advance of $0-10,000.** Publishes book 4 months after acceptance. Accepts simultaneous submissions. Reports in 1 month on queries and proposals, 2 months on manuscripts. Manuscript guidelines for #10 SASE.
Tips: How-to and self-help information.
Imprint(s): Compact Books (contact Donald Lessne); Fell Publishers; Lifetime Periodicals.

LIVINGSTON PRESS

Station 22
University of West Alabama
Livingston, AL 35470
E mail: just@univ.westal.edu
Web site: *http://livingstonpress.westal.edu*
Acquisitions: Joe Taylor, director. Estab. 1984. Publishes hardcover and trade paperback originals. **Publishes 4-6 titles/year; imprint publishes 1 title/year. 20% of books from first-time authors; 90% from unagented writers. Pays 12 1/2% of book run.** Publishes book 18 months after acceptance of manuscript. Accepts simultaneous submissions. Reports in 1 month on queries; 1 year on manuscripts. Query. *All unsolicited manuscripts returned.*

Tips: Livingston Press publishes topics such as Southern literature and quirky fiction. Currently emphasizing short stories. De-emphasizing poetry. **Imprint(s):** Swallow's Tale Press.

LONE EAGLE PUBLISHING CO.

2337 Roscomare Road, Suite 9
Los Angeles, CA 90077-1851
Phone: 310-471-8066
Fax: 310-471-4969
E-mail: info@loneeagle.com
Web site: *http://www.loneeagle.com*

Acquisitions: Jeff Black, editor. Estab. 1982. Publishes perfectbound and trade paperback originals. **Publishes 15 titles/year. Receives 100 submissions/year. 80% of books from unagented writers. Pays 10% royalty minimum on net income wholesale. Offers $500-1,000 average advance.** Publishes book 1 year after acceptance of manuscript. Accepts simultaneous submissions. Reports quarterly on queries.

Tips: Lone Eagle Publishing Company publishes reference directories that contain comprehensive and accurate credits, personal data, and contact information for every major entertainment industry craft. Lone Eagle also publishes many how-to books for the film production business, including books on screenwriting, directing, budgeting and producing, acting, editing, etc.

LONGSTREET PRESS, INC.

2140 Newmarket Parkway, Suite 122
Marietta, GA 30067
Phone: 770-980-1488
Fax: 770-859-9894
Web site: *http://www.lspress.com*
President/Editor: Chuck Perry.

Acquisitions: Editorial Department. Estab. 1988. Publishes hardcover and trade paperback originals. **Publishes 45 titles/year. Receives 2,500 submissions/year. 10% of books from first-time authors; none from unagented writers. Pays royalty.** Publishes book 1 year after acceptance of manuscript. Accepts simultaneous submissions. Reports in 3 months. Manuscript guidelines for #10 SASE.

Tips: Although Longstreet Press publishes a number of genres, their strengths have been humor, business, guidebooks, cookbooks, and fiction. Southern publishers looking for regional material.

LOOMPANICS UNLIMITED

P.O. Box 1197
port Townsend, WA 98368-0997
Fax: 360-385-7785
E-mail: loompseditor@olympus.net
Web site: *http://www.loompanics.com*
President: Michael Hoy. **Acquisitions:** Vanessa McGrady, chief editor. Estab. 1975. Publishes trade paperback originals. **Publishes 15 titles/year. Receives 500 submissions/year. 40% of books from first-time authors; 100% from unagented writers. Pays 10-15% royalty on wholesale or retail price or makes outright pur-** chase of $100-1,200. **Offers $500 average advance.** Publishes book 1 year after acceptance of manuscript. Accepts simultaneous submissions. Reports in 2 months. Author guidelines free.

Tips: No more secrets—no more excuses—no more limits! How-to books with an edge. Always looking for beat-the-system books on crime, tax avoidance, survival, drug manufacture, revenge, and self-sufficiency.

THE LOVE AND LOGIC PRESS, INC.

Cline/Fay Institute, Inc.
2207 Jackson Street
Golden, CO 80401
Phone: 800-LUV-LOGIC
Fax: 303-278-3894
Web site: *http://www.loveandlogic.com*

Acquisitions: Nancy Lucero, president/publisher (multiculturalism, social change, community organizing, progressive social work practice); Jeannie Jacobson, product development specialist (education, design). Publishes hardcover and trade paperback originals. **Publishes 5-12 titles/year. 10% of books from first-time authors; 100% from unagented writers. Pays 7 1/2-12% royalty on wholesale price. Offers $500-5,000 advance.** Publishes book 18 months after acceptance of manuscript. Accepts simultaneous submissions. Reports in 1 month on queries and proposals; 3 months on manuscripts.

Tips: Titles that empower parents, teachers, and others who help young people, and that help these individuals become more skilled and happier in their interactions with children. Titles stress building personal responsibility in children and helping them become prepared to function well in the world. Currently emphasizing parenting, classroom management. De-emphasizing psychology, self-help.

THE LYONS PRESS

31 West 21st Street
New York, NY 10010
Phone: 212-620-9580
Fax: 212-929-1836
Web site: *http://www.gorp.com/lyonspress*

Acquisitions: Christopher Pavone, managing editor, Bryan Oettel, editor in chief (outdoor activity, adventure, sports); Lilly Golden, senior editor (sports, cooking); Bryan Oettel, senior editor, (all subjects); Becky Koh, editor (sports, health). Estab. 1984 (Lyons & Burford), 1997 (The Lyons Press). Publishes hardcover and trade paperback originals and reprints. **Publishes 110-120 titles/year. 30% of books from first-time authors; 60% from unagented writers. Pays varied royalty on retail price.** Publishes book 1 year after acceptance of manuscript. Accepts simultaneous submissions. Reports in 3 weeks on queries. Allow 2 months for reply.

Tips: The Lyons Press publishes practical and literary books, chiefly centered on outdoor subjects—natural history, all sports, gardening, horses, fishing. Currently emphasizing adventure, sports. De-emphasizing hobbies, travel.

MACMURRAY & BECK

Altacourt
1490 Lafayette St.
Ste. 108
Denver, CO 80218
Phone: 303-832-2152
Fax: 303-832-2158
E-mail: ramey@macmurraybeck.com
Web site: *http://www.macmurraybeck.com*
Acquisitions: Frederick Ramey, executive editor; Leslie Koffler, associate editor; Greg Michelson, fiction. Estab. 1989. Publishes hardcover and trade paperback originals. **Publishes 5-8 titles/year. 90% of books from first-time authors; 20% from unagented writers. Pays 8-12% royalty on retail price. Offers $2,000-5,000 advance.** Publishes book 18 months after acceptance of manuscript. Accepts simultaneous submissions. Reports in 3 months on queries and proposals, 4 months on manuscripts. Manuscript guidelines free.
Tips: Reflective personal narrative of high literary quality, both fiction and nonfiction. Submit outline and 2 sample chapters with SASE. Reviews artwork/photos as part of manuscript package. Send photocopies.
Imprint(s): Divina (speculative, spiritual, and metaphysical, contact Leslie Koffler).

MAGE PUBLISHERS INC.

1032 29th Street NW
Washington, D.C. 20007
Phone: 202-342-1642
Fax: 202-342-9269
E-mail: info@mage.com
Web site: *http://www.mage.com*
Acquisitions: Amin Sepehri, assistant to publisher. Estab. 1985. Publishes hardcover originals and reprints, trade paperback originals. **Publishes 4 titles/year. Receives 40 queries and 20 manuscripts/year. 10% of books from first-time authors; 95% from unagented writers. Pays variable royalty. Offers $250-1,500 advance.** Publishes book 8-16 months after acceptance of manuscript. Accepts simultaneous submissions. Reports in 1 month on queries and proposals, 3 months on manuscripts.
Tips: Mage publishes books relating to Persian/Iranian culture.

MANATEE PUBLISHING

P.O. Box 6467
Titusville, FL 32782
Phone: 407-267-9800
Fax: 407-267-8076
Web site: *http://www.fourseasonspub.net/ manateehomepage.html*
Acquisitions: Crystal Holton, editor (children's stories). Publishes trade paperback originals and reprints. **Publishes 6 titles/year. Receives 200 queries and 100 manuscripts/year. 90% of books from first-time authors; 100% from unagented writers. Pays 10-15% royalty on wholesale price.** Publishes book 1 year after acceptance of manu-

script. Accepts simultaneous submissions. Reports in 1 month. Manuscript guidelines for #10 SASE.
Nonfiction: Children's/juvenile, illustrated book. Subjects include child guidance/parenting, education. Submit complete manuscript. Query with SASE. Reviews artwork/photos as part of manuscript package. Send photocopies.
Fiction: Juvenile, picture books, children's books. Submit complete manuscript. Query with SASE.
Tips: Specializes in books that *deserve* to be published.

MARCH STREET PRESS

3413 Wilshire
Greensboro, NC 27408
Phone: 336-282-9754
Fax: 336-282-9754
E-mail: rbixby@aol.com
Web site: *http://users.aol.com/marchst*
Acquisitions: Robert Bixby, editor/publisher. Publishes literary chapbooks. **Publishes 6-10 titles/year. Receives 12 queries and 30 manuscripts/year. 50% of books from first-time authors; 100% from unagented writers. Pays 15% royalty. Offers advance of 10 copies.** Estab. 1988. Publishes book 6 months after acceptance of manuscript. Accepts simultaneous submissions. Reports in 3 months on manuscripts. Manuscript guidelines for #10 SASE.
Tips: March Street publishes poetry chapbooks.

MASTERS PRESS, NTC/Contemporary Group

1214 West Boston post Road, #302
Mamaroneck, NY 10543
Phone: 914-834-8284
Web site: *http://www.masterspress.com*
Editorial Director: John T. Nolan.
Acquisitions: Ken Samelson, acquisitions editor. Estab. 1986. Publishes hardcover and trade paperback originals. **Publishes 45-50 titles/year; imprint publishes 20 titles/year. Receives 60 queries and 50 manuscripts/year. 25% of books from first-time authors; 75% from unagented writers. Pays 10-15% royalty. Offers $1,000-5,000 advance.** Publishes book 1 year after acceptance of manuscript. Accepts simultaneous submissions. Reports in 2 months on proposals.
Tips: Sports enthusiasts and participants, people interested in fitness.

McDONALD & WOODWARD PUBLISHING CO.

325 Dorrence Road
Granville, OH 43023
Phone: 740-321-1140
Fax: 740-321-1141
Web site: *http://www.mwpubco.com*
Acquisitions: Jerry N. McDonald, managing partner/publisher. Estab. 1986. Publishes hardcover and trade paperback originals. **Publishes 8 titles/year. Receives 100 queries and 20 manuscripts/year. 50% of books from first-time authors; 100% from unagented writers. Pays 10% royalty on net receipts.** Publishes book 1 year

after acceptance of manuscript. Accepts simultaneous submissions. Reports in 2 weeks.

Tips: McDonald & Woodward publishes books in natural and cultural history. Currently emphasizing travel, natural history. De-emphasizing self-help. Interested in additional titles in the "Guides to the American Landscape" series.

McGAVICK FIELD PUBLISHING

P.O. Box 854
Allyn, WA 98524-0854
Phone: 360-275-4081
Fax: 360-705-8006
E-mail: nannies@abc.nanny.com
Web site: *http://www.abcnanny.com*

Acquisitions: Phyllis McGavick, co-owner (children's issues), Frances Hernan, co-owner (human resource issues regarding all forms of child care). **Publishes 2 titles/1999; 6 planned for 2000. 75% of books from first-time authors; 75% from unagented writers. Pays 15-25% royalty on sliding scale on retail price. Advance varies.** Publishes book 9 months after acceptance of manuscript. Accepts simultaneous submissions. Manuscript guidelines free.

Tips: Looking for caring writers with professional backgrounds in all forms of hiring and employing child care.

McGREGOR PUBLISHING

4532 W. Kennedy Boulevard, Suite 233
Tampa, FL 33609
Phone: 813-805-2665
Fax: 813-832-6177
E-mail: mcgregpub@aol.com

Acquisitions: Dave Rosenbaum, acquisitions editor. Publishes hardcover and trade paperback originals. **Publishes 4-6 titles/year. Receives 100 queries and 20 manuscripts/year. 75% of books from first-time authors; 80% from unagented writers. Pays 10-12% on retail price; 13-16% on wholesale price. Advances vary.** Publishes book 1 year after acceptance of manuscript. Accepts simultaneous submissions. Reports in 2 months on queries and proposals, 3 months on manuscripts. Manuscript guidelines free.

Tips: Nonfiction books that tell the story behind the story.

MERLOYD LAWRENCE BOOKS

Perseus Book Group
102 Chestnut Street
Boston, MA 02108
Web site: *http://www.perseusbooksgroup.com*

Acquisitions: Merloyd Lawrence, president. Estab. 1982. Publishes hardcover and trade paperback originals. **Publishes 7-8 titles/year. Receives 400 submissions/year. 25% of books from first-time authors; 20% from unagented writers. Pays royalty on retail price.** Publishes book 1 year after acceptance of manuscript. Accepts simultaneous submissions.

Nonfiction: Child development, health/medicine, nature/environment, psychology, social science. Query with SASE only. *All queries with SASE read and answered.* No unsolicited manuscripts read.

Tips: quality, literary titles, both fiction and nonfiction.

MIDDLE ATLANTIC PRESS

10 Twosome Drirve
P.O. Box 600
Moorestown, NJ 08057
Web site: *http://www.koen.com/midatintro.html*

Acquisitions: Terence Doherty, acquisitions editor. Publishes trade paperback originals and mass market paperback originals. **Publishes 4-6 titles/year. Receives 50 queries and 12 manuscripts/year. 5% of books from first-time authors; 50% from unagented writers. Offers $3,000-5,000 advance.** Publishes book 3 months after acceptance of manuscript. Accepts simultaneous submissions. Reports in 1 week on queries, 1 month on proposals.

Tips: Middle Atlantic Press is a regional publisher focusing on New York, New Jersey, Pennsylvania, and Delaware.

MIDMARCH ARTS PRESS

300 Riverside Drive
New York, NY 10025-5239
Phone: 212-666-6990

Acquisitions: S. Moore, editor (art/literature). Estab. 1975. Publishes hardcover and trade paperback originals. **Publishes 4-6 titles/year. Receives 60-100 queries and 15 manuscripts/year. 1% of books from first-time authors; 100% from unagented writers. Pays 10% minimum royalty on retail price.** Publishes book 3 months after acceptance of manuscript. Reports in 3 months. Manuscript guidelines for #10 SASE.

Tips: Midmarch Arts Press publishes books on the arts, art history, criticism, and poetry.

MILKWEED EDITIONS

430 First Avenue North, Suite 400
Minneapolis, MN 55401-1743
Phone: 612-332-3192
Web site: *http://www.milkweed.org*

Acquisitions: Emilie Buchwald, publisher; Elisabeth Fitz, manuscript coordinator (fiction, children's fiction, poetry); City as Home editor (literary writing about cities); World as Home editor (literary writing about the natural world). Estab. 1980. Publishes hardcover originals and paperback originals and reprints. **Publishes 20 titles/year. Receives 2,000 submissions/year. 30% of books from first-time authors; 70% from unagented writers. Pays 7½% royalty on list price. Advance varies.** Publishes work 1-2 years after acceptance. Accepts simultaneous submissions. Reports in 6 months. Manuscript guidelines for SASE.

Tips: Milkweed Editions publishes literary fiction for adults and middle-grade readers, nonfiction, memoir, and poetry. Currently emphasizing nonfiction about the natural world.

MILKWEEDS FOR YOUNG READERS

Imprint of Milkweed Editions
430 First Avenue North, Suite 400
Minneapolis, MN 55401-1743
Phone: 612-332-3192
Fax: 612-332-6248
Web site: *http://www.milkweed.org*
Children's Reader: Elisabeth Fitz. Estab. 1984. Publishes hardcover and trade paperback originals. **Publishes 1-2 titles/year. 25% of books from first-time authors; 70% from unagented writers. Pays 7 1/2% royalty on retail price. Advance varies.** Publishes book 1 year after acceptance of manuscript. Accepts simultaneous submissions. Reports in 2 months on queries, 6 months on manuscripts. Manuscript guidelines for #10 SASE.
Tips: Milkweeds for Young Readers are works that embody humane values and contribute to cultural understanding. Currently emphasizing natural world, urban environments. De-emphasizing fantasy.

MILLENNIUM PRESS, Skeptics Society

P.O. Box 338
Altadena, CA 91001
Phone: 818-794-3119
Acquisitions: Michael Shermer, editor. Estab. 1988. Publishes hardcover and trade paperback originals. **Publishes 4 titles/year. Receives 100 queries and 10 manuscripts/year. 30% of books from first-time authors; 100% from unagented writers. Pays 10% or negotiable royalty on retail price. Offers negotiable advance.** Publishes book 8 months after acceptance of manuscript. Accepts simultaneous submissions. Reports in 1 month on queries, 2 months on proposals, 3 months on manuscripts. Manuscript guidelines free.
Imprint(s): Skeptic Magazine.
Nonfiction: Reference, technical. Subjects include history, religion, science. Submit outline, 1 sample chapter, proposal package, including table of contents and author biography. Reviews artwork/photos as part of the manuscript package. Send photocopies.
Tips: "Millennium Press strives to publish skeptical/scientific books supporting and embodying the scientific method and critical thinking."

MOON PUBLICATIONS, INC.

Avalon Publishing Group
330 Wall Street
Chico, CA 95928
Phone: 530-345-3778
Fax: 530-345-6751
E-mail: tmarch@moon.com
Web site: *http://www.moon.com*
Acquisitions: Taran March, executive editor. Estab. 1973. Publishes trade paperback originals. **Publishes 15 titles/year. Receives 100-200 submissions/year. 50% from first-time authors; 95% from unagented writers. Pays royalty on net price. Offers advance of up to $10,000.** Publishes book an average of 9 months after acceptance.

Accepts simultaneous submissions. Reports in 2 months. Proposal guidelines for 7 1/2 x 10 1/2 SASE with 2 first-class stamps.
Tips: Comprehensive, articulate travel information to North and South America, Asia, and the Pacific.

MUSTANG PUBLISHING CO.

P.O. Box 3004
Memphis, TN 38173
Phone: 901-521-1406
Fax: 901-521-1412
E-mail: MustangPub@aol.com
Acquisitions: Rollin Riggs, editor. Estab. 1983. Publishes hardcover and trade paperback originals. **Publishes 10 titles/year. Receives 1,000 submissions/year. 50% of books from first-time authors; 90% of books from unagented writers. Pays 6-8% royalty on retail price.** Publishes book 1 year after acceptance. Accepts simultaneous submissions. Reports in 1 month. Allow 2 months for reply. No phone calls, please.
Tips: Mustang publishes general interest nonfiction for an adult audience.

NARWHAL PRESS, INC.

1629 Meeting Street
Charleston, SC 29405-9408
Phone: 803-853-0510
Fax: 803-853-2528
E-mail: shipwrex@aol.com
Web site: *http://www.shipwrecks.com*
Acquisitions: Dr. E. Lee Spence, chief editor (marine archaeology, shipwrecks); Dr. Terry Frazier, managing editor (novels, marine histories, military); Roni L. Smith, associate editor (novels, children's books). Estab. 1994. Publishes hardcover and trade paperback originals. **Publishes 10 titles/year. Receives 100 queries and 50 manuscripts/year. 75% of books from first-time authors; 100% from unagented writers. Pays 10-15% royalty on wholesale price. Offers $1,000-2,000 advance.** Publishes book 3 months after acceptance of manuscript. Accepts simultaneous submissions. Reports in 2 weeks on queries, 1 month on manuscripts.
Tips: Narwhal Press specializes in books about shipwrecks and marine archaeology and history.

NEW HORIZON PRESS

P.O. Box 669
Far Hills, NJ 07931
Phone: 908-604-6311
Fax: 908-604-6330
Web site: *http://www.hooked.net/~lore/mar/ newhorizonpress.html*
Acquisitions: Dr. Joan S. Dunphy, publisher (nonfiction, social cause, true crime). Estab. 1983. Publishes hardcover and trade paperback originals. **Publishes 12 titles/year. 90% of books from first-time authors; 50% from unagented writers. Pays standard royalty on**

net price. **Pays advance.** Publishes book 2 years after acceptance of manuscript. Accepts simultaneous submissions. Manuscript guidelines free.
Tips: New Horizon publishes adult nonfiction featuring true stories of uncommon heroes, true crime, social issues, and self-help. Introducing a new line of children's self-help.
Imprints: Small Horizons.

NEXT DECADE, INC.
39 Old Farmstead Road
Chester, NJ 07930
Phone: 908-879-6625
Fax: 908-879-6625
Web site: *http://www.nextdecade.com*
Acquisitions: Barbara Kimmel, president (reference, self-help, how-to). Publishes trade paperback originals. **Publishes 2-4 titles/year. Receives 50 queries and 10 manuscripts/year. 50% of books from first-time authors; 10% from unagented writers. Pays 10-15% royalty on wholesale price. Advances vary.** Publishes book 1 year after acceptance of manuscript. Accepts simultaneous submissions. Reports in 1 month.
Tips: Reference/how-to books that have broad mass market appeal. We are a small, award-winning press that successfully publishes a handful of books each year.

NO STARCH PRESS
555 Dettaro Street, Suite 250
San Francisco, CA 94107
Phone: 415-863-9900
Fax: 415-863-9950
E mail: info@nostarch.com
Web site: *http://www.nostarch.com*
Acquisitions: William pollock, publisher. Estab. 1994. Publishes trade paperback originals. **Publishes 6-10 titles/year. Receives 100 queries and 5 manuscripts/year. 80% of books from first-time authors; 90% from unagented writers. Pays 10-15% royalty on wholesale price. Offers negotiable advance.** Publishes book 4 months after acceptance of manuscript. Accepts simultaneous submissions.
Tips: No Starch Press publishes informative, easy to read computer books for noncomputer people to help them get the most from their hardware and software. Currently de-emphasizing trade nonfiction related to the technology business and/or cyberculture.
Imprint(s): No Starch Comix.

NODIN PRESS, Micawber's Inc.
525 North Third Street
Minneapolis, MN 55401
Phone: 612-333-6300
Fax: 612-359-5737
Acquisitions: Norton Stillman, publisher. Publishes hardcover and trade paperback originals. **Publishes 4 titles/year. Receives 20 queries and 20 manuscripts/year. 75% of books from first-time authors; 100% from unagented writers. Pays 10% royalty. Offers $250-**

1,000 advance. Publishes book 20 months after acceptance of manuscript. Accepts simultaneous submissions. Reports in 6 months on queries. Manuscript guidelines free.
Tips: Nodin Press publishes Minnesota guidebooks.

NORTHEASTERN UNIVERSITY PRESS
360 Huntington Avenue, 416CP
Boston, MA 02115
Phone: 617-373-5480
Fax: 617-373-5483
Web site: *http://www.neu.edu/nupress*
Acquisitions: William Frohlich, director (music, criminal justice); John Weingartner, senior editor (history, law and society); Terri Teleen, editor (women's studies). Estab. 1977. Publishes hardcover originals and trade paperback originals and reprints. **Publishes 40 titles/year. Receives 500 queries and 100 manuscripts/year. 50% of books from first-time authors; 90% from unagented writers. Pays 5-15% royalty on wholesale price. Offers $500-5,000 advance.** Publishes book 1 year after acceptance of manuscript. Accepts simultaneous submissions. Reports in 1 month. Manuscript guidelines free.
Tips: Northeastern University Press publishes scholarly and general interest titles in the areas of American history, criminal justice, law and society, women's studies, African-American literature, ethnic studies, and music. Currently emphasizing American studies. De-emphasizing literary studies.

NORTHLAND PUBLISHING CO., INC.
P.O. Box 1389
Flagstaff, AZ 86002-1389
Phone: 520-774-5251
Fax: 520-774-0592
E-mail: editorial@northlandpub.com
Web site: *http://www.northlandpub.com*
Acquisitions: Stephanie Bucholz, adult editor (Western and Southwestern art and cookery); Aimee Jackson, kids editor (picture books, especially humor). Estab. 1958. Publishes hardcover and trade paperback originals. **Publishes 25 titles/year. Imprint publishes 10 titles/year. Receives 4,000 submissions/year. 25% of books from first-time authors; 50% from unagented writers. Pays royalty on net receipts. Offers advance.** Publishes book 2 years after acceptance. Accepts simultaneous submissions. Reports in 3 months. Call for manuscript guidelines.
Tips: A publisher of quality nonfiction books on the material culture and indigenous peoples of the American West, including fine art, history, natural history, and cookbooks. Rising Moon publishes picture books with universal themes for children.
Imprint(s): Rising Moon (books for young readers).

OCEAN VIEW BOOKS

P.O. Box 102650
Denver, CO 80250
Editor: Lee Ballentine. Publishes hardcover originals and trade paperback originals. **Publishes 2 titles/year. 100% from unagented writers. Pays negotiable royalty.** Reports in 2 months on queries.
Tips: Literary, science fiction, fiction about the 1960s. Ocean View Books is an award-winning publisher of new speculative and slipstream fiction, poetry, criticism, surrealism, and science fiction.

THE OLIVER PRESS, INC.

5707 West 36th Street
Minneapolis, MN 55416-2510
Phone: 612-926-8981
Fax: 612-926-8965
E-mail: theoliverpress@mindspring.com
Web site: *http://www.oliverpress.com*
Acquisitions: Denise Sterling, editor. Estab. 1991. Publishes hardcover originals. **Publishes 10 titles/year. Receives 100 queries and 20 manuscripts/year. 10% of books from first-time authors; 100% from unagented writers. Makes outright purchase of $800-2,000.** Publishes book 1 year after acceptance of manuscript. Accepts simultaneous submissions. Reports in 2 months on queries. Manuscript guidelines for #10 SASE.
Tips: Biographies for ages 10 and up. Currently emphasizing science, business, government. Audience is primarily junior and senior high school students who are writing reports. Query with SASE.

ONJINJINKTA PUBLISHING

The Betty Eadie Press
P.O. Box 25490
Seattle, WA 98125
Phone: 206-433-8978
Fax: 206-246-4088
E-mail: peter@embracedbythelight.com
Web site: *http://www.Embracedbythelight.com*
Acquisitions: Peter Orullian, senior editor. Publishes hardcover, trade paperback and mass market paperback originals and reprints. **Publishes 8-12 titles/year; imprint publishes 4-6 titles/year. Receives 500 queries and 100 manuscripts/year. 50% of books from first-time authors; 80% from unagented writers. Pays 5-15% royalty on retail price. Offers $1,000-10,000 advance.** Publishes book 18 months after acceptance of manuscript. Accepts simultaneous submissions. Reports in 2 months on queries and proposals, 3 months on manuscripts. Manuscript guidelines for #10 SASE.
Tips: Onjinjinkta publishes the future work of Betty Eadie (*Embraced by the Light*) and inspirational works by other writers.
Imprint(s): Wambly Publishing (contact Peter Orullian, editor).

ORCHISES PRESS

P.O. Box 20602
Alexandria, VA 22320-1602
Phone: 703-683-1243
E-mail: rlathbur@osfl.gmu.edu
Web site: *http://mason.gmu.edu/~rlathbur*
Acquisitions: Roger Lathbury, editor in chief. Estab. 1983. Publishes hardcover and trade paperback originals and reprints. **Publishes 4-5 titles/year. Receives 600 queries and 200 manuscripts/year. 1% of books from first-time authors; 95% from unagented writers. Pays 36% of receipts after Orchises has recouped its costs.** Publishes book 1 year after acceptance. Accepts simultaneous submissions. Reports in 3 months.
Tips: Orchises Press is a general literary publisher specializing in poetry (but not new fiction), with selected reprints and textbooks.

OZARK MOUNTAIN PUBLISHING, INC.

P.O. Box 754
Huntsville, AR 72740
Phone: 501-738-2348
Fax: 501-738-2348
Web site: *http://www.ozarkmt.com*
Acquisitions: Nancy Garrison. Publishes hardcover and trade paperback originals and mass market paperback reprints. **Publishes 3-4 titles/year. Receives 100 queries and 100 manuscripts/year. 25% of books from first-time authors; 90% from unagented writers. Pays 10% royalty on wholesale price. Offers $500 advance.** Publishes book 18 months after acceptance of manuscript. Accepts simultaneous submissions. Reports in 3 months.
Nonfiction: Biography. Subjects include spirituality, new age/metaphysical. Query with SASE or submit proposal package, including outline and 2 sample chapters.
Tips: Americana focusing on the Ozark Mountain region.

PACIFIC VIEW PRESS

P.O. Box 2657
Berkeley, CA 94702
Web site: *http://www.pacificviewpress.com*
Acquisitions: Pam Zumwalt, acquisitions editor. Estab. 1992. Publishes hardcover and trade paperback originals. **Publishes 4-6 titles/year. 50% of books from first-time authors; 100% from unagented writers. Pays 10% maximum royalty on net. Offers $1,000-5,000 advance.** Publishes book 1 year after acceptance. Accepts simultaneous submissions. Reports in 2 months on queries and proposals. Writer's guidelines for #10 SASE.
Tips: Pacific View Press publishes books on the growing importance of the Pacific Rim and/or the modern culture of these countries, especially China.

PALADIN PRESS

P.O. Box 1307
Boulder, CO 80306-1307
Phone: 303-443-7250
Fax: 303-442-8741
E-mail: editorial@paladin-press.com
Web site: *http://www.paladin-press.com*
President/Publisher: Peder C. Lund.

Acquisitions: Jon Ford, editorial director. Estab. 1970. Publishes hardcover and paperback originals and paperback reprints. **Publishes 50 titles/year. 50% of books from first-time authors; 100% from unagented writers. Pays 10-12-15% royalty on net sales.** Publishes book 1 year after acceptance. Accepts simultaneous submissions. Reports in 2 months.

Tips: Paladin Press publishes the "action library" of nonfiction in military science, police science, weapons, combat, personal freedom, self-defense, survival, "revenge humor." Currently emphasizing personal freedom, financial freedom.

Imprint(s): Sycamore Island Books.

PASSPORT PRESS

P.O. Box 1346
Champlain, NY 12919-1346
Phone: 514-937-3868
Fax: 514-931-0871
E-mail: travelbook@bigfoot.com
Web site: *http://www.geocities.com/TheTropics/Paradise/2100*

Acquisitions: Jack Levesque, publisher. Estab. 1975. Publishes trade paperback originals. **Publishes 4 titles/year. 25% of books from first-time authors; 100% from unagented writers. Pays 6% royalty on retail price.** Publishes book 9 months after acceptance.

Tips: Passport Press publishes practical travel guides on specific countries. Currently emphasizing offbeat countries.

PAUL S. ERIKSSON, PUBLISHER

P.O. Box 125
Forest Dale, VT 05745-4210
Phone: 802-247-4210
Fax: 802-247-4256

Acquisitions: Paul S. Eriksson, publisher/editor; Peggy Eriksson, associate publisher/co-editor. Estab. 1960. Publishes hardcover and paperback trade originals, paperback trade reprints. **Publishes 5 titles/year. Receives 1,500 submissions/year. 25% of books from first-time authors; 95% from unagented writers. Pays 10-15% royalty on retail price. Offers advance if necessary.** Publishes book 6 months after acceptance of manuscript.

Nonfiction: Americana, birds (ornithology), art, biography, business/economics, cooking/foods/nutrition, health, history, hobbies, how-to, humor, nature, politics, psychology, recreation, self-help, sociology, sports, travel. Query with SASE.

Fiction: Serious, literary. Query with SASE.

Tips: Serious, literary, Americana.

PEACHTREE CHILDREN'S BOOKS

Imprint of Peachtree Publishers, Ltd.
494 Armour Circle NE
Atlanta, GA 30324
Phone: 404-876-8761
Fax: 404-875-2578
E-mail: peachtree@mindspring.com
Web site: *http://peachtreebooks.com*
President/Publisher: Margaret Quinlin.

Acquisitions: Helen Harriss, submissions editor. Publishes hardcover and trade paperback originals. **Publishes 18-20 titles/year. 25% of books from first-time authors; 25% from unagented writers. Pays royalty on retail price. Advance varies.** Publishes book 18 months after acceptance of manuscript. Accepts simultaneous submissions. Reports in 3 months on queries, 4 months on manuscripts. Manuscript guidelines for #10 SASE.

Imprint(s): Free Stone, Peachtree Jr.

Nonfiction: Children's/juvenile. Subjects include health, history, regional. Submit complete manuscript with SASE. Query with SASE first.

Fiction: Juvenile, picture books, young adult. Submit manuscript with SASE.

Tips: Juvenile and young adult books only.

PENNYWHISTLE PRESS

P.O. Box 734
Tesuque, NM 87574
Phone: 505-982-0000
Fax: 505-982-0066
E-mail: pnywhistle@aol.com

Acquisitions: Victor di Suvero, publisher. **Publishes 6 titles/year. Receives 400 queries and 500 manuscripts/year. 50% of books from first-time authors; 100% from unagented writers. Pays $100, chapbook plus 50 copies of book to author.** Publishes book 1 year after acceptance. Accepts simultaneous submissions. Reports in 1 month on queries, 2 months on proposals, 3 months on manuscripts. Manuscript guidelines free.

Tips: Pennywhistle publishes only poetry chapbooks.

THE PERMANENT PRESS/SECOND CHANCE PRESS

4170 Noyac Road
Sag Harbor, NY 11963
Phone: 516-725-1101
Web site: *http://www.thepermanentpress.com*

Acquisitions: Judith Shepard, editor. Estab. 1978. Publishes hardcover originals. **Publishes 12 titles/year. Receives 7,000 submissions/year. 60% of books from first-time authors; 60% from unagented writers. Pays 10-15% royalty on wholesale price. Offers $1,000 advance for Permanent Press books; royalty only on Second Chance Press titles.** Publishes book 18 months after acceptance. Accepts simultaneous submissions. Reports in 6 months on queries. Manuscript guidelines for #10 SASE.

Tips: Permanent Press publishes literary fiction. Second Chance Press devotes itself exclusively to republishing fine books that are out of print and deserve continued recognition. Currently emphasizing literary fiction. De-emphasizing poetry, short story collections.

PERSPECTIVES PRESS

P.O. Box 90318
Indianapolis, IN 46290-0318
Phone: 317-872-3055
E-mail: ppress@iquest.net
Web site: *http://www.perspectivespress.com*
Acquisitions: Pat Johnston, publisher. Estab. 1982. Publishes hardcover and trade paperback originals. **Publishes 4 titles/year. Receives 200 queries/year. 95% of books from first-time authors; 95% from unagented writers. Pays 5-15% royalty on net sales.** Publishes book 1 year after acceptance. Reports in 1 month on queries to schedule a full reading. Writer's guidelines for #10 SASE with 2 first-class stamps or on Web site.
Tips: Books on and about infertility issues and alternatives, adoption, and closely related child welfare issues.

PICCADILLY BOOKS

P.O. Box 25203
Colorado Springs, CO 80936-5203
Phone: 719-550-9887
Web site: *http://www.piccadillybooks.com*
Publisher: Bruce Fife. **Acquisitions**: Submissions Department. Estab. 1985. Publishes hardcover and trade paperback originals and trade paperback reprints. **Publishes 5-8 titles/year. Receives 200 submissions/year. 70% of books from first-time authors; 95% from unagented writers. Pays 10% royalty on retail price.** Publishes book 1 year after acceptance. Accepts simultaneous submissions. Responds only if interested.
Tips: Picadilly publishes books on humor, entertainment, performing arts, skits and sketches, and writing.

PINEAPPLE PRESS, INC.

P.O. Box 3899
Sarasota, FL 34230
Phone: 941-359-0886
Web site: *http://www.pineapplepress.com*
Acquisitions: June Cussen, editor. Estab. 1982. Publishes hardcover and trade paperback originals. **Publishes 20 titles/year. Receives 1,500 submissions/year. 20% of books from first-time authors; 80% from unagented writers. Pays 6 1/2-15% royalty on retail price. Seldom offers advance.** Publishes book 18 months after acceptance. Accepts simultaneous submissions. Reports in 3 months.
Tips: Quality nonfiction on diverse topics for the library and book-trade markets of a regional (Florida) nature.

PLEXUS PUBLISHING, INC.

143 Old Marlton Pike
Medford, NJ 08055-8750
Phone: 609-654-6500
Fax: 609-654-4309
Web site: *http://plexuspublishing.com*
Acquisitions: Thomas Hogan, editorial director. Estab. 1977. Publishes hardcover and paperback originals. **Publishes 4-5 titles/year. Receives 10-20 submissions/year. 70% of books from first-time authors; 90% from unagented writers. Pays 10-20% royalty on wholesale price; buys some booklets outright for $250-1,000. Offers $500-1,000 advance.** Accepts simultaneous submissions/year. Reports in 3 months. Guidelines for 10x13 SASE with 4 first-class stamps.
Tips: Will give serious consideration to well-written manuscripts that deal even indirectly with biology/nature subjects.

POPULAR CULTURE INK

P.O. Box 1839
Ann Arbor, MI 48106
Phone: 734-677-6351
Acquisitions: Tom Schultheiss, publisher. Estab. 1989. Publishes hardcover originals and reprints. **Publishes 4-6 titles/year. Receives 50 queries and 20 manuscripts/year. 100% of books from first-time authors; 100% from unagented writers. Pays variable royalty on wholesale price. Offers variable advance.** Publishes book 2 years after acceptance. Accepts simultaneous submissions. Reports in 1 month. Manuscript guidelines free.
Tips: popular Culture Ink publishes directories and reference books for radio, TV, music, and other entertainment subjects. Audience is libraries, avid collectors.

PROSTAR PUBLICATIONS

P.O. Box 67571
Los Angeles, CA 90067
Phone: 310-577-1975
Fax: 310-577-9272
Web site: *http://www.nauticalbooks.com*
Acquisitions: Peter Griffes, president (marine-related/how- to/business); Cathryn Pisarski, editor (history/memoirs). Estab. 1965. Publishes trade paperback originals. **Publishes 35 titles/year; imprint publishes 10-15. Receives 60 queries and 25 manuscripts/year. 50% of books from first-time authors; 100% from unagented writers. Pays 15% royalty on wholesale price. Rarely offers advance.** Publishes book 1 year after acceptance of manuscript. Accepts simultaneous submissions. Reports in 1 month on queries, 3 months on proposals.
Tips: ProStar originally published only nautical books. Expanding to any quality nonfiction book.
Imprints: Lighthouse Press (Peter Griffes).

PRUETT PUBLISHING
7464 Arapahoe Road, Suite A-9
Boulder, CO 80303
Phone: 303-449-4919
Fax: 303-443-9019
E-mail: pruettbks@aol.com
Web site: *http://www.pruettpublishing.com*
Publisher: Jim Pruett. **Acquisitions**: Robert Sheldon, editor. Estab. 1959.
Publishes hardcover paperback and trade paperback originals and reprints.
Publishes 10-15 titles/year. 60% of books are from first-time authors; 100% from unagented writers. Pays 10-12% royalty on net income. Publishes book 18 months after acceptance of manuscript.
Accepts simultaneous submissions. Reports in 2 months on queries. manuscript guidelines free.
Tips: Pruett Publishing strives to convey to its customers and readers a respect of the American West, in particular the spirit, traditions, and attitude of the region.

QUITE SPECIFIC MEDIA GROUP LTD.
260 Fifth Avenue, Suite 703
New York, NY 10001
Phone: 212-725-5377
Fax: 212-725-8506
E-mail: info@quitespecificmedia.com
Web site: *http://www.quitespecificmedia.com*
Acquisitions: Ralph Pine, editor in chief. Estab. 1967. Publishes hardcover originals, trade paperback originals and reprints. **Publishes 12 titles/year. Receives 300 queries/year and 100 manuscripts/year. 75% of books from first-time authors; 85% from unagented writers. Pays royalty on wholesale price. Advance varies.**
Publishes book 18 months after acceptance. Accepts simultaneous submissions. Reports as quickly as possible. manuscript guidelines free.
Tips: Quite Specific Media Group is an umbrella company of five imprints specializing in costume and fashion, theater, and design.
Imprint(s): Costume & Fashion Press, Drama Publishers, By Design Press, Entertainment Pro, Jade Rabbit.

RAGGED MOUNTAIN PRESS
International Marine/The McGraw-Hill Companies
P.O. Box 220
Camden, ME 04843-0220
Phone: 207-236-4837
Fax: 207-236-6314
Web site: *http://www.pbg.mcgrawhill.com/rmp*
Acquisitions: Thomas McCarthy, acquisitions editor; Jonathan Eaton, editorial director. Estab. 1969. Publishes hardcover and trade paperback originals and reprints. **Publishes 40 titles/year; imprint publishes 15, remainder are International Marine. Receives 200 queries and 100 manuscripts/year. 30% of books from first-time authors; 90% from unagented writers. Pays 10-15% royalty on net price. Offers advance.** Publishes book 1 year after acceptance of manuscript.

Accepts simultaneous submissions. Reports in 1 month on queries. Allow 2 months for reply. Manuscript guidelines for #10 SASE.
Tips: Ragged Mountain Press publishes books that take you off the beaten path.
Nonfiction: Outdoor-related how-to books, guidebooks, essays.

RAINBOW BOOKS, INC.
P.O. Box 430
Highland City, FL 33846
Phone: 941-648-4420
Fax: 941-648-4420
E-mail: rbibooks@aol.com
Acquisitons: Betsy A. Lampe, editorial director. Estab. 1979. Publishes hardcover and trade paperback originals. **Publishes 12- 15 titles/year. Receives 300 queries and 100 manuscripts/year. 90% of books from first-time authors; 80% from unagented writers. Pays 6-12% royalty on retail price. Offers advance.** Publishes book 1 year after acceptance of manuscript. Accepts simultaneous submissions. Reports in 1 month on queries and proposals, 2 months on manuscripts. Manuscript guidelines for #10 SASE.
Tips: Rainbow Books publishes self-help/how-to books for the layperson, and is also interested in seeing the same type of nonfiction books for ages 8 to 14 years. Has begun a limited line of mystery fiction, up to approximately eighty thousand words. No other fiction.

RED HEN PRESS
Valentine Publishing Group
P.O. Box 902582
Palmdale, CA 93590-2582
Phone: 818-831-0649
Fax: 818-831-0649
E-mail: redhen@vpg.net
Web site: *http://www.vpg.net*
Acquisitions: Mark E. Cull, publisher/editor (fiction); Katherine Gale, poetry editor (poetry, literary fiction). Estab. 1993. Publishes trade paperback originals. **Publishes 6 titles/year. Receives 2,000 queries and 500 manuscripts/year. 10% of books from first-time authors; 90% from unagented writers. Pays 10% royalty on retail price.**
Publishes book 1 year after acceptance of manuscript. Accepts simultaneous submissions. Reports in 1 month on queries, 2 months on proposals, 3 months on manuscripts. Manuscript guidelines free.
Tips: Red Hen Press specializes in literary fiction and poetry.

REFERENCE PRESS INTERNATIONAL
P.O. Box 4126
Greenwich, CT 06831
Phone: 203-622-6860
Fax: 203-622-5983
E-mail: ml2626@aol.com
Acquisitions: Cheryl Lacoff, senior editor. Publishes hardcover and trade paperback originals. **Publishes 6 titles/year. Receives 50 queries and 20 manuscripts/year. 75% of books from first-time authors;**

90% from unagented writers. Pays royalty or makes outright purchase. Advance determined by project. Publishes book 6 months after acceptance. Accepts simultaneous submissions. Reports in 3 months.

Tips: Reference Press specializes in instructional, reference, and how-to titles.

SARABANDE BOOKS, INC.

2234 Dundee Road, Suite 200
Louisville, KY 40205
Phone: 502-458-4028
Fax: 502-458-4065
E-mail: sarabandeb@aol.com
Web site: *http://www.sarabandebooks.org*

Acquisitions: Sarah Gorham, editor in chief. Publishes hardcover and trade paperback originals. **Publishes 8 titles/year. Receives 500 queries and 2,000 manuscripts/year. 35% of books from first-time authors; 75% from unagented writers. Pays 10% royalty on actual income received. Offers $500-2,000 advance.** Publishes book 18 months after acceptance of manuscript. Accepts simultaneous submissions. Reports in 3 months on queries, 6 months on manuscripts. Manuscript guidelines for #10 SASE.

Fiction: Literary, novellas, short story collections. No novels. Query with 1 sample story, 1 page bio, listing of publishing credits, and SASE. *Submissions in September only.*

poetry: poetry of superior artistic quality. Query and submit 10 sample poems. *Submissions in September only.*

Tips: Literary material of high standard.

SEAL PRESS

3131 Western Avenue, Suite 410
Seattle, WA 98121
Phone: 206-283-7844
Fax: 206-285-9410
E-mail: sealprss@scn.org
Web site: *http://www.sealpress.com*

Acquisitions: Faith Conlon, editor/publisher. Jennie Goode, managing editor. Publishes hardcover and trade paperback originals. **Publishes 14 titles/year. Receives 500 queries and 500 manuscripts/year. 25% of books from first-time authors; 80% from unagented writers. Pays 6-10% royalty on retail price. Offers $500-1,000 advance.** Publishes book 18 months after acceptance of manuscript. Accepts simultaneous submissions. Reports in 2 months on queries. Manuscript guidelines for SASE.

Tips: An independent feminist book publisher interested in original, lively, radical, empowering, and culturally diverse nonfiction by women addressing contemporary issues from a feminist perspective or speaking positively to the experience of being female. Currently emphasizing women outdoor adventurists, young feminists. De-emphasizing fiction unless lesbian.

Imprint(s): Adventura Books, Djuna Books, Live Girls.

SEASTONE, Ulysses Press

P.O. Box 3440
Berkeley, CA 94703
Phone: 510-601-8301
Fax: 510-601-8307
E-mail: ulypress@aol.com
Web site: *http://www.ulyssespress.com*

Acquisitions: Ray Riegert, editorial director. Publishes trade paperback originals. **Publishes 10 titles/year. Receives 100 queries and 10 manuscripts/year. 10% of books from first-time authors; 75% from unagented writers. Pays 12-16% royalty on wholesale price. Offers $2,000-8,000 advance.** Publishes book 6 months after acceptance of manuscript. Accepts simultaneous submissions. Reports in 2 months on proposals.

Nonfiction: Religion, spirituality. Submit proposal package, including outline, 2 sample chapters, and market analysis with SASE. Reviews artwork/photos as part of manuscript package. Send photocopies.

Tips: Travel off the beaten path, particularly spiritualy inclined.

SEAWORTHY PUBLICATIONS, INC.

507 Sunrise Drive
port Washington, WI 53074
Phone: 414-268-9250
Fax: 414-268-9208
E-mail: publisher@seaworthy.com
Web site: *http://www.seaworthy.com*

Acquisitions: Joseph F. Janson, publisher. Publishes trade paperback originals, hardcover originals and reprints. **Publishes 8 titles/year. Receives 60 queries and 20 manuscripts/year. 60% of books from first-time authors; 100% from unagented writers. Pays 15% royalty on wholesale price. Offers $1,000 advance.** Publishes book 6 months after acceptance of manuscript. Reports in 1 month. Manuscript guidelines for #10 SASE.

Tips: Seaworthy Publications is a nautical book publisher that primarily publishes books of interest to recreational boaters and serious bluewater cruisers, including cruising guides, how-to, and first-person adventure. Currently emphasizing guidebooks, how-to. De-emphasizing first-person adventure.

SEVEN STORIES PRESS

140 Watts Street
New York, NY 10013
Phone: 212-226-8760
Web site: *http://www.sevenstories.com*

Acquisitions: Daniel Simon, Greg Ruggiero, Paul Abruzzo, Michael Maurkin. Estab. 1995. Publishes hardcover and trade paperback originals. **Publishes 20-25 titles/year. 15% of books from first- time authors; 15% from unagented writers. Pays 7-15% royalty on retail price.** Publishes book 1-3 years after acceptance. Accepts simultaneous submissions. Reports in 3 months. Manuscript guidelines free.

Tips: Seven Stories Press publishes literary/activist fiction and nonfiction.

THE SMITH, The Generalist Association, Inc.

69 Joralemon Street
Brooklyn, NY 11201-4003
Phone: 718-834-1212
Web site: *http://members.aol.com/thesmith1*
Acquisitions: Harry Smith, publisher/editor; Michael McGrinder, associate editor. Estab. 1964. Publishes hardcover and trade paperback originals. **Publishes 3-5 titles/year. Receives 2,500 queries/year. 50% of books from first-time authors; more than 90% from unagented writers. Pays royalty. Offers $500-1,000 advance.** Publishes book 9 months after acceptance. Accepts simultaneous submissions. Reports in 3 months. Guidelines for #10 SASE.
Nonfiction: Literary essays, language and literature. "The 'how' is as important as the 'what.'" Query with proposal package including outline and sample chapter. Reviews artwork/photos as part of manuscript package. Send photocopies. No registered mail.
Fiction: Experimental, literary. Query with 1 sample chapter. *No complete manuscripts. No registered mail.*
poetry: Submit 7 to 10 sample poems. No complete manuscript. Do not send registered mail.
Tips: Literary material of high quality.

SOHO PRESS, INC.

853 Broadway
New York, NY 10003
Phone: 212-260-1900
Web site: *http://www.sohopress.com*
Acquisitions: Juris Jurjevics, publisher/editor in chief; Laura Hruska, associate publisher; Melanie Fleishman, editor/director of marketing. Estab. 1986. Publishes hardcover and trade paperback originals. **Publishes 35 titles/year. Receives 5,000 submissions/year. 75% of books from first-time authors; 50% from unagented writers. Pays 7 1/2-15% royalty on retail price. Offers advance.** Publishes book within 1 year after acceptance. Accepts simultaneous submissions. Reports in 2 months.
Tips: Soho Press publishes literary fiction, mysteries set overseas, and in the United States, multicultural fiction and nonfiction.

SOUTH END PRESS

7 Brookline Street
Cambridge, MA 02139
Phone: 617-547-4002
Fax: 617-547-1333
Acquisitions: **Acquisitions** Department. Estab. 1977. Publishes hardcover and trade paperback originals and reprints. **Publishes 15 titles/year. Receives 400 queries and 100 manuscripts/year. 50% of books from first-time authors; 95% from unagented writers. Pays 11% royalty on wholesale price. Occasionally offers $500-2,500 advance.** Publishes book 9 months after acceptance. Accepts simultaneous submissions. Reports in up to 3 months on queries and proposals. Manuscript guidelines free.
Tips: South End Press publishes nonfiction political books with a new left/feminist/multicultural perspective.

SPINSTERS INK

32 East First Street, #330
Duluth, MN 55802
Phone: 218-727-3222
Fax: 218-727-3119
E-mail: spinsters@spinsters-ink.com
Web site: *http://www.spinsters-ink.com*
Acquisitions: Nancy Walker. Estab. 1978. Publishes trade paperback originals and reprints. **Publishes 6 titles/year. Receives 400 submissions/year. 50% of books from first-time authors; 95% from unagented writers. Pays 7-11% royalty on retail price.** Publishes book 18 months after acceptance. Reports in 4 months. Manuscript guidelines for SASE.
Tips: Spinsters Ink publishes novels and nonfiction works that deal with significant issues in women's lives from a feminist perspective. They are committed to publishing works by women writing from the periphery, fat women, Jewish women, lesbians, old women, poor women, rural women, women examining classism, women of color, women with disabilities, women who are writing books that help make the best in our lives more possible. Submit outline/synopsis and sample chapters.

STARBURST PUBLISHERS

P.O. Box 4123
Lancaster, PA 17604
Phone: 717-293-0939
Fax: 717-293-1945
E-mail: starburst@starburstpublishers.com
Web site: *http://www.starburstpublishers.com*
Acquisitions: David A. Robie, editor in chief. Estab. 1982. Publishes hardcover and trade paperback originals. **Publishes 15- 20 titles/year. Receives 1,000 queries and manuscripts/year. 50% of books from first-time authors, 75% from unagented writers. Pays 6-16% royalty on wholesale price. Advance varies.** Publishes book 1 year after acceptance of manuscript. Accepts simultaneous submissions. Reports in 1 month on queries. Manuscript guidelines for #10 SASE.
Tips: Starburst publishes quality self-help, health and inspirational titles for the trade and religious markets. Currently emphasizing inspirational gift books. De-emphasizing fiction.

STEMMER HOUSE PUBLISHERS

2627 Caves Road
Owings Mills, MD 21117
Phone: 410-363-3690
E-mail: stemmerhouse@home.com
Web site: *http://www.stemmer.com*
Acquisitions: Barbara Holdridge, president (design, natural history, children's books, gardening, cookbooks). Estab. 1975. Publishes hardcover and trade paperback originals. **Publishes 3-5 titles/year; imprint publishes 2 titles/year. Receives 2,000 queries and 1,500 manuscripts/year. 50% of books from first-time authors; 90% from unagented writers. Pays 5-10% royalty on wholesale price. Offers $300 advance.** Publishes book 1-2 years after acceptance of

manuscript. Accepts simultaneous submissions. Reports in 2 weeks. Manuscript guidelines for #10 SASE.

Tips: Stemmer House publishes nonfiction illustrated books for adults and children in the arts and humanities, cookbooks, gardening, children's books, and audio cassettes. Currently emphasizing natural history. De-emphasizing adult and children's fiction.

Imprints: The International Design Library, The NatureEncyclopedia Series.

STONE BRIDGE PRESS

P.O. Box 8208
Berkeley, CA 94707
Phone: 510-524-8732
Fax: 510-524-8711
E-mail: sbp@stonebridge.com
Web site: *http://www.stonebridge.com/*

Acquisitions: Peter Goodman, publisher. Estab. 1989. Publishes hardcover and trade paperback originals. **Publishes 6 titles/year; imprint publishes 2 titles/year. Receives 100 queries and 75 manuscripts/year. 15-20% of books from first-time authors; 90% from unagented writers. Pays royalty on wholesale price. Advance varies.** Publishes book 2 years after acceptance. Accepts simultaneous submissions. Reports in 1 month on queries and proposals, 4 months on manuscripts.

Tips: High-quality informational tools about Japan.

Imprint(s): The Rock Spring Collection of Japanese Literature.

STONEWALL INN, St. Martin's Press

175 Fifth Avenue
New York, NY 10010
Phone: 212-674-5151
Web site: *http://www.stonewallinn.com*

Acquisitions: Keith Kahla, general editor. Publishes trade paperback originals and reprints. **Publishes 20-23 titles/year. Receives 3,000 queries/year. 40% of books from first-time authors; 25% from unagented writers. Pays standard royalty on retail price. Advance varies.** Publishes book 1 year after acceptance of manuscript. Accepts simultaneous submissions. Reports in 6 months on queries.

Tips: Stonewall Inn is an imprint for gay and lesbian themed fiction, nonfiction, and mysteries. Currently emphasizing literary fiction. De-emphasizing mysteries.

STOREY PUBLISHING

Schoolhouse Road
pownal, VT 05261
Phone: 802-823-5200
Fax: 802-823-5819
Web site: *http://www.storey.com*

Acquisitions: Margaret J. Lydic, editorial director; Deborah Balmuth (natural beauty and healing/health, crafts, herbs); Deborah Burns (animals, horses, birds, farming); Gwen Steege (gardening, crafts); Dan Callahan (building). Estab. 1983. Publishes hardcover and trade paperback originals

and reprints. **Publishes 45 titles/year. Receives 350 queries and 150 manuscripts/year. 25% of books from first-time authors; 80% from unagented writers. Pays royalty or makes outright purchase.** Publishes book within 2 years of acceptance. Accepts simultaneous submissions. Reports in 1 month on queries, 3 months on proposals and manuscripts. Manuscript guidelines free.

Tips: Practical information that encourages personal independence in harmony with the environment.

STYLUS PUBLISHING, LLC

22883 Quicksilver Drive
Sterling, VA 20166
Web site: *http://www.styluspub.com*

Acquisitions: John von Knorring, publisher. Estab. 1996. Publishes hardcover and trade paperback originals. **Publishes 6-10 titles/year. Receives 50 queries and 6 manuscripts/year. 50% of books from first-time authors; 100% from unagented writers. Pays 5-10% royalty on wholesale price.** Publishes book 6 months after acceptance of manuscript. Reports in 1 month. Manuscript guidelines free.

Tips: Stylus specializes in books on higher education and business training.

SUCCESS PUBLISHING

3419 Dunham Road
Warsaw, NY 14569-9735
Phone: 716-786-5663
Web site: *http://www.successpublishing.com*

Acquisitions: Allan H. Smith, president (home-based business); Ginger Smith (business); Dana Herbison (home/craft), Robin Garretson (fiction). Estab. 1982. Publishes mass market paperback originals. **Publishes 6 titles/year. Receives 175 submissions/year, 10 manuscripts/year. 90% of books from first-time authors; 100% from unagented writers. Pays 7-12% royalty. Offers $500-1,000 advance.** Publishes book 10 months after acceptance. Accepts simultaneous submissions. Reports in 2 months. Manuscript guidelines for #10 SASE with 2 first-class stamps.

Tips: Success publishes guides that focus on the needs of the home entrepreneur to succeed as a viable business. Currently emphasizing starting a new business. De-emphasizing self-help/motivation books. The audience is made up of housewives, hobbyists, and owners of home-based businesses.

SUDBURY PRESS

Profitable Technology, Inc.
40 Maclean Drive
Sudbury, MA 01776
Fax: 978-443-0734
E-mail: press@intertain.com
Web site: *http://www.sudburypress.com*

Acquisitions: Susan Gray, publisher. Publishes hardcover and mass market paperback originals. **Publishes 4 titles/year. Receives 100 queries and 100 manuscripts/year. 100% of books from first-time**

authors; 100% from unagented writers. Pays 10% royalty on wholesale price. Offers $3,000 advance. Publishes book 6 months after acceptance. Reports in 3 months.

Tips: Sudbury Press publishes only cozy mysteries and autobiographies and biographies of women.

THE SUMMIT PUBLISHING GROUP

2000 East Lamar Boulevard, Suite 600
Arlington, TX 76006
Phone: 817-588-3013
Web site: *http://www.summitbooks.com*

Acquisitions: Jill Bertolet, publisher; Veronica Palmer, acquisitions editor; DeNell Russell, submissions editor; Katherine Bear, submissions editor. Estab. 1990. Publishes hardcover originals, trade paperback originals and reprints. **Publishes 35 titles/year. 40% of books from first-time authors; 80% from unagented writers. Pays 5-20% royalty on wholesale price. Offers $2,000 and up advance.** Publishes book 6 months after acceptance of manuscript. Accepts simultaneous submissions. Reports in 1 month on queries and proposals, 3 months on manuscripts.

Tips: Contemporary books with a nationwide appeal. Adult market with biography, self-help, how-to, gift, and coffee table books. Currently emphasizing self-help, biography, cookbooks. De-emphasizing children's/juvenile.

Imprints: Legacy Books (corporate private-label organizational publications).

SWAN-RAVEN & CO.

Blue Water Publishing, Inc.
P.O. Box 190
Mill Spring, NC 28756
Phone: 828-894-8444
Fax: 828-894-8454
E-mail: bluewaterp@aol.com
Web site: *http://www.5thworld.com/bluewater*

Acquisitions: Pamela Meyer, publisher. Publishes trade paperback originals. **Publishes 6 titles/year. Receives 40 queries and 25 manuscripts/month. 80% of books from first-time authors; 90% from unagented writers. Pays 5-12% royalty on wholesale price.** Publishes book 16 months after acceptance of manuscript. Accepts simultaneous submissions. Reports in 2 months on manuscripts. Manuscript guidelines for SASE with 55¢ postage.

Tips: Swan-Raven publishes books that draw on the ancient wisdom of indigenous cultures to bring information from the otherworlds to our world.

SYSTEMS CO., INC.

P.O. Box 339
Carlsborg, WA 98324
Phone: 360-683-6860

Acquisitions: Richard H. Peetz, Ph.D., president. Estab. 1981. Publishes hardcover and trade paperback originals. **Publishes 3-5 titles/year. 50% of books from first-time authors; 100% from unagented writers. Pays 20% royalty on wholesale price after costs.** Publishes book 6 months after acceptance of manuscript. Accepts simultaneous submissions. Reports in 2 months. Manuscript guidelines for $1.

Tips: Succinct and well-organized technical and how-to books with minimum filler. De-emphasizing business/economics, health/medicine.

TAYLOR PUBLISHING COMPANY

1550 West Mockingbird Lane
Dallas, TX 75235
Phone: 214-819-8560
Fax: 214-819-8580
Web site: *http://www.taylorpub.com*
President: Craig Von Pelt. Publisher/Editorial Director: Lynn Brooks.

Acquisitions: Michael Emmerich, senior editor (sports, history, pop culture, gardening, health); Camille N. Cline, editor (pop culture, history, health, gardening). Estab. 1981. Publishes hardcover and softcover originals. **Publishes 35 titles/year. Receives 1,500 submissions/year. 25% of books from first-time authors; 25% from unagented writers.** Publishes book 1-2 years after acceptance. Accepts simultaneous submissions. Reports in 3 months. Manuscript guidelines for 10x13 SASE.

Tips: Solid, practical books that should backlist well. Looks for authors who are experts in their field and already have some recognition through magazine articles, radio appearances, or their own TV or radio show.

TEXAS STATE HISTORICAL ASSOCIATION

2.306 Richardson Hall, University Station
Austin, TX 78712
Phone: 512-471-1525
Web site: *http://www.tsha.utexas.edu*

Acquisitions: George B. Ward, assistant director. Estab. 1897. Publishes hardcover and trade paperback originals and reprints. **Publishes 8 titles/year. Receives 50 queries and 50 manuscripts/year. 10% of books from first-time authors; 95% from unagented writers. Pays 10% royalty on net cash proceeds.** Publishes book 1 year after acceptance. Reports in 2 months on manuscripts. Manuscript guidelines free.

Tips: Interested in scholarly historical articles and books on any aspect of Texas history.

TIDEWATER PUBLISHERS

Cornell Maritime Press, Inc.
P.O. Box 456
Centreville, MD 21617-0456
Phone: 410-758-1075
Fax: 410-758-6849

Acquisitions: Charlotte Kurst, managing editor. Estab. 1938. Publishes hardcover and paperback originals. **Publishes 7-9 titles/year. Receives 150 submissions/year. 41% of books from first-time authors; 99% from unagented writers. Pays 7 1/2-15% royalty on retail price.** Publishes book 1 year after acceptance. Reports in 2 months.

Tips: Tidewater Publishers issues adult nonfiction works related to the Chesapeake Bay area, Delmarva or Maryland in general. Juvenile fiction with a regional focus. Query or submit outline/synopsis and sample chapters.

TRICYCLE PRESS, Ten Speed Press

P.O. Box 7123
Berkeley, CA 94707
Phone: 510-559-1600
Fax: 510-524-1052
Web site: *http://www.tenspeed.com*
Acquisitions: Nicole Geiger, publisher. Publishes hardcover and trade paperback originals. **Publishes 12-14 titles/year. 20% of books from first-time authors; 60% from unagented authors. Pays 15-20% royalty on wholesale price (lower if book is illustrated). Offers $0-9,000 advance.** Publishes book 1 year after acceptance of manuscript. Accepts simultaneous submissions. Reports in 3 months on submissions (no query letters Manuscript guidelines for #10 SASE.
Tips: Tricycle Press looks for something outside the mainstream; books that encourage children to look at the world from a possibly alternative angle.

TSR, INC., Wizards of the Coast

P.O. Box 707
Renton, WA 98057-0707
Phone: 425-226-6500
Executive Editor: Mary Kirchoff.
Acquisitions: Novel Submissions Editor. Estab. 1975. Publishes hardcover and trade paperback originals and trade paperback reprints. **Publishes 40-50 titles/year. Receives 600 queries and 300 manuscripts/year. 25% of books from first-time authors; 35% from unagented authors. Pays 4-8% royalty on retail price. Offers $4,000-6,000 average advance.** Publishes book 1 year after acceptance of manuscript. Accepts simultaneous submissions. Reports in 2 months on queries. Guidelines for #10 SASE.
Tips: TSR publishes science fiction and fantasy titles.
Imprint(s): Dragonlance Books; Forgotten Realms Books; Grayhawk Novels; Legend of the Fire Rings Novels; Magic: The Gathering Books; Star*Drive Books.

ULYSSES PRESS

P.O. Box 3440
Berkeley, CA 94703
Phone: 510-601-8301
Fax: 510-601-8307
E-mail: ulysses@ulyssespress.com
Web site: *http://ulyssespress.com*
Acquisitions: Ray Riegert, editorial director. Estab. 1982. Publishes trade paperback originals. **Publishes 10-15 titles/year. 25% of books from first-time authors; 75% from unagented writers. Pays 12-16% royalty on wholesale price. Offers $2,000-4,000 advance.** Publishes book 6 months after acceptance. Accepts simultaneous submissions. Reports in 2 months on proposals.
Tips: Ulysses publishes travel, spirituality, and health books.
Imprint(s): Seastone (hidden travel series).

THE UNIVERSITY OF AKRON PRESS

374B Bierce Library
Akron, OH 44325-1703
Phone: 330-972-5342
Fax: 330-972-5152
E-mail: press@uakron.edu
Web site: *http://www.uakron.edu/uapress*
Acquisitions: Elton Glaser, director. Estab. 1988. Publishes hardcover and trade paperback originals. **Publishes 4-5 titles/year. Receives 40-60 queries and over 500 manuscripts/year** (because of poetry contest). **20% of books from first-time authors; 100% from unagented writers. Pays 4-10% royalty on wholesale price.** Publishes book 14 months after acceptance of manuscript. Accepts simultaneous submissions (only for poetry contest.) Reports in 1 month on queries, 2 months on proposals, 5 months on manuscripts. Manuscript guidelines for #10 SASE.
Tips: Currently emphasizing technology and the environment, Ohio history and culture, poetry. De-emphasizing fiction. Query. Reviews artwork/photos as part of manuscript package. Send photocopies.

UNIVERSITY OF MAINE PRESS

5717 Corbett Hall
Orono, ME 04469-5717
Phone: 207-581-1408
Acquisitions: Director. Publishes hardcover and trade paperback originals and reprints. **Publishes 4 titles/year. Receives 50 queries and 25 manuscripts/year. 10% of manuscripts from first-time authors; 90% from unagented writers.** Publishes book 1 year after acceptance of manuscript. Accepts simultaneous submissions.
Tips: Interested in scholarly works and fiction on regional history, regional life sciences, Franco-American studies. Query.

UNIVERSITY OF SCRANTON PRESS

University of Scranton
Scranton, PA 18510-4660
Phone: 717-941-4228
Fax: 717-941-4309
E-mail: rousseaur1@uofs.edu
Web site: *http://www.viamall.com*
Acquisitions: Richard Rousseau, director. Estab. 1981. Publishes hardcover and paperback originals. **Publishes 5 titles/year. Receives 200 queries and 45 manuscripts/year. 60% of books from first-time authors; 100% from unagented writers. Pays 10% royalty.** Publishes book 1 year after acceptance. Reports in 1 month on queries. Manuscript guidelines free.
Tips: The University of Scranton Press, a member of the Association of Jesuit University Presses, publishes primarily scholarly monographs in theology, philosophy, and the culture of northeast Pennsylvania.
Imprint(s): Ridge Row Press.

VANDAMERE PRESS

AB Associates International, Inc.
P.O. Box 5243
Arlington, VA 22205
Phone: 703-538-5750
Fax: 703-538-5750
Web site: *http://www.vandamere.com*

Acquisitions: Jerry Frank, editor. Estab. 1984. Publishes hardcover and trade paperback originals and reprints. **Publishes 8-15 titles/year. Receives 750 queries and 2,000 manuscripts/year. 25% of books from first-time authors; 90% from unagented writers. Pays royalty on revenues generated**. Publishes book 1-3 years after acceptance of manuscript. Accepts simultaneous submissions. Reports in 6 months.

Tips: Vandamere publishes general fiction as well as nonfiction of historical, biographical, or regional interest. Currently emphasizing history and biography. No response without SASE.

VIKING STUDIO (formerly Penguin Studio)

Penguin Putnam, Inc.
375 Hudson Street
New York, NY 10014
Phone: 212-366-2191
Web site: *http://www.penguinputnam.com*

Acquisitions: Christopher Sweet, executive editor (art, music, history, photography, fashion, religion); Cyril Nelson, senior editor (arts and crafts, decorative arts); Marie Timell, senior editor (nonfiction general interest, astrology, new age); Rachel Tsutsumi, associate editor (art, architecture, photography, fashion, design, travel). Publishes hardcover originals. **Publishes 35-40 titles/year. Receives 300 submissions/year. Less than 10% of books are from first-time authors; less than 5% from unagented writers.** Publishes book 1 year after acceptance. Accepts simultaneous submissions. Reports in 2 months.

Tips: Viking Studio publishes high-quality nonfiction, illustrated hardcover/trade books.

VISTA PUBLISHING, INC.

422 Morris Avenue, Suite #1
Long Branch, NJ 07740
Phone: 732-229-6500
Fax: 732-229-9647
E-mail: czagury@vistapubl.com
Web site: *http://www.vistapubl.com*

Acquisitions: Carolyn Zagury, president. Estab. 1991. Publishes trade paperback originals. **Publishes 12 titles/year. Receives 200 queries and 125 manuscripts/year. 75% of books from first-time authors; 100% from unagented writers. Pays 50% royalty on wholesale or retail price.** Publishes book 2-3 years after acceptance of manuscript. Accepts simultaneous submissions. Reports in 3 months on manuscripts. Manuscript guidelines free.

Tips: Vista publishes books by nurses and allied health professionals. Currently emphasizing clinical nursing issues and topics. De-emphasizing fiction and mysteries.

VOYAGEUR PRESS

123 North Second Street
Stillwater, MN 55082
Phone: 651-430-2210
Fax: 651-430-2211
E-mail: mdregni@voyageurpress.com or tberger@voyageurpress.com
Web site: *http://www.voyageurpress.com*

Acquisitions: Michael Dregni, editorial director. Todd R. Berger (regional travel and photography. Estab. 1972. Publishes hardcover and trade paperback originals. **Publishes 30 titles/year. Receives 1,200 queries and 500 manuscripts/year. 10% of books from first-time authors; 90% from unagented writers. Pays royalty.** Publishes book 1 year after acceptance of manuscript. Accepts simultaneous submissions. Reports in 3 months. Manuscript guidelines free.

Tips: Publisher of quality natural history, wildlife, and regional books.

WESCOTT COVE PUBLISHING CO.

P.O. Box 130
Stamford, CT 06904
Phone: 203-322-0998

Acquisitions: Julius M. Wilensky, president. Estab. 1968. Publishes trade paperback originals and reprints. **Publishes 4 titles/year. Receives 15 queries and 10 manuscripts/year. 25% of books from first-time authors; 95% from unagented writers. Pays 5-10% royalty on retail price. Offers $1,000-1,500 advance.** Publishes book 1 year after acceptance of manuscript. Accepts simultaneous submissions. Reports in 1 month on queries.

Tips: All titles are nautical books; half of them are cruising guides. Westcott Cove seeks out authors knowledgeable in sailing, navigation, and cartography, in a particular area are commissions them to write a book. Query with outline, 1 to 2 sample chapters, author's credentials, and SASE.

WESLEYAN UNIVERSITY PRESS

110 Mount Vernon Street
Middletown, CT 06459
Phone: 860-685-2420
Web site: *http://www.weslyan.edu/wespress*

Acquisitions: Suzanna Tamminen, editor in chief. Estab. 1957. Publishes hardcover originals and paperbacks. **Publishes 25-30 titles/year. Receives 1,500 queries and 1,000 manuscripts/year. 10% of books from first-time authors; 80% from unagented writers. Pays 0-10% royalty. Offers up to $3,000 advance.** Publishes book 1 year after acceptance of manuscript. Accepts simultaneous submissions. Reports in 1 month on queries, 2 months on proposals, 3 months on manuscripts. Manuscript guidelines for #10 SASE.

Tips: Wesleyan University Press is a scholarly press with a focus on cultural studies.

WESTCLIFFE PUBLISHERS

P.O. Box 1261
Englewood, CO 80150
Phone: 303-935-0900
Fax: 303-935-0903
E-mail: westclif@westcliffepubishers.com
Web site: *http://www.westcliffepublishers.com*
Acquisitions: Linda Doyle, associate publisher; Kristin Iverson, managing editor. Estab. 1981. Publishes hardcover originals, trade paperback originals and reprints. **Publishes 23 titles/year. Receives 100 queries and 60 manuscripts/year. 75% of books from first-time authors; 100% from unagented writers. Pays 3-15% royalty on retail price. Offers advance of up to 50% of the first year's royalties.** Publishes book 18 months after acceptance of manuscript. Accepts simultaneous submissions. Reports in 1 month.
Tips: High-quality regional photography and essays for coffee-table books and calendars. Currently emphasizing children's regional books.

WHISPERING COYOTE PRESS, L.P.

300 Crescent Court, Suite 1150
Dallas, TX 75201
Phone: 214-871-5599
Fax: 214-871-5577 or 214-319-7298
Web site: *http://www.charlesbridge.com*
Acquisitions: Mrs. Lou Alpert, editor. Estab. 1990. **Publishes 6 titles/year. 20% of books from first-time authors; 90% from unagented writers. Pays 8% royalty on retail price of first 10,000 copies, 10% after (combined author and illustrator). Offers $2,000-8,000 advance (combined author, illustrator).** Publishes book 2 years after acceptance of manuscript. Accepts simultaneous submissions. Reports in 3 months. Manuscript guidelines for #10 SASE with 55¢ postage.
Tips: Children's picture books ages 4 to 11. Recently purchased by Charlesbridge Publishing.

WHITE CLIFFS MEDIA, INC.

Editorial Department
400 Del Verde, Circle #2
Sacramento, CA 95833
Acquisitions: Lawrence Aynesmith. Estab. 1985. White Cliffs publishes music titles for an academic and general audience. Publishes hardcover and trade paperback originals. **Publishes 5-10 titles/year. 50% of books from first-time authors; 50% from unagented writers. Pays 5-12% royalty or makes outright purchase.** Publishes book 1 year after acceptance. No simultaneous submissions. Reports in 2 months on queries, 4 months on proposals, 6 months on manuscripts.
Nonfiction: Biography, textbook. Subjects include anthropology, ethnic, music/dance. Query. Reviews artwork/photos as part of manuscript package. Send photocopies.

WHITE MANE BOOKS

White Mane Publishing Company Inc.
63 W. Burd Street
P.O. Box 152
Shippensburg, PA 17257
Phone: 717-532-2237
Fax: 717-532-7704
Acquisitions: Martin K. Gordon, president (White Mane Books); Harold Collier, vice president (other imprints). Estab. 1987. Publishes hardcover, and trade paperback originals and reprints. **Publishes 60 titles/year; each imprint publishes 12-18 titles/year. Receives 300 queries and 50 manuscripts/year. 50% of books from first-time authors; 75% from unagented writers. Pays royalty on monies received.** Publishes book 18 months after acceptance of manuscript. Accepts simultaneous submissions. Reports in 1 month on queries and proposals, 3 months on manuscripts. Manuscript guidelines free.
Tips: Books on military history with the emphasis on the American Civil War. Currently emphasizing World War II.
Imprints: Back Street Books (military history, emphasis on American Civil War); Ragged Edge Press (religious); WMkids (historically based children's fiction).

WILD FLOWER PRESS

Blue Water Publishing
P.O. Box 190
Mill Spring, NC 28756
Phone: 828-894-8444
Fax: 828-894-8454
E-mail: bluewaterp@aol.com
Web site: *http://www.5thworld.com*
President: Pam Meyer.
Acquisitions: Brian Crissey; Julie Sherar, editor. Publishes hardcover originals and trade paperback originals and reprints. **Publishes 6 titles/year. Receives 50 queries and 25 manuscripts/month. 80% of books from first-time authors; 90% from unagented writers. Pays 7 1/2-15% royalty.** Publishes book 16 months after acceptance of manuscript. Accepts simultaneous submissions. Reports in 2 months on manuscripts. Manuscript guidelines for SASE with 55¢ postage.
Tips: Books about extraterrestrial research and experiences. Submit outline. Reviews artwork/photos as part of manuscript package. Send photocopies.

WILDERNESS PRESS

2440 Bancroft Way
Berkeley, CA 94704-1676
Phone: 510-843-8080
Fax: 510-548-1355
E-mail: mail@wildernesspress.com
Web site: *http://www.wildernesspress.com*
Acquisitions: Caroline Winnett, publisher. Mike Jones, associate publisher. Estab. 1967. Publishes paperback originals. **Publishes 10 titles/year. Receives 150 submissions/year. 20% of books from**

first-time authors; 95% from unagented writers. **Pays 8-10% royalty on retail price. Offers $1,000 average advance.** Publishes book 8 months after acceptance of manuscript. Reports in 1 month. Manuscript guidelines for SASE.

Tips: Books about the outdoors. Most are trail guides for hikers and backpackers, but also how-to books about the outdoors. The manuscript must be accurate. The author must research an area in person. If writing a trail guide, you must walk all the trails in the area the book is about. Outlook must be strongly conservationist. Style must be appropriate for a highly literate audience. Request proposal guidelines.

WILLOW CREEK PRESS

P.O. Box 147
9931 Highway 70 West
Minocqua, WI 54548
Phone: 715-358-7010
Fax: 715-358-2807
E-mail: ljevert@newnorth.net
Web site: *http://www.willowcreekpress.com*
Acquisitions: Laura Evert, managing editor. Estab. 1986. Publishes hardcover and trade paperback originals and reprints. **Publishes 25 titles/year. Receives 400 queries and 150 manuscripts/year. 15% of books from first-time authors; 50% from unagented writers. Pays 6-15% royalty on wholesale price. Offers $2,000-5,000 advance.** Publishes book 10 months after acceptance of manuscript. Accepts simultaneous submissions. Reports in 2 months.

Tips: Willow Creek specializes in nature, outdoor, and animal books, cookbooks, calendars, and videos with high-quality photography.

WINDSOR BOOKS, Windsor Marketing Corp.

P.O. Box 280
Brightwaters, NY 11718-0280
Phone: 516-321-7830
Web site: *http://www.windsorpublishing.com*
Acquisitions: Jeff Schmidt, managing editor. Estab. 1968. Publishes hardcover and trade paperback originals, reprints, and very specific software. **Publishes 8 titles/year. Receives approximately 40 submissions/year. 60% of books from first-time authors; 90% from unagented writers. Pays 10% royalty on retail price; 5% on wholesale price (50% of total cost). Offers variable advance.** Publishes book an average of 6 months after acceptance of manuscript. Accepts simultaneous submissions. Reports in 2 weeks on queries. Manuscript guidelines free.

Tips: Books are for serious investors.

WINSLOW PRESS

770 East Atlantic Avenue, Suite 201
Delray Beach, FL 33483
Phone: 561-274-8084
Fax: 561-274-8533
Web site: *http://www.winslowpress.com*

Publishes hardcover originals. **Publishes 3-5 titles/year. Receives 150 queries and 2,000 manuscripts/year. 80% of books from first-time authors; 80% from unagented writers. Pays royalty. Sometimes offers advance.** Accepts simultaneous submissions. Reports in 1 month on queries and proposals, 3 months on manuscripts.

Nonfiction and Fiction: Children's/juvenile. History subjects. Query with SASE. Reviews artwork/photos as part of manuscript package. Send photocopies. Adventure, ethnic, fantasy, historical, humor, multicultural, mystery, picture books, poetry, science fiction, sports, suspense, young adult. Submit complete manuscript.

WOODBINE HOUSE

6510 Bells Mill Road
Bethesda, MD 20817
Phone: 301-897-3570
Fax: 301-897-5838
E-mail: info@woodbinehouse.com
Web site: *http://www.woodbinehouse.com*
Acquisitions: Susan Stokes, editor. Estab. 1985. Publishes hardcover and trade paperback originals and reprints. **Publishes 8 titles/year. 90% of books from unagented writers. Pays 10-12% royalty.** Publishes book 18 months after acceptance of manuscript. Accepts simultaneous submissions. Reports in 2 months. Manuscript guidelines for 6x9 SASE with 3 first-class stamps.

Tips: Publishes books for and about children and adults with disabilities. No personal accounts or general parenting guides. Submit outline and 3 sample chapters with SASE. Reviews artwork/photos as part of manuscript package.

Fiction: Children's picture books. Submit entire manuscript with SASE.

WOODHOLME HOUSE PUBLISHERS

131 Village Square I
Village of Cross Keys
Baltimore, MD 21210
Phone: 410-532-5018
Fax: 410-532-9741
E-mail: info@woodholmeshouse.com
Acquisitions: Gregg A. Wilhelm, director. Estab. 1996. Publishes hardcover and trade paperback originals. **Publishes 5 titles/year. Receives 100 queries and 50 manuscripts/year. 50% of books from first-time authors; 80% from unagented writers. Pays 5-15% royalty on retail price.** Publishes book 9 months after acceptance of manuscript. Accepts simultaneous submissions. Reports in 1 month on queries, 3 months on manuscripts. Manuscript guidelines for #10 SASE.

Tips: Woodholme is a regional-interest publisher (mid-Atlantic/Chesapeake Bay area) covering a variety of genres, nonfiction and fiction.

Additional Resources for Writers

American Black Book Writers Association
P.O. Box 10548
Marina Del Rey, CA 90295
E-mail: staff@blackbookworld.com
Web site: *http://www.iwaysol.com/xblackbookworld/*

American Society of Journalists and Authors
1501 Broadway, Suite 302
New York, NY 10036
Phone: 212-997-0947
Fax: 212-768-7414
E-mail: execdir@asja.org
Web site: *http://www.asja.org/*

Associated Writing Programs
Tallwood House, MSN 1E3
George Mason University
Fairfax, VA 22030
Phone: 703-993-4301
Fax: 703-993-4302
E-mail: awp@gmu.edu
Web site: *http://web.gmu.edu/departments/awp/*

Authors Guild, Inc.
330 West 42nd Street, 29th floor
New York, NY 10036
Phone: 212-563-5904
Fax: 212-564-5363
E-mail: staff@authorsguild.org
Web site: *http://www.authorsguild.org/*

International Women's Writing Guild
P.O. Box 810
Gracie Station
New York, NY 10028-0082
Phone: 212-737-7536
Fax: 212-737-9469
E-mail: iwwg@iwwg.com
Web site: *http://www.iwwg.com/*

National Endowment for the Arts (NEA)
1100 Pennsylvania Avenue, NW
Washington, D.C. 20506
Phone: 202-682-5451
Web site: *http://arts.endow.gov/*

National Endowment for the Humanities (NEH)
1100 Pennsylvania Avenue, NW
Washington, D.C. 20506
Phone: 202-606-8400 or 1-800-NEH-1121
Fax: 202-606-8240
E-mail: info@neh.gov
Web site: *http://www.neh.fed.us/*

National League of American Pen Women
Pen-Arts Building
1300 17th Street, NW
Washington, D.C. 20036-1973
Web site: *http://members.aol.com/penwomen/pen.htm*

National Writers Association Inc.
1450 South Havana, Suite 424
Aurora, CO 80012
Phone: 303-751-7844
Fax: 303-751-8593
Web site: *http://lcweb.loc.gov/loc/cfbook/coborg/nwa.html*

PEN American Center
568 Broadway
New York, NY 10012-3225
Phone: 212-334-1660
Fax: 212-334-2181
E-mail: pen@pen.org
Web site: *http://www.pen.org*

Poets & Writers, Inc.
72 Spring Street
New York, NY 10012
Phone: 212-226-3586
Fax: 212-226-3963
E-mail: infocenter@pw.org
Web site: *http://www.pw.org/*

The Writer's Center
4508 Walsh Street
Bethesda, MD 20815-6006
Phone: 301-654-8664
Fax: 301-654-8667
E-mail: postmaster@writer.org
Web site: *http://www.writer.org*

Index

A

AAR. see Association of Authors'
    Representatives
ABPA. see American Book
    Producers Association
Acceptance. see also Manuscript;
    Submissions
    in general, 158-160
Advertising, 204. see also
    Marketing
Agents
    author/agent agreement,
      sample, 121-122
      agency clause, sample, 122
      letter of agreement,
        sample, 122-126
    benefits of using, 115
    contacting, 116-117
    duties and responsibilities,
      111-114
    expectations for, 118-120
    in general, 110-111
    list of, 126-142
    locating, 120
    locating and working with,
      114-116
    questions to ask, 119
    "reading fees" charges, 116
    researching, ix
    rights and, 214
    types of, 118
American Book Producers
    Association (ABPA), 228, 231
American Society of Journalists
    and Authors, contact
    information, 11
Artwork, contract requirements
    for, 172-173
Assistant editor. see Editorial
    assistant
Associated Writing Programs (AWP)
    list of programs, 18-33
    member writing programs,
      17-18
    Web page URL, 7
Association of Authors'
    Representatives (AAR), 112, 121
    Web page URL, 7, 61

Association of Electronic
    Publishers (AEP). see also
    Electronic publishing
    membership rules, 237-239
    resources, 236
Audience. see also Market research
    determining, 38, 60-62
    likes and dislikes, 49, 51-52,
      64-65
    testing material before, 5
Audio rights, 164, 218. see also
    Rights
Author. see also Writers
    biographical information
      requirements, 198
    book sales by, 68
    personality types, viii
    promotional efforts by, 151
Author/agent agreement, sample,
    121-122. see also Agents
Author biography, including in
    proposal, 79
Author's compensation, contract
    requirements for, 184-189
Author's free copies, contract
    requirements for, 172
Author's Guild, contact
    information, 11
Author's representative. see Agents
Author's statements
    contract requirements for,
      177-179
    royalty checks and, 220-221
AWP. see Associated Writing
    Programs

B

Backlist, 54. see also Publishing list
Back matter, 145
Bacon's Media, 208
Bartlett's Familiar Quotations, 4, 9
Bestseller, 55
"Bestseller bonus," 185
Bible, online reference source for, 7
Binding
    hardcover/cloth, 12
    paperback, 12-14
Biography
    all fiction as, 52
    discussed, 44-45

reading list recommendations, 56
"Blues," 198
Book clubs
    discussed, 16
    rights for, 217
    Web sites, 57
Book packagers, discussed,
    228-229
Book production timetable, 66, 73
Books. see also Manuscript
    about writing, 17
    annual U.S. production of, 8, 37
    author's right to buy, 179-180
    basic publishing procedure,
      viii-xi
    categories and genres, in
      general, 37-39
    coffee table, 12
    fiction, 36-37
    hardcover/cloth, 12
    nonfiction, 37
    paperback, 12-14
    for writing instruction, 4
Book scouts, 214
Book signings, 207
Books in Print, 62
Bookstores. see also
    Conglomerates
    book display in, 202, 203
    getting your book into, 200
    independent, 201, 202
    noticing book people in, vii
    online Web sites, 61
    researching in, vii, 37-38, 62,
      65, 201-202
Business
    publishing as, 81, 147-148, 149, 150
    reading list recommendations, 56

C

Catalogs, requesting, 65
Categories. see also Genres;
    Reading list
    biography, 44-45
    cookbooks, 46
    crime novels, 41-42, 67
    in general, 37-39
    historicals, 41
    horror, 39
    how-to books, 45

    humor, 47
    memoirs, 45
    mystery, 80
    nonfiction, 43-44
    pop culture, 46-47
    reference, 46
    romance, 39, 67
    science fiction and fantasy, 40, 67
    series, 49
    thrillers, 42-43
    travel, 46
    true crime, 44, 47-48, 67
    westerns, 40-41
    young adult/children, 43, 67
Chains, 201. see also Bookstores;
    Conglomerates
Changes. see also Page proofs;
    Revisions
    contract requirements for, 171
    making to manuscript, x, xi,
      117, 193
Chapters, including samples in
    proposal, 79
Chicago Manual of Style, 195
Classes, opportunities at, 5
Clippings, including with proposal, 75
In Cold Blood (Capote), 44
Competing works, contract
    language for, 174-175
Competition
    analyzing, 62-64, 77-78
    within genres, 38, 73-74
Conferences. see also Seminars;
    Workshops
    guides to, 7
    opportunities at, 5, 120, 152
    for sales and editorial staffs, 198
Conglomerates. see also
    Bookstores
    discussed, 15-16
    influence on book selection,
      150, 200-201
    problems with, 148
Contracts, 154
    cancellation of, 70-71
    for e-publishing, 234
    negotiating with agent, 115
    requirements for, 159, 160-161
    sample, 162-189
Cookbooks
    discussed, 46

reading list recommenda-
tions, 53-56
Copyediting
contract requirements for, 171
living with results of, xi, 195
online sources for, 7
subsequent procedures,
196-198
Copyright. see also Rights
contract requirements for,
173-174
Cover letter. see also Query
letter
including in proposal,
79-80
Covers, 151, 197. see also Titles
Craft of Writing, Web page
URL, 7
Crashing, 151
Creativity, developing, 6
Crime novels, discussed, 41-42

D
Delays, coping with, 192
Dell, relation with Doubleday,
15
Design department, 151
Dispute resolution. see also
Contracts
contract requirements for,
181-182
Distribution department, 152
Distributors, online Web sites, 61
Doubleday, relation with Dell, 15

E
Editorial assistant, review of
manuscripts by, 145-146, 195
Editorial department. see also
Publishing
operations of, 144, 148-149
Editorial Freelance
Association, contact
information, 116
Editorial meetings, in general,
146-148
Editors
as agents, 118
employment opportunities
for, 16, 120
hierarchy of, 148
relations with agents, 114

relations with book
buyers, 150
Electronic book (E-book), 188
resources for, 235, 236
Electronic publishing. see
also Publishing
choosing an e-publisher,
233-234
commercial, 231
in general, 230-231
pros and cons, 232-233
resources, 233
subsidiary, 231-232
Electronic rights. see also
Rights
discussed, 218-219
protecting, 165
The Elements of Style
(Strunk/White), 4
e-mail, recommendations for
using, 86
Endorsements. see also
Testimonials
soliciting, 206
EText, 231, 232
Expertise, in specific
categories, 47-48

F
Feedback. see also Audience;
Market research
from live audience, 5
Fiction
described, 36-37
query letter for, 82-83
reading list
recommendations,
53-56
sample proposal, 98-102
Friends
compared to your agent,
118-119
marketing assistance from,
205-206
Frontlist, 63, 64
Front matter, 145

G
Genres. see also Categories;
Reading list
being an expert in, 47-48
in general, 37-39

Goals, reader expectations
for, 52
Grant of rights, contract
requirements for, 163-164,
165-166
Groups, benefits of, 5, 6

H
Handwritten documents,
recommendations against,
4, 86, 194
Hardcover/cloth, described, 12
HarperCollins, cancellation of
contracts, 70-71
Hemingway, Ernest, 6
Historicals
discussed, 41
reading list
recommendations, 56
Hooks, discussing in
proposal, 75, 83
Horror novels, described, 39
How-to books, discussed, 45
Humor
discussed, 47
reading list
recommendations, 57

I
Ideas
bad
familiarity, 50
in general, 50
importance, 50
truth, 51
fiction reading list
recommendations for,
53-56
good, identifying, 51-52, 68
good and bad, in general,
48-49
higher concept, 52-53
suggested sources for, 53
Independent Literary Agents
Association, 121
Independents, 201, 202. see
also Bookstores
Information Please, Web page
URL, 7
In print/out of print, 217, 222
The Insider's Guide to Getting
Published (Boswell), 36

Internet, doing research on, 6
Interviews, 203, 208, 209
do's and don'ts for,
210-211

K
King, Stephen, 39, 42, 67, 72, 216

L
Lawyers, as agents, 118
Letter of agreement. see also
Cover letter; Query letter
between author and agent,
122-126
Letter of endorsement, 206
Library card, using, 9
Literary agent. see Agents
Literary Market Place (LMP),
65, 121
LMP. see Literary Market Place
Lunch, significance of, 113-114

M
Magazines, 64, 207
Management, agent assistance
with, 115
Manuscript. see also
Submissions
checking for mistakes, 194
contract requirements for,
168-169
submitting without agent,
152-153
trail of through publishing
house, 144-147, 192-196
Marketing. see also Publicity;
Sales; Sales and marketing
agent's assistance with, 115
author's efforts for,
204-205
contract requirements for,
180
how a book gets into
stores, 200
in nontraditional
publishing, 224-226
numbers game and,
201-203
publicist concerns for,
209-210

publicity hints and tips,
206-207, 206-208
publisher's responsibilities for,
203-204
for self-publishing, 224-228
Marketing analysis, including with
proposal, 77
Market research. see also
Audience; Research
analysis of competition, 62-64
author sales projections, 68
book production timetable, 66
in general, 60
talking to booksellers, 65
titles, 65, 66
Web sites for, 61
Meetings
editorial, 146-147
secrets of, 147-148
Memoirs, discussed, 45
Mistakes, in manuscripts, 194
Multimedia, 188-189
Mystery, 80
Mythology, online sources for, 7

N

Names, getting correctly, 83, 86
National Writer's Union, contact
information, 13
Net Amount Received, 189
Networking, 120
New Age. see Religion
Newspapers, 64, 207
Niche publishing, 67, 153
Nonfiction
discussed, 43-44
in general, 36, 37
query letter for, 83-85
reading list recommendations
biography, 56
business, 56
cooking, 56
history, 56
humor, 57
parenting, 57
pop culture, 57
psychology, 57
reference, 56
religion and spirituality, 57
science, 57
selected classics, 58
self-help, 57
sports, 58

travel, 58
sample proposal, 87-97
Nontraditional publishing,
marketing to, 224-226
Novel, 36. see also Fiction
Novelists, Inc., contact
information, 11

O

Offers. see also Acceptance
responding to, x
Options, contract language for,
175-176
Originals, security for, 80, 193

P

Page proofs. see also Changes
checking, 197-198
Paperbacks
discussed, 12-14
mass market, 14
rights for, 217
trade format, 12-14
Parenting, reading list
recommendations, 57
Parody, 58
"Pass through," from subsidiary
rights, 187
Payments, advance against
royalties, xi
Performance bonus, 185
Pocket Books, 15
Pop culture
discussed, 46-47
reading list recommendations, 57
Press releases, 207
Print-on-Demand edition, 189
Print-outs, recommendations for, 193
Production department. see also
Publishing
operations of, 150-152
Professionalism, maintaining, 86
Profit and loss statement (P&L), 81
Project Gutenberg, 231, 232, 234
Promotion of works. see Marketing
Proposals
benefits section, 75
byline, 75
competing books, 77-78
hook overview, 75, 83
larger overview, 76

marketing analysis, 77, 206
title page, 75
do's and don'ts, 86
features section, 75
author biography, 79
chapter-by-chapter
descriptions, 78-79
cover letter, 79-80
sample chapters, 79
table of contents, 78
fiction
preparing, 80-81
sample proposal, 98-102
in general, 70-71
nonfiction, sample proposal,
87-97
preparing
fiction, 80-81
format for, 74-75
in general, 73-74
query letters for, 81-83
as sales tool, 71-73
sample proposal, nonfiction,
87-97
time frame for, 66-67
Psychology, reading list
recommendations, 57
Publication date, contract
requirements for, 170-171
Publicist, considerations for using,
209-210
Publicity. see also Marketing
hints and tips for, 206-208
Publicity department, operations
of, 151, 194, 203-204
Publishers Weekly, 8, 61
Publishing. see also Electronic
publishing
basic procedure for book
publishing, viii-xi
business aspects of, 9, 81,
147-148, 149, 150
design department, 151
distribution department, 152
editorial department, 148-149
editorial offices, 144
in general, 8-9, 144-147
personalities and specialties, 113
production department, 150-152
publicity department, 151, 194,
203-204, 206-208
reasons for interest in, vii-viii
sales and marketing
department, 149-150

subsidiary rights department, 152
vertical, 14-15
Publishing list, 14, 219. see also
Backlist
Publishing terms
book clubs, 16
conglomerates, 15-16
hardcover/cloth, 12
paperback, 12-14
publishing list, 14
remaindering, 15
returns, 12
royalty advance, 9-10, 17
royalty rate, 10
sell through, 10-12
subsidiary rights, 16-17
vertical publishing, 14-15
Publish-It-Yourself Handbook
(Henderson), 225

Q

Query letter. see also Cover letter
for fiction, 82-83
for nonfiction, 83-85
for proposals, 81-83, 194

R

Radio-TV Interview Report,
contact information, 208, 211
Reading, personal history of, xi
"Reading fees" charges, 116. see
also Agents
Reading list recommendations.
see also Categories; Genres
fiction, 53-56
nonfiction
biography, 56
business, 56
cooking, 56
history, 56
humor, 57
parenting, 57
pop culture, 57
psychology, 57
reference, 56
selected classics, 58
religion and spirituality, 57
science, 57
self-help, 57
sports, 58
travel, 58

Reference
    discussed, 46
    reading list
        recommendations, 56
Reference material. see also
    Research
    online sources for, 7
    recommendations for, 4, 9
Rejection. see also Returned
    work
    discussed, 154-156
Religion
    online sources for, 7
    spirituality and, reading list
        recommendations, 57
Remainders, discussed, 15, 222
Research. see also Market
    research; Reference material
    using Internet for, 6, 7
Returned work. see also
    Rejection
    procedures for, 80
Returns, 149
    discussed, 12, 220-221
Reviews, 61, 207, 227
Revisions. see also Changes
    contract language for,
        176-177
Rights. see also Contracts;
    Copyright; Subsidiary
    rights
    adaptation, 219
    audio, 218
    book clubs, 217
    commercial and
        merchandising, 218
    electronic, 218-219
    first and second serial,
        215-216
    in general, 214-215
    North American, 216
    open market, 216
    other book publication,
        217-218
    performance/dramatic, 218
    protecting in contract,
        163-178
    reprint, paperback, 217
    reversion of, 179
    translation/foreign, 216
    world, 217
    world English language, 216
RocketBooks, 230, 231-232
Roget's Thesaurus, 4, 9

Romance novel, described, 39
Romance Writers of America,
    208
Routine, for writing, 6
Royalty, 111
    agent-audited, 115
    self-published, 227
Royalty advance, 158
    discussed, 9-10
    with e-books, 232-233
    paying back, 17
Royalty checks, statements
    and, 220-221
Royalty rate, discussed, 10

S

Sales. see also Marketing
    by author, 68
    from self-publishing, 225
    hardcover novels, 12
    mass market paperbacks, 14
    role of proposal in, 70,
        71-73
Sales and marketing
    department. see also
    Marketing
    impact on book's
        prospects, 148
    operations, 149-150
Sales reps, operations of, 200,
    201, 202
SASE, recommendations for
    using, 80, 87
Science, reading list
    recommendations, 57
Science fiction and fantasy,
    discussed, 40
Self-help
    in general, 38
    reading list
        recommendations, 57
Self-publishing
    compared to vanity press,
        226-228
    discussed, 224-226
    economics of, 225-226
    electronic, 232
    tips for, 227
Sell through, 149
    discussed, 10-12
    for mass market
        paperback, 14

Seminars. see also
    Conferences
    opportunities at, 5, 225
Series, 49
ShawGuides, Inc., Web page
    URL, 7
Sisters in Crime (SinC), contact
    information, 208, 209
Small press
    submitting manuscript to,
        153-154
    submitting proposal to, 73
Spell checker, 4, 194
Sports, reading list
    recommendations, 58
Style, developing, 4-5
Style sheets, 192
Submissions, 71. see also
    Acceptance; Manuscript
    exclusive, 117
    multiple, 117
        agent-assisted, 115
    without agent, 152-153
Subsidiary houses, operations
    of, 227
Subsidiary publishing,
    electronic, 231-232
Subsidiary rights. see also
    Rights
    discussed, 16-17
    "pass through" from, 187
    retaining, 115
Subsidiary rights department, 152
Synopsis, 75

T

Table of contents, in
    proposal, 78
Telephone calls, suggestions
    about, 86, 194
Television interviews. see also
    Interviews
    do's and don'ts for,
        210-211
Testimonials. see also
    Endorsements
    including with proposal, 75
Title page, preparing, 75
Titles. see also Covers
    discussed, 66, 196
    examples of, 65
Travel
    discussed, 46

reading list
    recommendations, 58
True crime, discussed, 44, 47-48

U

Unagented submissions, 71
University presses, 152

V

Vanity press
    compared to
        self-publishing, 226-228
    options for, 224-226

W

Web sites, for writers, 7
Webster's Tenth New
    Collegiate Dictionary, 4, 9
    Web page URL, 7
Westerns, discussed, 39-41
Word processor, 4
Words into Type, 195
Work for hire, discussed,
    228-229
Workshops. see also
    Conferences
    for skill development, 5
Writer, 4
Writers. see also Author
    Web sites for, 7
Writer's Digest, 4, 87
    Web page URL, 7
Writer's groups, benefits of
    joining, 5, 6
Writer's Internet Resource
    Guide, Web page URL, 7
The Writer's Chronicle, 17
Writing
    books about, 17
    establishing routine for, 6
    nuts and bolts of, ix
Writing organizations,
    recommendations for, 11
Writing tools, discussed, 4-5

Y

Young adult/children's books,
    discussed, 43

THE EVERYTHING SERIES!

BUSINESS

Everything® **Business Planning Book**
Everything® **Coaching and Mentoring Book**
Everything® **Fundraising Book**
Everything® **Home-Based Business Book**
Everything® **Leadership Book**
Everything® **Managing People Book**
Everything® **Network Marketing Book**
Everything® **Online Business Book**
Everything® **Project Management Book**
Everything® **Selling Book**
Everything® **Start Your Own Business Book**
Everything® **Time Management Book**

COMPUTERS

Everything® **Build Your Own Home Page Book**
Everything® **Computer Book**
Everything® **Internet Book**
Everything® **Microsoft® Word 2000 Book**

COOKBOOKS

Everything® **Barbecue Cookbook**
Everything® **Bartender's Book, $9.95**
Everything® **Chinese Cookbook**
Everything® **Chocolate Cookbook**
Everything® **Cookbook**
Everything® **Dessert Cookbook**
Everything® **Diabetes Cookbook**
Everything® **Indian Cookbook**
Everything® **Low-Carb Cookbook**
Everything® **Low-Fat High-Flavor Cookbook**
Everything® **Low-Salt Cookbook**
Everything® **Mediterranean Cookbook**
Everything® **Mexican Cookbook**
Everything® **One-Pot Cookbook**
Everything® **Pasta Book**
Everything® **Quick Meals Cookbook**
Everything® **Slow Cooker Cookbook**
Everything® **Soup Cookbook**
Everything® **Thai Cookbook**
Everything® **Vegetarian Cookbook**
Everything® **Wine Book**

HEALTH

Everything® **Alzheimer's Book**
Everything® **Anti-Aging Book**
Everything® **Diabetes Book**
Everything® **Dieting Book**
Everything® **Herbal Remedies Book**
Everything® **Hypnosis Book**
Everything® **Massage Book**
Everything® **Menopause Book**
Everything® **Nutrition Book**
Everything® **Reflexology Book**
Everything® **Reiki Book**
Everything® **Stress Management Book**
Everything® **Vitamins, Minerals, and Nutritional Supplements Book**

HISTORY

Everything® **American Government Book**
Everything® **American History Book**
Everything® **Civil War Book**
Everything® **Irish History & Heritage Book**
Everything® **Mafia Book**
Everything® **Middle East Book**
Everything® **World War II Book**

HOBBIES & GAMES

Everything® **Bridge Book**
Everything® **Candlemaking Book**
Everything® **Casino Gambling Book**
Everything® **Chess Basics Book**
Everything® **Collectibles Book**
Everything® **Crossword and Puzzle Book**
Everything® **Digital Photography Book**
Everything® **Easy Crosswords Book**
Everything® **Family Tree Book**
Everything® **Games Book**
Everything® **Knitting Book**
Everything® **Magic Book**
Everything® **Motorcycle Book**
Everything® **Online Genealogy Book**
Everything® **Photography Book**
Everything® **Pool & Billiards Book**
Everything® **Quilting Book**
Everything® **Scrapbooking Book**
Everything® **Sewing Book**
Everything® **Soapmaking Book**

HOME IMPROVEMENT

Everything® **Feng Shui Book**
Everything® **Feng Shui Decluttering Book, $9.95 ($15.95 CAN)**
Everything® **Fix-It Book**
Everything® **Gardening Book**
Everything® **Homebuilding Book**

All Everything® books are priced at $12.95 or $14.95, unless otherwise stated. Prices subject to change without notice.
Canadian prices range from $11.95–$31.95, and are subject to change without notice.

Everything® **Home Decorating Book**
Everything® **Landscaping Book**
Everything® **Lawn Care Book**
Everything® **Organize Your Home Book**

EVERYTHING® KIDS' BOOKS

All titles are $6.95

Everything® **Kids' Baseball Book, 3rd Ed.** ($10.95 CAN)
Everything® **Kids' Bible Trivia Book** ($10.95 CAN)
Everything® **Kids' Bugs Book** ($10.95 CAN)
Everything® **Kids' Christmas Puzzle & Activity Book** ($10.95 CAN)
Everything® **Kids' Cookbook** ($10.95 CAN)
Everything® **Kids' Halloween Puzzle & Activity Book** ($10.95 CAN)
Everything® **Kids' Joke Book** ($10.95 CAN)
Everything® **Kids' Math Puzzles Book** ($10.95 CAN)
Everything® **Kids' Mazes Book** ($10.95 CAN)
Everything® **Kids' Money Book** ($11.95 CAN)
Everything® **Kids' Monsters Book** ($10.95 CAN)
Everything® **Kids' Nature Book** ($11.95 CAN)
Everything® **Kids' Puzzle Book** ($10.95 CAN)
Everything® **Kids' Riddles & Brain Teasers Book** ($10.95 CAN)
Everything® **Kids' Science Experiments Book** ($10.95 CAN)
Everything® **Kids' Soccer Book** ($10.95 CAN)
Everything® **Kids' Travel Activity Book** ($10.95 CAN)

KIDS' STORY BOOKS

Everything® **Bedtime Story Book**
Everything® **Bible Stories Book**
Everything® **Fairy Tales Book**
Everything® **Mother Goose Book**

LANGUAGE

Everything® **Inglés Book**
Everything® **Learning French Book**
Everything® **Learning German Book**
Everything® **Learning Italian Book**
Everything® **Learning Latin Book**
Everything® **Learning Spanish Book**
Everything® **Sign Language Book**
Everything® **Spanish Phrase Book,** $9.95 ($15.95 CAN)

MUSIC

Everything® **Drums Book (with CD),** $19.95 ($31.95 CAN)
Everything® **Guitar Book**
Everything® **Playing Piano and Keyboards Book**
Everything® **Rock & Blues Guitar Book (with CD),** $19.95 ($31.95 CAN)
Everything® **Songwriting Book**

NEW AGE

Everything® **Astrology Book**
Everything® **Divining the Future Book**
Everything® **Dreams Book**
Everything® **Ghost Book**
Everything® **Love Signs Book,** $9.95 ($15.95 CAN)
Everything® **Meditation Book**
Everything® **Numerology Book**
Everything® **Palmistry Book**
Everything® **Psychic Book**
Everything® **Spells & Charms Book**
Everything® **Tarot Book**
Everything® **Wicca and Witchcraft Book**

PARENTING

Everything® **Baby Names Book**
Everything® **Baby Shower Book**
Everything® **Baby's First Food Book**
Everything® **Baby's First Year Book**
Everything® **Breastfeeding Book**

Everything® **Father-to-Be Book**
Everything® **Get Ready for Baby Book**
Everything® **Getting Pregnant Book**
Everything® **Homeschooling Book**
Everything® **Parent's Guide to Children with Autism**
Everything® **Parent's Guide to Positive Discipline**
Everything® **Parent's Guide to Raising a Successful Child**
Everything® **Parenting a Teenager Book**
Everything® **Potty Training Book,** $9.95 ($15.95 CAN)
Everything® **Pregnancy Book, 2nd Ed.**
Everything® **Pregnancy Fitness Book**
Everything® **Pregnancy Organizer,** $15.00 ($22.95 CAN)
Everything® **Toddler Book**
Everything® **Tween Book**

PERSONAL FINANCE

Everything® **Budgeting Book**
Everything® **Get Out of Debt Book**
Everything® **Get Rich Book**
Everything® **Homebuying Book, 2nd Ed.**
Everything® **Homeselling Book**
Everything® **Investing Book**
Everything® **Money Book**
Everything® **Mutual Funds Book**
Everything® **Online Investing Book**
Everything® **Personal Finance Book**
Everything® **Personal Finance in Your 20s & 30s Book**
Everything® **Wills & Estate Planning Book**

PETS

Everything® **Cat Book**
Everything® **Dog Book**
Everything® **Dog Training and Tricks Book**
Everything® **Golden Retriever Book**
Everything® **Horse Book**
Everything® **Labrador Retriever Book**
Everything® **Puppy Book**
Everything® **Tropical Fish Book**

All Everything® books are priced at $12.95 or $14.95, unless otherwise stated. Prices subject to change without notice. Canadian prices range from $11.95–$31.95, and are subject to change without notice.